The South in the
History of the Nation

The South in the History of the Nation

A READER

VOLUME ONE: THROUGH RECONSTRUCTION

Edited by

William A. Link
University of North Carolina at Greensboro

and

Marjorie Spruill Wheeler
University of Southern Mississippi

BEDFORD/ST. MARTIN'S   BOSTON ❧ NEW YORK

43.95

For Bedford/St. Martin's

History Editor: Katherine E. Kurzman
Developmental Editor: Ellen Kuhl
Production Editor: Lori Chong Roncka
Production Supervisor: Catherine Hetmansky
Marketing Manager: Charles Cavaliere
Editorial Assistant: Molly Kalkstein
Production Assistant: Helaine Denenberg
Copyeditor: Ara Salibian
Text Design: Geri Davis, The Davis Group Inc.
Cover Design: Diana Coe
Cover Art: Vicksburg, Mississippi, Western Scenery. From the Collections of the St. Louis
   Mercantile Library Association.
Composition: ComCom, an RR Donnelley & Sons Company
Printing and Binding: Haddon Craftsmen, Inc.

President: Charles H. Christensen
Editorial Director: Joan E. Feinberg
Director of Editing, Design, and Production: Marcia Cohen
Managing Editor: Elizabeth M. Schaaf

Library of Congress Catalog Card Number: 98–87545

For information, write: Bedford/St. Martin's, 75 Arlington Street, Boston, MA 02116 (617-426-7440)

ISBN: 0–312–13357–X (Volume One)
      0–312–15787–8 (Volume Two)

PREFACE

This book is intended for use in the U.S. history survey course, but a quick perusal of its contents will reveal that it is not a typical reader. Like most of the available survey readers, *The South in the History of the Nation* is organized by topics that most instructors cover, from early encounters between Europeans and Native Americans to social changes in our own time. The readings are split between two volumes, which overlap at the Civil War and Reconstruction.

In many respects, though, this is a very different book. To help students become engaged more fully with the study of American history, we have tried to place it into a more familiar, accessible context. In every chapter, readings relate local and regional developments to themes of national importance, showing that the historical forces that propelled events such as colonial development, Jacksonian democracy, Progressivism, and the New Deal had unique manifestations in the South. Yet these developments, and others, were part of a larger national picture, affecting all Americans in one way or another.

While these two volumes can easily be used in courses about the South, we have designed them primarily for American history survey courses. The reader will be especially interesting to students and instructors in the South, as it "brings home" national themes and issues, but it is intended to be helpful to students and teachers in any part of the nation who are interested in regionalism in American history. Each of the two volumes contains fifteen chapters, organized around topics that are standard fare in American history courses all across the country. Brief chapter introductions provide context for the regional documents and connect the chapter topic to larger themes in American history. Exercises (under the heading *As you read*) at the end of the introductions prepare students to read the documents actively. Each document is preceded by a headnote that provides background on the source and its relevance to the chapter topic. And each chapter concludes with a brief list of secondary sources in which students can find further information.

The primary source materials in *The South in the History of the Nation* are, we believe, unique in other respects. We have aimed for balance and ease of use by instructors and students throughout both volumes. The readings include social and political history, and they reflect diverse voices—black and white, Native and European, male and female, rich and poor—that mirror our diverse national history. Finally, we believe these documents are eminently readable and should prove exciting as well as informative to students, providing the basis for meaningful and spirited class discussions.

Intentionally, we have used a broad conception of "the South." We include the eleven states that seceded from the Union in 1860–61 and formed the Confederacy: Virginia, North Carolina, South Carolina, Georgia, Florida, Alabama, Mississippi, Louisiana, Tennessee, Arkansas, and Texas. Although Texas was as much western as southern, we believe that it offers a rich study of the blending of regional characteristics. We also include border states that could be considered "southern" but did not secede, such as Maryland and Kentucky. Documents from these thirteen states together represent the diversity of the region, illustrating the different experiences encountered within the South while collectively reflecting the broader national experience.

Founded on the novel concept that regional materials can aid the teaching of a national history, *The South in the History of the Nation* required an unusual amount of planning and careful organization. As editors, we quickly became conscious of creating a new kind of reader. We restructured the book several times and tried out materials on our own students, receiving useful feedback. We conferred extensively with the editors at Bedford/St. Martin's on many different occasions, and only after considerable discussion did we settle on a format for presenting these regional materials that, we believe, will be very helpful in the teaching of American history.

Acknowledgments

The successful completion of this book depended on the support and advice of a large number of people. We thank graduate student assistants Jason Dawsey of the University of Southern Mississippi (USM), and Chris Patterson and Brett Rumble of the University of North Carolina at Greensboro (UNCG), who assisted in locating the documents for the book and shared our enthusiasm about the project. Lori Wright and Christine R. Flood of UNCG and Sheila Smith of USM were unfailingly helpful through several years. While Scott Spruill Wheeler contributed as a research assistant, Josie M. Link helped with last-minute copyediting.

Historians Ed Ayers, William A. Blair, Emily Clark, Karen Cox, Leesha Faulkner, Glenda Gilmore, Steve Hochman, Karen Leatham, Jon Sensbach, James "Pat" Smith, and Lisa Tolbert all contributed ideas. UNCG archivist Betty Carter and USM's Yvonne Arnold provided materials on short notice. We would also like to thank the University of Southern Mississippi and the University of North Carolina at Greensboro for various forms of institutional support for the project. We are particularly grateful to USM history department chair Orazio Ciccarelli; former UNCG history department head Steven F. Lawson; UNCG dean Walter H. Beale; former USM vice president for academic affairs Karen Yarbrough; UNCG provost Ed Uprichard; USM president Horace Fleming; and UNCG chancellor Pat Sullivan.

Without the patience, prodding, and constant support of Bedford/St. Martin's and its very talented editorial and production staff this project would never have reached fruition. The original conception of this book came from conversations with Chuck Christensen and Joan Feinberg, and their continuing enthusiasm sustained us over the course of several years. Niels Aaboe and Katherine Kurzman also helped in the development and completion of the book. Ellen Kuhl contributed unflagging support, dogged persistence, and frequent editorial interventions that were instrumental in the project's completion. We are also very grateful to Lori Chong Roncka for overseeing the production of the final book copy and to Elizabeth Schaaf, the managing editor; we are indebted to Ara Salibian for his expert copyediting. Others at B/SM who helped include Fred Courtright, Helaine Denenberg, Molly Kalkstein, Ed Tonderys, Elizabeth Marcus, Jennifer Rush, and Jo Swanson. We also greatly appreciate the aid of historians around the country who provided input while the book was being designed: Ed Ayers, Anne Bailey, Robert Becker, Kathleen Berkeley, William A. Blair, W. Fitzhugh Brundage, Robert Calvert, Valerie Jean Conner, John Daly, Charles Eagles, Sarah Gardner, Glenda Gilmore, William Harris, Mark Hill, Susan Hult, Wallace Hutcheon, Mary Carroll Johansen, Stephen Kneeshaw, Jessica Kross, Janice Leone, Carl Moneyhon, James Tice Moore, Fred Roach, Dennis Rousey, Jon Sensbach, Bryant Simon, Sheila Skemp, Marcia Synnott, Lisa Toland, and Harold Wilson. Finally, as always, we have depended on the love and support of our spouses, Susannah Link and David Wheeler, and our children, Percy, Maggie, and Josie Link, and Scott and Jesse Wheeler.

William A. Link, Greensboro, N.C.

Marjorie Spruill Wheeler, Hattiesburg, Miss.

CONTENTS

Preface   v

CHAPTER ONE
CULTURES IN CONFLICT
Indian-European Encounters in the American South   1

1. The Spanish and the Indians in "La Florida"
   Garcilaso de la Vega, the Inca, On Hernando de Soto's
   Expedition, 1605   3

2. Indians in Virginia
   Powhatan, Address to John Smith, 1608   11

3. The English in Virginia
   John Smith, Description of Indian Life and Culture, 1612   13

4. The French on the Gulf Coast
   Pierre Le Moyne, Sieur d'Iberville, Journal Entries, 1699   17

CHAPTER TWO
COLONIZATION
Religion and the Founding of Maryland   23

5. Catholic Intentions
   Cecil Calvert, Lord Baltimore, Instructions to His
   Colonists, 1633   25

6. Jesuit Missionaries
   Father Edward Knott, S.J., From the "Annual Letter of the
   English Province of the Society of Jesus," 1638   29

7. A Violent Confrontation
    Leonard Strong, Babylon's Fall, 1655   33

CHAPTER THREE
THE CRISIS OF THE LATE SEVENTEENTH CENTURY
Social Tensions and Rebellion in Virginia   40

8. The Servant's Experience
    *James Revel, "The Poor Unhappy Transported Felon's
    Sorrowful Account of His Fourteen Years Transportation
    at Virginia in America," c. 1680*   42

9. The Lawne's Creek Rising
    *Evidence from the Surry County Deed Book and the Surry
    County Order Book, January 1674*   49

10. Two Women View the Frontier
    *Elizabeth Bacon and Mary Horsmanden Byrd, Letters,
    1676*   54

11. Bacon's Rebellion
    *The Royal Commissioners, "A True Narrative of the Late
    Rebellion in Virginia," 1677*   56

CHAPTER FOUR
THE EIGHTEENTH CENTURY
Prosperity and the Planter Elite   62

12. A Life of Leisure
    William Byrd, Entries from His Secret Diary, 1709   64

13. A Woman Planter in South Carolina
    *Eliza Pinckney, Letters to Her Children, to George Morly,
    and to Mrs. Evance, 1758–1760*   69

14. A Plantation Owner's Difficulties
    Landon Carter, Entries from His Diary, 1766   76

CHAPTER FIVE
PRE-REVOLUTIONARY AMERICA
The Regulators and the Carolina Backcountry in Turmoil   81

15. Pre-Revolutionary Turmoil: The North Carolina Regulators
    *Edmund Fanning and Samuel Spencer, Letters to William
    Tryon, 1768*   83

16. The Regulator Critique
Joshua Teague et al., Letter to Harmon Husbands, 1769   89
17. A Regulator Perspective
Harmon Husbands, Introduction to A Fan for Fanning and
a Touch-Stone to Tryon, *1771*   92
18. The Hillsborough Riot
Richard Henderson and the Virginia Gazette, *Reports of the
Riot, 1770*   95

CHAPTER SIX

THE REVOLUTION

A Proposal for Arming Slaves   **102**

19. The British Call Slaves to Arms
John Murray, Earl of Dunmore, Proclamation, 1775   105
20. A Patriot's "Scheme"
*Henry Laurens and John Laurens, Correspondence between
a Slaveholder and His Son, 1776–1779*   106
21. Extreme Measures for Difficult Times
*Alexander Hamilton, Henry Laurens, George Washington,
Christopher Gadsden, John Laurens, and David Ramsay,
Letters, 1779*   115
22. Defeated by a "Triple-Headed Monster"
*John Laurens and George Washington, Correspondence,
1782*   121

CHAPTER SEVEN

THE CREATION OF THE AMERICAN REPUBLIC

Slavery and the Constitution   **125**

23. Slavery and Representation
*James Madison, Debates in the Federal Convention,
June 11–July 12, 1787*   127
24. The African Slave Trade
*James Madison, Debates in the Federal Convention,
August 21–25, 1787*   134
25. A Southerner Opposes the Three-Fifths Clause
Luther Martin, "Genuine Information," 1788   138
26. Ratification
*Debates in South Carolina, Virginia, and North Carolina,
1788*   140

CHAPTER EIGHT

THE NEW REPUBLIC

The Americanization of New Orleans?   **148**

27. Explaining the French Decision
     Pierre Clément Laussat, Proclamation in the Name of the
     French Republic, to the Louisianians, 1803   151

28. Establishing a Government for Orleans Territory
     Thomas Jefferson and William C. C. Claiborne,
     Correspondence, 1804   154

29. Fears for the Church in a Secular Republic
     The Ursulines of New Orleans and Thomas Jefferson,
     Correspondence, 1804   160

30. Creoles Demand the Civil Law
     Legislative Council of the Territory of Orleans, Resolution,
     1806   163

31. Changes in New Orleans Society
     Benjamin Latrobe, Entries from His Diary, 1819   168

CHAPTER NINE

THE AGE OF JACKSON

The Removal of the Cherokees   **173**

32. The Civilized State of the Cherokees
     John Ridge, Letter to Albert Gallatin, 1826   176

33. Disputing Georgia's Claim
     Chief John Ross, Annual Message to the Cherokee Nation,
     1828   182

34. Justifying Removal
     Wilson Lumpkin and Andrew Jackson, Arguments for
     Removal, 1830   185

35. The Trail of Tears
     Evan Jones, Letters, 1838   191

CHAPTER TEN

ANTEBELLUM REFORM

Religion and Morality in the Debate over Slavery   **196**

36. A Minister Defends Slavery
     Richard Furman, The Biblical Justification for Slavery,
     1822   198

37. Slavery Defended as Moral and Beneficial
    George Fitzhugh, "Slavery Justified, by a Southerner," 1850   202

38. An Expatriate Urges Southern Women to Oppose Slavery
    *Angelina Grimké, From "Appeal to the Christian Women of the
    South," 1836*   207

39. A Former Slave Exposes Hypocrisy
    *Frederick Douglass, "What to the Slave Is the Fourth of
    July?" 1852*   214

CHAPTER ELEVEN
WESTWARD EXPANSION
The Texas Frontier   221

40. Texas and the Union
    *Stephen F. Austin, Address Delivered at Louisville,
    Kentucky, 1836*   223

41. Going to Texas
    Ann Raney Thomas Coleman, A Frontier Marriage, 1830s   229

42. Life in Texas
    Frederick Law Olmsted, "Route across Eastern Texas," 1857   235

CHAPTER TWELVE
THE SLAVE SOUTH
The Case of Jordan Hatcher   242

43. Trial and Conviction
    Trial Record from the Case of Jordan Hatcher, 1852   244

44. Pleading for Justice
    Petitions for and against Commutation, 1852   248

45. The Commutation
    *Governor Joseph Johnson, Messages to the Legislature,
    1852*   250

46. Virginians React
    Newspaper Articles, 1852   253

CHAPTER THIRTEEN
THE SECTIONAL CRISIS
John Brown's Raid, True Womanhood, and the
Alienation of North and South   259

47. A Plea from Massachusetts
     Lydia Maria Child, Letter to Governor Wise, 1859   261

48. The Virginia Governor's Response
     Governor Henry A. Wise, Letter to Lydia Maria Child, 1859   263

49. What Is a True Woman to Do?
     Margaretta Mason and Lydia Maria Child,
     Correspondence, 1859   265

CHAPTER FOURTEEN
THE CIVIL WAR
The Minds and Hearts of the Southern People   **275**

50. A Confederate Officer
     William L. Nugent, Letters to Eleanor Smith Nugent,
     1861–1865   278

51. A Confederate Soldier
     John Dooley, Journal Entries, 1862 and 1863   289

52. A Young Woman in Occupied New Orleans
     Clara Solomon, From Her Diary, 1862   293

53. A Unionist from Tennessee
     W. G. Brownlow, Explaining Union Support from the
     Border States, 1862   300

54. Black Loyalists in Louisiana
     Letters and Petition, 1862 and 1864   305

CHAPTER FIFTEEN
RECONSTRUCTION
Black Freedom and the Ku Klux Klan   **311**

55. The Rise of the Klan
     Alexander K. Davis and Lydia Anderson, Testimony for the
     Joint Select Committee in Macon, Mississippi, 1871   314

56. A Northern View
     Harper's Weekly, "The Ku-Klux Conspiracy," 1872   323

57. Missionary Women and Black Education
     Maria Waterbury, From Seven Years among the Freedmen,
     1890   327

58. The Legacy of the Klan
     Albion W. Tourgée, "The Causes, Character, and
     Consequences of the Ku-Klux Organization," 1880   330

The South in the History of the Nation

CHAPTER ONE

CULTURES IN CONFLICT

Indian-European Encounters in the American South

W hen the first European explorers reached the part of North America we know as the American South in the early 1500s, it was already inhabited by approximately two million people. Dubbed "Indians" by the Spanish, they had developed the most culturally and socially advanced civilization in North America, including large and powerful confederacies headed by the queen of the Cofitachequi in present-day South Carolina and by Powhatan in what is now Virginia. Conflict between these Native Americans and the Spanish, English, and French who staked claim to and began to colonize the region was inevitable, given the extreme cultural differences and competing claims to the land. But Indian-European interaction varied greatly — from the creation of alliances to brutal struggles for survival — as each group assessed the other's nature and motives and pursued its own goals.

The Spanish were the first Europeans to explore the southeastern part of North America and to have extensive contact with the Indians. Although Spain later established several colonies and missions to convert the Indians to Christianity and to strengthen its territorial claims, its early expeditions were devoted solely to exploration. The explorers failed to discover the deposits of gold and silver they had hoped for, and met fierce resistance from the native population.

Hernando de Soto led one of the most famous expeditions, from 1539 to 1543. More than six hundred men, including two hundred cavalry, took nearly four years to make their way through what is now Florida, Georgia, the Carolinas, Alabama, Tennessee, Mississippi, Louisiana, Arkansas, and Texas. A veteran plunderer of Central America and Peru, de Soto used the same brutal methods in North America. His barbarous behavior provoked fierce resistance from the Indians; in 1541 the Choctaw led de Soto and his men into a trap and nearly destroyed them. As the severely weakened expedition straggled westward, de Soto died of fever and was buried in the Mississippi River; the survivors eventually made it to Mexico.

England was slower to show interest in establishing a New World colony. Its Jamestown Colony in Virginia was founded in 1607 as a commercial venture; the settlers made little effort to convert the Indians, whom they regarded — quite accurately — as dangerous adversaries. The English happened to have settled in the midst of the Algonquian confederation led by Powhatan. The Indians had every right to resent the settlers, who were often brutal, encroached upon Indian lands, and spread devastating diseases. Powhatan could have easily crushed the English colony in its infancy, but he saved the starving colonists by exchanging food (especially corn) for English goods; historians speculate that Powhatan decided against a full-scale attack because of his desire for English iron and steel weapons. After Powhatan's death, however, his brother Opechancanough succeeded him and made a concerted attempt to destroy the colony in 1622, killing a third of the white population. Intermittent warfare between the English and the Indians would continue for many years.

France began to emerge as a major power in the colonial South toward the end of the seventeenth century. In 1698 a young French Canadian naval hero and explorer, Pierre Le Moyne, Sieur d'Iberville, led an expedition of four ships and two hundred people to explore the Lower Mississippi Valley and establish a French military outpost. Like other French colonists in the New World, d'Iberville and his brother, Jean Baptiste Le Moyne, Sieur de Bienville, were well aware of England's and Spain's competing claims and the need to be able to counter their activities. Thus they understood better than many in France the need to establish a defensible colony at the mouth of the Mississippi. The brothers also recognized the need for good relations with the Indians. The French outposts in Louisiana (named after Louis XIV) were based on trade rather than agriculture, and the French needed firm alliances with the Indians against their European rivals. Landing first near Pensacola, d'Iberville's crew encountered a small Spanish fort; they sailed westward, exploring the Gulf Coast, seeking alliances with the Indians against the Spanish, and consulting with them about the location of the mouth of the Mississippi River (which they eventually located on Mardi Gras of 1699). D'Iberville's expedition established several French outposts along the Gulf Coast and the Mississippi River; his brother, de Bienville, founded New Orleans in 1718.

The readings in this chapter suggest the different impressions that Europeans had of Indian life and customs. Garcilaso de la Vega's account of de Soto's expedition, John Smith's descriptions of Indian life and culture, and d'Iberville's journal address topics as varied as religion, government, gender relations, food production, lodging, character traits, physical attributes, dress, weapons, and warfare. Garcilaso's account and Powhatan's speech to John Smith also give some idea of what the Indians thought of the Europeans, though we must remember that these are secondhand versions of Indian ideas and attributes as recorded by Europeans. Together these documents remind us that the relationships between Indians and Europeans varied greatly and were a crucial factor in determining the success or failure of the groups competing for land and power in the colonial South.

As you read, consider the following questions. What Indian customs and characteristics did the Europeans admire, and what did they dislike? What did the Indians think of the Europeans, and how did previous experiences shape their attitudes? How did the differing motives and circumstances of the three European nations affect their approaches to the Indians they encountered?

1. The Spanish and the Indians in "La Florida"

GARCILASO DE LA VEGA, THE INCA
On Hernando de Soto's Expedition
1605

Garcilaso de la Vega, a historian of the conquest of the Americas, was the son of a Spaniard who fought in Peru and an Inca woman descended from the emperor Tupac Inca Yupanqui. Garcilaso's voluminous account of the de Soto expedition, La Florida *(1605), based upon the recollections of participants, depicts Spaniards and Indians locked in an epic struggle. This work has been called the first American literary classic.*

La Florida reflects Garcilaso's mixed heritage. In these four excerpts, he clearly casts de Soto in a favorable light while also celebrating the achievements and the courage of the Indians: he describes the general characteristics of the native inhabitants of North America, comparing them to the people of Peru; he re-

Garcilaso de la Vega, *La Florida* (1605). Reprinted in *The De Soto Chronicles: The Expedition of Hernando de Soto to North America in 1539–1543,* ed. Lawrence A. Clayton, Vernon James Knight Jr., and Edward C. Moore, vol. 2 (Tuscaloosa: University of Alabama Press, 1993), 67–71, 143–45, 304–6, 313–14.

counts an incident in which the cacique, *or "lord," of the Acuera Indians of central Florida forcefully declined de Soto's dubious offer of friendship; and he describes the impressive culture of the Cofitachequi (also spelled Cofachiqui) in what is now South Carolina, recounting the warm reception given the Spanish by the Indian queen. (Unlike others who wrote about de Soto, Garcilaso fails to mention that the explorer rewarded the queen's generosity by stealing pearls and other valuables and by taking her as a hostage to secure safe passage for the continued expedition.)*

Concerning Still Others Who Have Made the Same Journey to La Florida, and Concerning the Customs and Usual Arms of Its Natives[1]

This, though brief, is the most accurate account that it has been possible to give of the land of La Florida, and of those who have gone there to discover and conquer it. Before going on, it will be well to describe some of the customs the Indians of that great kingdom had in common, at least those the adelantado[2] Hernando de Soto discovered. In almost all of the provinces he traversed those customs are the same, and if they differ in some places, we shall take care to note them in the course of our *History*; but in general they all follow almost the same manner of life.

These Indians are a heathen race and idolaters; they worship the sun and the moon as chief deities but without ceremonies involving idols, or sacrifices, or prayers, or other superstitions such as other heathens practice. They had temples that served them as burial places rather than as houses of prayer where, for pomp and display, besides being sepulchers for their dead, they kept all the best and richest of their treasures. These tombs and temples were held in extreme veneration, and they placed at their doors trophies of the victories that they won over their enemies.

In general they married only one woman, and she was obliged to be most faithful to her husband under penalty imposed by the laws they had for the punishment of adultery, which in some provinces was a cruel death and in others very ignominious punishment. . . . Because of their privileged position, the rulers had the right to take as many wives as they wished, and this law or privilege of the rulers was observed throughout the Indies in the New World, but always it was with the distinction of the principal legitimate wife from the others, who were more concubines than wives. Thus they acted as servants, and the children whom they bore were neither legitimate nor equal in honor or inheritance to those of the principal wife.

---

[1]Book 1, chapter 4.
[2]**adelantado:** governor.

Throughout El Perú the common people married only one woman, and he who took two incurred the death penalty. The Incas, who were those of royal blood, and the *curacas*, who were the overlords of vassals, had the privilege of having as many wives as they wished or could support, but with the distinction described above of the legitimate wife from the concubines. And like heathen, they said that this custom was permitted and provided among them because it was necessary that the nobles have many wives in order to have many children; in order to make war and govern the commonwealth and augment their empire they affirmed that they must have many nobles, because it was they who spent themselves in war and died in battle; to carry burdens, till the soil, and act as servants there were more than enough of the common people, who (because they were not a people who were employed in the dangerous pursuits in which the nobles engaged), however few of them might be born, still multiplied greatly. They were useless for government, nor was it legal for them to concern themselves with it, which would be an offense against the office itself, because governing and dispensing justice was the function of persons of noble birth and not of plebeians.

Returning to those of La Florida, their ordinary food is maize, in place of bread, and their viands are beans and calabashes of the variety they call here *romana*, and a great deal of fish because of the many rivers they possess. There is a scarcity of meat, for they have no species of domesticated cattle. They kill in the chase with their bows and arrows red deer, fallow deer, and roe deer, which are numerous and larger than those of Spain. They kill many kinds of birds, both in order to eat the flesh and to adorn their heads with the feathers, which they wear in showy, multicolored headdresses half a fathom tall; thereby they distinguish the nobles from the plebeians in time of peace, and the soldiers from those who are not such in time of war. Their drink is clear water, just as nature gives it to them, without the admixture of anything else. The meat and the fish they eat must be very well dressed and cooked, and the fruit very ripe. They will never eat it green or half-ripe and laugh at the Castilians for eating green fruit.

Those who say that they eat human flesh attribute this to them falsely, at least to those of the provinces our governor discovered. On the contrary they abominate it, as Alvar Núñez Cabeza de Vaca[3] notes in . . . his *Naufragios*, where he says that certain Castilians who were lodged apart died of hunger and that their remaining companions ate those who had died, except for the buttocks, which none of them would eat, whereupon, he says, the Indians were so scandalized that they were on the point of killing all those who were left in another lodging. It may be that they eat it at places where our people did not go; La Florida is so large and extensive that there is room for all.

They go about naked except for some garments of chamois-skin of various colors almost like very short breeches, which cover them decently, as much as necessary, in front and behind. In the place of a cloak they wear mantles clasped at the throat, which reach halfway down the leg; they are of extremely fine marten-skins, which give off the odor of musk. They also make them of small skins

---

[3]**Alvar Núñez Cabeza de Vaca:** Cabeza de Vaca was one of only four survivors of a disastrous 1527 Spanish expedition, which he described in his work *Naufragios* (The Shipwrecked).

of various animals, such as several kinds of cat, fallow deer, roe deer, red deer, bears, lions, and of skins of cattle. Those hides they dress to such extreme perfection that the skin of a cow or a bear, with the hair on it, they prepare in a manner that leaves it so pliant and soft that it can be worn as a cloak, and it serves them for bed-covering at night. Their hair grows long and they wear it gathered up into a large knot on top of their heads. For a headdress they wear a thick skein of thread in whatever color they desire, which they wind about their heads and tie the ends over the forehead in two half-knots, so that one end hangs down over either temple as far as the ears. The women dress in chamois-skin, having the whole body decently covered.

The arms these Indians carry are bows and arrows, and — although it is true that they are skillful in the use of the other weapons they have, such as pikes, lances, darts, halberds, the sling, club, broadsword, and staff, and other similar ones, if there are others except the harquebus and crossbow which they do not possess — with all this they do not use any other arms except the bow and arrow, because for those who carry them they are the greatest embellishment and ornament. The ancient heathen for the same reason depicted their most beloved gods, as Apollo, Diana, and Cupid, with bows and arrows, for besides that which these arms signify in themselves, they are very beautiful and add to the grace and elegance of him who carries them. For all these reasons, and because of the effectiveness of these arms, which are superior to all others at both short and long range, in retreating or attacking, in fighting in battle or in the recreation of the hunt, these Indians carry them, and these arms are much used throughout the New World.

The bows are of the same height as he who carries them, and as these Indians of La Florida are generally of large stature, their bows are more than two *varas*[4] in length and thick in proportion. They make them of oak and of various other hard and very heavy woods they have. They are so hard to bend that no Spaniard, however much he tried, was able to pull the cord back so that his hand touched his face, but the Indians through their long experience and skill drew back the cord with the greatest ease to a point behind the ear and made such valiant and wonderful shots. . . .

They make the cords of the bows from deerskin, taking a strip two finger-breadths in width from the hide, running from the tip of the tail to the head. After removing the hair they dampen and twist it tightly; one end they tie to the branch of a tree, and from the other they hang a weight of four or five *arrobas*,[5] and they leave it thus until it becomes about the thickness of the larger strings of a bass viol. These cords are extremely strong. In order to shoot safely in such a manner that when the cord springs back it may not injure the left arm, they wear as a protection on the inner side a half-bracer, which covers them from the wrist to the part of the arm that is usually bled. It is made of thick feathers and attached to the arm

[4]*varas:* yardsticks.
[5]*arrobas:* weights of about twenty-five pounds each.

with a deerskin cord, which they give seven or eight turns at the place where the cord springs back most strongly.

This, in short, is what can be said of the life and customs of the Indians of La Florida. . . .

The Insolent Reply of the Lord of the Province of Acuera[6]

The whole army having assembled in Acuera, while the men and horses were recovering from the hunger they had suffered in the days past, which was no small thing, the governor with his accustomed clemency sent messages to the cacique Acuera with some of his Indians whom he had captured, saying that he begged him to come out peaceably and to consent to have Spaniards for friends and brothers; that the latter were a warlike people and brave, who, if their friendship was not accepted, could do much harm and damage to his lands and vassals. At the same time he was to understand and be convinced that they did not have the intention of injuring anyone, as they had not done in the provinces they had left behind them, but on the contrary felt a strong friendship for those who had been willing to receive it. Their chief intention was to reduce through peace and friendship all the provinces and nations of that great kingdom to the obedience and service of the most powerful emperor and king of Castilla, their lord, whose servants they were; and the governor desired to see and speak with him in order to tell him these things more fully and to give him an account of the order that his king and lord had given him to deal and communicate with the lords of that land.

The cacique replied haughtily, saying that he had already had much information from other Castilians who had come to that country years before as to who they were, and he knew very well about their lives and customs, which consisted in occupying themselves like vagabonds in going from one land to another, living from robbing, pillaging, and murdering those who had not offended them in any way. He by no means desired friendship or peace with such people, but rather mortal and perpetual warfare, and even though they might be as brave as they boasted of being, he had no fear of them because he and his vassals considered themselves no less valiant, as proof of which he promised to wage war against them during all the time that they might see fit to remain in his province, not in the open nor in a pitched battle, although he could do so, but by waylaying and ambushes, taking them off guard. Therefore he warned and admonished them to watch and be on their guard against him and his people, whom he had ordered to bring him every week two heads of Christians, and no more; that this would satisfy him because by beheading two of them every eight days, he thought to put an end to all of them within a few years, for although they might settle and make establishments they could not perpetuate themselves because they brought no

---

[6]Book 2, part 1, chapter 16.

women to have children and carry the next generation onward. To what they said about giving obedience to the king of Spain, he replied that he himself was king in his own country and there was no necessity for becoming the vassal of another who had as many as he. Those who put themselves under a foreign yoke when they could live free he regarded as very mean-spirited and cowardly. He and all his people protested that they would die a thousand deaths to maintain their liberty and that of their country; and he gave that reply once and for all. With regard to their vassalage and their statement that they were servants of the emperor and king of Castilla, and that they were going about conquering new lands for his empire, he said that it was well and good that they were all of this; that now he held them in less esteem, since they admitted being servants of another and that they were laboring and gaining kingdoms so that others might rule them and enjoy the fruits of their labors. Inasmuch as they were undergoing hunger, fatigue, and other hardships in such an enterprise, and risking their lives, it would be better and more honorable and profitable for them to win and acquire these things for themselves and their descendants than for strangers; and since they were so mean-spirited that, being so far away, they did not abjure the name of servants, they need not hope for friendship at any time, for he could not bestow it in such a mean way, nor did he wish to know the order of their king. He knew what he might do in his own country and the manner in which he must treat them; therefore they should leave as quickly as they could if they did not all wish to die at his hands.

On hearing the Indian's reply, the governor was amazed to see with what arrogance and pride of spirit a barbarian was able to say such things, for which reason from that time forward he attempted more insistently to win his friendship, sending him many messages couched in affectionate and courteous terms. But the curaca said to all the Indians who went to him that he had sent his reply the first time and that he intended to give no other response, nor did he.

The army was in this province twenty days, resting from the hardship and hunger of their past march and collecting the things necessary for passing on. During these days the governor was engaged in obtaining information and reports concerning the province. He sent runners in every direction to observe carefully and diligently and note the good parts of it, and they brought favorable news.

In those twenty days the Indians were not sleeping; on the other hand they did not fail to carry out the threats and menaces their curaca had made against the Castilians, and so that the latter might see that they had not been empty ones, they were so watchful and astute in their stratagems that no Spaniard wandered a hundred paces from the camp that they did not shoot him with arrows and immediately behead him, and as quickly as his people went to his assistance they found themselves without their heads, which the Indians carried off to present to their cacique, as he had ordered them to do.

The Christians interred the bodies of the dead where they found them. The Indians returned the following night, disinterred them, cut them in pieces, and hung them from the trees where the Spaniards could see them. By such acts they complied well with what their cacique had ordered them, namely, that they bring him two heads of Christians every week, for in two days they brought him four, two at a time, and fourteen during the whole space of time the Spaniards were in his country, not counting those whom they wounded, who were many more. They came out to make these assaults so safely and so near their haunts, which were the woods, that they could return to them very easily, having done as much damage as possible, without losing a single opportunity that was offered them. From this the Castilians came to verify the truth of the words that the Indians whom they found all along the road through the great swamp had shouted to them: "Go on, thieves, traitors; in Acuera and farther on in Apalache they will treat you as you deserve; they will cut you all in quarters and pieces and hang you from the highest trees along the road."

The Spaniards, however they might try, did not kill fifty Indians in that whole time, because they were very cautious and vigilant in their stratagems.

The Army Leaves Cofachiqui
in Two Divisions[7]

In the sixth room there was nothing except bows and arrows wrought in all the extreme perfection and care with which they make them. For arrowheads, they used points of wood, of the bones of land and sea animals, and of flint. . . . Besides these kinds of arrowheads made of copper, such as those they put on darts in Spain, there were others with harpoons, also made of copper, and in the form of small chisels, lances, and Moorish darts, which looked as if they had been made in Castilla. They noted also that the arrows with flint tips had different kinds of heads; some were in the form of a harpoon, others of small chisels, others were rounded like a punch, and others had two edges like the tip of a dagger. The Spaniards examined all these curiously and wondered how they could fashion such things out of a material as resistant as flint, though in view of what Mexican history says about the broadswords and other arms that the Indians of that land made of flint, a part of this wonderment of ours will be lost. The bows were handsomely made and enameled in various colors, which they do with a certain cement that gives them such a luster that one can see himself in them. In speaking of this temple, Juan Coles says the following: "And in one apartment there were more than fifty thousand bows with their cases or quivers full of arrows."

Not satisfied with this lustrous finish, they put on the bows many circles of pearls and seed pearls placed at intervals, these circles or rings beginning at the handles and going in order to the tips in such manner that the first circles were of large pearls and made seven or eight turns, the second were of smaller pearls and had fewer turns, and thus they went on decreasing to the last ones, which were near the tips and were of very small seed pearls. The arrows also had circles of seed pearls at intervals, but not of pearls, there being seed pearls only. . . .

The general and his captains, having seen and noted the grandeur and sumptuousness of the temple and its riches, the multitude of the arms, and the elaboration and order with which everything was made and arranged, asked the Indians what was the significance of such ostentation and pomp. They replied that the

[7]Book 3, chapter 17.

lords of that kingdom, especially those of that province and of others that they would see beyond, regarded the ornateness and magnificence of their burial places as the greatest [sign of] their dignity, and thus they endeavored to embellish them with all the arms and wealth they could, as they had seen in that temple. Because this one was the richest and most superb of all those that our Spaniards saw in La Florida, I have seen fit to write of it at such length, and particularly of the things that were in it, and also because he who gave me the account ordered me to do so. For, as he said, it was among the grandest and most wonderful of all the things that he had seen in the New World, in having traveled over most and the best part of México and El Perú, though it is true that when he passed through those two kingdoms they had already been sacked of their most valuable wealth, and their chief grandeurs had been destroyed.

The officials of the imperial hacienda discussed taking the fifth of the pearls and seed pearls and the rest of the wealth in the temple that belonged to his Majesty's hacienda and carrying it with them. The governor told them that taking it would serve only to load the army down with useless burdens, when they could not carry even the necessary ones of their arms and munitions. They were to leave it all as it was, for at present they were not parceling out the land, but discovering it, and when they should distribute and settle it then he who received it by lot would pay the fifth. Thus they did not touch anything that they had seen, and they went back to where the lady [the queen of Cofachiqui] was, having wonders to tell of the magnificence of her burial place. . . .

Where Is Recounted Some
of the Magnanimity of Spirit
of the Lady of Cofachiqui[8]

But to return to the lady of Cofachiqui, whose seigniories we have not yet left: because it is fitting that her generosities be recorded, we say that, not content with having served and entertained the general and his captains and soldiers in her own house and court, nor satisfied with having provided the supplies that they would need for the march when her country was suffering such want as it did, nor with giving him Indian carriers to serve him throughout the fifty leagues of the province of Xuala, she ordered her vassals to carry from Xuala, where there was plenty of food, without any recompense whatever, all that the Spaniards might request for the twenty leagues of uninhabited country they would have to pass through before reaching Guaxule, and that they give them Indian servants and everything else necessary as if to her own person. Along with this she directed that four principal Indians go with the general, whose care would be to control and give orders to the servants so that the Spaniards might be better attended on their march. She made all these preparations for her own provinces.

But now it must be understood that neither did she overlook the others [i.e., other provinces], desiring that the Spaniards receive the same attentions in all of

---

[8]Book 3, chapter 19.

them. To this end she ordered the four principal Indians that, having entered the province of Guaxule, which bordered upon hers in that direction, they go on ahead and, acting as her ambassadors, charge the curaca of Guaxule that he serve the governor and all his army as she herself had done; otherwise she threatened him with war, with fire and bloodshed. The governor was ignorant of this embassy until the four principal Indians, after they had passed through the uninhabited country, asked his permission to go on ahead to carry it out. When the governor and his captains learned of this it caused them wonder and new gratification to see that that Indian lady had not been content with the service and entertainment she had given them in her own house and country with such affection and good will, but had also provided for it in other [provinces]. From this they came to understand more clearly the will and desire that this lady always had to serve the governor and his Castilians, for thus it was that though she did everything she could to please them, and they saw it, she always asked the general's pardon for being unable to do as much as she wished for them, which so afflicted and depressed her that the Spaniards themselves had to console her. By these manifestations of a generous spirit and others that she showed toward her vassals, according to what they themselves said publicly, she showed herself to be a woman truly worthy of the states she possessed and of other greater ones, and undeserving of being left in her heathenism. The Castilians did not offer her baptism because, as has been said already, they had the intention of preaching the faith after having made settlements and an establishment in that country, and marching continually as they did from one province to another, without stopping, they had little opportunity for preaching.

2. Indians in Virginia

POWHATAN
Address to John Smith
1608

Powhatan was the ruler of approximately fourteen thousand Algonquians called Powhatans, who lived in villages near the Chesapeake Bay. Though he had shown a willingness to trade with the tiny Jamestown colony, he was still uneasy about the

John Smith, *A Map of Virginia, With a Description of the Countrey, the Commodities, People, Government, and Religion* . . . (Oxford, 1612). Reprinted in *The English Experience: Its Record in Early Printed Books Published in Facsimile*, no. 557 (New York: Da Capo Press, 1973), 59–63. (Some spelling and punctuation has been modernized.)

settlers' intentions when Captain John Smith approached him seeking provisions in the winter of 1608. Powhatan had reason to be wary of Europeans: his brother Opechancanough had been captured by the Spanish and taken to Mexico. He was returned during the Spanish attempt to settle near the Chesapeake and soon led an attack that wiped out the newly established colony. It is likely that Opechancanough, who retained an abiding hatred of whites, advised his brother against aiding or trusting the English. In addition, Powhatan had lost many loved ones to European diseases even before Jamestown was settled. And finally, the colonists tended to seize corn by force if it was not readily available by trade.

This passage recounts Powhatan's reaction to Smith's plea for help. Among other things, the chief urged an end to hostilities and issued a subtle warning that, if the English continued to raid his villages in search of food, Indian tolerance and trade would end. Smith, who transcribed the speech, included it in his Map of Virginia, With a Description of the Countrey, the Commodities, People, Government, and Religion, first published in England in 1612.

... Captaine *Smith,* ... some doubt I have of your coming hither, that makes me not so kindly seeke to relieve you as I would; for many do informe me, your coming is not for trade, but to invade my people and possess my Country, who dare not come to bring you corn, seeing you thus armed with your men. To clear us of this feare, leave aboard your weapons, for here they are needlesse we being all friends and for ever *Powhatans.* ...

Captaine *Smith* you may understand, that I, having seene the death of all my people thrice, and not one living of those 3 generations, but my selfe, I know the difference of peace and war, better than any in my Country. But now I am old, and ere long must die; my brethren, namely *Opichapam, Opechankanough,* and *Kekataugh,* my two sisters, and their two daughters, are distinctly each others' successours. I wish their experiences no lesse than mine, and your love to them, no lesse than mine to you; but this brute from *Nansamund*[1] that you are come to destroy my Country, so much affrighteth all my people, as they dare not visit you. What will it availe you, to take that perforce, you may quietly have with love, or to destroy them that provide you with food? What can you get by war, when we can hide our provision and flee to the woodes, whereby you must famish by wronging us your friends; and why are you thus jealous of our loves, seeing us unarmed, and both do, and are willing still to feed you with that you cannot get but by our labours? Think you I am so simple not to knowe it is better to eat good meat, lie well, and sleepe quietly with my women and children, laugh and be merrie with you, have copper hatchets, or what I want, being your friend; than be forced to fly from all, to lie cold in the woods, feed upon acorns, roots, and such trash, and be so hunted by you, that I can neither rest, eat, nor sleepe; but my tired men must

---

[1]**brute from Nansamund:** rumor originating from the Nansemond Indians.

watch, and if a twig but breake, every one cry there comes Captaine *Smith.* Then must I flee I knowe not wither, and thus with miserable feare end my miserable life, leaving my pleasures to such youths as you, which through your rash unadvisedness, may quickly as miserably ende, for want of that you never knowe how to find? Let this therefore assure you of our loves and every yeare our friendly trade shall furnish you with corn, and now also if you would come in friendly manner to see us, and not thus with your guns and swords, as to invade your foes. . . .

Captaine *Smith,* I never used any of *werewances,*[2] so kindly as yourselfe; yet from you I receive the least kindnesse of any. Captaine *Newport* gave me swords, copper, cloths, a bed, tooles, or what I desired, ever taking what I offered him, and would send away his guns when I intreated him: none doth deny to lay at my feet (or do) what I desire, but only you, of who I can have nothing, but what you regard not, and yet you will have whatsoever you demand. Captaine *Newport* you call father, and so you call me, but I see for all us both, you will do what you list, and we must both seeke to content you: but if you intend so friendly as you say, sende hence your armes that I may believe you, for you see the love I bear you doth cause me thus nakedly forget my selfe.

[2]***werewances:*** lesser chiefs subordinate to Powhatan in the Algonquian confederacy; also spelled "werowances."

3. The English in Virginia

John Smith
Description of Indian Life and Culture
1612

The eventual improvement in English relations with Powhatan was largely owed to Captain John Smith, one of the few Englishmen in Virginia who studied the neighboring Indians' language. An experienced soldier and diplomat before coming to Jamestown, Smith had fought against the Spanish in the Netherlands and against the Turks in Hungary. A man of many talents, he is widely credited with saving

John Smith, A Map of Virginia, With a Description of the Countrey, the Commodities, People, Government, and Religion . . . (Oxford, 1612). Reprinted in The English Experience: Its Record in Early Printed Books Published in Facsimile, no. 557 (New York: Da Capo Press, 1973), 19–36. (Some spelling and punctuation has been modernized.)

Jamestown from starvation by forcing the colonists to work and persuading the Indians to supply them with food. Severe injuries from a gunpowder explosion forced Smith to leave Jamestown and return to England in 1609. Yet he continued to aid the struggling colony — and modern historians — by publishing a number of promotional tracts designed to enhance Virginia's poor reputation in England. Like Powhatan's speech, this passage describing Smith's impressions of Indian life and culture is from his 1612 Map of Virginia.

The land is not populous, for the men be fewe; their far greater number is of women and children. Within 60 miles of James Towne there are about some 5,000 people, but of able men fit for their wars scarce 1,500. To nourish so many together they have yet no means because they make so small a benefit of their land, be it never so fertile, 6 or 700 have beene the most hath beene seene together, where they gathered themselves to have surprised Captaine Smith at Pamavuke, having but 15 to withstand the worst of their fury. As small as the proportion of ground that hath yet been discovered, is in comparison of that yet unknowne. The people differ very much in stature, especially in language, as before is expressed. Some being very great as the *Sesquesahamocks*; others very little, as the *Wighcocomocoes*: but generally tall and straight, of a comely proportion, and of a colour browne when they are of any age, but they are borne white. Their haire is generally black, but few have any beards. The men weare halfe their heads shaven, the other halfe long; for Barbers they use their women, who with 2 shells will grate away the haire, of any fashion they please. The women are cut in many fashions agreeable to their yeares but ever some part remaineth long. They are very strong, of an able body and full of agility, able to endure to lie in the woods under a tree by the fire, in the worst of winter, or in the weedes and grasse, in *Ambuscado* in the Summer. They are inconstant in every thing, but what feare constraineth them to keepe. Crafty, timorous, quicke of apprehension, and very ingenious. Some are of disposition fearefull, some bold, most cautious, all *Savage*. Generally covetous of copper, beads, and such like trash. They are soone moved to anger, and so malicious that they seldome forget an injury: They seldome steale one from another, least their conjurers should reveale it, and so they be pursued and punished. That they are thus feared is certaine, but that any can reveale their offences by conjuration I am doubtfull. Their women are carefull to not bee suspected of dishonesty without the leave of their husbands. Each household knoweth their owne lands and gardens, and most live of their owne labours. For their apparell, they are some time covered with skinnes of wilde beasts, which in winter are dressed with hair, but in summer without. The better sort use large mantels[1] of deer skins not much differing in fashion from the Irish mantels. Some embroidered with white beads, some with copper, other painted after their man-

---

[1]**mantels:** cloaks.

ner. But the common sort have scarce to cover their nakednesse but with grasse, the leaves of trees, or such like. We have seen some use mantels made of Turky feathers, so prettily wrought and woven with threads that nothing could bee discerned but the feathers. That was exceedingly warme and very handsome. But the women are always covered about their middles with a skin and very shamefast to be seene bare. They adorne themselves most with copper beads and paintings. Their women some have their legs, hands, breasts, and face cunningly embroidered with divers workes, as beasts, serpentes, artificially wrought into their flesh with blacke spots. In each eare commonly they have 3 great holes, whereat they hang chaines, bracelets, or copper. Some of their men weare in those holes, a small greene and yellow coloured snake, neare halfe a yard in length, which crawling and lapping herselfe about his necke often times familiarly would kisse his lips. Others wear a dead Rat tied by the tail. Some on their heads weare the wing of a bird, or some large feather with a Rattle. Those Rattles are somewhat like the shape of a Rapier butlesse,[2] which they take from the taile of a snake. Many have the whole skinne of a hawke or some strange fowle, stuffed with the wings abroad. Others a broad piece of copper, and some the hand of their enemy dried. Their heads and shoulders are painted red with the roote *Pocone* braied[3] to powder mixed with oil, this they hold in summer to preserve them from the heate, and in winter from the cold. Many other formes of paintings they use, but he is the most gallant that is the most monstrous to behould.

Their buildings and habitations are for the most part by the rivers or not farre distant from some fresh spring. Their houses are built like our Arbors or small young springs bowed and tyed, and so close covered with mats, or the barkes of trees very handsomely, that notwithstanding either winde, raine, or weather, they are as warm as stoves, but very smoky, yet at the toppe of the house there is a hole made for the smoke to goe into right over the fire.

Against the fire they lie on little hurdles of Reedes covered with a mat borne from the ground a foote and more by a hurdle of wood. On these round about the house they lie heads and points one by the other against the fire, some covered with mats, some with skins, and some starke naked lie on the ground. Some 20, some 40, some 100, some 200. Some more, some lesse, some times from 2 to 100 of those houses together, or but a little separated by groves of trees. Neare their habitations is little small wood or old trees on the ground by reason of their burning of them for fire. So that a man may gallop a horse amongst these woods any way, but where the creekes or Rivers shall hinder.

Men, women, and children have their severall names according to the severall humor of their Parents. Their women (they say) are easily delivered of childe, yet do they love children very dearly. To make them hardy, in the coldest mornings they wash in the rivers and by painting and ointments so tanne their skins, that after a year or two, no weather will hurt them.

---

[2]**Rapier butlesse:** probably "rapier but less," meaning the shape of a rapier, but smaller.
[3]**braied:** crushed, ground.

The men bestowe their times in fishing, hunting, wars, and such manlike exercises, scorning to be seen in any woman like exercise, which is the cause that the women be very painefull and the men often idle. The women and children do the rest of the worke. They make mats, baskets, pots, mortars, pound their corne, make their bread, prepare their victuals, plant their corne, gather their corne, beare all kind of burdens, and such like. . . .

Their fishing is much in Boats. These they make of one tree by bowing and scratching away the coals with stones and shells till they have made it in forme of a Trough. Some of them are an elne[4] deepe, and 40 or 50 foot in length, and some will beare 40 men, but the most ordinary are smaller and will bear 10, 20, or 30 according to their bigness. Instead of oares, they use paddles and sticks with which they will row faster than our Barges. . . .

Their manner of trading is for copper, beades, and such like, for which they give such commodities as they have, as skins, fowle, fish, flesh, and their country corne. But their victuall is their chiefest riches. . . .

There is yet in *Virginia* no place discovered to bee so *Savage* in which the *Savages* have not a religion, Deer and Bow, and Arrowes. All things that were able to do them hurt beyond their prevention, they adore with their kinde of divine worship; as the fire, water, lightning, thunder, our ordinance, pieces, horses, etc. But their chiefe God they worship is the Devil. Him they call *Oke* and serve him more of feare than love. They say they have conference with him, and fashion themselves as neare to his shape as they can imagine. In their Temples they have his image evill favouredly carved, and then painted and adorned with chaines copper, and beades, and covered with a skin, in such manner as the deformity may well suit with such a God. By him is commonly the sepulcher of their kings. Their bodies are first bowelled, then dried upon hurdles till they bee very dry, and so about the most of the jointes and necke they hang bracelets or chaines of copper, pearle, and such like, shall not live after death. . . .

Although the country people be very barbarous, yet have they amongst them such government, as that their Magistrates for good commanding, and their people for due subjection, and obeying, excell many places that would be counted very civill. The forme of their Common wealth is a monarchicall governement, one as Emperour ruleth over many kings or governours. Their chiefe ruler is called *Powhatan*. . . .

His kingdome descendeth not to his sons nor children, but first to his brethren, whereof he hath 3, namely *Opitchapan, Opechancanough,* and *Catataugh,* and after their decease to his sisters. First to the eldest sister then to the rest and after then to the heires male and female of the eldest sister, but never to the heirs of the males.

He nor any of his people understand any letters whereby to write or read, only the lawes whereby he ruleth is custum. Yet when he listeth his will is a law and must bee obeyed: not only as a king but as halfe a God they esteeme him. His in-

[4]**elne:** a hogshead or barrel.

feriour kings whom they call *werowances* are tied to rule by custums, and have power of life and death as their command in that nature. But this word *Werowance* which we call and confer for a king, is a common worde whereby they call all commanders: for they have but fewe words in their language, and but few occasions to use any officers more than one commander, which commonly they call *werowances*. They all knowe their severall landes, and habitations, and limits, to fish, fowle or hunt in, but they hold all of their great *Werowances Powhatan*, unto whom they pay tribute of skinnes, beades, copper, pearle, deare, turkies, wild beasts, and corne. What he commandeth they dare not disobey in the least thing. It is strange to see with what great feare and adoration all these people do obey this Powhatan. For at his feet they present whatsoever hee commandeth, and at the least frowne of his browe, their greatest spirits will tremble with feare: and no marvell, for he is very terrible and tyrannous in punishing such as offend him.

4. The French on the Gulf Coast

PIERRE LE MOYNE, SIEUR D'IBERVILLE
Journal Entries
1699

Pierre Le Moyne, Sieur d'Iberville, was well aware that his mission to solidify French claims in Louisiana depended largely upon the recruitment of Indian allies. He took care not to alarm the Indians he encountered and tried to impress them by giving gifts, firing cannon, and igniting brandy. He carefully observed and practiced Indian rituals. After first making friends with the Annocchy (Biloxi), Moctoby, and Chozetta (Pascagoula) tribes, the expedition encountered Indians from the Bayogoula and Mougoulacha tribes west of the Mississippi who, fortunately for d'Iberville, were hunting in the area. The French and the Indians exchanged gifts, officially creating alliances between France and tribes both east and west of the Mississippi. The French then left with the Bayogoula to seek the mouth of the Mississippi. They soon encountered the Ouma and Quinipassa tribes, who gave them an elaborate welcome.

A Comparative View of French Louisiana, 1699 and 1762: The Journals of Pierre Le Moyne d'Iberville and Jean-Jacques-Blaise d'Abbadie, ed., trans., and annot. Carl A. Brasseaux, rev. ed. (Lafayette: Center for Louisiana Studies, University of Southwestern Louisiana, 1981), 31–55.

The following passages are taken from d'Iberville's journal, in which he recorded daily the progress of his expedition. They describe the successful methods the French used to befriend the Indians and at the same time provide valuable information about Indian tribes along the Gulf Coast.

The twelfth.   Midday. We have seen a campfire along the shore of an island, five and a half leagues distant to the northeast.

The thirteenth.   I crossed to the shore four leagues north of here with my *biscayenne*[1] and eleven men, while my brother sailed there in a birchbark canoe with two men. Putting ashore, I found two sets of fresh Indian tracks, which I followed with a single companion. My brother, in the canoe, and the *biscayenne* followed us one-half league to the rear, to avoid frightening the Indians. I trailed them for two leagues, traveling in an easterly direction. At that point, I was overtaken by nightfall and camped. From the vessels to this shore are four leagues distance to the north. Between them I found about sixteen feet of muddy water; however, the approach to the coast is very shallow, with only four feet of water one-half league offshore. This shoreline extends to the west, one-quarter southwest; and east, one-quarter northeast. The woods there are very pretty. Mixed vegetation. There, we see numerous blooming plum trees, turkey tracks, partridges which are only as large as quails, hares comparable to those of France, and fairly good oysters.

February 14.   I continued to follow the Indians' tracks, having left two hatchets, four knives, two packages of porcelain beads, and a little vermilion at my campsite, not doubting that the two Indians, who had come at daybreak to observe me at three hundred paces, would go there when we would depart. While walking in the same manner as the previous day, one and a half leagues from my campsite, I sighted a canoe, which crossed to an island, and several Indians who awaited its arrival there in five additional canoes. Together they crossed to the northern shore. As my position was separated from it by a bay one league wide and four leagues long, I embarked aboard my canoe, and I pursued the Indians' canoes which I overtook as they landed. The Indians then fled into the woods, abandoning their boats and baggage. I disembarked five hundred paces beyond the place where they were concealed near their canoes. There, I encountered an ancient and very ill Indian who was unable to stand up. We conversed through sign language. I gave him something to eat and to smoke; he informed me that he wanted a campfire, which I provided as well as a hut, near which I placed him with his entire baggage and a number of sacks of corn and beans that they had brought in their canoes. I made him understand that I would sleep one-half league from there, where my launch would join me. I sent my brother and two Canadians after the fugitives in an attempt to make them reappear or to capture one of their num-

---

[1]*biscayenne:* a small two-masted boat of the sort used by French fishermen in the Bay of Biscay west of France and north of Spain.

ber. At nightfall, he brought me a woman, whom he had seized in the woods three leagues away. I conducted her to the elder, where I left her, after having given her presents and tobacco to take to her people.

The fifteenth.　　Three of these Indians and two women, having been captured by one of my Canadians, came to chant words of peace. The elder died at ten A.M. One of these men chanted while holding aloft a bleached stick. He then presented it to me. I conducted them to their canoes, where they made sagamité from maize in order to feast us. I also sent for things to feast them and made them a present of hatchets, knives, shirts, tobacco, pipes, *batte-feu,*[2] and beads. Other members of their tribe joined them, and they camped one-half league away.

The morning of the sixteenth.　　Overcast weather and rain. I went ashore to join them. There, I found only ten men clothed in loincloths. All of their canoes and baggage had been removed, indicating that they distrusted me. We smoked once again, although I never smoke. I persuaded three of them to come aboard our vessels, having left the remaining warriors my brother and two Canadians as hostages. I went aboard at two P.M.; they were astounded at everything they saw there. I fired several cannon loaded with solid shot for them. This greatly impressed them.

The seventeenth.　　Noon. I returned to join my brother and to return the three Indians who belong to the Annocchy and Moctoby tribes. They are three-and-a-half days' journey from their village. They mentioned a village of their neighbors, the Chozetta, located on the banks of a river, which they call the Pascoboula, whose mouth lies nine leagues to the east. I gave them some presents to take to their tribes. They assured me that there are four fathoms of water in this river.

At six P.M., I arrived at my brother's campsite. There, I found a Bayogoula chief, his men, and the Mougoulacha, who live along the banks of the Mississippi. They had arrived early last night; while hunting on this side of the island, the Mougoulacha had heard the report of the cannon and had come to see who we were. They repeatedly showered with attention my brother who had given them [tobacco] to smoke and who had feasted them the preceding night. They asked him if he had come in the birchbark canoe which they saw there and if he was one of the people living along the Upper Mississippi, which, is called Malbanchya in their language. He indicated that he was. Having arrived at my brother's campsite, the chief or captain of the Bayogoula came to the seashore to pay me compliments and civilities in their customary manner, which is to pause near you and rub their hands on your face and chest. They then place their hands upon yours, after which they lift them skyward, rubbing them and kissing them again. I repeated the ceremony, having seen it done to the others; they greeted the Annocchy, their friends, in the same manner. After our encounter and the exchange of civilities, we went to my brother's tent, where all of the Bayogoula called to proffer their kind regards to myself and my men, embracing one another. I made them smoke, and we all smoked my iron peace pipe, made in the form of a ship with a white flag

---

[2] *batte-feu:* a tool for starting a fire.

marked with a *fleur de lys*, and embellished with beads. I then gave them a present, consisting of hatchets, knives, blankets, shirts, beads, and other things valued by them, and made them understand that with this calumet I had rendered them united with the French and that we were now one nation. I made them sagamité with plums and gave them some brandy and wine, but they drank very little. They were astounded by the brandy, which we ignited. At eight P.M., the chief and several others came to chant the calumet and to deliver a present, three or four muskrat blankets, allying me with four tribes west of the Mississippi, the Mougoulacha, Ouacha, Toutymascha, Yagueschito, and, to the east of the river, the Bilocchy, Moctoby, Ouma, Pascoboula, Techloel, Bayacchito, and Amicous. The Indians and my men sang at my hut until midnight.

February 18.   After showing these Indians maps in order to ascertain the location of the eastern fork of the Mississippi, we think that the one which they indicated is the Pascoboula River. Since then, I have suspected that this is what they wanted to tell me, that they used this riverway to reach the Mississippi through rivers which communicate with it. I made them understand that I would go to its mouth in my launch in order to take soundings, that I would return to join them, and that my brother and three men would remain with them in the birchbark canoe. The Bayogoula chieftain came to tell me that he would depart on a buffalo and turkey hunt, and that he would return in four days to my first campsite, where we would entertain one another. . . .

The nineteenth.   Today, we traveled six and a half leagues and camped at nightfall on the left riverbank. Three leagues from the Ouma landing, I fired one shot from the swivel gun to notify them of my arrival; I did not wish to surprise them. We fought the unrelenting current for thirteen hours today. My men are exhausted, having eaten only sagamité. They swear and inveigh against the authors of the spurious reports which are the cause of my determination to press onward.

The twentieth.   At 10:30 A.M., I arrived at the Ouma village landing, three leagues from my campsite, where I found five men — three Ouma and [two] Quinipissa awaiting my arrival with a peace pipe. They had come from the village upon hearing the discharge of the swivel gun. As soon as they sighted us, they began singing, and the Bayogoula who accompanied me sang on my behalf. Upon landing, we were embraced and we saluted one another in the customary manner, and we smoked the calumet together. At eleven o'clock, I set out for the village; the Bayogoula and these people escorted us the length of the pathway. The Ouma deputies walked ahead of us, singing constantly although we were constrained to travel over a very primitive trail, replete with very steep hills or small mountains through most of the journey. At one P.M., we were within sight of the village; four hundred paces beyond this point, I encountered three men commissioned to present me with the peace pipe. Protocol required ceremonial smoking of the calumet while seated upon a mat. This fatigued me, never having smoked. The three new singers conducted me to a hilltop, three hundred paces distant from the village, where there were three huts. There they detained me, forwarded notification of my arrival to the chief, and awaited his instructions. A man subsequently came and told us to enter the village. Upon our arrival, the three singers walked in advance of our party, singing and presenting the calumet of peace to the village by elevating it at an arm's length overhead. The chief and two of the most eminent villagers appeared before me at the entrance to the village, each holding a white cross in their hand. They saluted me in their customary manner, and subsequently took me by the arm and conducted me to the mats placed at the center of the settlement, where the entire village had assembled. There, we smoked the peace pipe again, and they exhibited many signs of their friendship. I gave them a small present, while awaiting the opportunity to present more substantial gifts, which I intend to distribute among them at the longboats. At four P.M., they held a ball of sorts in our honor at the center of the settlement, before the assembled villagers. They brought rattles to the center of the assembly. These instruments are gourds, containing dried seeds and have a cane handle. They produce a gentle sound and serve to mark the cadence. A number of singers subsequently appeared and, shortly thereafter, were followed by twenty young men, twenty to thirty years of age, and fifteen of the prettiest young women. Magnificently adorned, by their standards, the females were completely nude, wearing only a strap, upon which they placed a one foot wide sash. The sashes are made of feathers and fur or bristles, painted red, yellow, and white. Their faces and bodies were tatooed or painted different colors, and they carried plumes in their hands, which are used as fans or to mark the cadence. Their hair was properly plaited and adorned with bouquets of plumes. The young men are naked, wearing only a sash like the girls, which partially conceals their nudity. Like the elders, these young males were auspiciously marked and their hair was attractively trimmed with bouquets of feathers. Several had cooking utensils in the form of flattened plates, in bundles of two or three, attached to their sashes. Hanging to the knees, these earthenware utensils made noise and aided in marking the cadence. They danced in this manner for three hours with a very cheerful and sportive mien. At nightfall, the chief lodged us in a cabin or house which he had built. After having dined on sagamité, they brought forth and lit a fifteen foot long torch, two feet in circumference and composed of bound canes. This flambeau, which adequately illuminated the site of the festivities, was erected at the center of the village. All of the local youths arrived with their bows and arrows, tomahawks, and instruments of war. In addition, several women or girls were present. Once again, they began dancing the war dances, which I deemed very pretty. The festivities continued until midnight, when the revelers retired to their homes, except the chief, who remained in his hut to sleep with us and all of the Bayogoula. . . .

Suggestions for Further Reading

Clayton, Lawrence A., Vernon James Knight Jr., and Edward C. Moore, eds. *The De Soto Chronicles: The Expedition of Hernando de Soto to North America in 1539–1543.* 2 vols. Tuscaloosa: University of Alabama Press, 1993.

Conrad, Glenn R., ed. *The Louisiana Purchase Bicentennial Series in Louisiana History.* Vol. 1, *The French Experience in Louisiana.* Lafayette: Center for Louisiana Studies, University of Southwestern Louisiana, 1995.

Hudson, Charles, and Carmen Chaves Tesser, eds. *The Forgotten Centuries: Indians and Europeans in the American South, 1521–1704.* Athens: University of Georgia Press, 1994.

Milanich, Jerald T. *Florida Indians and the Invasion from Europe.* Gainesville: University Press of Florida, 1995.

Milanich, Jerald T., and Susan Milbrath, eds. *First Encounters: Spanish Explorations in the Caribbean and the United States, 1492–1570.* Gainesville: University Press of Florida, 1989.

Whayne, Jeannie M., ed. *Cultural Encounters in the Early South: Indians and Europeans in Arkansas.* Fayetteville: University of Arkansas Press, 1995.

Wood, Peter H., Gregory A. Waselkov, and M. Thomas Hatley, eds. *Powhatan's Mantle: Indians in the Colonial Southeast.* Lincoln: University of Nebraska Press, 1989.

CHAPTER TWO

COLONIZATION

Religion and the Founding of Maryland

T he earliest English efforts at colonization were unimpressive. Sponsored by Sir Walter Raleigh, colonists were dispatched in the 1580s to Roanoke Island, a site in present-day North Carolina. Poor planning, bad relations with local Indian tribes, and the colonists' inability to feed themselves led to disastrous results, and the English abandoned the Roanoke Island effort (later known as the "Lost Colony") by 1590. Although Jamestown presented a rocky beginning for the Virginia Colony, by the 1620s it had established itself as a permanent colony. By 1629, meanwhile, the English had planted settlements in Plymouth and around Massachusetts Bay, which was populated by Puritan immigrants.

The motives for English colonization were economic, social, political, and cultural, but religion was also undeniably important. While religious concerns played little or no role in the settlement of the Virginia Colony, an important goal in New England was to create a "Zion on the Hill," an example of godly government in the New World. In both the Plymouth and Massachusetts Bay colonies, churches formed the basis of social and political organization; towns were settled around congregations, and lay church leaders were also the colonies' political leaders.

The Chesapeake developed differently. Economically, the Maryland Colony established itself much like the Virginia Colony to the south, and very soon it depended on tobacco cultivation; within fifty years of its founding, Marylanders relied predominantly on African slave labor. But Maryland also provides a different example of English colonization, particularly in the important — and unique — role that religion played in it. George Calvert, the first Lord Baltimore, was an important political figure during the reigns of James I and Charles I. In 1625 he converted to Roman Catholicism and became determined to found a colony that would welcome Catholics into the New World. After an unsuccessful attempt at establishing a colony in Newfoundland, he began to lay the plans for another in the northern Chesapeake. Two months after Calvert's death in 1632, Charles I granted a charter to Calvert's elder son, Cecil Calvert, the second Lord Baltimore, who organized the Maryland Colony the following year. From the outset the new Lord Baltimore wanted to make the colony a center for immigration by English Roman Catholics, though he did not expect that Catholicism would be the only form of organized religion.

The Maryland Colony offered a new model of religious pluralism. Lacking a single dominant method of worship, it was shaped by the pronounced and often bitter struggle between Protestants and Catholics for religious and political dominance. The early settlers competed with Protestants from Virginia, led by the English trader William Claiborne, who had established themselves in the northern Chesapeake as fur traders and planters. The two groups clashed militarily in 1635, and the Marylanders succeeded in subduing the Virginians within the next two years. Conditions for the spread of Roman Catholicism beyond the upper-class English who immigrated were not auspicious, and events worked to undermine Calvert's plans. Within two decades of the founding of the colony, a majority of the English inhabitants were Protestants, most of them hostile to "Papist" — a disparaging term for "Catholic" — rule. By 1637 Maryland's expanding Protestant majority, which included some Puritans, had organized itself into a one-house colonial assembly. Like other such assemblies in the British empire, the Maryland assembly enacted the colony's laws and levied taxes.

Maryland then became entangled in the English Civil War, in which supporters of the Parliament and of King Charles I fought a protracted and bitter war for supremacy. A group of Protestant Parliamentarians arrived in Maryland in 1645 and declared the Calvert government illegitimate because of its royalist connections; the Protestant interlopers were soon driven out, but the political-religious instability continued. After the Calverts' proprietary rule ended in 1652, the colony was ruled by a ten-man Puritan council, which in October 1654 repealed the Toleration Act and prohibited Roman Catholics from practicing their faith. Led by local officeholder William Stone, Catholic settlers rebelled and fought a losing battle with Puritans at the Severn River in March 1655. The conflict ended in 1657, when rule by the Calverts was reestablished and the principle of religious toleration for all Christian sects was restored.

As the documents in this chapter illustrate, establishing colonies was not an easy process anywhere. It evoked basic conflicts, such as religious differences between Protestants and Roman Catholics, and contradictions arose between original objectives and the actual ways in which colonization occurred. Lord Baltimore's instructions lay out the Calverts' objectives in establishing the colony: not all of those objectives were religious, and Calvert was realistic enough to understand the limits of how far he could go in establishing Roman Catholicism in the

New World. Nonetheless, Maryland's subsequent development strayed from Baltimore's intentions, as shown by Father Edward Knott's description of the Catholic experience and by a Protestant partisan's perspective, in "Babylon's Fall," of the intense Protestant-Catholic conflict that erupted in the Maryland Colony.

As you read, trace the Calverts' original intentions in settling Maryland, especially with regard to religion, and the effects conditions in the developing colony had on the fulfillment of their goals. How did the colony try to deal with Protestant-Catholic conflict? How did religious conflict shape Maryland and make its development unique?

5. Catholic Intentions

CECIL CALVERT, LORD BALTIMORE
Instructions to His Colonists
1633

After Charles I granted a charter authorizing the new colony of Maryland, Cecil Calvert, the second Lord Baltimore, worked hard to recruit an expedition that would realize his father's dream of establishing a Catholic colony in North America. Although he wanted to accompany the colonists himself, Calvert decided to remain in England in order to protect the colony from political attacks. Those who did go were divided into two classes: gentlemen, most of whom were Catholic, and indentured servants, most of whom were Protestant. Before they set sail in November 1633, Calvert provided them with a set of instructions. (In the English colonies, it was frequent practice for officials to whom the colonists were responsible — in this case, Lord Baltimore — to detail their expectations in writing.) Baltimore's instructions do more than outline how he thought Maryland should be organized and governed: they reveal the role he envisioned for religion in this new colony.

Narratives of Early Maryland: 1633–1684, ed. Clayton Colman Hall, Original Narratives of Early American History (New York: Charles Scribner's Sons, 1910), 16–23. (Some spelling and punctuation has been modernized.)

Instructions 13 Novem: 1663 directed by the Right Honorable Cecilius Lo: Baltimore and Lord of the Provinces of Mary Land and Avalon unto his well beloved Brother Leo: Calvert Esquire his Lordship Deputy Governor of his province of Mary Land and unto Jerom Hawley and Thomas Cornwaleys Esquires, his Lordship's Commissioners for the government of the said Province.

1. INPRI:[1] His Lordship requires his said Governor and Commissioners that in their voyage to Mary Land they be very carefull to preserve unity and peace amongst all the passengers on Shipboard, and that they suffer no scandall nor offence to be given to any of the Protestants, whereby any just complaint may hereafter be made, by them, in Virginea or in England, and that for that end they cause all Acts of Roman Catholic Religion to be done as privately as may be, and that they instruct all the Roman Catholics to be silent upon all occasions of discourse concerning matters of Religion; and that the said Governor and Commissioners treat the Protestants with as much mildness and favor as Justice will permit. And this to be observed at Land as well as at Sea. . . .

3. That as soon as it shall please God they shall arrive upon the coast of Virginea, they be not persuaded by the master or any other of the shipp, in any case or for any respect whatsoever to go to James Towne, or to come within the command of the fort at Poynt-Comfort: unless they should be forced into it by some extremity of weather (which god forbidd) for the preservation of their lives and goods, and that they find it altogether impossible otherwise to preserve themselves: But that they come to an Anchor somewhere about Accomack,[2] so as it be not under the command of any fort; and to send ashore there, to inquire if they can find any to take with them, that can give them some good information of the Bay of Chesapeake and Pattawomeck River, and that may give them some light of a fit place in his Lordship's Country to set down on; wherein their chief care must be to make choice of a place first that is probable to be healthfull and fruitfull, next that it may be easily fortified, and thirdly that it may be convenient for trade both with the English and savages. . . .

6. That when they have made choice of the place where they intend to settle themselves and that they have brought their men ashore with all their provisions, they do assemble all the people together in a fit and decent manner and then cause his majesties letters patents[3] to be publicly read by his Lordship's Secretary John Bolles, and afterwards his Lordship's Commission to them, and that either the Governor or one of the Commissioners presently after make some short declaration to the people of his Lordship's intentions which he means to pursue in this his intended plantation, which are first the honor of god by endeavoring the conversion of the savages to Christianity, secondly the augmentation of his majesties Empire and Dominions in those parts of the world by reducing them under the subjection of his Crown, and thirdly by the good of such of his Countrymen as are

---

[1] **INPRI:** misspelled abbreviation of the Latin *imprimis,* "in the first place."
[2] **Accomack:** located on the eastern shore of Chesapeake Bay.
[3] **letters patents:** documents from the king authorizing the colony's establishment.

willing to adventure their fortunes and themselves in it, by endeavoring as he can, to assist them, that they may reap the fruits of their charges and labors according to the hopefulness of the thing, with as much freedom, comfort, and encouragement as they can desire; and with all to assure them, that his Lordship's affection and zeal is so great to the advancement of this Plantation and consequently of their good, that he will imploy all his endeavors in it, and that he would not have failed to have come himself in person along with them this first year, to have been partaker with them in the honor of the first voyage thither, but that by reasons of some unexpected accidents, he found it more necessary for their good, to stay in England some time longer, for better establishment of his and their right, then it was fit that the shipp should stay for him but that by the grace of god he intends without fail to be with them the next year: And that at this time they take occasion to minister an oath of Allegeance to his majestie unto all and every one upon the place, after having first publicly in the presence of the people taken it themselves; letting them know that his Lordship gave particular directions to have it one of the first things that were done, to testify to the world that none should enjoy the benefit of his majesties gracious Grant unto his Lordship of that place, but such as should give a public assurance of their fidelity and allegeance to his majestie. . . .

9. That where they intend to settle the Plantation they first make choice of a fit place and a competent quantity of ground for a fort within which or near unto it a convenient house, and a church or a chapel adjacent may be built for the seat of his Lordship or his Governor or other Commissioners for the time being in his absence, both which his Lordship would have them take care should in the first place be erected, in some proportion at least, as much as is necessary for present use though not so compleate in every part as in fine afterwards they may be and to send his Lordship a Platt[4] of it and of the situation, by the next opportunity, if it be done by that time, if not or but part of it nevertheless to send a Platt of what they intend to do in it. That they likewise make choice of a fit place neer unto it to seat a towne.

10. That they cause all the Planters to build their houses in as decent and uniform a manner as their abilities and the place will afford, and neer adjoining one to another, and for that purpose to cause streets to be marked out where they intend to place the towne and to oblige every man to build one by another according to that rule and that they cause divisions of Land to be made adjoyning on the back sides of their houses and to be assigned unto them for gardens and such uses according to the proportion of every ones building and adventure and as the conveniency of the place will afford which his Lordship refers to their discretion, but is desirous to have a particular account from them what they do in it, that his Lordship may be satisfied that every man hath justice done unto him.

11. That as soon as conveniently they can they cause his Lordship's surveyor Robert Simpson to survey out such a proportion of Land both in and about the intended towne as likewise within the Countrey adjoyning as will be necessary to be

---

[4]**Platt:** probably "plan."

assigned to the present adventurers, and that they assigne every adventurer his proportion of Land both in and about the intended towne, as also within the Countrey adjoyning, according to the proportion of his adventure and the conditions of plantation propounded by his Lordship to the first adventurers, which his Lordship in convenient time will confirme unto them by Pattent. And herein his Lordship wills his said Governor and Commissioners to take care that in each of the aforesaid places, that is to say in and about the first intended Towne and in the Countrey adjacent they cause in the first and most convenient places a proportion of Land to be sett out for his Lordship's owne proper use and inheritance according to the number of men he sends this first yeare upon his owne account; and as he alloweth unto the adventurers, before any other be assigned his part; with which (although his Lordship might very well make a difference of proportion between himself and the adventurers) he will in this first colony, content himself, for the better encouragement and accommodation of the first adventurers, unto whom his Lordship conceive himself more bound in honor and is therefore desirous to give more satisfaction in everything then he intends to do unto any that shall come hereafter. That they cause his Lordship's surveyor likewise to draw an exact mapp of as much of the countrey as they shall discover together with the soundings of the rivers and Baye, and to send it to his Lordship.

12. That they cause all the planters to imploy their servants in planting of sufficient quantity of corne and other provision of victuall and that they do not suffer them to plant any other commodity whatsoever before that be done in a sufficient proportion which they are to observe yearly.

13. That they cause all sorts of men in the plantation to be mustered and trained in military discipline and that there be days appoynted for that purpose either weekly or monthly according to the conveniency of other occasions; which are duly to be observed and that they cause constant watch and ward to be kept in places necessary.

14. That they informe themselves whether there be any convenient place within his Lordship's precincts for the making of Salt, whether there be proper earth for the making of saltpeter and if there be in what quantity; whether there be probability of Iron oare or any other mines and that they be carefull to find out what other commodities may probably be made and that they give his Lordship notice together with their opinions of them.

15. That in fine they be very carefull to do justice to every man without partiality, and that they avoid any occasion of difference with those of Virginea and to have as little to do with them as they can this first yeare that they connive and suffer little injuries from them rather than to engage themselves in a public quarrell with them, which may disturbe the business much in England in the Infancy of it. And that they give unto his Lordship an exact account by their letters from time to time of their proceedings both in these instructions from Article to Article and in any other accident that shall happen worthy his Lordship's notice, that thereupon his Lordship may give them farther instructions what to do and that by every conveyance by which they send any letters as his Lordship would not have them to omitt any they send likewise a Duplicate of the letters which they writt

by the last conveyance before that, least they should have failed and not be come to his Lordship's hands.

6. Jesuit Missionaries

FATHER EDWARD KNOTT, S.J.
From the "Annual Letter of the English Province of the Society of Jesus"
1638

Accompanying the Calverts into Maryland were members of the Society of Jesus — the Jesuits — who constituted the Roman Catholic Church's chief missionary organization. Although Jesuits accompanied French fur traders in Canada and the Mississippi Valley and could be found throughout the Spanish colonies, they were not active in English North America until settlers first arrived in Maryland in 1634. To a large degree, they operated without much supervision by Calvert and his officials. With a majority of the white population Protestant and deeply suspicious of Catholics, the Jesuit fathers traveled in Maryland under false identities and wrote their reports in great secrecy. They maintained detailed records of their work and reported regularly to their superior in Maryland, Edward Knott, who in turn annually described their progress to the General Society in Rome. The following excerpts from Knott's letter for 1638 recount the condition of Roman Catholicism in Maryland four years after the colony's founding, including experiences with Native Americans and Protestant settlers, and suggest something about the obstacles that confronted Roman Catholics in the New World.

Four fathers belonged to this mission, with one coadjutor in temporal concerns. And he indeed, after enduring severe toils for the space of five years with the greatest patience, humility, and ardent love, chanced to be seized by the disease prevailing at the time, and happily exchanged this wretched life for an immortal one.

Narratives of Early Maryland: 1633–1684, ed. Clayton Colman Hall, Original Narratives of Early American History (New York: Charles Scribner's Sons, 1910), 119–24. (Some spelling and punctuation has been modernized.)

He was also shortly followed by one of the fathers, who was young indeed, but on account of his remarkable qualities of mind, evidently of great promise. He had scarcely spent two months in this mission, when, to the great grief of all, he was carried off by the common sickness prevailing in the colony, from which no one of the three remaining priests has escaped unharmed; yet we have not ceased to labor, to the best of our ability, among the neighboring people.

And though the rulers of this colony have not yet allowed us to dwell among the savages, both on account of the prevailing sicknesses, and also because of the hostile acts which the barbarians commit against the English, they having slain a man from this colony, who was staying among them for the sake of trading, and having also entered into a conspiracy against our whole nation; yet we hope that one of Ours will shortly secure a station among the barbarians. Meanwhile, we devote ourselves more zealously to the English; and since there are Protestants as well as Catholics in the colony, we have labored for both, and God has blessed our labors.

For, among the Protestants, nearly all who have come from England in this year 1638, and many others, have been converted to the faith, together with four servants, whom we purchased in Virginia (another colony of our kingdom), for necessary services, and five mechanics, whom we hired for a month, and have in the meantime won to God. Not long afterwards, one of these, after being duly prepared for death, by receiving the sacraments, departed this life. And among these persons hardly anything else worth mentioning has occurred. The following occurrences are more remarkable.

A certain man, entirely unknown to us, but a zealous disciple of the Protestant religion, was staying with a friend who was still more zealous; and having been bitten by one of the snakes which abound in these parts, was expecting immediate death. One of Ours, finding this out, took with him a surgeon, and hurried to the sick man, who, it was reported, had already lost his senses, with the intention of ministering to his soul in any way that he could. But the host, divining his intention, tried to thwart his pious efforts. And the priest, as he could find no other opportunity, determined to stay all night with the sick man. But the host prevented this too, and, lest the Father should be admitted at night, he appointed a guard to sleep on a bed, laid across the door of the chamber occupied by his friend. Nevertheless, the priest kept on the watch for every opportunity of approach; and going at the dead of night, when he supposed the guard would be especially overcome by sleep, he contrived, without disturbing him, to pass in to the sick man; and, at his own desire, received him into the Church. And although, under the circumstances, it was impossible that the sick man should be taught much, or be firmly established in his belief, yet when, contrary to all expectation, he had been cured by our surgeon, the grace of God prevailed with him, and he chose rather to be put out of his friend's house than to retract what he had done; nay, he even came to us of his own accord, and happily completed the work he had begun.

Another man, when one of Ours tried to bring him to the orthodox faith, repulsed him with the answer, "that he had vowed that he never would embrace that faith." A short time afterwards this wretched man was attacked by disease, and brought to the last extremity, before the Father was advised of his sickness. He, however, hastens to the sick man with all speed, and finds him entirely insensible, yet still breathing. Accordingly he instructs the attendants to put some nourishment into the mouth of the sick man, every now and then, and to summon him if at any time he returned to consciousness. This was done early the next morning, and the Father runs to him, and, while talking to him, perceives that he is in some measure recognized by him, and receives from him, at times, an answer to a short question (for he could not take in too long a discourse at once). The Father therefore determined to make use of the present opportunity, inasmuch as he could not hope for another one afterwards. And when by various communications he had obtained (as he judged) the consent of the sick man, understanding from him that he wished to be made a Catholic, that he was sorry for his sins, and that he wished to be absolved from them, he absolved him from his sins and anointed him with the sacred oil. After this had been done, the sick man, in a day or two, was perfectly restored to his senses. And when he was asked what he had done, or what he had perceived to have been done around him, he answered with so great joy and such heart-felt emotion, that he had been admitted into the Catholic Church, and that he intended to remain in it even to his last breath, that all who were present were affected with no small admiration. Afterwards, when the Father came again, he expressed the same joy to him; and to his great satisfaction performed the other things necessary for completing the work he had begun. From that time he gradually recovered; but, since he had scarcely any proper remedies, and lay for a long time on his back, a dreadful ulcer broke out over his whole body. Wherefore we procured necessaries for him, as far as we could, at our own expense, and sent a surgeon to cure his malady. And although the surgeon removed a great many worms from the ulcer, yet by his skilful attention and the watchful care of others the sick man was cured, and now he is a strong servant, sound, as we trust, both in mind and body.

Another man, who was of noble birth, had been reduced to such poverty by his own unrestrained licentiousness, that he sold himself into this colony. Here, when he had been recalled by one of Ours, to the right faith and the fruit of good living, he always anxiously doubted whether he had entered upon the safe road; and on one occasion, when he had intrusted himself to the sea in a small skiff, and a frightful storm arose, such as he had never seen, although he had often met with storms at sea, and certain shipwreck seemed already at hand, he earnestly prayed to God, that in confirmation of the faith he had lately received — if it was really true — he would ward off the impending danger. God heard his prayer, and turning the storm in another direction, confirmed his wavering mind with tranquil peace. Not long afterwards, this man was brought to the last extremity by a severe disease, and after taking all the sacraments, about an hour before his death asked his Catholic attendant to pray for him. It is probable that an evil angel presented himself to his sight; for almost at the very point of death he called the same attendant and said, with a cheerful voice: "Don't you see my good angel? Behold him standing near to carry me away; I must depart"; and thus, happily (as we are permitted to hope) he breathed his last. Since his burial, a very bright light has often been seen at night around his tomb, even by Protestants.

Besides these, one of Ours, going out of the colony, found two Frenchmen, one of whom had been without the sacraments of the Catholic Church for three entire years; the other, who was already near death, having spent fifteen whole years among heretics, had lived just as they do. The Father aided the former with the sacraments and confirmed him in the Catholic faith as much as he could. The latter he restored to the Catholic Church, and, administering all the sacraments, prepared him for dying happily.

As for the Catholics, the attendance on the sacraments here is so large, that it is not greater among the Europeans, in proportion to the number of Catholics. The more ignorant have been catechised, and catechetical lectures have been delivered for the more advanced every Sunday; and on feast days sermons have been rarely neglected. The sick and the dying, who have been very numerous this year, and who dwelt far apart, we have assisted in every way, so that not even a single one has died without the sacraments. We have buried very many, and baptized various persons. And, although there are not wanting frequent occasions of dissension, yet none of any importance has arisen here in the last nine months, which we have not immediately allayed. By the blessing of God, we have this consolation, that no vices spring up among the new Catholics, although settlements of this kind are not usually supplied from the best class of men.

We bought off in Virginia two Catholics who had sold themselves into bondage, nor was the money ill-spent, for both are showing themselves good Christians: one, indeed, surpasses the ordinary standard. Some others have performed the same duty of charity, buying thence Catholic servants, who are very numerous in that country. For every year very many sell themselves thither into bondage, and living among men of the worst example and being destitute of all spiritual aid, they generally make shipwreck of their souls.

Several of the chief men by spiritual exercises have been formed by us to piety, a fruit not to be repented of. In the case of one, we adore the remarkable providence and mercy of God, which brought a man encompassed in the world with very many difficulties, and now at length living in Virginia, almost continually without any aid to his soul, to undertake these exercises, not long before his death; by which he profited so much that he determined on the very best mode of spending his life thenceforth. This design a severe sickness prevented, which he bore with the greatest patience, with a mind generally fixed on God; and at length having properly received all the sacraments, in the most peaceful manner, contrary to the usual course of his life, which had been so full of troubles and disquietudes, renders back his soul to his Creator.

A noble matron also has died, who, coming with the first settlers into the colony, with more than woman's courage bore all difficulties and inconveniences. She was given to much prayer, and most anxious for the salvation of her neighbors — a perfect example of right management as well in her self as in her domestic concerns — she was fond of our society while living, and a benefactor to it when dying — of blessed memory with all, for her notable examples, especially of charity to the sick, as well as of other virtues.

7. A Violent Confrontation

LEONARD STRONG
Babylon's Fall
1655

The eruption of Protestant-Catholic tensions during the 1640s and 1650s profoundly affected the Maryland colonists. Babylon's Fall, one of several pamphlets published in England at the time, was part of another war — a war of words — between English Catholics and Protestants vying to win support for their cause. Calvert's supporters lobbied to preserve Maryland's charter — the legal basis for proprietary rule — while his opponents sought to invalidate it. Some observers favored a general reconciliation of the two sides. The author of the document reprinted here, Leonard Strong, was a member of the ten-man Puritan council that governed Maryland during part of the 1650s. He also served as the agent for the Protestant cause in London, and in 1655 wrote this pamphlet urging an invalidation of Calvert's charter.

Babylon's Fall in Maryland: a Fair Warning to Lord Baltimore; or a Relation of an Assault made by divers Papists, and Popish Officers of the Lord Baltimore's against the Protestants in Maryland; to whom God gave a great Victory against a greater force of Souldiers and armed Men, who came to destroy them.
Published by Leonard Strong, Agent for the people of Providence in Maryland. Printed for the Author, 1655.

In the yeer 1649, many, both of the congregated Church, and other well-affected people in Virginia, being debarred from the free exercise of Religion under the Government of Sir William Barkely, removed themselves, Families, and

Narratives of Early Maryland: 1633–1684, ed. Clayton Colman Hall, Original Narratives of Early American History (New York: Charles Scribner's Sons, 1910), 235–44. (Some spelling and punctuation has been modernized.)

Estates into the Province of Maryland, being thereunto invited by Captain William Stone, then Governor for Lord Baltamore, with promise of Liberty in Religion and Priviledges of English Subjects.

An Oath to the Lord Baltamore was urged upon this people soon after their coming up, which if they did not take, they must have no Land, nor abiding in the Province. This Oath was very scrupulously looked upon: first, In regard it bindes to acknowledge and be subject to a Royal Jurisdiction and absolute Dominion of the Lord Baltamore, and to defend it and him against all power whatsoever. This was thought far too high for him, being a Subject, to exact upon such terms as it was exacted and too much unsuitable to the present liberty which God had given the English Subjects from Arbitrary and Popish Government as the Lord Baltamore's Government doth plainly appear to be. Secondly, It was exceedingly scrupled on another account *viz.*: That they must swear to uphold that Government and those Officers who are sworn to countenance and uphold Antichrist, in plain words exprest in the Officers Oath, the Roman Catholick Religion. And for these people to own such by an Oath, whom in their hearts they could by no means close with; what could it be accounted but Collusion?

Yet nevertheless the people that were then come up to Providence, considering Lord Baltamore to be Lord of the soil, and willing to acknowledge him, and pay him his due Rents and Services; upon that account took an Oath which was much qualified and moderated from its former rigour: but this, though it was accepted by Captain Stone, the Lord Baltamore's Lieutenant, yet utterly rejected by his Lordship, who gave order, That the Oath absolutely should be urged; and gave special instructions and charge to his Lieutenant to proclaim, That all that would not take the Oath within three Months after publication, and pay Rents, and sue out Patents,[1] should be expulsed the Province, and the Land seized to his Lordships use; who required his Officers to see the contents of the Proclamation executed.

Now the people having been formerly sensible of such yokes, imposed contrary to what was promised them before they came into the Province, complained by their Agent in England.

First, to the Lord Baltamore, desiring his Lordship, That such burdens as the Oath and other great inconveniences mentioned in our instructions, might be removed. But the Lord Baltamore rejected the motion. Our Agent presented a Petition to the Council of State, where it hath been depending neer four yeers, without any hearing, Answer or Relief; which hath brought unspeakable troubles upon this Province, and now at last occasioned the Shedding of much English blood, yea, of the Saints in Maryland. God grant that Right and Justice may have a more open course to flow into all the Dominions of England, without obstructions, and that innocent blood be not shed any more for want thereof. . . .

Then the Lord Baltamore's Officers, and the Popish party began to divulge abroad, and boast much of power which came in that ship from his Highness the Lord Protector to confirm the Lord Baltamore's Patent to him, and to re-establish

---

[1]**Patents:** land patents, legal documents validating land titles.

his Officers in their former places under him: which pretended power they assumed to themselves; Captain Stone and the rest giving out threatning speeches, That now the Rebels at Putuxent and Severne, should know that he was Governour again; giving Order, That neither Act of the said Assembly should be observed, nor Writ from the power established by the Commissioners aforesaid obeyed, but what should issue forth in the name of the Lord Proprietory, *viz.* Lord Baltamore. And further, the said Captain Stone gave several Commissions to the Papists and other desperate and bloody fellows, to muster and raise men in arms to be ready upon all occasions, giving out that he would go to Putuxent and seize the Records of the Province at the place where they were appointed to be kept by an Act of the Assembly, and to apprehend Mr. Richard Preston also, at whose house they were; which shortly after was effected by Vertue of a Warrant in Captain Stone's name, without Proclaiming, or showing any power by which he acted such high Robberies. But in threatning speeches declared, That they would have the Government; and for the terror of others, would hang some of the Commissioners, which were entrusted with the Government by the Commissioners of the Commonwealth of England, under his Highness the Lord Protector, namely Captain William Fuller, Mr. Richard Preston, and Mr. William Durand.

About this time Captain William Fuller, Mr. William Durand, Mr. Leonard Strong, and Mr. Richard Ewen, to whom among others the Government was committed, sent two Messengers of quality and trust with Letters to Captain Stone in a way of peace and love; desiring him to make it known by what power he surprised the Records; and desiring him, the said Captain Stone, to give an Answer, as by the Letter, relation thereunto being had, more at large appeareth: But the said Captain Stone, instead of giving a satisfactory Answer, imprisoned the Messengers, and in much wrath and fury said he would show no power: at last he affirmed, that he acted by a power from Lord Baltamore; and that the Lord Protector had confirmed the Lord Baltamore's power. If so, Sir, said one of the Messengers, if it be confirmed, let that appear and it will satisfie. Confirmed, said Captain Stone, I'll confirm it; and so sent them home. After this the said Captain Stone and his Officers proceeded in their wicked design; yet to colour it over, the said Captain Stone published a Proclamation to deceive the amazed and distracted people at Putuxent; wherein he called God to witness, that he intended not to use any hostile way to them or the people at Providence. Which Protestation, how false and feigned it was, the following proceedings of himself and Officers will clearly evidence to all the World: for notwithstanding this Proclamation and Protestation, the said Captain Stone sent up to Putuxent one William Eltonhead and Josias Fendall, and with them twenty men in Arms, who did beset and entered the house of Mr. Richard Preston, with intent to surprise him; but not finding him at home, took away in Guns, Swords, and Ammunition to the value of 30 *l.* sterling; ransacked every place in and about the house, to seek for the said Richard Preston; and as some of the Company then said with purpose to hang him for his rebellion against the Lord Baltamore. At the same time they surprised John Sutton, who was appointed by the Assembly and Secretary to attend the Records for any that should have occasion to use them either for search or Copy; and carried him away Prisoner with such Guns and Ammunition he had, and kept him about twenty dayes; even so they dealt with Lieutenant Peter Johnson; several other houses at Putuxent, they served in the like kinde. And when they were desired to show by what power or Commission they so acted, they would in a proud bravado clap their hands on their swords, and say, Here is a Commission. This was no sooner effected at Putuxent, but presently they mustered in Arms two hundred or two hundred and fifty men at the house of the aforesaid Eltonhead, which Eltonhead and Fendall sent up by night several Boats with armed men, and forced many of Putuxent whether they would or not to go with them upon their warlike Expedition to Providence; taking all the Guns, Powder, Shot, and Provision, they could anywhere finde. And when they had done what they pleased at Putuxent, they bent all their forces towards Providence, the chief place of the residence of most of the Commissioners, and people that were forced out of Virginia by Sir William Barkely for conscience sake, Some of the said Company marching by Land, others by Water; they that marched by Land, did much spoil and robbery in all the Houses and Plantations where they came, breaking open Doors, Trunks, and Chests. In this barbarous manner, they carried it for about forty miles.

Now again the Commissioners at Providence sent other Messengers with a Letter to Capt. Stone, still complaining his proceedings and seeking the knowledge of his power; and that some better accommodation might be attended to prevent the ruine and desolation of the whole Province, which this course was very likely to bring to pass. If he were resolved to come to no Parley or Treaty they protested in the said writing, that by the help of God, they were resolved to commit themselves into the hand of God, and rather die like men, than live like slaves. This was also rejected by the said Captain Stone and his Accomplices, the Messengers apprehended, their Boat seized, and only three of six escaped to bring the report of their desperate and bloody design, and that they were upon their march in a hostile way.

Capt. Stone and his Company still drew neerer to Providence, into a place called Herring-Creek, where they apprehended one of the Commissioners, and forced another man of quality to flee for his life, having threatened to hang him up at his own door; and not finding the man, affrighted his wife, and plundered the house of Ammunition and Provision, threatning still what they would do to the people at Providence, and that they would force the rebellious factious Roundheads to submit; and then they would show their power.

Having now left the Country behinde them bare of men, save only such as fled into the Woods from their cruelty and raping, as also of Arms and Ammunition; the poor women urging this to them, What should they do if the Indians should come upon them, being thus strip'd of men and Arms to defend them; and in what a sad and sorrowful condition they were left: These merciless men answered scoffingly, It matters not, your sorrow is our joy.

And indeed, it is too apparent, that the Indians waited upon their motions, and by examination it was found at Providence, that the Indians were resolved in themselves, or set on by the Popish faction, or rather both together to fall upon us:

as indeed after the fight they did, besetting houses, killing one man, and taking another prisoner.

Now the people at Providence perceiving such a tempest ready to fall upon them, and all messages rejected, prepared for their coming, looking up and crying to the Lord of Hosts and King of Zion, for counsel, strength, and courage, being resolved in the strength of God to stand on their Guard, and demand an account of these proceedings; seeing no other remedy, for so great a mischief, could be found.

About this time Captain Stone sent two men to publish a Proclamation quite against the Law established by the Commissioners of the Commonwealth of England, and against an Act of a lawful Assembly; which being read, and having no other Treaty to offer, they were quietly dismissed to their own Company, to whom they might have gone if they would.

That night Captain Stone and his Army appeared in the River of Severne at Providence, with eleven or twelve Vessels, greater and lesser, some of which had plundered by the way, in which their whole Army were wafted.

Capt. Fuller and the Council of War appointed at Providence Mr. Wil. Durand, Secretary, to go aboard the *Golden Lion,* which then lay at Anchor in the River, and to fix a Proclamation in the main mast, directed to Captain Heamans, Commander of the said Ship, wherein he was required in the name of the Lord Protector, and Commonwealth of England, and for the maintenance of the just Libertyes, Lives, and Estates of the free Subjects thereof against an unjust power to be aiding and assisting in this service.

The said Captain Heamans at first was unwilling; but afterwards seeing the equity of the Cause, and the groundless proceedings of the Enemy, he offered himself, Ship, and Men for that service, to be directed by the said William Durand.

The enemy was come within the command of the Ship at the shutting in of the evening: the Captain of the Ship was required to command them aboard by a piece of Ordnance.[2] The enemy with a great noise rejected the warning. Then another Piece was levelled where they heard the Boats rowing; the Shot whereof lighting something neer, but doing no hurt; A Messenger came aboard; but had nothing of any message to deliver, save only that Captain Stone thought the Captain of the Ship had been satisfied. To which the Captain answered, Satisfied, with what? I never saw any power Captain Stone had, to do as he hath done; but the Superscription of a Letter. I must, and will, appear for these in a good Cause.

That night the Enemy run into the Creek, where they landed out of reach of the Ship.

But in the morning; all their Vessels were block'd up by a small Barque with two pieces of Ordnance, which was commanded to lie in the mouth of the Creek, and so kept from coming out.

---

[2]**Ordnance:** larger weapons, usually artillery.

The same day, being the first day of the week, and the 25 of March, the Enemy appeared in a body upon a narrow neck of the Land, neer their Vessels, and with Drums and shoutings said, *Come ye Rogues, come ye Rogues, Round-headed Dogs;* which caused the Captain of the Ship to give fire at them, and forced them to march further off, into the neck of Land.

In the meantime Capt. Will. Fuller with his company came up the River with shoutings and couragious rejoycings, and landed with a hundred and twenty men, six mile distant from the Enemy: and immediately sent away all their Sloops and Boats, committing themselves into the hand of God: he marched directly where the Enemy lay waiting for him. The Enemies Sentry shot; immediately they appeared in order. Captain Fuller still expecting that then at last possibly they might give a reason of their coming, commanded his men upon pain of death not to shoot a Gun, or give the first onset; setting up the Standard of the Commonwealth of England: against which the Enemy shot five or six Guns, and killed one man in the front before a shot was made by the other. Then the word was given *In the name of God fall on; God is our Strength,* that was the word for Providence; the Marylanders Word was *Hey for Saint Maries.* The Charge was fierce and sharp for the time; but through the glorious presence of the Lord of Hosts manifested in and towards his poor oppressed people, the Enemy could not endure, but gave back; and were so effectually charged home, that they were all routed, turned their backs, threw down their Arms, and begged mercy. After the first Volley of shot, a small Company of the Enemy, from behinde a great tree fallen, galled us, and wounded divers of our men, but were soon beaten off. Of the whole Company of the Marylanders there escaped only four or five, who run away out of the Army to carry news to their Confederates. Captain Stone, Colonel Price, Captain Gerrard, Captain Lewis, Captain Hendall, Captain Guither, Major Chandler, and all the rest of the Councillors, Officers, and Souldiers of the Lord Baltamore among whom, both Commanders and Souldiers, a great number being Papists, were taken, and so were all their Vessels, Arms, Ammunition, provisions; about fifty men slain and wounded. We lost only two in the field; but two died since of their wounds. God did appear wonderful in the field, and in the hearts of the people; all confessing him to be the only Worker of this victory and deliverance.

> *Examinatur per me,*
> WILLIAM DURAND,
> *Secretary of Maryland.*

Suggestions for Further Reading

Brugger, Robert J. *Maryland, A Middle Temperament, 1634–1980.* Baltimore: Johns Hopkins University Press, 1988.

Foster, James W. *George Calvert: The Early Years.* Baltimore: Maryland Historical Society, 1983.

Lahey, R. J. "The Role of Religion in Lord Baltimore's Colonial Enterprise." *Maryland Historical Magazine* 72 (1977): 492–511.

Land, Aubrey C. *Colonial Maryland, A History.* Millwood, N.Y.: KTO Press, 1981.

Tate, Thad W., and David L. Ammerman, eds. *The Chesapeake in the Seventeenth Century: Essays on Anglo-American Society.* Chapel Hill: University of North Carolina Press, 1979.

CHAPTER THREE

THE CRISIS OF THE
LATE SEVENTEENTH CENTURY

Social Tensions and Rebellion
in Virginia

The English colonies experienced major changes at the close of the seventeenth century. As Massachusetts and Virginia became the two largest centers of white population, their settlers discovered ways to sustain themselves and, in doing so, even earn a profit. Over time, the two colonies acquired distinct identities. Massachusetts Bay Colony, founded as the ideological center of New England Puritanism, remained bound to the mission of establishing a government and society run by Reformed leaders. It also developed into a commercial center for many of the Atlantic trade's merchant-capitalists. Particularly after 1650, as Boston developed into a port of considerable importance, merchants came to dominate much of the trade between North America and the outside world. Virginia also found a path to prosperity: European demand for Chesapeake tobacco fueled an export boom, and planters rushed to develop the land and to organize an exploitable labor force.

Whether in New England or the Chesapeake, economic development led to a heightened degree of class and racial hierarchy. The first generation of English colonists had primarily faced a struggle for survival; when their sons and daughters discovered ways not only to survive but also to make fortunes, new issues arose, such as who would have access to resources key to wealth and what sources of labor existed to perpetuate its creation. In Virginia, the answers to these questions became clearer during the second half of the seventeenth century, by which time it was apparent that wealth depended on tobacco. With the rapid expansion of plantation agriculture, tobacco exports from Virginia increased by 1,600 percent between 1620 and 1640 and by 3,500 percent between 1640 and 1700.

The growth of tobacco culture depended on two resources: land and labor. From the earliest days of the Virginia Colony, the headright system — whereby each settler received fifty acres of land — provided a means to acquire both: a planter could acquire additional acreage for every servant imported into the colony. The more successful planters were able to amass large tracts of land, and on that basis establish themselves and their families as the dominant class in the colony.

But tobacco cultivation required constant and laborious work to plant, maintain, and harvest crops. From the outset, planters sought workers whose tenure would bind them to the land. For much of the seventeenth century, they depended on white labor, particularly indentured servants. In exchange for a sum of money (which was often used to pay the cost of passage), aspiring colonists in England agreed to a term of service — usually four to seven years. Thousands of English immigrants crossed the Atlantic to Virginia in this way, and they composed by far the largest segment of the colony's population.

As the welfare of planters improved, that of indentured servants declined. There were few incentives to provide good conditions for bond servants, and an appalling rate of mortality persisted in the Virginia Colony for most of the seventeenth century. Conditions included overwork, poor housing and diet, beatings and physical abuse from masters and overseers, and other consequences associated with a system that encouraged the exploitation of the labor force. Frequently, servants resisted bad treatment by running away, stealing, and violently resisting the master's authority. This system therefore provided both a harsh existence for the servants and an insecure labor system for the planters.

Meanwhile, immigrants who survived the length of their indentures were swelling the ranks of recently freed bondsmen. More free whites meant increased pressure on land resources, which, because the colony was encircled by still-powerful Indians, were limited. Small-scale challenges to the colonial regime — and to the newly emerging planter elite — erupted periodically. The Lawne's Creek Rising, in early 1674, for example, pitted smaller planters aggrieved at high taxes against the government, which the rebels regarded as inept. By the 1670s, the focus on Virginia's social and political dynamics of land and labor had shifted to the frontier, where unruly former indentured servants and other white colonists on the make congregated. The situation was ripe for conflict. Among the best-known incidents of seventeenth-century discontent was Bacon's Rebellion, in which the general discontent of much of the white population coalesced around the overthrow of Virginia's legal colonial government. (The 1670s were crucial in yet another respect: because of the crisis in its labor system, Virginia began to use African slaves more extensively.)

The conditions in Virginia resembled those elsewhere: the coalescence of new social systems with newly arrived elites; a growing gap between haves and have-nots; increasing pressure on land resources; and rising conflicts with Indians. The following documents illustrate the acute social and political instability that characterized late-seventeenth-century English North America. James Revel supplies a telling account of the harsh conditions that indentured servants faced and suggests that class differences, arising out of a scarcity of land — and therefore of opportunity — were becoming more apparent. For aspiring planters, Native Americans were an obstacle to obtaining land, and during this era relations between whites and Indians worsened. Two women on the frontier, Elizabeth Bacon and Mary Horsmanden Byrd, comment on the extent of the hostility that simmered in the 1670s. The deterioration of relations among whites, and between whites and Indians, was tied to an eroding sense of confidence in the colonial government: the documents from the Lawne's Creek Rising reveal the tenuous hold the government had on colonists and the propensity of colonists to challenge its authority. Finally, the royal commissioners' 1677 report illustrates how these conditions came together in the famous Bacon's Rebellion.

———————

As you read, try to determine the following: What was the nature and source of class tensions in 1670s Virginia? How were class attitudes among whites related to racial attitudes toward Native Americans? What similarities were there between the events at Lawne's Creek and Bacon's Rebellion? Were conditions in Virginia and the Chesapeake unique, or were there parallels to conditions prevailing in the rest of English North America?

8. The Servant's Experience

JAMES REVEL
"The Poor Unhappy Transported Felon's Sorrowful Account of His Fourteen Years Transportation at Virginia in America"
c. 1680

Because accounts of indentured servants' experiences rarely appeared in their own words, James Revel's "Sorrowful Account" provides an unusual historical perspective. Although it is possible that Revel's story is fictional, historians have accepted it as the authentic testimony of a mid-seventeenth-century transportee. In criminal cases in England, convicted offenders — usually in lieu of death — could be "transported."

Under this arrangement, felons went to the colonies — often to the Chesapeake — and served a specified sentence bound to a master. Revel, who was born in London, was at the age of thirteen convicted of thievery and sentenced to fourteen years in the colonies. The date of his sentence remains uncertain; royal officials banned the transportation of convicted felons in 1671, so it seems likely that he is describing an experience that occurred sometime during the 1650s or 1660s.

Part I

My loving Countrymen pray lend an Ear,
    To this Relation which I bring you here,
My sufferings at large I will unfold,
Which tho' 'tis strange, 'tis true as e'er was told,
    Of honest parents I did come (tho' poor),
Who besides me had never Children more;
Near Temple Bar was born their darling son,
And for some years in virtue's path did run.
    My parents in me took great delight,
And brought me up at School to read and write,
And cast accompts[1] likewise, as it appears,
Until that I was aged thirteen years.
    Then to a Tin-man I was Prentice bound,
My master and mistress good I found,
They lik'd me well, my business I did mind,
From me my parents comfort hop'd to find.
    My master near unto Moorfields did dwell,
Where into wicked company I fell;
To wickedness I quickly was inclin'd
Thus soon is tainted any youthful mind.
    I from my master then did run away,
And rov'd about the streets both night and day:
Did with a gang of rogues a thieving go,
Which filled my parents' heart with grief and woe.
    At length my master got me home again,
And used me well, in hopes I might reclaim, . . .
I promis'd fair, but yet could not refrain,
    But to my vile companions went again: . . .
One night was taken up one of our gang,

[1]**cast accompts:** to count, to calculate.

John Melville Jennings, ed., *Virginia Magazine of History and Biography* 56 (1948): 189–94. Reprinted in *The Old Dominion in the Seventeenth Century: A Documentary History of Virginia, 1606–1689*, ed. Warren M. Billings (Chapel Hill: Institute of Early American History and Culture; University of North Carolina Press, 1975), 137–41. (Some spelling and punctuation has been modernized.)

Who five impeach'd and three of these were hang'd.
    I was one of the five was try'd and cast,
Yet transportation I did get at last; . . .
    In vain I griev'd, in vain my parents weep,
For I was quickly sent on board the Ship:
With melting kisses and a heavy heart,
I from my dearest parents then did part.

Part II

In a few Days we left the river quite,
    And in short time of land we lost the sight,
The Captain and the sailors us'd us well,
But kept us under lest we should rebel.
    We were in number much about threescore,
A wicked lowsey crew as e'er went o'er;
Oaths and Tobacco with us plenty were,
For most did smoak, and all did curse and swear.
    Five of our number in our passage died,
Which were thrown into the Ocean wide:
And after sailing seven Weeks and more,
We at Virginia all were put on shore.
    Where, to refresh us, we were wash'd and cleaned
That to our buyers we might the better seem;
Our things were gave to each they did belong,
And they that had clean linnen put it on.
    Our faces shav'd, comb'd out our wigs and hair,
That we in decent order might appear,
Against the planters did come down to view,
How well they lik'd this fresh transported crew.
The Women separated from us stand,
As well as we, by them for to be view'd;
And in short time some men up to us came,
Some ask'd our trades, and others ask'd our names.
    Some view'd our limbs, and others turn'd us round
Examening like Horses, if we're sound,
What trade are you, my Lad, says one to me,
A Tin-man, Sir, that will not do, says he.
    Some felt our hands and view'd our legs and feet,
And made us walk, to see we were compleat;
Some view'd our teeth, to see if they were good,
Or fit to chew our hard and homely Food.
    If any like our look, our limbs, our trade,
The Captain then a good advantage made:
For they a difference made it did appear.

'Twixt those for seven and for fourteen year.
    Another difference there is alow'd,
They who have money have most favour show'd;
For if no cloaths nor money they have got,
Hard is their fate, and hard will be their lot.
    At length a grim old Man unto me came,
He ask'd my trade, and likewise ask'd my Name:
I told him I a Tin-man was by trade,
And not quite eighteen years of age I said.
    Likewise the cause I told that brought me there,
That I for fourteen years transported were,
And when he this from me did understand,
He bought me of the Captain out of hand.

Part III

Down to the harbour I was took again,
    On board of a sloop, and loaded with a chain;
Which I was forc'd to wear both night and day,
For fear I from the Sloop should get away.
    My master was a man but of ill fame,
Who first of all a Transport thither came,
In Reppahannock county we did dwell,
Up Reppahannock river known full well,
    And when the Sloop with loading home was sent
An hundred mile we up the river went
The weather cold and very hard my fare,
My lodging on the deck both hard and bare,
    At last to my new master's house I came,
At the town of Wicoccomoco call'd by name,
Where my Europian clothes were took from me,
Which never after I again could see.
    A canvas shirt and trowsers then they gave,
With a hop-sack frock in which I was to slave:
No shoes nor stockings had I for to wear,
Nor hat, nor cap, both head and feet were bare.
    Thus dress'd into the Field I next must go,
Amongst tobacco plants all day to hoe,
At day break in the morn our work began,
And so held to the setting of the Sun.
    My fellow slaves were just five Transports more,
With eighteen Negroes, which is twenty four:
Besides four transport women in the house,
To wait upon his daughter and his Spouse,
    We and the Negroes both alike did fare,

Of work and food we had an equal share;
But in a piece of ground we call our own,
The food we eat first by ourselves were sown,
     No other time to us they would allow,
But on a Sunday we the same must do:
Six days we slave for our master's good,
The seventh day is to produce our food.
     Sometimes when that a hard day's work we've done,
Away unto the mill we must be gone;
Till twelve or one o'clock a grinding corn,
And must be up by daylight in the morn.
     And if you run in debt with any one,
It must be paid before from thence you come;
For in publick places they'll put up your name,
That every one their just demands may claim,
     And if we offer for to run away,
For every hour we must serve a day;
For every day a Week, They're so severe,
For every week a month, for every month a year
But if they murder, rob, or steal when there,
Then straightway hang'd, the Laws are so severe;
For by the Rigour of that very law
They're much kept under and to stand in awe.

Part IV

At length, it pleased God I sick did fall
But I no favour could receive at all,
For I was Forced to work while I could stand,
Or hold the hoe within my feeble hands.
     Much hardships then in deed I did endure,
No dog was ever nursed so I'm sure,
More pity the poor Negroe slaves bestowed
Than my inhuman brutal master showed.
     Oft on my knees the Lord I did implore,
To let me see my native land once more;
For through God's grace my life I would amend
And be a comfort to my dearest friends.
     Helpless and sick and being left alone,
I by myself did use to make my moan;
And think upon my former wicked ways,
How they had brought me to this wretched case.
     The Lord above who saw my Grief and smart,
Heard my complaint and knew my contrite heart,
His gracious Mercy did to me afford,

My health again was unto me restor'd.
    It pleas'd the Lord to grant me so much Grace,
That tho' I was in such a barbarous place,
I serv'd the Lord with fervency and zeal,
By which I did much inward comfort feel.
    Thus twelve long tedious years did pass away,
And but two more by law I had to stay:
When Death did for my cruel Master call,
But that was no relief to us at all.
    The Widow would not the Plantation hold,
So we and that were both for to be sold,
A lawyer rich who at James-Town did dwell,
Came down to view it and lik'd it very well.
    He bought the Negroes who for life were slaves,
But no transported Fellons would he have,
So we were put like Sheep into a fold,
There unto the best bidder to be sold.

Part V

A Gentleman who seemed something grave,
Unto me said, how long are you to slave;
Not two years quite, I unto him reply'd,
That is but very short indeed he cry'd.
    He ask'd my Name, my trade, and whence I came
And what vile Fate had brought me to that shame?
I told him all at which he shook his head,
I hope you have seen your folly now, he said,
    I told him yes and truly did repent,
But that which made me most of all relent
That I should to my parents prove so vile,
I being their darling and their only child.
    He said no more but from me short did turn,
While from my Eyes the tears did trinkling run,
To see him to my overseer go,
But what he said to him I do not know.
    He straightway came to me again,
And said no longer here you must remain,
For I have bought you of that Man said he,
Therefore prepare yourself to come with me.
    I with him went with heart oppressed with woe,
Not knowing him, or where I was to go;
But was surprised very much to find
He used me so tenderly and kind.
    He said he would not use me as a slave,

But as a servant if I well behav'd;
And if I pleased him when my time expir'd,
He'd send me home again if I required.
     My kind new master did at James Town dwell;
By trade a Cooper, and liv'd very well:
I was his servant on him to attend.
Thus God, unlook'd for raised me up a friend.

Part VI

Thus did I live in plenty and at ease,
     Having none but my master for to please,
And if at any time he did ride out,
I with him rode the country round about.
     And in my heart I often cry'd to see,
So many transport fellons there to be;
Some who in England had lived fine and brave,
Were like old Horses forced to drudge and slave.
     At length my fourteen years expired quite,
Which fill'd my very soul with fine delight;
To think I should no longer there remain,
But to old England once return again.
     My master for me did express much love,
And as good as his promise to me prov'd:
He got me ship'd and I came home again
With joy and comfort tho' I went asham'd,
     My Father and my Mother wel I found,
Who to see me, with Joy did much abound:
My Mother over me did weep for Joy,
My Father cry'd once more to see my Boy;
     Whom I thought dead, but does alive remain,
And is returned to me once again;
I hope God has so wrought upon your mind,
No more wickedness you'll be inclined,
     I told them all the dangers I went thro'
Likewise my sickness and my hardships too;
     Which fill'd their tender hearts with sad surprise,
While tears ran trinkling from their aged eyes.
     I begg'd them from all grief to refrain,
Since God had brought me to them home again,
The Lord unto me so much grace will give,
For to work for you both While I live,
     My country men take warning e'er too late,
Lest you should share my hard unhappy fate;

Altho' but little crimes you here have done,
Consider seven or fourteen years to come,
    Forc'd from your friends and country for to go,
Among the Negroes to work at the hoe;
In distant countries void of all relief,
Sold for a slave because you prov'd a thief.
    Now young men with speed your lives amend,
Take my advice as one that is your friend:
For tho' so slight you make of it while here,
Hard is your lot when once they get you there.

9. The Lawne's Creek Rising

Evidence from the Surry County Deed Book and the Surry County Order Book
January 1674

On the expiration of the term of their indenture, servants could look forward to the possibility of freedom. Yet in the late seventeenth century, prospects for those recently freed diminished considerably. The 1670s were a decade of discontent and periodic outbreaks of violence. The Lawne's Creek incident resulted from the circumstances of the Third Anglo-Dutch War. In July 1673, a Dutch fleet arrived at the mouth of the James River and burned a fleet laden with tobacco. Many colonists were out-raged at the inability of local authorities to defend the fleet, despite what colonists considered burdensome taxation. Disaffection focused particularly on Governor William Berkeley; when the Virginia Assembly assessed new taxes for defense, local resentment boiled over. Some fourteen residents of the Lawne's Creek Parish de-cided to mount a protest. On December 12, 1673, the protesters attempted to pre-vent the collection of taxes and the local authorities ordered them to disband. When they gathered a second time, magistrates arrested them for unlawful assembly and obstructing the sheriff. The documents below describe the reasons for this drastic ac-tion. Although they were convicted in court and assessed heavy fines, in September 1674 Berkeley commuted the sentences on the condition that the protesters publicly admit their error.

ARREST WARRANTS

Surry

Whereas a Company of rude and disorderly persons to the Number of Four-teene did unlawfully Assemble on or about the 12th day of December last at the parish Church of Lawnes Creeke in this County with Intent to alter the Late Levy, or not to pay the Same: and that they Expected divers others of their Con-federates to meete with them and for that it appears by the Confession of Mathew Swan, John Barnes, William Hancock, Robert Lacy, John Grigory, Thomas Cley, Michael Upchurch, John Sheppard, William Tooke, George Peters, William Lit-tle, John Greene, and James Chessett that they did meete at the Time and place aforesaid, and for that the greatest part of the persons aforesaid did this day also Ri-ottously meete together in the field, commonly called the Devil's field, notwith-standing some of them were advertised to the Contrary, Which we Conceive to be against the peace of our said Sovereign Lord the King, and the quiett of this County. These are Therefore in the Kings Majesties name to will and require you to take into your Custody the bodyes of the Severall persons before named, and them in Safe Custody to Keepe, until they Enter into Bond with Sufficient Secu-rity for their appearance at the Ware Neck on Tuesday the 6th Instant[1] at the Court there; there to be proceeded against according to Law and also that they be of the good behavior and Keepe the peace of our Sovereign Lord the King, and for so doing this shall be your warrant. Given under our hands this 3rd January 1673.

Lawrence Baker
Robert Spencer

To the Sheriff of the Said County or his deputy
Vera Recordat
Teste William Edwards Clerk of Court

Surry County

Whereas by the Examination and Confession of Roger Delke and by the Tes-timony of William Sherwood Sub Sheriff of this County, it is Apparent that the said Delk (being one of the unlawfull Assembly on the 12th December last) did this day discoursing of that meeting, Justifye the same and said we will burne all, before one shall Suffer, which words being Spoken in A Terrifying manner and tending to the breach of his Majesties peace, being also spoken by the said Delke before us. These are Therefore in the Kings Majesties Name to will and require

---

[1]**Instant:** the current month; in this case, January.

Surry County Deed Book, 1671–1684, fols. 41–42. Reprinted in *The Old Dominion in the Seventeenth Century: A Documentary History of Virginia, 1606–1689*, ed. Warren M. Billings (Chapel Hill: Insti-tute of Early American History and Culture; University of North Carolina Press, 1975), 263–64. (Some spelling and punctuation has been modernized.)

you to take into your Custody the Body of the said Roger Delk, and him in Safe Custody to Keepe untill the next Court to be held for this County on Tuesday the Sixth of this Instant, and that you have Delke at the said Court there to be Dealt with according to Law, unless he find good Security for his personall appearance at the Court and that he be of the good behavior and keep the peace of our Sovereigne Lord the King, and for your so doing this shall be your Sufficient Warrant. Given under our hands this 3d January 1673.

Lawrence Baker
Robert Spencer

To the Sheriff of the said County or his deputy these
Vera Recordat. Teste William Edwards Clerk of Court

FRANCIS TAYLOR'S DEPOSITION

The deposition of Francis Taylor being Called before Captain Lawrence Baker, Mr. Robert Caufield, and Captain Robert Spencer, to swear his true Knowledge concerning a meeting of some of the parish on Friday the 12th December 1673 at Lawnes Creek parish Church is as followeth: That being at home at my lodging looking out I Spied John Grigory going through the field, and called him to desire him to make me a waistcoat, which he told me he would, but he asked me If I would not be at the Church for there was to be a great part of the parish met there this morning concerning the Levies. I told him I knew nothing of it Neither was I Concerned in it as being no housekeeper, but I did not much care if I went with him to see what was done. He told me he was going to Mr. Caufield's to take measure of one of his men, to make his freedom Clothes, and he would hallow for me as he Came back, which Accordingly he did and we went together. And when we Came there we found about halfe A Score of men Sitting there, and asking them how they did, and what they met for, they said they did Expect some more to come Intending Civilly to Treate Concerning the Levy, for that they did understand, that there was Several Officers to be paid tobacco out of the Levy, which they Knew no Reason for, by Reason they were put to as much Trouble and Expense as they were, and that Colonel Swan was to have five Thousand pounds of tobacco for his trouble and Charge, that which tobacco for the Officers and the Colonel was to be Levied on this parish only, their Company not meeting they stayed about an hour, and so resolved to Speake about it on the next Sab-

Surry County Deed Book, 1671–1684, fol. 43. Reprinted in *The Old Dominion in the Seventeenth Century: A Documentary History of Virginia, 1606–1689*, ed. Warren M. Billings (Chapel Hill: Institute of Early American History and Culture; University of North Carolina Press, 1975), 264–65. (Some spelling and punctuation has been modernized.)

bath being Sermon day. In the Interim on the Saturday, I being at Mr. Sherwoods, requested him to see the list of the Levy, which he did show me, and there I saw that the Charge was Levied on the whole County, which I spoke of at the Church, they hearing that said no more and further Saith not.

Francis Taylor

[names of the dissidents omitted]

Jurat Coram Nobis
January 3d 1673
Lawrence Baker
Robert Caufield
Robert Spencer

Vera Recordat   Teste William Edwards Clerk of Court

THE COURT'S VERDICT

Whereas a Certain Company of giddy headed and Turbulent persons Inhabiting in Lawnes Creeke Parish to the number of 14, Tis to say Mathew Swan, John Barnes, William Hancock, Robert Lacy, John Grigory, Thomas Cley, Michael Upchurch, John Sheppard, William Tooke, George Peters, William Little, John Greene, James Chessett, and Roger Delke, upon the 12 of December last, factiously and in contempt of Governor and contrary to the peace of our sovereign Lord the King and to the Disturbance of this county, and the bad example of [others?], did unlawfully assemble themselves at the parish church of Lawnes Creeke with intent and designe to oppose not only the just and lawfull order of this court but also the sheriff in the due execution of his office, but a greater number being by now invited and expected, which by reason of the weather did not come, they perswaded John Grigory one of the above named to list and give number of men and appoynted a second meeting or unlawful assembly, but being by the Sheriff, by order from Capt. Lawrence Baker and Capt. Robert Spenser commanded to appeare before them and ordered by the Sheriff not to go above two or three together, did not stand planning to meet the most part of them in the Devil's field, and go before the magistrates with great clubs, where being come they demeaned themselves of great stubborness and contempt, and were bound out by the magestrates to answer their Offenses at this court, and according to per-

Surry County Order Book, 1671–1691, fols. 41–42. Reprinted in *The Old Dominion in the Seventeenth Century: A Documentary History of Virginia, 1606–1689*, ed. Warren M. Billings (Chapel Hill: Institute of Early American History and Culture; University of North Carolina Press, 1975), 265–66. (Some spelling and punctuation has been modernized.)

sons being of this day brought before the said court and after a long serious admonition of the dangerous and mischevious effecte of such unlawful and factious proceedings, and being also desired by the court to show the cause of their aggrievance and the intent of their meeting, they answered the levy was unjustly laid upon them, and they met with intent to remedy that oppression, but the court having publickly repeated the order according to Record, every particular of the levy which they pretended unjust, and Showed by them as justness and reasonabless there of and their bond, and [how] carefull they had been not to impose one pound of tobacco upon the county but [what] Justice and nessessity required. And that all which they complained of did not exceed three pounds of tobacco, some of them answered that they were exceeding well satisfied in the case, and were heartily sorry for what they had done and the rest were stubborn and silent and went out in the sheriff's custody.

And being called again one by one and strictly examined how and by whom and to the unlawful assembly was projected, and set on foot, it appeared, that the said Mathew Swan, John Sheppard, and William Hancock at the house of the said John Barnes, did first resolve and conclude upon the meeting, and that the rest (of a great many more whom they Intended to perswade were only drawn in from the beginning) the said John Grigory, Robert Lacy, James Chessett, Thomas Cley, Michael Upchurch, William Tooke, William Little, and John Greene, it is therefore ordered and resolved by this court that the said John Grigory, Robert Lacy, James Chessett, Thomas Cley, Michael Upchurch, William Tooke, William Little, and John Greene, for which they are sorry for their offence and were not [the] projection of the same, be comitted untill they give bond for their future good behavior and pay court [expenses] and be dismissed and that the said John Barnes, John Sheppard, and William Hancock be committed untill they give the like bond and pay each of them one thousand pounds of tobacco fine to the use of his Majesty and for the said Roger Delke although he were no ring leader in the faction, yet for saying after much faire admonition that if one of them suffered they would burne all, he shall stand comitted untill he give the like bond and pay the like fine of one thousand pounds of tobacco and for the said Mathew Swan[, who] was the chief projector of the design and being asked if he were convinced of his offence, he answered that he was not convinced and said that the court had unjustly proceeded in the levy and charged the court therewith at the [word illegible], it is therefore ordered that he stand comitted untill he give bond with security for his appearance on the 3rd day of the next General Court before the Right Honorable the Governor and Council for his Dangerous Contempt and unlawful project and his wicked persisting in the same and that the order be enforced for every single person herein named according to this general order.

10. Two Women View the Frontier

ELIZABETH BACON AND
MARY HORSMANDEN BYRD
Letters
1676

The rising population of recently freed indentured servants realized that their success depended on access to resources, the most important of which was land. But by the end of the seventeenth century, increased population — caused by immigration and decreased mortality rates — created tremendous pressure on land resources, pushing the white population westward into closer proximity with Indians. In separate letters, two elite Virginia women explain how in 1676 relations with Indians grew worse on the northern and western frontiers. The first was written by Elizabeth Bacon, wife of Nathaniel Bacon and cousin of Governor Berkeley; the second by Mary Byrd, who was married to the planter William Byrd I. These documents are unusual: few letters written by seventeenth-century women survive, and because Bacon and Byrd were literate and relatively prosperous, they were atypical of colonial women. But both letters describe how whites became more insistent about having access to their land and how Indians responded with attacks on the settlers' encroachments.

ELIZABETH BACON

Dear Sister,

I pray God keep the worst Enemy I have from ever being in such a sad condition as I have been in since my former to thee: occasioned by the troublesome Indians, who have killed one of our Overseers at an outward plantation which we had, and we have lost a great stock of cattle, which we had upon it, and a good crop that we should have made there, such plantation Nobody durst come nigh, which is a very great loss to us.

If you had been here, it would have grieved your heart to hear the pitiful complaints of the people, The Indians killing the people daily the Govern: not taking any notice of it for to hinder them, but let them daily do all the mischief they can: I am sure if the Indians were not cowards, they might have destroyed all the upper plantations, and killed all the people upon them; the Governour so much their friend, that he would not suffer anybody to hurt one of the Indians; and the poor people came to your brother to desire him to help against the Indians, and he being very much concerned for the loss of his Overseer, and for the loss of so many

Major Problems in American Colonial History, ed. Karen Ordahl Kupperman (Lexington, Mass.: D.C. Heath & Co., 1993), 202–3. (Some spelling and punctuation has been modernized.)

men and women and children's lives every day, he was willing to do them all the good he could; so he begged of the Governour for a commission in several letters to him, that he might go out against them, but he would not grant one, so daily more mischief done by them, so your brother not able to endure any longer, he went out without a commission. The Governour being very angry with him put out high things against him, and told me that he would most certainly hang him as soon as he returned, which he would certainly have done; but what for fear of the Governour's hanging him, and what for fear of the Indians killing him brought me to this sad condition, but blessed be God he came in very well, with the loss of a very few men; never was known such a fight in Virginia with so few men's loss. The fight did continue nigh a night and a day without any intermission. They did destroy a great many of the Indians, thanks be to God, and might have killed a great many more, but the Governour were so much the Indians' friend and our enemy, that he sent the Indians word that Mr. Bacon was out against them, that they might save themselves. After Mr. Bacon was come in he was forced to keep a guard of soldiers about his house, for the Governour would certainly have had his life taken away privately, if he would have had opportunity; but the country does so really love him, that they would not leave him alone anywhere; there was not anybody against him but the Governour and a few of his great men, which have got their Estates by the Governour; surely if your brother's crime had been so great, all the country would not have been for him, you never knew any better beloved than he is. I do verily believe that rather than he should come to any hurt by the Governour or anybody else they would most of them willingly lose their lives. The Governour has sent his Lady into England with great complaints to the King against Mr. Bacon, but when Mr. Bacon's and all the people's complaints be also heard, I hope it may be very well. Since your brother came in he hath sought to the Governour for commission, but none would be granted him, so that the Indians have had a very good time, to do more mischief. They have murdered and destroyed a great many whole families since, and the men resolving not to go under any but your brother, most of the country did rise in Arms, and went down to the Governour, and would not stir till he had given a commission to your brother which he has now done. He is made General of the Virginia War, and now I live in great fear, that he should lose his life amongst them. They are come very nigh our Plantation where we live. . . .

MARY HORSMANDEN BYRD

Mrs. Bird's relation, who lived nigh Mr. Bacon in Virginia, and came from there July last for fear of the Indians.

Who saith, that before ever Mr. Bacon went out against the Indians, there were said to be above two hundred of the English murdered by the barbarous Indians, and

Major Problems in American Colonial History, ed. Karen Ordahl Kupperman (Lexington, Mass.: D.C. Heath & Co., 1993), 203–4. (Some spelling and punctuation has been modernized.)

posts came in daily to the Governour, giving notice of it, and yet no course was taken to secure them, till Mr. Bacon went out against them. And that her husband had 3 men killed by the Indians before Mr. Bacon stirr'd, which was made known to the Governour, who notwithstanding was so possessed to the contrary, that he would not believe it to be any other than a mere pretence, for to make war against the Indians, and that the said 3 men were alive and well, and only shut up in a chamber to make the world believe they were murdered. She further affirmed that neither Mr. Bacon nor any with him had injured any English man in their persons or Estates, and that the country was generally well pleased with what they had done, and she believed most of the council also, so far as they durst show it.

That the most of them with Mr. Bacon were substantial housekeepers who bore their own charges in this war against the Indians. And that so soon as Mr. Bacon had receiv'd his commission from the Governour he went out to the people (as she heard) and told them that though he had no power before to restrain some of their too lavishly tongues, they should now find he would make use of his power, to punish any man severely, that should dare to speak a word against the Governour or Government.

11. Bacon's Rebellion

THE ROYAL COMMISSIONERS
"A True Narrative of the Late Rebellion in Virginia"
1677

Bacon's Rebellion shook the social and political order in colonial Virginia. Finding fertile ground in the growing number of discontented white Virginians, Nathaniel Bacon led a war against the Indians that soon turned against and overthrew the colonial government. Following the rebellion, royal authorities in England sought to reestablish order in the colony. Governor William Berkeley was recalled and replaced by a new governor with extensive pardoning and military powers. But as royal authorities discovered the degree of discontent in Virginia, they concluded that even stronger measures were necessary. England appointed an official commission (composed of naval commander Captain John Berry, military commander and governor

Narratives of the Insurrections, 1675–1690, with Three Facsimiles, ed. Charles M. Andrews, Original Narratives in Early American History (New York: Charles Scribner's Sons, 1967), 105–11. (Some spelling and punctuation has been modernized.)

Colonel Herbert Jeffreys, and former acting governor of Virginia Francis Moryson)
to restore order and investigate the causes of the rebellion. They landed in Virginia
in January 1677 with a fleet of three ships and more than eleven hundred men. Berry
and Moryson returned to England in July 1677 and presented the commission's
final report, excerpted below, to the Privy Council in October of that year.

A True Narrative of the Rise, Progresse, and Cessation of the Late Rebellion in
Virginia, Most Humbly and Impartially Reported by his Majestyes Commissioners Appointed to Enquire into the Affaires of the Said Colony.

In all due observance of his Most Sacred Majesties commands, we have imployed our best endeavours to informe ourselves (for his Royal Satisffaction) by the
most knowing, credible, and indifferent Persons in Virginia of the true state of affairs in that his Majestyes Colony, and of such other matters as occasioned the late
unhappy Divisions, Distractions, and Disorders among the People there; which
as far as we can possibly collect from a strict Inquiry, observation, examination, and
the most probable impartial Reports by us made and received during our stay
upon the Place, seems to take its original Rise, as followeth, *vizt:*

Few or none had been the Damages sustained by the English from the Indians, other than occasionally had happen'd sometimes upon private quarrels and
provocations, untill in July, 1675, certain Doegs and Susquahanok Indians on
Maryland side, stealing some Hoggs from the English at Potomake on the Virginia
shore (as the River divides the same), were pursued by the English in a Boate,
beaten or kill'd, and the hoggs retaken from them; whereupon the Indians re-
pairing to their owne Towne, report it to their Superiors, and how that one Mathewes (whose hoggs they had taken) had before abused and cheated them, in not
paying them for such Indian trucke[1] as he had formerly bought of them, and that
they took his hogs for Satisfaction. Upon this (to be Reveng'd on Mathews) a war
Captain with some Indians came over to Potomake and killed two of Mathewes
his servants, and came also a second time and kill'd his son.

It happen'd hereupon that Major George Brent and Col. George Mason pursued some of the same Indians into Maryland, and marching directly up to the Indian Towne with a Party of 30 Virginians came to a certaine House and there
killed an Indian King and 10 of his men upon the place; the rest of the Indians
fled for their lives. On this occasion the Governor of Maryland writes a Letter to
Sir Wm. Berkeley, complayning of this rash action and intrusion of the Virginians
on his Province without his leave or knowledge, the Indians and them being at that
time in Peace. By what authority Brent and Mason went over into Maryland and

---

[1]**trucke:** goods.

kill'd those Indians is an Article of Inquiry in the Rappahanock Grievances and the supposed originall cause of the many murders that ensued in that county as themselves complaine.

The Indians persisting to Revenge themselves Inforted in Maryland and now began to be bold and formidable to the English who Besieged them; their Boldness and daring behavior of late tymes and their promptnesse to Fire arms, being (indeed) wonderfull, over what they seem'd formerly induced with, which doubtlesse was of some advantage extraordinary to them considering their Small Body, the Virginians and Marylanders that Besieged them being said to make a neer a thousand men. The siege held 7 weekes, during which tyme the English lost 50 men, besides some Horses which the Indians tooke, and serv'd themselves to subsist on. But Provisions growing very scarce with them during this siege the Indians sent out 5 greate men to Treate of Peace, who were not Permitted to return to the Fort, but being kept Prisoners Some tyme were at last murdered by the English.

At length (whether through negligence or cowardize) the Indians made their escape through the English, with all their wives, children, and goods of value, wounding and killing some at their sally and going off. After which the English returning (as Report Saith), the Marylanders composed a Peace with the Savages, and so diverted the war from themselves.

As yet the General Peace and Government of Virginia continued undisturb'd, only some ignorant People grumbl'd at the 60 *lb.* of Tob. p. pole,[2] that necessary Tax, raised at two paym'ts to take off the Patents granted to the Lord Arlington and Lord Culpepper and the Earl of St. Albans and Lord Berkly etc.

But about the beginning of January, 1675–6, a Party of those abused Susquahanocks in Revenge of the Maryland businesse came suddenly down upon the weak Plantations at the head of Rappahanock and Potomaque and killed at one time 36 persons and then immediately (as their Custome is) ran off into the woods.

No sooner was this Intelligence brought to the Governour but he immediately called a court and ordered a competent force of horse and foot to pursue the Murderers under the Comand of Sir Henry Chicheley and some other Gentlemen of the County of Rappahanock, giving them full Power by Comission to make Peace or War. But the men being ready to march out upon this Service the Governor on a sudden recalls this comission, Causes the men to be disbanded, and without any effectual course being taken for present Preservation, refers all to the next assembly; in the meantime leaving the Poor Inhabitants under continual and deadly feares and terrors of their Lives.

In so much that in the upper Parts of the Parish of Citternborne in Rappahanock which consisted of 71 Plantations, on the 24th of Jan., 1675–6, by the 10th of Febr following was reduced to eleven what with those that ran away into the heart of the country, and such as stay'd and were cut off by the Enemy.

The assembly met to consult for the Safety and defence of the Country against the Incursions and destructions of the Indians, dayly Comitted upon the

---

[2]**Tob. p. pole:** a poll tax, which was assessed on all male heads of households.

Inhabitants of Virginia, there having been within the space of about 12 months before, neer 300 Christian persons murder'd by the Indians Enemy. What care the Assembly tooke to prevent these massacres was only to build Forts at the heads of each River and on the Frontiers and confines of the country, for erecting of which and maintaining Guards on them a heavy levy was laid by act of Assembly on the People; throughout the country universally disliked before the name of that Imposture Bacon was heard of, as being a matter from which was expected great charge and little or no security to the Inhabitants, the Situation of the Virginian Plantations being invironed with thick woods, swamps, and other covert, by the help of which the enemy might at their Pleasure make their approaches undiscover'd on the most secure of their habitations, as they have often done not only on the Frontiers but in the very heart and centre of the country, their sculking nature being apt to use these advantages.

The Murders, Rapes, and outrages of the Indians became so much the more Barbarous, fierce, and frequent, by how much the more they perceived the Public Preparations of the English against them, Prosecuting their mischiefs upon the extreme Plantations thereby forcing many to desert them to their Ruines, and destroying those that adventur'd to stay behind.

The unsatisfied People finding themselves still lyable to the Indian Crueltyes, and the cryes of their wives and children growing grievous and intollerable to them, gave out in Speeches that they were resolved to Plant tobacco rather than pay the Tax for maintaining of Forts, and that the erecting of them was a great Grievance, Juggle, and cheat, and of no more use or service to them than another Plantation with men at it, and that it was merely a Design of the Grandees to engrosse all their Tobacco into their owne hands.

Thus the sense of this oppression and the dread of a common approaching calamity made the giddy-headed multitude mad, and precipitated them upon that rash overture of Running out upon the Indians themselves, at their owne voluntary charge and hazard of their Lives and Fortunes, only they first by Petition humbly craved leave or comission to be led by any comander or comanders as the Governor should please to appoint over them to be their Chieftaine or Generall. But instead of Granting this Petition the Governor by Proclamation under great Penalty forbade the like Petitioning for the future.

This made the People jealous that the Governor for the lucre of the Beaver and otter trade etc. with the Indians, rather sought to protect the Indians than them, Since after publick Proclamation prohibiting all trade with the Indians (they complaine) he privately gave comission to some of his Friendes to truck with them, and that those persons furnished the Indians with Powder, Shott, etc. so that they were better provided than his Majestye's Subjects.

The People of Charles City County (neer Merchants Hope) being denyed a Commission by the Governor although he was truly informed (as by a Letter of his to his Majesty he confesseth) of Several formidable Bodies of Indians coming downe on the heads of James River within 50 or 60 miles of the English Plantations, and knew not where the Storme would light, they begin to beat up drums for Volunteers to go out against the Indians and so continued Sundry days drawing into armes, the Magistrates being either so remise or of the Same faction, that they suffered this disaster without contradiction or endeavouring to prevent so dangerous a begining and going on.

The Rout being got together now wanted nor waited for nothing but one to head and lead them out on their design. It so happen'd that one Nathaniel Bacon Junr, a person whose lost and desperate fortunes had thrown him into that remote part of the world about 14 months before, and fram'd him fit for such a purpose, as by the Sequel will appeare, which may make a short character of him no impertinent Digression.

He was a person whose erratic fortune had carryed and shown him many Foreign Parts, and of no obscure Family. Upon his first coming into Virginia he was made one of the Councill, the reason of that advancement (all on a sudden) being best known to the Governour, which honor made him the more considerable in the eye of the Vulgar, and gave some advantage to his pernicious designs. He was said to be about four or five and thirty years of age, indifferent tall but slender, blackhair'd, and of an ominous, pensive, melancholly Aspect, of a pestilent and prevalent Logical discourse tending to atheism in most companyes, not given to much talke, or to make sudden replies, of a most imperious and dangerous hidden Pride of heart, despising the wisest of his neighbours for their Ignorance, and very ambitious and arrogant. But all these things lay hid in him till after he was a councillor, and untill he became powerfull and popular.

Now this man being in Company with one Crews, Isham, and Bird, who growing to a height of Drinking and making the Sadnesse of the times their discourse, and the Fear they all lived in, because of the Susquahanocks who had settled a little above the Falls of James River, and comitted many murders upon them, among whom Bacon's overseer happen'd to be one, Crews and the rest persuaded Mr. Bacon to go over and see the Soldiers on the other Side James river and to take a quantity of Rum with them to give the men to drinke, which they did, and (as Crews etc. had before laid the Plot with the Soldiers) they all at once in field shouted and cry'd out, a Bacon! a Bacon! a Bacon! which taking Fire with his ambition and Spirit of Faction and Popularity, easily prevail'd on him to Resolve to head them, His Friends endeavouring to fix him the Faster to his Resolves by telling him that they would also go along with him to take Revenge upon the Indians, and drink Damnation to their Soules to be true to him, and if he could not obtain a Comission they would assist him as well and as much as if he had one; to which Bacon agreed.

This Forwardnesse of Bacons greatly cheer'd and animated the People, who looked upon him as the only Patron of the Country and preserver of their Lives and Fortunes.

For he pretended and boasted what great Service he would do for the country, in destroying the Common Enemy, securing their Lives and Estates, Libertyes, and such like fair frauds he subtily and Secretly insinuated by his owne Instruments over all the country, which he seduced the Vulgar and most ignorant People to believe (two thirds of each county being of that Sort) So that their whole hearts and hopes were set now upon Bacon. Next he charges the Governour as negligent and wicked, treacherous and incapable, the Lawes and Taxes as unjust and oppressive, and cryes up absolute necessity of redress.

Thus Bacon encouraged the Tumult and as the unquiet crowd follow and adhere to him, he listeth them as they come in upon a large paper, writing their name circular wise, that their Ring-Leaders might not be found out.

Having conjur'd them into this circle, given them Brandy to wind up the charme, and enjoyn'd them by an oath to stick fast together and to him, and the oath being administered, he went and infected New Kent County ripe for Rebellion.

Bacon having got about 300 men together in armes prepared to go out against the Indians, the Governour and his Friends endeavour to divert his designs, but cannot.

Suggestions for Further Reading

Galenson, David W. *Traders, Planters, and Slaves: Market Behavior in Early English North America.* New York: Cambridge University Press, 1986.

Jernegan, Marcus W. *Laboring and Dependent Classes in Colonial America, 1607–1783.* Chicago: University of Chicago Press, 1931. Reprint, Westport, Conn.: Greenwood Press, 1980.

Kulikoff, Allan. *Tobacco and Slaves: The Development of Southern Cultures in the Chesapeake, 1680–1800.* Chapel Hill: University of North Carolina Press, 1986.

Morgan, Edmund S. *American Slavery, American Freedom: The Ordeal of Colonial Virginia.* New York: W. W. Norton, 1975.

Nash, Gary B. *Red, White, and Black: The Peoples of Early America.* Englewood Cliffs, N.J.: Prentice-Hall, 1974.

Washburn, Wilcomb E. *The Governor and the Rebel: A History of Bacon's Rebellion in Virginia.* Chapel Hill: Published for the Institute of Early American History and Culture at Williamsburg by the University of North Carolina Press, 1957. Reprint, New York: W. W. Norton, 1972.

CHAPTER FOUR

THE EIGHTEENTH CENTURY

Prosperity and the Planter Elite

I n contrast to the late seventeenth century, when social unrest and political tur-
bulence had prevailed across the continent, the half century between 1700
and 1750 witnessed the widespread maturation of colonial institutions and the
achievement of a degree of stability. Americans became part of a worldwide economy in which ideas and goods were exchanged with growing frequency. The English Parliament had constructed a mercantilist system around the Navigation Acts,
creating a very profitable economic empire in which American colonies produced raw materials for export to England and England sent manufactured goods
to American markets.

By the end of the 1700s, the system had brought substantial benefits to the
colonies. Although they sacrificed autonomy — particularly the ability to manu-
facture and finish goods — Americans gained access to a protected European market through England. Politically, this was a system of "salutary neglect": English
colonial officials paid little attention to the growth of American political institutions from 1700 to 1750. Across the continent, colonial assemblies composed of
elected representatives of taxpayers and landholders grew in strength, leadership,
and power. Although royal officials tightened control over many of the colonies
and appointed royal governors, they acknowledged the powers of the colonial assemblies, which joined the English Parliament as the only legitimate and constitutional bodies able to levy taxes on the colonists.

The first half of the eighteenth century was a period of marked demographic
and economic growth. Population grew rapidly — from 250,000 to 2 million between 1700 and 1770 — owing in part to the relatively large size of American
families and decreasing child mortality rates, and in part to heavy non-English immigration, including coerced Africans and land-hungry Germans and Scots-Irish

drawn to the expanding economy. Land, the basis of economic opportunity, became more available as Native American tribes declined. At the same time, towns and cities grew more important. The focal point of urban development was the ports, through which the Atlantic trade flowed. The expanding urban economy was accompanied by an increasing differentiation between rich and poor. On the one hand, the ports attracted a more prominent class of poor — moreso than existed in rural areas — as well as a proud class of skilled workers and artisans. On the other hand, consumption and political leadership came to be concentrated in a wealthy class of merchants that emerged in the coastal ports of Boston, New York, Philadelphia, and Charleston.

While the status of ordinary folk — poor whites, small landholders, and enslaved African Americans — improved only slightly, it changed enormously for the South's new economic elite, composed not only of merchants but also of what were becoming known as "great" planters. Particularly in the tobacco and rice plantations of Virginia and South Carolina, southern planters came to possess more disposable wealth and became conspicuous consumers of furniture, books, porcelain, and other luxury items purchased from English merchants. Directly connected to the Atlantic economy, these planters consciously produced goods for a world market and took pains to ally themselves closely with the elites of other North American colonies.

Dominant families in Virginia — most notably the Lees, the Carters, the Fitzhughs, and the Randolphs — established themselves as the "First Families of Virginia" and built large tobacco plantations near the commonwealth's major rivers. Planters in South Carolina cultivated rice in the marshes of the coastal "low country"; the most successful built large plantation homes along the coast and in the colony's largest urban center, Charleston. Because tobacco and rice planters created their prosperity on the backs of imported African labor, they needed to sustain the slave system in order to perpetuate their way of life. The slave population expanded rapidly in the 1700s; South Carolina, for example, had become a majority slave society by the end of the first decade of the eighteenth century. Increasingly, in the colonies south of the Chesapeake, slavery came to define social relations — and even the political system.

The documents in this chapter take a closer look at the world of prosperous Southerners up to the eve of the American Revolution. The first, excerpted from William Byrd II's famous diary, recounts a typical month in the life of a member of one of Virginia's leading families. Eliza Lucas Pinckney's letters, written between 1758 and 1760, describe how a South Carolina widow took on the running of a family and a plantation. Landon Carter's diary, written a half-century after Byrd's, provides another view of the challenges of plantation management.

As you read the documents in this chapter, what changes do you notice in lifestyle between the time of William Byrd and that of Landon Carter? What values do Byrd, Pinckney, and Carter share? What values do they *not* share? How are Byrd, Pinckney, and Carter similar or different as consumers? What are their preferences? What are their dislikes?

12. A Life of Leisure

WILLIAM BYRD
Entries from His Secret Diary
1709

William Byrd II, a member of Virginia's ruling class, inherited substantial wealth in land and slaves. He acquired much of his sophistication and polish from an English education. When he returned to Virginia in 1705, he took up residence on his Tidewater estate, Westover, where he maintained himself as one of the colony's wealthiest and best-known gentlemen. On his death, Byrd owned more than 179,000 acres in Virginia and North Carolina. He served as a member of the Virginia House of Burgesses, a member of the colony's Council, and an agent for the colony in London. Byrd's diary, which he kept in shorthand, is the earliest surviving account that details the life of a colonial Southerner. Though Byrd was consumed with the maintenance of his vast holdings, he also made time for leisure, as these entries from his diary show.

November 1709

    1.   I rose at 8 o'clock because I could not leave my wife sooner. Then I ate milk for breakfast.[1] I neglected to say my [prayers] nor could I read anything. About 11 o'clock I went to Williamsburg and about 12 took my place in court. I sat there till about 4 and could not go out of town because I had accounts to settle with several people. About 5 o'clock we went to dinner and I ate boiled beef.

[1]**milk for breakfast:** probably a reference to eating curds.

William Byrd, *The Secret Diary of William Byrd of Westover, 1709–1712*, ed. Louis B. Wright and Marion Tinling (Richmond, Va.: Dietz Press, 1941), 101–12.

Then the President took us home to his house, where I played at cards and won 35 shillings. We were very merry and in that condition went to the coffeehouse and again disturbed Colonel Churchill. About 11 o'clock I went home and said a short prayer. I had good health, good thoughts, and good humor, thanks be to God Almighty.

2. I rose at 6 o'clock and read a chapter in Hebrew and some Greek in Lucian. I said my prayers and ate milk for breakfast, and settled some accounts, and then went to court where we made an end of the business. We went to dinner about 4 o'clock and I ate boiled beef again. In the evening I went to Dr. [Barret's] where my wife came this afternoon. Here I found Mrs. Chiswell, my sister Custis, and other ladies. We sat and talked till about 11 o'clock and then retired to our chambers. I played at [r-m] with Mrs. Chiswell and kissed her on the bed till she was angry and my wife also was uneasy about it, and cried as soon as the company was gone. I neglected to say my prayers, which I should not have done, because I ought to beg pardon for the lust I had for another man's wife. However I had good health, good thoughts, and good humor, thanks be to God Almighty.

3. I rose at 6 o'clock and without ceremony went away to court to hear the orders read. However I ate my breakfast in milk first. We had likewise a short Council. I settled accounts with Colonel Digges and Mr. President. Then I took leave of the Council and returned to Dr. [Barret's], from whence I waited on the ladies to Queen's Creek where my mother Parke's things were divided between my wife and her sister. My uncle Ludwell was there with us. Then we went to Mr. Blair's where we found Mr. Holloway and Mr. Robinson. I ate boiled pork for supper. Then we played at cards and about 10 o'clock went to bed. I neglected to say my prayers but had good health, good thoughts, and good humor, thanks be to God Almighty. . . .

7. I rose at 7 o'clock and said my prayers. I ate chocolate for breakfast. We walked about till dinner and then I ate roast beef. We had intended to go over the river again but my sister Custis asked me to [move] her over the Bay and I said I would if Mr. Burwell would. He said he would if his wife would, and she agreed to go and drew us all into the frolic. In the afternoon we rode to my Cousin Berkeley's with design to take him and his wife with us but he escaped by being from home. His wife was at home and gave us a good supper. I ate boiled beef. Then we had some cherries which had been scalded in hot water which did not boil and then [put] in bottles without water in them. They were exceedingly good. I neglected to say my prayers but had good health, good humor, good thoughts, and good humor, thanks be to God Almighty.

8. I rose at 7 o'clock and said a short prayer. I ate chocolate for breakfast. Then we took our leave of Mrs. Berkeley and went in a [boat] to York where there is a stone church. Then we went over the river to Gloucester Town and about noon went aboard the shallop and sailed down the river with a fair wind. When we came to the mouth of the river it grew calm so that we came to anchor but soon after the wind began to blow again. We saw a [c-l-n] sloop in the bay which soon

put aboard us and the men were so rude we kept them off because we took them for privateers. I ate roast beef for dinner, but the women were [so] frightened with the boat that they could not eat. We lay in the shallop all night but about 5 o'clock in the morning we dropped anchor in [Pigot's] Hole. I recommended myself and all the company to God Almighty and had good health, good thoughts, and good humor, thanks be to God Almighty.

9.　　I turned out about 7 o'clock and Mr. Burwell and I rowed ourselves ashore because the men were all gone for horses. We went to Mr. Littleton's where I ate milk for breakfast. About 10 o'clock the horses came from my brother Custis and we rode to Arlington which is a great house within sight of the Bay and really a pleasant plantation but not kept very nicely. We walked all over the plantation in which the hogs had done great damage. My brother Custis received us kindly. I ate goose for dinner. In the afternoon, we walked again and in the evening Mr. Dunn and his wife came to see us. We ate oysters and were merry together till about 11 o'clock. I neglected to say my prayers but had good health, good thoughts, and good humor, thanks be to God Almighty.

10.　　I rose about 7 o'clock and read some Greek in Anacreon. I said my prayers shortly and ate roasted potatoes for breakfast. About 10 o'clock we rode to the Cape with design to go to Smith Island but it blew too hard. Among the . . . here and everywhere on this shore is a tree called [p-l] tree, a suffusion of whose bark will cause a salivation. The leaves and berries smell of spice. We were kindly treated at George Freshwater's where I ate beef and potatoes for dinner. Parson Dunn was sick here, who is a man of no polite conversation, notwithstanding he be a good Latin scholar. From hence we rode to Mr. [Harris] who gave us a bottle of good wine, of which he was very generous. Then we went home, where we were merry till 11 o'clock. I neglected to say my prayers but had good health, good thoughts, and good humor, thanks be to God Almighty.

11.　　I rose at 7 o'clock and read some Greek in Anacreon. I said a short prayer and about 11 o'clock we went to breakfast and I ate goose. In the afternoon we went to visit Colonel Waters, a very honest man, who lives about six miles off. He gave us some good wine called [Saint George's] wine. We took a walk by the side of the Bay and then went to supper and I ate some roast beef. Then we returned in the dark to Arlington where we found some of the women sick and some out of humor and particularly my wife quarreled with Mr. Dunn and me for talking Latin and called it bad manners. This put me out of humor with her which set her to crying. I wholly made the reconciliation. The parson was more affronted than I, and went to bed. I neglected to say my prayers but had good health, good thoughts, and indifferent good humor, thanks be to God Almighty.

12.　　I rose about 7 o'clock and read some Greek in Anacreon. I said a short prayer and about 11 o'clock ate some goose for breakfast again. Then we rode on bad horses to Hungars to visit Colonel Custis who is 20 miles off Arlington. It began to rain before we got there. We were very kindly received by all the family. The Colonel is an honest well-meaning man. About 3 o'clock we went to dinner and I ate boiled beef. Then we took a walk about the plantation. Colonel Waters met us here. In the evening we danced and were very merry till about 10 o'clock. I neglected to say my prayers but had good health, good thoughts, and good humor, thanks be to God Almighty.

13.   I rose about 7 o'clock but could read nothing because we were in haste to go to church. I ate milk for breakfast notwithstanding it was here not very good. About 10 o'clock we rode to church which is six miles off. There was the biggest congregation I ever saw in the country. The people look half dead since the sickness which they had last year. Mr. Dunn preached a good sermon. After church we returned to Colonel Custis's again. About 3 o'clock we dined and I ate boiled beef. In the evening we drank a bottle of wine pretty freely and were full of mirth and good humor and particularly Colonel Waters. However we were merry and wise and went to bed in good time by my means. I neglected to say my prayers but had good health, good thoughts, and good humor, thanks be to God Almighty. . . .

25.   I rose about 6 o'clock because the wind was come fair again. I said a short prayer, gave the servants money, and we all rode away to the Hole with expedition. About 8 we took leave of Mr. Custis and went on board the shallop, notwithstanding the wind was very scanty and blew hard. This made us all very sick and particularly the women. In about five hours we made a shift to reach Back River, for the wind would not permit us to reach York. We went ashore at Mr. Wallace's who was not at home himself, but his wife was very kind to us and gave us a good supper. I ate roast beef. In the evening Mr. Wallace came home and gave us some excellent cider. I said a short prayer and had good health, good thoughts, and good humor, thank God Almighty.

26.   I rose about 7 o'clock and because we were in haste to go I neglected to say my prayers. I [ate] toast and cider for breakfast. The parson was so kind as to provide us with six horses and would hardly part with us so that it was noon before we could get away. He lives very neatly and is very kind to all that come to his house. At 12 we mounted and it was my fortune to have a horse that would not run away with me. We all got safe in the evening to Major Burwell's, where we found abundance of company. I was grieved to hear my daughter had received a fall and hurt her forehead but I was comforted again with a letter from Bannister that told me she and all the family was well. I ate exceedingly much boiled beef for supper. I neglected to say my prayers but had good health, good thoughts, and good humor, thanks be to God Almighty.

27.   I rose about 7 o'clock but neglected to say my prayers. I could read nothing but wrote some notes for Major Burwell. So soon as Mr. Burwell sent my [papers] over the river I thought to go away, but I ate milk for breakfast and likewise stayed to dinner and I ate mutton. About 4 o'clock we took leave of Major Burwell and Mrs. Burwell, who is a well-humored woman that I had not seen once out of humor since our voyage. We rode to Williamsburg and had a little rain by the way. Mr. [?] nor his wife were at home so that we were forced to tarry till it was dark, when they came. Here I saw honest Mr. Clayton, Mr. Jones, and Mr. Robinson. Mr. Clayton was so kind as to lend me his horse to Green Springs, because mine was lame. We got there about 7 o'clock. Here I was a little out of humor

without any reason. I neglected to say my prayers but had good health and good thoughts, thanks be to God Almighty.

28.   I rose about 7 o'clock and said a short prayer. About 8 o'clock we played at cricket and lost five shillings. At 10 o'clock we went to breakfast and I ate goose. We stayed till noon and then took our leave of all the company. My wife was uneasy and much out of humor by the way. We got home by 5 o'clock where we found all well, thanks be to God. Poor old Ben died ten days ago and I learned that Mr. Isham Eppes died likewise about the same time. I examined into all my business and was well satisfied with it. I ate some milk for supper. I neglected to say my prayers in form, but had good health, good thoughts, and good humor, thanks be to God Almighty.

29.   I rose about 7 o'clock and settled some accounts and put all my matters in order. I neglected to say my prayers but did not neglect to eat milk for breakfast. I thought to go to Falling Creek but I learned that [G-r-l] had laid a wager that he would saw 1,000 feet of planks in ten hours with two saws and by way of . . . afterwards performed it in six hours, to the confusion of Webb and Woodson, that had laid with him. I ate fish for dinner. In the afternoon I walked about the plantation to see what my negroes had done and was not displeased. In the evening I read some Greek in Homer and a chapter in Hebrew. I said my prayers and had good health, good thoughts, and good humor, thanks be to God Almighty.

30.   I rose at 3 o'clock and read two chapters in Hebrew and some Greek in Cassius. I went to bed again and lay till 7. I said my prayers, danced my dance, and ate milk for breakfast. Eugene was whipped for pissing in bed and Jenny for concealing it. I settled several accounts. I ate boiled beef for dinner. In the afternoon I played at billiards with my wife and then took a walk about the plantation to look over my affairs. I said my prayers. In the evening I read some Italian. About 8 o'clock we went to bed and I had good health, good thoughts, and good humor, thanks be to God Almighty.

13. A Woman Planter in South Carolina

ELIZA PINCKNEY
*Letters to Her Children, to George Morly,
and to Mrs. Evance*
1758–1760

Eliza Lucas Pinckney was among the most accomplished women in the American colonies. In 1739 — a year after moving from the West Indies to South Carolina with her father, George Lucas — young Eliza assumed direction of her father's plantation at Wappoo. In the very unusual position of a woman managing a plantation, Eliza became known for her innovative experimentation with indigo, a new crop being grown in the West Indies that produced a blue dye very popular with consumers in England. The production of indigo grew rapidly in South Carolina during the 1740s, and in 1747 some 135,000 pounds were produced in the colony. Eliza married Charles Pinckney, a forty-five-year-old widower, in 1744. A prosperous lawyer, member of the colonial assembly, chief justice of the colony, agent for the colony in England, and planter, Charles built Eliza and their family a large townhouse in Charleston; they also occupied a plantation on the nearby Cooper River. After his death, the subject of the first letter reprinted here, Eliza took charge of the family. Her letters describe the life of a South Carolina woman planter on the eve of the Revolution.

August 1758

To My dear Children Charles and Thomas Pinckney

How shall I write to you! What shall I say to you! My dear, my ever dear Children! but if possible more so now than Ever, for I have a tale to tell you that will peirce your tender infant hearts! You have mett with the greatest loss, my children, you could meet with upon Earth! Your dear, dear father, the best and most valueable of parents, is no more!

God Almighty support your tender minds in this terrible distress, and enable you to put your whole trust and confidence in Him, enable you to rely on him that he will be your father, your comfort, and support. Endeavour to submit to the Will of God in the best manner you can, and let it be a comfort to you, my dear babes, as long as you live that you had such a father! He has set you a great and good example. May the Lord enable you both to follow it, and may God Almighty fulfill

Eliza Pinckney, *The Letterbook of Eliza Lucas Pinckney, 1739–1762*, ed. Elise Pinckney with the editorial assistance of Marvin R. Zahniser (Chapel Hill: University of North Carolina Press, 1972), 94–95, 142–49. (Some spelling and punctuation has been modernized.)

all your pious father's prayers upon both your heads. They were almost incessant for blessings both spiritual and temporal on you both. He never mentioned you but with repeated blessings, and with up lifted Eyes and hands to heaven; God bless them, God bless them was his constant prayer when ever he named you, and that was very often. His affection for you was as great as ever was upon Earth! And you were good children and deserved it. He thought you so; he blessed and thanked God for you, and had most comfortable hopes of you. And he left you in the care and protection of the Great and Good God, who had been his merciful Father and Guide through life, and whom he truely loved and served with sincerity — whose merceys to him had been without number through all his life, and did not forsake him when he stood in most need of support: in the hour of Death!

His sickbed and dying moments were the natural conclusion of such a life as his was; for that God whom he had served, enabled him to put the firmist trust and confidence in him. His patience was great and uncommon, and he had the most perfect resignation to the Will of his God that ever man had. He met the king of terrors without the least terror or affright, and without agony, and went like a Lamb into eternity, into a blessed Eternity! where I have not the least doubt he will reap immortal joy for Ever and Ever. Such was the end of this Good man, this pious Christian, your father — the best of husbands and of fathers, and equally good in every relation and connection in life; and this treasure was ours!

We have, my dear children, mett with the greatest of human Evils, but we must drink of the cup it has pleased God to Give us, a bitter Cup indeed! but alloted us by Infinite Wisdom, and let us ever remember, terrible and grievous as the stroke is, we have still reason to thank the hand from whence it comes for all his mercys to him, through life and through death, and to us for having given us this inestimable blessing, for having spared him so long to us, for all the Graces and Virtues he endowed him with, for the goodness of his understanding, and the soundness of his judgement, for all his aimable qualities, for one of the best hearts that ever informed the human body, for all he was and had; he and we are indebted to the infinitely wise and good God, and above all for the most comfortable and joyous hope that we shall meet in Glory never never more to be seperated!

This hope, This expectation, is the support and comfort of my life, a life which I will endeavour as much as is in my power to preserve, not only as a duty to the God that gave it, but as a duty due from me to the remains of your dear dear father, to you and your dear Sister; and I hope the Almighty will enable me to do my duty in every instance by you, and that all my future life may be spent to do you good, and in showing to you, the dear pledges of the sincerest affection that ever was upon Earth, how much, how truely, I loved and honoured Your dear father by my affection and care of you.

Adieu, my beloved children! God Almighty bless, guide, and protect you! Make you his own children, and worthy such a father as yours was, and comfort you in this great affliction is the fervent and constant prayer of Your ever affectionate tho' greatly afflicted Mother

Eliza. Pinckney

March [1760]

My dear Children

The fleet being just upon sailing (and I lately so hurry'd about other matters that I began late to write to England) will prevent my writing to you so fully as my inclination leads me to do and as your pretty letters of the [blank] demand. Be assured I shall answer them more particularly very soon. In the meantime I hope my dear Charles will readily acquiesce in changing his school as the air of Camberwell does not agree with his dear little brother. I know your grateful and affectionate temper and know it will give you a good deal of pain to leave Mr. Gerrard, but your affection to your brother and the deference you will, I know, always pay to the judgment of our friends in England who advise it and can more properly judge of matters than I can at this distance. Rely intirely on their friendship and judgement in the case — which I hope will make you the more readily give up your own judgment and inclination to theirs.

I dont yet know where you are fixt or would write to your Master to whom pray pay my Compliments and inform him so. My Lady Carew was so good to inform me you wrote to me the day before she did in Dec. last, but your letters are not yet come to hand. I impatiently expect them. You know, my dearest boys, how near my heart you lie, and that all the happiness I have upon Earth is centered in you and your dear Sister. Let me then hear from you as often as possible if 'tis but 2 lines to say you are both well.

And now, my dear little Tomm, your Mama has one petition to make to you. 'Tis to think of her frequently when you are tempted to eat unripe or too much fruit. If you knew how much anguish I suffer upon every apprehension of your want of health I am sure you would punish your self to give me this consolation. You and your dear brother are the dayly — almost hourly — subject of my prayer and thoughts. Do not therefore forget to take care of your selves and joyn with me in imploring the Divine blessing upon you.

Your Sister is, I thank God, well and will write to you if the ships stay a day or two longer. Be good children, mind your learning, and love one another; and that the Almighty will bless you both with your dear Sister, protect and guide you and make you his children is the most devout petition that is put up to Heaven by, my dear boys,

Your ever affectionate Mother
Eliza. Pinckney

By Mr. T. Smith

March 14th, 1760

Dear Sir [Mr. Morly]

Since mine of the 3rd o' Nov. by the Brig Spy, Capt. Lyford, to Bristol inclosing 3 letters, one to Sir Richard Lyttleton, one to Miss McCartney, and one to Mr. Onslow, I received your favour of the 31st of Aug. inclosing Copies of 3 I had before received dated the 29th May, 5th June, and 17th July, for all which pray accept my most grateful thanks.

I was in hopes to have inclosed you a bill for a hundred pound sterling by the last ships but could not prevail on the person I was to have them from to draw before the fleet sailed. I now inclose them and beg the favour as soon as you receive it to present Doctor K with 6 Guineas for his attendance on my children, and Mr. Gerrard with the value in lieu of a barrel of Rice which he ought to have had long ago, and Miss Bartlett the ramainder of the Legacy of ten pound. I am very much obliged to you for what you advanced her of it before. It was very kind and you may be sure what I must approve.

The beginning of this Year there was such a fine prospect on our plantations of a great Crop that I was hopeful of clearing all the money that was due upon the Estate, but the great drought in most parts of the Country, such as I never remember here, disapointed those expectations so much that all that we make from the planting interest will hardly defray the charges of the plantations. And upon our arrival here we found they wanted but every thing and [were] every way in bad order, with ignorant or dishonest Over Seers.

My Nephew had no management of the planting interest, and my brother who had, by a stroke of the palsey, had been long incapable of all business. I thank God there is now a good prospect of things being differently conducted. I have prevailed upon a conscientious good man (who by his industry and honesty has raised a fine fortune for 2 orphan children my dear Mr. Pinckney was guardian to) to undertake the direction and inspection of the overseers. He is an excellent planter, a Dutchman, originally Servant and Overseer to Mr. Golightly, who has been much solicited to undertake for many Gentlemen; but as he has no family but a wife and is comfortable enough in his circumstances, refuses to do it for any but women and children that are not able to do it for themselves. So that if it please God to prosper us and grant good Seasons, I hope to clear all next year.

I find it requires great care, attention, and activity to attend properly to a Carolina Estate, tho' but a moderate one, to do ones duty and make it turn to account, that I find I have as much business as I can go through of one sort or other. Perhaps 'tis better for me, and I believe it is. Had there not been a necessity for it, I might have sunk to the grave by this time in that Lethargy of stupidity which had seized me after my mind had been violently agitated by the greatest shock it ever felt. But a variety of imployment gives my thoughts a relief from melloncholy subjects, tho' 'tis but a temporary one, and gives me air and exercise, which I believe I should not have had resolution enough to take if I had not been roused to it by motives of duty and parental affection.

I have not yet proved the Will and am advised not to do it as it would be attended with much trouble in taking particular Inventory of every thing, the most minute, which must be returned upon oath; and the proving of it 'tis said is unnecessary as there is but little due from the Estate and nobody to call me to account. And the Will it self must remain good and in force as it is a record. However if you think it best, I shall not mind the trouble but will still do it, as I would perform the Sacred trust to the utmost of my ability in every Tittle in the best manner I can.

I hope you received mine of the 19th Septr., acknowledging the receipt of yours that inclosed several from my other friends, the answers to some of which and some former ones I have last month and now trouble you with.

The long experience I have — and still daily have — of the friendly part you take in our concerns has occationed you the trouble of so long a letter. Be so good to pay my Compliments and thanks to Mr. Chatfield for his management of our little affairs at Riply and for the trouble he and Mrs. Chatfield are so good to give themselves to indulge my dear boys. I am really ashamed to give Mr. Chatfield so much trouble about the house. I should be much obliged to you to do for me what you think I should do in the case either to make him, as he is a man of business, an acknowledgment for the trouble by way of commissions or in what way you think best.

I wrote you a short letter in Febr. last in such a hurry that I kept no copy by Capt. Cramp, and Copy by Lambert Tree, inclosing several letters in each packet, Viz: one to Miss Lyttelton, 3 in two packets to Miss Mackartney, one to Mrs. King, one to Miss Varier, one to Mr. Keat, one to Dr. Kirkpatrick, and one to Mr. Gerrard.

Your favour of the 19 Novr. by way of Bristol gave me great pleasure as it informed me of my dear boys health. Indeed, Sir, 'tis not only friendly but really charitable to let me hear as often as you can from them. My heart bleeds at our separation but it must be so for a time.

The day after I wrote the foregoing I received your favour of the 31st of Decr. by Capt. Rains and another from my friend Mrs. Evance by the same opportunity; but none from Dr. Kirkpatrick or my children as you imagined I should. You may be sure, My good Sir, that I acquiesce in every thing you and my other friends do with regard to my children. You are upon the spot and must be better judges of their care than I possibly can be at this distance. The prospect of the change of air's establishing my dear little babes health is of it self a sufficient reason for removing him and I should not choose to have the brothers separated if I could help it. I have always heard a great character of Harrow school, but if that at Kensington is equally good as there is fewer scholars and tis nearer London and the air aproved for tender constitutions I should think that would be to be prefered.

You are very good to have given your self so much trouble about the 30 £ bill on Mr. Davison. My poor brother has been very ill many months, so that matter must rest for the present.

My best Compliments to the D. and Mrs. E.

I am

I received Lady C. letter
Sent this letter by Mr. T. Smith, inclosing bills for a hundred pound, and the Copy by the Trent with a 2nd Set of bills.

March 15th, [17]60

[To Mrs. Evance]

With how much pleasure I receive your letters, My Dear friend, I wont attempt to say, and the comfort I have at hearing my dear children are well your own maternal heart can better conceive than I express. So far I can with great truth affirm that 'tis the greatest felicity I have upon Earth. In consequence of this tender attachment I am under very frequent apprehensions for my dear, dear little Tomm from the tenderness of his constitution. Pray God Almighty bless and restore him. Mrs. King, Mr. Morly, etc., all inform me of your great care of and tenderness for him. You have obliged me, my dear friend, beyond all acknowledgement by your goodness to them. May the Almighty bless and reward you in sending every blessing both spiritual and temporal on you and yours, and enable me to convince you you have not bestowed the most acceptable of all services on an ungrateful heart. You make me very happy by the account you give me of my dear Charles.

I saw Mr. Raven the day he arrived. I went every where in pursuit of him till I found him and had the satisfaction to hear from him that you and all yours as well as my own children were well. He called once afterwards; I happened to be out. I imagine he has been in the Country and very busy or he would have let me see him, since in all this time I had a hundred little Chit chat questions to ask him about you all.

How could that strange woman treat you so! You desire me not to be concerned at it; I really cant help being so and beg of you, my dear Madam, not to lay your self open to her ill usage to save me a little money. I would much rather pay it than have my friend treated in an ungentile way.

I joyn very cordially with you in the great opinion you have of Mr. Gerrard. I am much concerned on his account and believe he has had great injustice done him. I know my self to be under great obbligations to him. He is, I verily believe, a good man, very capable of all he undertakes, and will do his utmost for my children. To his knowledge I am sure there will be no neglect, but if there should be any thing material with regard to their health, etc. which he cant know I rely on your friendship in a thing of so much consequence to me as to inform him of it; and if my dear little Creatures state of health should be too tender for a boarding school, will you, my dear Madam, extend your charity so far to take him home and let him go to an academy in London in the day and be with you at Nights till his health is mended. What ever you think proper to charge for his board I will with the greatest cheerfulness and thankfulness repay. If I can procure a bill of twenty pound to send you by this fleet I will do it; but if not now, as soon as I can.

A great cloud seems at present to hang over this province. We are continually insulted by the Indians on our back settlements, and a violent kind of small pox rages in Charles Town that almost puts a stop to all business. Several of those I have to transact business with are fled into the Country, but by the Divine blessing I hope a month or two will change the prospect. We expect shortly troops from Gen. Amherst, which I trust will be able to manage these savage Enemies. And the small pox, as it does not spread in the Country, must be soon over for want of subjects.

I am now at Belmont to keep my people out of the way of the violent distemper for the poor blacks have died very fast even by inocculation. But the people in Charles Town were inocculation mad, I think I may call it, and rushed into it with such presipitation that I think it impossible they could have had either a proper preparation or attendance had there been 10 Doctors in town to one. The Doctors could not help it — the people would not be said nay.

We lose with this fleet our good Gov. Lyttelton. He goes home in the Trent man of war before he goes to his Government at Jamaica.

My sincere thanks to Mr. and Mrs. Watson.

Poor John Mott who was inocculated in England is now very bad with the small pox; it could never have taken then to be sure.

I had but just finished the above when I received your favour of the 3rd Decr. by Capt. Rains, and beg leave to assure you, however great my oppinion of and partiallity to Mr. Gerrard, I absolutely aprove what you and my other friends have done in removing my children, if there were no other reason in the world for it but the air's not agreeing with Tommy. I always thought my self very much obliged to Mr. G for his care and tenderness to them and really think him too reasonable a man to wish them to continue when the circumstance of health is in the case. I would inlarge but the ships are so near sailing, and I must write a line to my dear boys, that I can only say I am

> Your truely obliged and affecte.
> E. Pinckney

My Compliments to the Lady at Kingston
March 18th, 1760
Memorandum. Had not time to Copy fully this letter.
Inclosed it to Mr. Morly by Mr. T. Smith.

14. A Plantation Owner's Difficulties

LANDON CARTER
Entries from His Diary
1766

Landon Carter benefited from a fortune created by his father, Robert "King" Carter. Like the Byrd fortune, the Carter wealth was in land and slaves, a result of profits from tobacco plantations. By the time King Carter died in 1732, he owned some 333,000 acres of land, making him perhaps the richest man in eighteenth-century North America. The fourth of King's sons, Landon Carter, was educated in London as a member of the English gentry; on his father's death, he inherited eight plantations in Tidewater Virginia. He subsequently increased his holdings so much that he became one of the wealthiest planters in Virginia himself. Sometime in the 1740s, Carter constructed one of the most elegant homes in pre-Revolutionary Virginia, Sabine Hall, located in Richmond County, above the Rappahannock River.

Written in the decade prior to the Revolution, the following excerpts from Carter's diary describe a prosperous commonwealth in which planters exerted nearly absolute power over their families, their slaves, and their plantations but also faced a number of uncertainties: profits from tobacco were declining, debt was increasing, and the future seemed less rosy.

April 1766

25. Friday. Cattle are now dying with poverty and how should it be other wise? All the winter food gone and no grass yet on the earth. 2 have lain down and expired, and two or three more very near it if my Lucern patch can't save them, where I have and must bring them. One of the dead cows has a calf which must be raised if I can. This is the general time of the year when cattle yield to their poverty; And I cannot see how it can be avoided, as it is impossible to provide food enough for any number of Cattle after such prodigeous dry years; And equally difficult to procure a green food for this time except perhaps a wheat field should be devoted purely for the very poor creatures at such a time. I fancy if I can once get that ready to be done from tailings, Rye, oats, or Barley, it may do.

Sowed a meadow plant patch this day [as be]fore. Plants fine in the fork meadow. I gave orders if the flye came in them to float them off as it can be done in a few hours.

Landon Carter, *The Diary of Colonel Landon Carter of Sabine Hall, 1752–1778*, vol. 1, ed. Jack P. Greene (Charlottesville: University Press of Virginia/Virginia Historical Society, 1965), 290–327.

The frosts on the 23 and 24 in the morning have scorcht a great deal of wheat from the tops of the blades pretty low down; so that it in all such places looks fowey. This is the 4th day we have been carting out dung; but a poor hand indeed.

My man Bart came in this day, he has been gone ever since New year's day. His reason is only that I had ordered him a whipping for saying he then brought in two load of wood when he was coming with his first load only. This he still insists on was truth Although the whole plantation asserts the contrary, and the boy with him. He is the most incorrigeable villain I believe alive, and has deserved hanging; which I will get done if his mate in roguery can be tempted to turn evidence against him.

Bart broke open the house in which he was tyed and locked up; he got out before 2 o'clock but not discovered till night. Talbot is a rogue. He was put in charge of him. I do imagine the gardiner's boy Sam, a rogue I have suspected to have maintained Bart and Simon all the while they have been out And I sent this boy with a letter to the Island ferry at breakfast, but he never returned although he was seen coming back about 12 and was seen at night by Hart George at night pretending to be looking for his Cattle. I kept this fellow up two nights about these fellows before And have given Rit the Miller a light whipping as having fed them by the hands of Gardiner Sam.

5 Cattle died yesterday and 3 or 4 more in a decaying Situation. I have had them up to my Lucern field. Perhaps that may save them. My overseer Davis was advised to give me notice of the Poverty of the creatures before they faltered; but he is a sorry fellow and I believe does not care though he pretends he does. He pretended the Creatures were out in the woods but they never went there; the wench never carried them out there at all in this day but he says it was his orders. I shall direct otherwise and get a man to see my orders obeyed. . . .

27. *Tuesday.* Began weeding corn at Mangorike with 10 hands, the rest weeding plant patches, and burying dung and turning hills for the next season.

Fork not yet weeding corn but burying Dung and hoeing hills for next season. I shall set in the corn tomorrow I hope.

Rain wanted though it rained the 22d in great plenty, but the cool winds after it have merely baked my soil, of such a nature it is. Weather now warm. I see nothing very promising for a crop, it has been in general too Cool and windy in every soil, but the stiff the worst. . . .

June 1766

This moon rather wet than dry and perhaps it will be wet at the end.

1. *Sunday.* Very cold after the rain. A hard wind at Northwest in the night and some rain. . . .

4. *Wednesday.* A Pretty season but so late and I do suppose my overseer stupid with liquor that I shall have very little done; although I have had some thousands of hills got ready by my Jobbers. At the Fork: No hills turned but a very few,

Jack Lubbar is a most lazy as well as stupid old fellow grown. All is my own fault to think a drunkard could be reclaimed, or a negroe honest enough to carry on any business long enough for more than one year. I must get new overseers every where and I will too that 1 more, god willing.

5. *Thursday.*   Fine rain in the night so that all that were planted will stand a good chance to live though but a few. A most Glorious season this day for many hours from between 6 and 7 till eight and past. But few hills turned at the fork but all hands turning and so at Thrift's. I believe I have hills enough to use all the plants fit; Certainly every thing will now grow, Wheat only in danger for some not quite done blooming. . . .

27. *Friday.*   . . . We had this day a domestic gust. My daughters, Lucy and Judy, mentioned a piece of impudent behaviour of little Landon to his mother; telling her when she said she would whip him, that he did not care if she did. His father heard this unmoved. The child denied it. I bid him come and tell me what he did say for I could not bear a child should be sawsy to his Mother. He would not come and I got up and took him by the arm. He would not speak. I then shook him but his outrageous father says I struck him. At Breakfast the Young Gent. would not come in though twice called by his father and once Sent for by him and twice by me. I then got up, and gave him one cut over the left arm with the lash of my whip and the other over the banister by him. Madame then rose like a bed-lamite that her child should be struck with a whip and up came her Knight Er-rant to his father with some heavy God damning's, but he prudently did not touch me. Otherwise my whip handle should have settled him if I could. Madam pre-tended to rave like a Madwoman. I shewed the child's arm was but commonly red with the stroke; but all would not do. Go she would and go she may. I see in her all the ill treatment my son gives and has given me ever since his marriage. Indeed I always saw this in her a girl a Violent, Sulkey, Proud, imperious Dutch so One fit to be the Queen of a Prince as the old ——always complimented her. As this child is thus encouraged to insult me, I have been at great expence hitherto in maintaining him but I will be at no more. And so I shall give notice.

28. *Saturday.*   No rain since the 22. Begins to be dry; though our crops are so weedy as not to want rain as yet; fine Corn and tobacco but very foul.
      Began to reap my wheat at Olivers branch, much injured by a trespass of all my creatures of my cow pen on the 23; by means of two Mischievous steers.
      Killed one of them as per yesterday. Reaped my Barley two days agoe.
      My Thermometer from 76 to 87 for two days past. Yesterday from 82 to 87. Three people fainted, but I believe they had foul stomachs gave them Vomits. One got out. The other a Purge today.

30. *Monday.*   Got down 11 acres at home this day by reap hooks, and scythes 5 mowers; but my horses so poor and so imployed in my Cornfields still very foul I could not set to carting it in. Therefore resolved upon treading as much as I could cut in the field; for which purpose I prepared a large treading floor more then 60

feet diameter; but could not quite finish one floor before night took us; however we took in 5 large sacks full and two empty tobacco hogsheads full which I had covered and secured against the rain and lockt up the loose untrod straw. The rest of the wheat I fixed in triangular Gavels in the high parts of the fields; that is 3 large sheeves in such a form laid that the heads of each sheeve lay on the butts of the other so that I hope they will not take much damage.

July 1766

20. *Wednesday.* Upon examining my sheep I have found out Mr. Owen [Griffith] to be a damned villain, setting down every day the number of sheep as if he actually counted them. But near a fortnight ago Davis counted them and found 7 short of the number Owen pretended. They were afterwards brought up and since then has in every day's note given in the particular number which was sheep, lambs, and fallow sheep: 83 in number. But now we can discover but 77, that is 47 Gang sheep, 11 fat sheep, 15 lambs with those in Johnny's house, and 4 Ewes that suckle them.

My Daughter Judy's illness began July 17 so that to this day there has been 32 days and the quantity of butter made in that time by Owen's Account is 113¾ pounds for 475 Gallons milk which Milk ought to have yielded 237 pounds butter. But there is a pretence of Milk for fools and which ought to impose on none but fools and evidently proves a roguery in my dairy. The quantity of butter weighed in 4 pots since my daughter's illness is

	167½ pounds — 48 pounds
weight of the pots leaves	119½ pounds — 21 pounds

used up in peck butter makes 140½ besides the pot made before my daughter's illness. In this whole affair there is a damned villany. And this rascal Owen by giving in Accounts over different from what he keeps in his book is consenting to it for which I will have him before a Justice.

Suggestions for Further Reading

Brewer, John, and Roy Porter. *Consumption and the World of Goods.* London and New York: Routledge, 1994.

Carson, Cary, Ronald Hoffman, and Peter J. Albert. *Of Consuming Interests: The Style of Life in the Eighteenth Century.* Charlottesville: University Press of Virginia, 1994.

Kulikoff, Allan. *Tobacco and Slaves: The Development of Southern Cultures in the Chesapeake, 1680–1800.* Chapel Hill: University of North Carolina Press, 1986.

Marambaud, Pierre. *William Byrd of Westover, 1674–1744.* Charlottesville: University Press of Virginia, 1971.

Ragsdale, Bruce A. *A Planters' Republic: The Search for Economic Independence in Revolutionary Virginia.* Madison, Wis.: Madison House, 1995.

Wood, Peter H. *Black Majority: Negroes in Colonial South Carolina from 1670 through the Stono Rebellion.* New York: Alfred A. Knopf, 1974.

CHAPTER FIVE

PRE-REVOLUTIONARY AMERICA

The Regulators and the Carolina Backcountry in Turmoil

Among the major social changes affecting pre-Revolutionary North Carolina was immigration. A large proportion of eighteenth-century white immigrants still originated in England, but by the eve of the Revolution, Scots-Irish and Germans were pouring into the American interior. They first settled in western Pennsylvania and soon streamed into the "backcountry" — a vast region stretching from western Maryland into Virginia's Shenandoah Valley, the Carolinas, and Georgia. North Carolina, in particular, attracted immigrants because the price of land there was as much as half that of land in Virginia, and a rush of development transformed the colony. The colony's population grew rapidly, from about 36,000 in 1730 to about 265,000 in 1775, placing severe stress on its social and political fabric.

By the 1760s, the narrowing of backcountry opportunities led to crisis. Much of the available land was taken. The end of the French and Indian War in 1763 occasioned higher taxes, which were levied to pay the high costs of fighting that war. The frenetic land boom had stimulated considerable price gouging in fees as well as other forms of petty corruption. Backcountry discontent culminated in the appearance of more or less organized bands of farmers who sought to supervise — or "regulate" — the functioning of government. In 1768, a group calling itself "Regulators" formally organized in Orange County and, within months, spread throughout much of the backcountry.

The Regulators — and the crisis in authority that accompanied them — exemplify the wider tensions pervading pre-Revolutionary America. Not all Americans were comfortable with the path being taken by the colonial leadership, which strongly resisted British rule. The prosperity of the eighteenth century touched Americans unevenly; access to political power affected the path to individual success and created major differences between classes. In many instances these differences were expressed geographically, as those in the more remote hinterlands resented the wealth and power held by those in port cities and coastal counties. Appearances to the contrary, Regulators were not an early version of Revolutionaries. In North Carolina, many of the subsequent leaders of the Revolution considered the Regulators a threat to their leadership. Regulators, for their part, accused anti–Stamp Act leaders of hypocrisy, asking whether it was appropriate to challenge British tyranny while oppressing backcountry farmers.

Much of the Regulators' hostility focused on local officials like Edmund Fanning and Samuel Spencer, whose corruption, they believed, was undermining the political system. No official attracted greater anger than Fanning. A prominent lawyer and officeholder often accused of charging excessive fees, he came to exemplify an emerging elite that, to Regulators, seemed oppressive and unrepresentative. Refusing to recognize the legitimacy of local government, Regulators openly defied it. Local officials responded in April 1768 by arresting Regulator leaders Harmon Husbands and William Butler for resisting tax payments. They also arrested Fanning for charging excessive fees. Hearing that a large assemblage of Regulators was prepared to descend on the Orange County courthouse in Hillsborough, Governor William Tryon dispatched a force of one thousand militiamen to maintain peace. Husbands was acquitted; Butler and two other Regulators were convicted; Fanning was convicted and charged a small fine. Tryon subsequently released the prisoners, suspended the fines, and issued a general pardon to all Regulators except the principal leaders.

Tryon's policy of leniency did not end the crisis, however. Indeed, defiance of authority grew more extensive and, to a large degree, local respect for authority broke down. In 1769, Regulators elected solid delegations from the backcountry counties of Orange, Granville, Anson, and Halifax. Even as governmental authority continued to deteriorate, particularly the ability to collect taxes, Regulators became increasingly frustrated by the unresponsiveness of the political and legal systems. In September 1770, their discontent erupted in the so-called Hillsborough Riot, a full-fledged defiance of the law and of established order that outraged colonial leaders. Regulator leaders resisted the payment of taxes, disrupted the operation of courts, and declared Fanning an outlaw. After four months of rebellion, the North Carolina assembly authorized the use of force to suppress the Regulators. Tryon assembled a militia of fourteen hundred men, marched into the backcountry, and decisively routed a disorganized group of about two thousand Regulators at the Great Alamance Creek. In response to his general offer of amnesty, an astounding number of Regulators — more than six thousand of them — came forward and laid down their arms.

The documents in this chapter illustrate how backcountry discontent grew into an all-out challenge to established authority. Aggrieved farmers calling themselves "Regulators" first emerged in 1768; letters from Edmund Fanning and

Samuel Spencer describe these farmers' deep-seated hostility toward and aversion for local officers. Regulators' conviction that corruption was perverting the political system — and their civil liberties — is apparent in Joshua Teague's petition and Harmon Husbands's pamphlet. Richard Henderson's letter and an account published in the *Virginia Gazette* describe in detail the violence of the Hillsborough Riot.

As you read, ponder the following questions. What were the sources of Regulator unhappiness? How seriously did Fanning and others regard the Regulator threat? How did Regulators express their discontent? What similarities and what differences are there between the Regulators and the Revolutionaries? What does the Regulator experience tell us about social and political tensions on the eve of the Revolution?

15. Pre-Revolutionary Turmoil: The North Carolina Regulators

Edmund Fanning and Samuel Spencer
Letters to William Tryon
1768

When the Stamp Act crisis ended in 1766, Governor William Tryon and the colonial assembly developed cordial relations; construction of a new capitol named "Tryon's Palace" in his honor seemingly reflected an era of harmonious politics in the colony. But within two years, inhabitants of the Carolina backcountry had become intensely aggrieved at what they regarded as unresponsive, dictatorial government. By 1768 thousands of backcountry planters were refusing to pay taxes, harassing local officials violently, and even disrupting the administration of justice.

In these two letters local officials describe the rapid spread of the Regulator movement and express alarm at its growing extent, particularly in Orange County. Edmund Fanning served as Orange County's representative to the colonial assembly and as registrar of deeds; Samuel Spencer was court clerk for Anson County. They had both emigrated from northern colonies (Fanning from New York, Spencer from

New Jersey). As officeholders and members of the backcountry social and political elite to which the Regulators objected, Fanning and Spencer viewed the Regulators as a serious threat. They both wrote to Tryon appealing for his help and, implicitly, for military support.

EDMUND FANNING TO WILLIAM TRYON

Hillsborough April 23rd 1768.

May it please your Excellency,

Sir,

I want words to express the concern I feel, while I communicate to your Excellency the wretched and deplorable situation of this County; this my present uneasiness is greatly aggravated from a sense of the concern it must give you, & being informed that the late orderly and well regulated County of Orange, is now (O my favourite County and people how art thou fallen) the very nest and bosom of rioting and rebellion — The People are now in every part and Corner of the County, meeting, conspiring, and confederating by solemn oath and open violence to refuse the payment of Taxes and to prevent the execution of Law, threatening death and immediate destruction to myself and others, requiring settlements of the Public, Parish, and County Taxes to be made before their leaders — Clerks, Sheriffs, Registers, Attornies, and all Officers of every degree and station to be arraigned at the Bar of their Shallow Understanding and to be punished and regulated at their Will, and in a word, for them to become the sovereign arbiters of right and wrong. This Contagion and spirit of rebellion (for surely Sir it is rank rebellion) took its rise in the lower part of Anson spread itself into Orange and encouraged by some of the principal men of Cumberland (as I am informed & verily believe) became considerable — On my return from Salisbury Superior Court hearing of the Conspiracy I convened four of the Head men before me and expatiated to them on the folly and madness of their conduct and three out of four readily acknowledged the impropriety of their conduct, confessed a clear conviction of their error, and made me a promise to put an end to it as far as in their Power. I dismissed them and expected to hear no more of it — But alas I find it was not to be effected — the restless Tools of Faction were and continue still at work in their dark cabals — The contagion (I am sorry to say it) is by indefatigable pains and industry extending itself far and wide through this part of the Province — For your Excellency's information of the manner of its taking its rise here again after

The Colonial Records of North Carolina, Published under the Supervision of the Trustees of the Public Libraries, by Order of the General Assembly, ed. William L. Saunders, vol. 7, *1765–1768* (Raleigh, N.C.: Josephus Daniels, Printer to the State, 1890), 713–16, 722–26. (Some spelling and punctuation has been modernized.)

I went to Halifax and the several stages of it since and the proceedings had thereon I beg leave to refer your Excellency to the inclosed copies of several Letters — I was unwilling as recommended in Letter from Mr. Hart and Mr. Nash[1] to trouble your Excellency before I came into the County Anticipating the pain I judged your Excellency would feel, and desirous if by any means practicable to suppress the insurrection without troubling of your Excellency, and I own, Sir, I thought it too inglorious a conduct in me and unworthy of the command that I am honored with by your Excellency for to go immediately to Brunswick without returning to my regiment — I therefore set out from Halifax the 20th and arrived here last night (retarded by heavy rains and great Freshes[2]) and this day got all the information in my power of the state situation and number of the regulators (as they are pleased to call themselves, tho' by Lawyers they must be termed rebels and Traitors) and learn that on this day they have a grand Association and that on the third day of May they are to environ the Town with fifteen hundred men & then to execute their vengeance on me and if not satisfied in every particular to their desire (which is impossible) why then to lay the Town in ashes etc. but I cannot believe them anything like so numerous, neither do I apprehend such inevitable death as the universal Panic and the popular cry seems to suggest and threaten — Colonel Gray, Major Lloyd, Captain Hart, Adjutant Nash, & Captain Thackston[3] seem to think that not above one hundred men can be raised in this County who will with spirit and courage oppose them, for say they those who are not for them will not fight against them. Unluckily for the cause of Government the County Court is next week to be held in this Town and considering the prevalency of that Party and the impossibility of enforcing any order among the tumultuous throng and rabble which ever attend Courts, I thought it most advisable to be silent until to-morrow week when in the evening I propose to send off a Detachment of the Trusty and loyal few that I can command for to apprehend three or four of the principals under the cover of the night, and to have them brought instantly to town where on the Tuesday following I verily expect an attack from the whole united force of the regulators or rebels at which time I intend, as do also the aforementioned Officers, to *bravely repulse them or nobly die* — If I can rally force to withstand one attack I then shall plume myself as being the commanding Officer in this County & then shall expect to be joined immediately by numbers who now think it desperately dangerous and almost inevitable death to oppose them, so powerful are they thought, and so alarming are the apprehensions of the Populace at this time — and was it not that they will be awed by their guilt and we supported and encouraged by our loyalty and attachment to the Constitution and Government our defeat would be indubitably certain and sure — They say they can command powerful and numerous aids from Anson, Rowan, and Mecklenburg and if so it becomes the important concern of Government and undoubtedly my duty early to apply to your Excellency for Orders to raise the Militia and if any

---

[1]**Mr. Hart and Mr. Nash:** probably local officials.
[2]**Freshes:** rushes of water.
[3]**Colonel Gray . . . Captain Thackston:** probably local officials.

will obey (which I think they will some few) to give them Battle immediately, and if any advantage can be once gained the show will be over I am convinced — And to do that, I think (tho' almost singly) that I need nothing but your Excellency's express orders, which I hope to be honored with by three o'clock in the afternoon on Sunday the first of May next — I should, considering the shortness of the time and exigency of affairs, have waited for another visit, if the legality of my raising the Militia on an Insurrection had not been doubted without your Excellency's express Orders and Directions under our present Militia Law — If any dangerous attempts are made at any time I shall immediately dispatch an Express with the particulars, and shall notwithstanding the threats of these traitorous Dogs bound to stand by and assist each other by the most solemn oaths oppose them with resolution & courage and if I have but your Excellency's orders I can't but flatter myself with success from the few recruits that can be raised even among ourselves, tho' it is except by three or four chosen leaders, thought impracticable but if from this Account of the matter it is thought fit by your Excellency, *I wish to make the Experiment.* I think it shamefull and I hope unnecessary to call in the aid of other forces to subdue the rebels of our own County but I shall wait and obey your Excellency's commands with punctuality and pleasure.

I thank your Excellency for favour by Mr. Lattiburn and shall endeavour to make his stay in Orange as safe and agreeable as possible. I have not seen that Gentleman as yet, but expect him to dine with me tomorrow. My duty to Her Excellency Mrs. Tryon and do me the favour to believe that I am most cordially and sincerely with the highest sense of Gratitude and respect most absolutely at your Excellency's full command.

Edmund Fanning.

Samuel Spencer to William Tryon

Anson County. 28. April 1768.

As my duty and allegiance to His Majesty: my respect to your Excellency's person and sincere attachment to your Administration prompt me to take the earliest opportunity to acquaint you with those matters which deeply concern the happiness of your Administration, the internal peace & security of the Province, and that Trust your Excellency has been pleased to repose in me, I beg leave to mention the unparalleled tumults, Insurrections, and Commotions which at present distract this County. There have been for some weeks past frequent rumours of the objections and oppositions of many People in this County and the County of Orange to the Payment of the Taxes now due from them. It is now beyond a doubt that this disaffection has been stirred up and principally promoted in this County by a certain man, who for several Elections past of representatives for this County has constantly set up for a candidate of such Elections, and has been as often disappointed except once, which was some time before the last Division of this County. He seems now to have got to his last shift; and expecting a new writ of Election will soon be sent to his County for choosing another representative, . . . and being I doubt superior to no degree of meanness that he can think sufficient to effect his Purpose he is bent upon making his last effort in this desperate manner, for carrying his Election. He has not yet appeared openly in the Mob, because as some of them say he fears if he should be elected on that plan, he would be expelled the House. In consequence of such encouragement and instigation a considerable number of transient Persons, New Comers, Desperadoes, and those who have not paid a tax for several years past were prevailed upon to resist the Sheriff in collecting the Taxes upon pretence that several parts of them were unjust. Clamours have been most industriously and maliciously raised against the Members of the Assembly, the Justices of the County, and all those who have had any hand in the present taxation. By which means many of the unthinking and unwary have been galled into the scheme of Insurrection, & rebellion, and consequently added to their number till at length matters have been carried to that height that upon Thursday last, the first day of this Term, they came up to the Court House to the number of about forty armed with Clubs and some Fire Arms and before the opening of the Court, took possession of the Court House and soon gave out that no Court should be held there. It grew late in the afternoon and a sufficient number of Justices not appearing to constitute a Court, it became necessary that one Justice should open the Court and adjourn till the next morning — I therefore declared my resolution, as did Mr. Medlock and some others, to enter the Court House for opening the Court at all Adventures, and I proceeded about half the way from my Office to the Court House door, and was met by some of my Friends, who entreated me to desist for a few minutes till they could inform the Mob of our full determination to fight our way through them. Whereupon I was persuaded to return to my Office where I stayed some minutes in infinitely more uneasiness from being entirely out of Action, than I felt in approaching the Mob, who besides their numbers had much the advantage of the Ground, but my friends for that time prevailed and the Mob being told of certain and inevitable Bloodshed if they persisted for that we would actually force our way to the Table and the Bench gave up the point, and we came in & opened the Court without resistance. This unparalleled Arrogance can hardly be accounted for but from a particular stratagem of the intended candidate above mentioned, and the readiness of those that constitute the Mob, to evade the payment of their debts by obstructing the Proceedings at Law. But this morning after the Court had met some time, the Mob appeared in a much larger number than they did the first day of the Court consisting of perhaps a hundred men, and came armed as before mentioned to the Court House Door, made a great deal of noise & uproar, behaved very saucy and arrogant & threatened to come in and take the Magistrates off the Bench. Whereupon I went to the door, & demanded of them what they would have. They told me they came to settle some matters in the County for which they wanted the use of the Court House, I immediately then proceeded to read to them a clause of the Act of Parliament . . . against riot and unlawful Assemblies, and procured the Proclamation therein prescribed, to be made for their dispersing themselves etc. They seemed greatly exasperated, and lifted up their clubs and threatened — But as I and some others with me appeared to be on the Defensive they seemed to de-sist a little, & proposed that a few of their Company should come into the Court House, and in the name of the whole set forth those Grievances, they wanted to have redressed. Accordingly I retired to the Table, for the transaction of the busi-ness of my Office, as Clerk of the Court, and after some time some of them came in, and after them came all the rest. They said among other things they desired to know what they were taxed for? Whereupon I rose up & explained to them the na-ture of Taxation, and whence the reasonableness and necessity of it was derived. And proceeded to give them an account of each particular for which they were taxed by the Assembly, and then showed them the several Articles for which the Court had taxed them, for defraying the Charges of the County. They declared they had nothing against me upon what I had said to them, but were dissatisfied with the several allowances the justices had made for raising the County Tax. Ac-cordingly one of them having desired to speak with Mr. Medlock privately he walked off the Bench, having before declared his intention of firing the first man through the Body who should offer to molest him in the execution of his Office as a justice of this Court — By this stratagem the only man was removed from the Bench from whom they expected any desperate resistance. Whereupon they im-mediately without ceremony took the other justices off the Bench, and entirely ob-structed the Proceedings of the Court — They offered no direct insult to me, but told me they did not desire to hurt me, nor my Papers and records. Though be-fore that they had signified their design of taking the records from me, and pe-rusing them, till I assured them that not one of them by any means should go out of my possession, but at the Peril of the life of him, that should take them from me. They then proceeded to appoint some Officers among themselves, and held sev-eral Debates and Consultations, and among the rest whether they should tear down the Court House and the Jail. The matter was very warmly debated, pro and con, but as some of them chose the Court House should be where it is, and some wanted it moved, they at length agreed to let it stand, and after declaring their res-olution to resist the Sheriff in serving any process or collecting of Taxes, Their right to know what Bills were sent to the Grand Jury, and their intention to meet again at the next Court, they marched out and soon after dispersed themselves. . . . Their Arrogance is insupportable and the whole County is thrown into such con-fusion that I am at a loss to tell what measures it will be prudent to take on this Occasion — It has been proposed to me to raise the Militia immediately and to quell the rioters by force of Arms, but whether the seeds of Disaffection to the Pay-ment of Taxes are not so generally sowed through the whole County that few can be found to resist the Mob with resolution and sincerity I am at a loss to say. And whether the appointment of a general muster at this juncture of time would not be likely to give the Disaffected an opportunity of being more mischievous and dangerous than otherwise I most humbly submit to your Excellency and should be extremely glad of your advice and direction on this occasion. And as I appre-hend the Writ of Election is not yet issued to this County for choosing another rep-resentative in the room of Mr. Crawford, I beg leave to entreat your Excellency not by any means to send up the Writ of Election till these unheard of and surprising commotions have at least in some measure subsided. For if an Election were now at hand it is hard to tell the number of ill consequences that must inevitably follow thereupon. I hope your Excellency will excuse the freedom and plainness of this letter, & that the peculiar circumstances of the times & the hurry of business I am at present in will apologise for the defects & incorrectness of it. For further particulars I must beg leave to refer your Excellency to Mr. Hooper who was present during the extraordinary transactions above related — I am obliged to a number of my friends who have with uncommon firmness and assiduity endeavoured with me to suppress the outrages & violence of the rabble on this occasion particularly Colonel Anthony Hutchins, Mr. Medlock, Mr. Dunn, Mr. Martin, and Mr. Hooper. I have by some of these Gentlemen's assistance procured a list of names of some of the Mob, subscribed to their Articles of Association & the oath they have thereupon taken which your Excellency finds herewith inclosed. I wait with impatience to know what measures your Excellency in your wisdom and prudence shall think fit to be taken in this respect.

I am, with the greatest respect, etc.,
Samuel Spencer.

16. The Regulator Critique

JOSHUA TEAGUE ET AL.
Letter to Harmon Husbands
1769

The Regulators' appeal for justice was crafted along lines familiar to eighteenth-century American colonists. They identified conditions of obvious injustice and described a worsening social and economic climate. In this and other documents, Regulators warned of the dangers of tyranny and despotism. When they spoke of "oppression," they portrayed it as part of a larger pattern of political corruption.

In this letter to Orange County Regulator Harmon Husbands, Regulators describe how, seeking justice, they accused local officials of levying excessive fees on

The Colonial Records of North Carolina, Published under the Supervision of the Trustees of the Public Libraries, by Order of the General Assembly, ed. William L. Saunders, vol. 8, 1769–1771 (Raleigh, N.C.: Josephus Daniels, Printer to the State, 1890), 68–70. (Some spelling and punctuation has been modernized.)

*local farmers. Written from Rowan County, southwest of Orange County, it illus-
trates the spread of the movement to the backcountry during the late 1760s and suggests that a degree of provincial coordination was emerging. That failure of the
Rowan correspondents to obtain redress through the legal system gave rise to a profound frustration, and perhaps to a willingness to adopt more extreme measures.*

Salisbury Sept. 14th 1769

Sir,

Agreeable to the Resolutions of the Committee, held at Joshua Teague's last
month; of putting in force the Laws against such Officers, as had transgress'd the
same: about 6 or 7 of us, attended at Salisbury General Court, for that purpose;
when to our astonishment, we found the Grand Jury to be composed of our most
inveterate Enemies & of such as had been our greatest Oppressors; no less than
five of the old Sheriffs on the Jury. In fine there are not above 2 or 3 on it, but what
are limbs of the Law, however we were resolved at all Events to try what Justice
could be obtained, as we have been so often referr'd thereunto by the Governor
and others of the first Rank in the Province, who had so repeatedly urged us to take
legal steps, assuring us that we should everywhere obtain the highest Justice, &
one particular Gentleman had always told us he would be there & see us have Justice, so Relying on those promises, & being Conscious to ourselves, that the Law
was in our favour, against our Enemies, who had repeatedly broke it. Besides the
Cries of the people were so great, & repeated for Justice, and we well knowing that
the oppression was so great, that we durst hardly return home, before trial made;
as we were nominated for that purpose by the people. In order therefore to proceed, we applied to Mr. Hooper Deputy Attorney General . . . who appeared well
pleased with our Designs, & assured us he would do everything in his power for
us. Accordingly he drew up a Bill of Indictment against Colonel Frohock[1] for Ex-
tortion, in taking £2 5s of the Widow Coo for the Cost of an Indictment, & the Bill
found Ignoramus;[2] the King proved by the Oath of Joseph Harrison,[3] that the said
Harrison paid the Money to one Linville, a Sub-Sheriff for the use of Colonel Frohock; John Dunn proved that he got the Receipt from the Widow some time ago,
in order to procure redress for her, but had lost it, but that it was for £2 5s; Abraham Crosson[4] proved that when the Colonel was about to make out the Bill of
Cost against the Widow, he asked said Crosson what circumstances the Widow
was in, who answered in very Good, & had money by her; if that be the Case said
the Colonel then I must double the Bill. However the Jury found the Bill ignoramus, and soon after some of the Jury came to us and wondered we would lay in
such Complaints without better proof, notwithstanding this disappointment we

[1]**Colonel Frohock:** an Orange County official, probably county sheriff.
[2]**Ignoramus:** presenting insufficient evidence.
[3]**Joseph Harrison:** a Rowan County resident.
[4]**Abraham Crosson:** a Rowan County resident.

kept up our spirits, our oppressors coming us to ever & anon, and begging we would make up with them in behalf of the Country, promising to return the Money they had illegally taken, & withal to lay in no more Complaints, as they hated to be recorded for Extortioners. Next Day we laid in a Complaint against William Frohock, Sub-Sheriff as follows, viz, That one Mook had taken out an Inferior Court Writ, for one Bools,[5] but that immediately on serving said Writ, (for 7 pounds) they compromised the matter, & paid the Cost to the amount of fifty four shillings; we produced the Receipt, & proved by the Oath of Joseph Harrison, however evident as this was, no Bill was found; we next brought in a Bill against Colonel Frohock as follows, viz, One Robins took out a Writ for one Robins and immediately the matter was agreed upon, & after paying the Lawyer, & Sheriff, their Respective Demands, then going to the Colonel as Clerk, to know his demand he asked & received, 16s 6d on payment of which he gave to Robins a Receipt, which was produced and proved, by the oath of Thomas Frohock, but this met the same fate with the others, & turned out NO BILL. On this we signified to the Chief Justice, that the Jury were combined against us, who said he was sorry for the Occasion, but that there was no help for it, especially at this Time; we told him now it would exasperate the Country, who were now fully become sensible of their Oppression, to see themselves thus debarr'd of Justice, and pass unnoticed, when groaning under the weight of their Oppressions. He begged of us to be quiet, & still, & to advise the people to be so, & to try some other Time, reminding us that that Jury would not be there always; we likewise acquainted the District Attorney General that we were creditably informed, that the now acting Jury, were not the Jurors chosen by the Court. This information we Procured from one of the Magistrates, who came to us & told us they were not the men appointed for that purpose, for said he, I was on the bench when the appointment was made, & was myself nominated, but when I came & offered my service I met a refusal. We next applied to one of the Burgesses, who agreed with the said Justice, saying it was true to his knowledge. However to leave no stone unturned, whereby to obtain Justice, we now resolved to laying a Complaint against the Colonel wherein he had confessed lately he had taken too much, & had paid back 11s 0d of the money, the Complaint stood thus, Elijah Teague took out a General Court Writ for one James, & on serving the Writ they immediately agreed, & the Writ return'd agreed, Joshua Teague went immediately to Frohock before execution, to pay of the Cost, who demanded & Received £4 2s. 4d; hereupon the Jury sent for the Case Book, but as there were a plenty of Clerks and Sheriffs among them, well acquainted with drawing up such Bills, this was likewise thrown out, on the old score NO BILL. So we concluded to return home, & then left them congratulating each other on their happy success & Deliverance. Thus you see my dear friend we can get no redress in what is called Courts of Justice, & seeing our Crafty & cruel Oppressors are so combined together that we think it impossible to obtain the least shadow of Justice among them. As you may plainly see, they

---

[5]**Mook . . . Bools:** two Rowan litigants.

take the power of the Court in their own hands, & try it themselves, or at least deprive us of the Benefit of bringing our matter to any Issue, and now Sir we apply to you as a Representative, to see if you can get any Redress from that Quarter, as for the present mode we expect none from it, & let us begg of you & the rest of that respectable Body, not to be afraid to alter the present form; for we are sure none can be worse than the present; for we are confidant, that it takes more in this County to prevent the poor oppressed people to obtain Justice, than it would take under an honest Administration to support it. And we remain Sir

Your very humble Servants
Joshua Teague
Abraham Crosson
Isaac Wainscot
Jos. Harrison
James Hunter

A true Copy

17. A Regulator Perspective

HARMON HUSBANDS
Introduction to **A Fan for Fanning
and a Touch-Stone to Tryon**
1771

Perhaps the most important North Carolina Regulator leader, Harmon Husbands was the oldest son of a wealthy Maryland planter and slaveholder. He became an active Quaker as a young man, moved to North Carolina in 1755, and eventually acquired ten thousand acres of land. Following his imprisonment and trial for resisting tax payments in 1768 in Hillsborough, he was elected twice to the assembly, but it voted to expel him. Husbands fled the colony in 1771, after the battle of Alamance. Under the name "Toscape Death," he exiled himself to western Pennsylvania, where he remained an active political radical and participated in the famous

Some Eighteenth Century Tracts Concerning North Carolina, with Introductions and Notes, ed. William K. Boyd (Raleigh, N.C.: Edwards and Broughton Co., 1927), 341–44. (Some spelling and punctuation has been modernized.)

Whiskey Rebellion of 1795. His lands were confiscated and he remained outlawed even after Governor Josiah Martin had pardoned all Regulators in 1775.

In this pamphlet, published prior to the battle of Alamance, Husbands defends the Regulators to a wider audience. He attempts to explain their grievances, motives, and goals in the movement.

———————

It will be readily granted, that the task of an Historian is a difficult one, and that because of its being almost impossible to obtain good, and proper information; nor does this always arise from a design to deceive in them, who furnish materials for History; but from an aptness in Men to inform us, not of the facts as they are in themselves, and immediately connected with their circumstances and causes, but of the impressions made upon their minds, by the effects of civil and political conduct. Hence it is, that one Historian is called a Jacobite, and a Tory, and another a Whig, and a friend to his Country, and an impartial writer; when such declarations do not ascertain the real character of the writer, they serve only to inform of what side and opinion He is, whom we hear thus judging, and what are the feelings of his mind. But however difficult the talk, the advantage of having even an imperfect History is so great as to be a sufficient counterpoise, and determine them, who have it in their power, to inform their Country, as fully as they can. And this it is that hath prompted me to undertake to give an account of what has been called the Regulation in North-Carolina. . . .

. . . [I]t may be proper, . . . as leading to our principal subject, to say something of the settlement and inhabitants of North Carolina. Its name points out the Prince that granted the Charter of the Province, who was Charles the Second after his restoration to the Crown of England. The grantees were the Earl of Claradon, Duke of Albemarle, Lord Craven, Lord Berkley, Lord Anthony Ashley Cooper, Sir George Carteret, Sir William Colleton, and their Heirs. The patent or grant appears to have been an *Exclusive* one; for the first Government was a kind of sovereignty; but this kind of regency proving very troublesome, the proprietaries, all save one, sold the Lordship to the Crown, and it has ever since been a royal Government. It was settled, as most new Countries are, by those who *would not live in their* OWN PLACE; who sat down upon the Sea-Coast, or places contiguous to navigable Water. And such has been the fate of Newbern, and other places, in North-Carolina, that for many Years they were accounted an Asylum for all such as fled from their Creditors, and from the hand of Justice, and such as would not live without working elsewhere. Men regardless of religion, and all moral obligation. Hence it was, that refugees from the western Governments, and from *Connecticut,* found a safe retreat in North-Carolina; particularly on the Sea Coast, and places adjacent. The settlement of the inland Country has been very slow, till since the last War, when families from Virginia, Maryland and, the lower government, Pennsylvania, Jersies, New-York, &c, have moved down, five or six hundred in a season; by which Orange County was populated; and by good industrious labouring Men; who knew the value of their property better than to let it go to enrich Pettyfogging Lawyers, extortionate and griping publicans or Tax gatherers, and such as delighted in building Palaces, at the expense of the honest Farmer, and Tradesman.

The above picture may perhaps be supposed too strongly represented, the dark part set too much to view. And therefore drawn by the pen of bitterness. If such thought should occur to any reader, I have only to ask of him, that he would suspend a judgment in the case, until he has heard the whole matter, and if then he shall think the writer deserving censure, he will please to remember that he who has seen, and heard from the sufferers own mouths must have feelings different from him who reads only, and that with a persuasion, that a bad story, however true, ought not to be told, especially when it effects publick characters.

The writer has thought it proper to give this short general description of North-Carolina, to prepare the mind of the reader, as well as to enable him to form a right judgment; as many things will occur in the course of these papers, that to a Man of Massachusetts will seem *unaccountable*. And perhaps nothing more so, than that from the year 1765, the people in different parts of Carolina, appeared against, openly against the most flagrant breaches of all law, on the side of the civil officers, and were not able to obtain any the least relief; and their complaints beginning at that time, show that the oppressions were of older date, and makes it probable that the Era of Carolina's misery commenced at that period, when the great Colonel Fanning, and the Magnanimous General Tryon, mistaking the designs of nature, in their formation, by a marvellous Metamorphosis became Politicians.

One hint I think necessary to give the reader in this introduction, and that is, that Governor Tryon does not appear to have acted in any part of his character which concerned the Regulators, under ministerial influence, save what might have been the effects of his own, and his Tools representations to the King's Ministers; but rather appears to have been so great a Fool, as to have been led by Fanning, or that he and Fanning with the rest of the civil officers were leagued together, Knaves alike, to fleece the people that they might build palaces, &c. For Fanning, when he arrived in Carolina, seven or eight years ago, was poor; he had before he left Carolina, the last summer amassed a fortune, of near ten thousand pounds Sterling, and all out of the people, as will appear by and by.

How unfortunate is that Prince, who is sorely wounded through the side of base designing wretches, who prostitute all things sacred and civil to deceive their King, and to get into places of important trust; and because they have spent much time in basely sycophanting to a noble Lord, and prostituting the honour and virtue of their family connections, when in place, run hard to bring up lost time, and the King's good subjects are made their beasts of burden and of prey.

How fortunate, on the other hand, is that Prince, and happy the people, when he that governs, is a wise and good man, and one who knows the bound of the peoples privilege, and limits of the rulers power. Should not they who are thus happy, prize and love such an one, and in every instance avoid giving him pain, remembering his anxiety and solicitude, for the prosperity of the King, his Master's subjects.

18. The Hillsborough Riot

RICHARD HENDERSON AND THE VIRGINIA GAZETTE
Reports of the Riot
1770

The most significant act of Regulator defiance occurred in Orange County in late September 1770, when 150 frustrated Regulators burst into the meeting of the Orange County superior court, physically assaulted officers of the court, and destroyed the home of Edmund Fanning. These documents provide two perspectives on the riot. The first is a letter from Richard Henderson, a self-made man who immigrated about 1740 to North Carolina from Virginia and became a lawyer and superior court judge. He was presiding over his courtroom in Hillsborough when the Regulators burst in; his letter to Governor Tryon was meant to convey the gravity of the crisis — and the need for intervention. The Virginia Gazette report, a secondhand description that also appeared in newspapers in Boston and London, was intended for a wider, more public audience. Still, both documents suggest some of the local officials' horror at the Regulators' defiance of law and established political authority.

RICHARD HENDERSON TO WILLIAM TRYON

Granville September 29, 1770

Sir

With the deepest Concern for my Country I have lately been Witness to a Scene which not only threatened the peace and well being of this province for the future, but was in itself the most horrid & audacious Insult to Government: perpetrated with such Circumstances of Cruelty & Madness, as (I believe) scarsely has been equaled at any Time.

However flattering Your Excellency's prospect may have been with respect to the People called Regulators, their late Conduct too sufficiently evince that a Wise, Mild, and Benevolent Administration come very far short of bringing them to a Sense of their Duty. They are abandoned to every principle of Virtue and desperately engaged not only in the most shocking Barbarities but a Total Subversion of the Constitution.

On Monday last being the second Day of Hillsborough Superior Court, early in the Morning the Town was filled with a great Number of these People, shouting, hallooing, and making a considerable Tumult in the Streets. At about

The Regulators in North Carolina: A Documentary History, 1759–1776, ed. William S. Powell, James K. Huhta, and Thomas J. Farnham (Raleigh, N.C.: State Department of Archives and History, 1971), 245–48. (Some spelling and punctuation has been modernized.)

11 O'Clock the Court was opened, and immediately the House filled as close as one Man could stand by another; some with Clubs, others with Whips and Switches, few or none without some Weapon! When the House had become so crowded that no more could well get in, one of them (whose Name I think is called Fields) came forward and told Me he had something to say before I proceeded to Business.—The Accounts I had previously received, together with the Manner and Appearance of these Men, and the abruptness of their Address rendered my Situation extremely Uneasy. Upon my informing Fields that He might speak on, He proceeded to let Me know that He spoke for the whole Body of the People called Regulators, That they understood I would not try their Causes, and that their Determination was to have them tried, for they had come down to see Justice done, and Justice They would have, and if I would proceed to try these Causes, it might prevent much Mischief; They also charged the Court with Injustice at the preceeding Term and objected to the Jurors appointed by the Inferior Court and said they would have them altered and others appointed in their room, with many other things too tedious to mention Here. Thus I found Myself under a necessity of attempting to soften and turn away the Fury of this mad People in the best Manner in my Power, and as much as could well be Pacify their Rage and at the same Time preserve the little remaining Dignity of the Court: The Consequence of which was that after spending upwards of half an Hour in this disagreeable Situation the Mobb Cried Out "Retire, Retire, and let the Court go on," upon which most of the Regulators went out and seemed to be in Consultation in a party by themselves. The little Hope of peace derived from this piece of Behavior were very Transient for in a few Minutes, Mr. Williams an Attorney of that Court was coming in and had advanced near the Door when they fell on him in a most furious Manner with Clubs and sticks of enormous Size and 'twas with great Difficulty He saved His Life by taking Shelter in a Neighbouring store House.—Mr. Fanning was next the Object of their Fury, Him they seized and took with a degree of Violence not to be described, from off the Bench where He had retired for protection and Assistance and with hideous Shouts of Barbarian Cruelty dragged him by the Heels, out of Doors, while others engaged in dealing out Blows with such Violence that I made no doubt His Life would instantly become a Sacrifice to their Rage and Madness; However Mr. Fanning by a Manly exertion miraculously broke hold and fortunately jumped into a Door that saved him from immediate Dissolution. During this Uproar several of them told Me with Oaths of great Bitterness that my Turn should be next — I will not deny but in this frightful Affair my Thoughts were much Engaged on my own protection, but it was not long before James Hunter[1] and some other of their Chieftains came and told Me not to be uneasy for that no Man should hurt Me on proviso, I would set and hold Court to the end of the Term. I took Advantage of this proposal and made no scruple at promising what was not in my Intention to perform: for the Terms they would admit Me to hold Court on were that no Lawyer, The Kings Attorney ex-

---

[1]**James Hunter:** a prominent Regulator leader.

cepted, should be admitted into Court, and that they would stay and see Justice impartialy done.

It would be impertinent to trouble Your Excellency with many circumstances that ocurred in this Barbarous Riot — Messers. Thomas Hart, Alexander Martin, Michael Holt, John Sitterell (Clerk of the Crown), and many others were severely whipped.—Colonel Gray, Major Lloyd, Mr. Francis Nash, John Cooke, Tyree Harris,[2] and sundry other persons Timously made their Escape, or would have shared this same Fate. In about four or five Hours their Rage seemed to subside a little and they permitted Me to adjourn Court and conducted Me with great parade to my Lodgings.—Colonel Fanning whom they had made a prisoner of was in the Evening permitted to return to His own House, on His Word of Honor to surrender Himself the next Day.

At about Ten O'clock that Evening, took an Opportunity of making my Escape by a back Way, and left poor Colonel Fanning and the little Borough in a wretched Situation.

Thus far May it please Your Excellency with Respect to what came within my own Knowledge, since my Departure many different and Authentical Accounts say that the Mobb not contented with the cruel Abuse they had already given Mr. Fanning, in which one of his Eyes was almost beaten out did the next Day actually determine to put Him immediately to Death, but some of them a little more Humane than the rest interfered and saved His Life. They turned Him out in the Street and spared His Life on no other Condition than that of his taking the Road and continuing to run until He should get out of their Sight. They soon after to consumate their wicked Designs, broke and entered His Mansion House, destroyed every Article of Furniture, and with Axes and other Instruments laid the Fabrick level with its Foundation, broke and entered His Cellar and destroyed the Contents, His Papers were carried into the Streets by Armfuls and destroyed, His wearing Apparel shared the same Fate; — I much fear His Office will be their next Object.—Have not yet heard where Colonel Fanning has taken Shelter, the last Advice was that He was a Mile or two from Town on Horseback, but the person by whom this came says that the Insurgents have scouting Parties constantly harrying the several Roads and Woods about Town, and should He unfortunately fall into their Hands the Consequence perhaps would be fatal. The Merchants and Inhabitants were chiefly run out into the Country, and expect their Stores and Houses without Distinction will be pillaged and laid Waste. The Number of Insurgents that Appeared when the Riot first began was, I think, about one hundred and fifty, tho they constantly increased for two Days and kept a Number with Fire Arms at about a Mile distance from Town ready to fall on whenever they were called for! This Account is contradicted by Some and believed by Others: certain it is that a large Number of Men constantly lay near the Town, whether They had Arms or not is not yet sufficiently determined.

As the Burden of conducting Hillsborough Superior Court fell on my shoulders alone, the Task was extremely hard and Critical I made every Effort in my

---

[2]**Thomas Hart . . . Tyree Harris:** all of these were prominent backcountry officials.

power consistent with my Office and the Duty the public is entitled to claim to preserve Peace and good Order, but as all attempts of that kind were quite ineffectual, thought it more adviseable to break up Court than sit and be made a mock Judge for the sport and entertainment of those Abondoned Wretches.

This Express has been delayed two Days in expectation of obtaining from Mr. Fanning a more particular Account of the Damage done him as well as the rest of the Inhabitants of that desolate Borough, but as the persons whom I sent for that purpose are not yet returned, think it my Duty to forward this with the utmost Expedition. Should my Conduct through these Transactions Merit Your Approbation it will greatly add to the Felicity of Sir

P.S. My Express has this Instant arrived from Hillsborough with the following Accounts. Colonel Fanning is alive & well as could be expected.—The Insurgents left the Town on Wednesday Night, having done very little Mischief after Spoiling Mr. Fannings House, except breaking the Windows of most of the Houses in Town, among which Mr. Edward's did not escape. The Merchants and others are taking possession of their shattered Tenaments. Mr. Fannings House is not quite down, a few Timbers support the lower Story, but they are cut off at the Sills and a small Breeze of Wind will throw down the little Remains.—Every Thing else that we heard respecting Mr. Fanning is true with this Addition that He lost upwards of two hundred pounds in Cash.

Enclosed is a petition presented me on Saturday by James Hunter, that being the first Day of the Court, the Answer was deferred till Monday. Your Excellency will best Judge if that paper may not be of Service at a future Day, there are many subscribers who are all without Dispute Regulators.

Virginia Gazette

October 25, 1770

Newbern, October 5, 1770

On Wednesday last a special messenger arrived in town from Granville county, to his Excellency the Governor, with the melancholy account of a violent insurrection, or rather rebellion, having broke out in Orange County, among a set of men who call themselves regulators, and who have for some years past given infinite disturbance to the civil government of this province, but now have sapped its whole foundation, brought its courts of Justice to their own controul, leaped the strong barrier of private property, and audaciously violated the laws of God and man.

These people have for a long time opposed paying all manner of taxes, have entertained the vilest opinion of the Gentlemen of the law, and often threatened them with their vengeance. Accordingly, as the Honourable Judge Henderson,

The Regulators in North Carolina: A Documentary History, 1759–1776, ed. William S. Powell, James K. Huhta, and Thomas J. Farnham (Raleigh, N.C.: State Department of Archives and History, 1971), 250–53. (Some spelling and punctuation has been modernized.)

and several other Gentlemen of the law, were returning from Salisbury circuit to Hillsborough, in order to hold the court there, they were waylaid by a number of them with their rifles; but happily, having notice of their hellish design, by taking a contrary route they eluded their bloody plot. They still gave out their threats of meeting them at Hillsborough, and wreaking their vengeance on them there.

These menaces were treated with contempt, or rather the violent ravings of a factious and discontented mob, than any settled and fixed resolution of men of property to commit so daring an insult to the laws of the country; and accordingly the court was opened and proceeded to business. But on Monday, the second day of the court, the tragical scene began; a very large number of these people, headed by men of considerable property, appeared in Hillsborough, armed with clubs, whips, loaded at the ends with lead or iron (a stroke from which would level the strongest man) and many other offensive weapons, and at once beset the courthouse. The first object of their revenge was Mr. John Williams, a Gentleman of the law, whom they assaulted as he was entering the courthouse; him they cruelly abused, with many and violent blows with their loaded whips on the head and different parts of his body, until he, by great good fortune, made his escape, and took shelter in a neighboring store. They then entered the courthouse, and immediately fixed their attention on Colonel Fanning as the next object of their merciless cruelty. He expected his fate, and had retired to the Judge's seat, as the highest part of the courthouse from which he might make the greatest defence against these bloodthirsty and cruel savages; but, poor Gentleman, vain were all his efforts, for after behaving with the most heroic courage he fell a sacrifice to numbers, and suffered a cruelty the richest language can but faintly paint. They seized him by the neck, dragged him down the steps, his head striking violently on every step, carried him to the door, and forcing him out, dragged him on the ground over stones and brickbats, struck him with their whips and clubs, kicked him, spit and spurned at him, and treated him with every possible mark of contempt and cruelty; until at length, by a violent effort of strength and activity, he rescued himself from their merciless claws, and took shelter in a house. The vultures pursued him there, and gave him a stroke that will probably destroy one of his eyes. In this piteous and grievously maimed condition, they left him for awhile, retreated to the courthouse, knocked down and very cruelly treated the deputy clerk of the Crown, ascended the bench, shook their whips over Judge Henderson, told him his turn was next, ordered him to pursue business, but in the manner they should prescribe, which was that no lawyers should enter the courthouse, no juries but what they should pick, and order new trials in cases where some of them had been cast for their malpractices. They then seized Mr. Hooper, a Gentleman of the law, dragged and paraded him through the streets, and treated him with every mark of contempt and insult. This closed the first day, but the second day presented a scene, if possible, more tragic. Immediately on their discovering that the Judge had made his escape from their fury, and refused to submit to the dictates of lawless and desperate men, they marched in a body to Colonel Fanning's house, and on a signal given by their ringleaders entered the house, destroyed ever[y] piece of furniture in it, ripped open his beds, broke and threw in the streets every piece of china and glass ware in the house, scattered all his papers and books in the wind, seized all his plate, cash, and proclamation money; entered his cellars, and after saturating and gorging their more than savage stomachs with his liquors, stove and strew in the streets the remainder. Being now drunk with rage, liquor, and lawless fury, they took his wearing clothes, stuck them on a pole, paraded them in triumph through the streets, and, to close the scene, pulled down and laid his house in ruins, Hunter and Butler, two of their chiefs, stripping in buff and beginning the heroick deed. They then went to a large handsome church bell that Colonel Fanning, at the expense of 60 or 70 £, had made a present of to the church of Hillsborough, and split it to pieces, and were at the point of pulling down the church, but their leaders, thinking it would betray their religious principles, restrained them. Their revenge being not yet satiated on this unhappy Gentleman, they again pursued him, cruelly beat him, and at length with dogs hunted him out of town, and with a cruelty more savage than bloodhounds stoned him as he fled. What heart but feels for the distresses of this unfortunate Gentleman! what hand that would not be uplifted in defense of such injured innocence.

When they had fully glutted their revenges on the lawyers, and particularly Colonel Fanning, to show their opinion of courts of justice they took from his chains a negro that had been executed some time, and placed him at the lawyer's bar, and filled the Judge's seat with human excrement, in derision and contempt of the characters that fill those respectable places. Would a Hottentot[1] have been guilty of such a piece of brutality! or is there the most savage nation on earth whose manners are less cultivated!

A paragraph of a letter from a Gentleman, who was eye witness of the above dismal scene, says: "The merchants' stores are broke and rifled, Mr. Cooke's house torn to pieces, and Mr. Edward's had not shared a better fate. The inhabitants have fled the town and the regulators live at their expense; they are in possession of their houses, and make the best use of the emergency to satiate their cursed passions, and appetites. Here my pen drops; I satiate with the painful recital."

In short, all civil government in Orange County is relaxed, the courts of justice totally stopped, and every thing reduced to the power and controul of a set of men who call them selves regulators; but are in fact no other than a desperate and cruel banditi, actuated by principles that no laws can restrain, no honour or conscience bind.

---

[1]**Hottentot:** a member of a nomadic Southwest African group; the term "Hottentot" was a derogatory characterization of Africans.

Suggestions for Further Reading

Douglass, Elisha P. *Rebels and Democrats: The Struggle for Equal Political Rights and Majority Rule during the American Revolution.* Chapel Hill: University of North Carolina Press, 1955.

Ekirch, A. Roger. *"Poor Carolina": Politics and Society in Colonial North Carolina, 1729–1776.* Chapel Hill: University of North Carolina Press, 1981.

Kay, Marvin L. Michael. "The North Carolina Regulation, 1766–1776: A Class Conflict." In *The American Revolution: Explorations in the History of American Radicalism,* ed. Alfred F. Young. DeKalb: Northern Illinois University Press, 1976.

Whittenburg, James P. "Planters, Merchants, and Lawyers: Social Change and the Origins of the North Carolina Regulation." *William and Mary Quarterly,* 3d Ser., 34 (1977): 215–38.

CHAPTER SIX

THE REVOLUTION

A Proposal for Arming Slaves

From the very beginning, the southern colonies played an integral role in the American Revolution. Nevertheless, the British initially blamed New England for their colonial problems and, counting on strong pro-British sentiment in the South, concentrated their efforts for the first three years on subduing the northern colonies.

There were, in fact, many loyalists in the South, but Britain's failure to establish a strong military presence there early in the war and to support loyalist campaigns against rebellious colonists lost them this initial advantage. Other British decisions, including an offer of freedom to slaves who were willing to serve the British army, further alienated white sympathizers in the South.

Just after fighting broke out at Lexington and Concord in April 1775, a group of slaves in Virginia offered its support to the royal governor, Lord Dunmore. He was reluctant to accept, correctly fearing that this would enrage white Virginians. Outnumbered by revolutionaries, and with little support from the British army, Dunmore soon changed his mind. In November 1775 he offered freedom to any indentured servant or slave who would bear arms in His Majesty's forces. This act provoked fear and anger among whites throughout the southern colonies; they reacted by tightening controls over their slaves, moving them away from British lines, and spreading rumors that the British actually intended to sell them into slavery in the West Indies. As the war progressed, thousands fled to the British.

In the early stages of the Revolution, black men also fought on the American side. Though the general practice in the decades preceding the Revolution had been to bar blacks from colonial militias, northern units often disregarded this policy. When the Continental army was established, however, southern soldiers and politicians insisted on the exclusion of blacks. Free blacks protested. General

George Washington, sympathetic to their claim, presented the matter to the Continental Congress, which in 1776 ruled that only free blacks who had already served could be accepted. As the war continued and it became increasingly difficult to raise troops, northern states again ignored the law and a few, led by Rhode Island, passed their own legislation authorizing the enlistment of slaves.

Rhode Island's example inspired John Laurens, an idealistic young officer from South Carolina, to develop a plan for arming slaves in his state, which was having considerable difficulty raising troops for the Continental army. In January 1778 Laurens requested that his father, Henry Laurens, then president of the Continental Congress, allow him to create "black battalions" from the slaves who were to be his inheritance. It was a well-known fact that South Carolina was poorly defended: some white men were loyalists, and even patriots were not eager to enlist for long terms that might take them far from home. In some parts of the Carolina low country, slaves outnumbered whites by as many as twenty to one, and fears of slave revolts or desertions to the British made white men reluctant to leave their farms or plantations. Laurens's proposal was a radical one, especially for the son of a major slaveholder from a state with a black majority. Most white Southerners viewed the arming of blacks, whether by the British or by Americans, as a dire threat. After months of discussion, Henry Laurens finally persuaded his son to back off from his plan. Of the southern states, only Maryland allowed the enlistment of blacks.

In late 1778, however, British leaders began planning a campaign against the highly vulnerable South. Laurens felt that the impending disaster called for extreme measures, and this time his father agreed. Laurens began promoting an expanded version of his "scheme," calling for South Carolina and Georgia to create battalions of slaves. The troops were to be furnished by slave owners in proportion to the number they possessed. In March 1779, the proposal won the support of a congressional committee that had been created (at Henry Laurens's suggestion) to make recommendations for the defense of the southern colonies. Congress approved it and promoted John Laurens, who was to command one of the proposed battalions, to lieutenant colonel.

Although Laurens (now a member of the South Carolina legislature) fought hard for the proposal, it was overwhelmingly rejected by state officials incensed that Congress responded to their pleas for troops by telling them to arm their slaves. Some even considered surrendering Charleston if the British would allow the city to remain neutral for the remainder of the war. Charleston was neither surrendered nor captured that year, but Laurens, knowing an attack was inevitable, continued to push for slave enlistment — to no avail. On May 12, 1780, General Benjamin Lincoln surrendered Charleston to the British in the worst defeat of the war.

John Laurens was among the 5,500 American soldiers captured. Freed in a prisoner exchange, Laurens was appointed by Congress as a minister to France, where he served from December 1780 to September 1781. He returned to America in time to serve again under General Washington during the siege of Yorktown and represent the American army during surrender negotiations in October 1781. The war was not yet over, however: the British still occupied Charleston, Wilmington (North Carolina), and Savannah (Georgia); and the South Carolina low country was the scene of small but savage battles between patriots and loyalists. Returning to his home state, Laurens again recommended raising a battalion of slaves, this time from the confiscated estates of loyalists. Instead, the state approved a plan to raise troops by awarding "contraband" slaves to white volunteers. (This action actually strengthened the institution of slavery by extending slave ownership to many who had not previously owned slaves.) Laurens refused to give up on his plan and was to present the idea in Georgia but was killed in a minor skirmish there in August 1782.

That same summer, the Americans advanced on Savannah and Charleston; the British withdrew, taking with them 3,800 loyalists and 5,000 slaves. White Southerners, who expected the British to return all contraband — including slaves — were infuriated. One of the Americans who pushed hard at the Paris peace talks for an article prohibiting the British from removing additional "property" from America was Henry Laurens.

This chapter brings together four sets of documents concerning the British offer to arm slaves and the deliberations among leading Americans over using slaves as soldiers: Dunmore's proclamation, selected correspondence between John and Henry Laurens, letters among Continental leaders, and an exchange between John Laurens and George Washington. These documents shed light not only on the difficulties of raising Southern troops during the Revolution, but also on late-eighteenth-century ideas about race.

As you read, keep in mind these questions. What were John Laurens's reasons for seeking to create slave battalions? What objections did he encounter? What do these documents reveal about Revolutionary-era attitudes concerning human nature in general and the nature of black slaves in particular? How do Laurens's arguments for freeing slaves reflect Enlightenment ideas about nature versus experience in shaping human attributes and republican ideas about civic virtue?

19. The British Call Slaves to Arms

JOHN MURRAY, EARL OF DUNMORE
Proclamation
1775

John Murray, Earl of Dunmore, was in the unenviable position of being the royal governor of Virginia when the Revolution began in April 1775. By autumn he had retreated from Williamsburg to a man-of-war anchored in the Norfolk harbor, from which he issued his famous proclamation promising freedom to slaves who fought on the British side. Despite strenuous efforts by the Virginians to prevent slave defections, hundreds of slaves responded to Dunmore's call. By December nearly three hundred slaves had enlisted in what was dubbed "Lord Dunmore's Ethiopian Regiment" and were outfitted in uniforms with the inscription "Liberty to Slaves" across their chests.

Off Norfolk, November 7, 1775

As I have ever entertained hopes that an accommodation might have taken place between Great Britain and this Colony, without being compelled by my duty to this most disagreeable, but now absolutely necessary step, rendered so by a body of armed men, unlawfully assembled, firing on His Majesty's Tenders; and the formation of an Army, and that Army now on their march to attack His Majesty's Troops, and destroy the well-disposed subjects of this Colony: To defeat such treasonable purposes, and that all such traitors and their abettors may be brought to justice, and that the peace and good order of this Colony may be again restored, which the ordinary course of the civil law is unable to effect, I have thought fit to issue this my Proclamation, hereby declaring, that until the aforesaid good purposes can be obtained, I do, in virtue of the power and authority to me given by His Majesty, determine to execute martial law, and cause the same to be executed throughout this Colony. And to the end that peace and good order may the sooner be restored, I do require every person capable of bearing arms to resort to His Majesty's standard, or be looked upon as traitors to His Majesty's crown and Government, and thereby become liable to the penalty the law inflicts upon such offences — such as forfeiture of life, confiscation of lands, etc., etc.: and I do hereby further declare all indented servants, Negroes or others, (appertaining to Rebels) free, that are able and willing to bear arms, they joining His Majesty's Troops as soon as may be, for the more speedily reducing this Colony to a proper sense of

Sources and Documents Illustrating the American Revolution, 1764–1788, and the Formation of the Federal Constitution, ed. Samuel Eliot Morrison (New York: Oxford University Press, 1965), 111.

their duty to His Majesty's crown and dignity. I do further order and require all His Majesty's liege subjects to retain their quit-rents, or any other taxes due, or that may become due, in their own custody, till such time as peace may be again restored to this, at present, most unhappy Country, or demanded of them for their former salutary purposes, by officers properly authorized to receive the same.

Given under my hand, on board the Ship *William*, off Norfolk, the 7th day of November, in the sixteenth year of His Majesty's reign.

Dunmore

God Save the King!

20. A Patriot's "Scheme"

HENRY LAURENS AND JOHN LAURENS
Correspondence between a Slaveholder and His Son
1776–1779

The following is a series of letters exchanged between a conservative and cautious father and his idealistic and daring son. At the time these letters were written, Henry Laurens was president of the Continental Congress and John was an aide-de-camp to General George Washington.

The elder Laurens had grown wealthy from trading in slaves and goods, but by 1770 had abandoned the slave trade and acquired vast rice plantations in South Carolina and Georgia. John, his eldest and favorite son, was educated in England and Switzerland. He chose to study law, believing it would enable him to gain fame while also serving the weak and oppressed. As a student in London, he was influenced by friends who admired America but abhorred slavery. Handsome, charming, and fearless, young Laurens became a favorite of Washington's. He earned a reputation for courage verging on recklessness: as General Lafayette observed after the battle of Brandywine, "it was not his fault that he was not killed or wounded; he did every thing that was necessary to procure one or t'other."

Henry Laurens to John Laurens

Charleston, S. C., 14th August, 1776

My Negroes, all to a man, are strongly attached to me; hitherto not one of them has attempted to desert; on the contrary, those who are more exposed hold themselves always ready to fly from the enemy in case of a sudden descent. Many hundreds of that colour have been stolen and decoyed by the servants of King George the Third. Captains of British ships of war and noble lords have busied themselves in such inglorious pilferage, to the disgrace of their master and disgrace of their cause. These Negroes were first enslaved by the English; acts of parliament have established the slave trade in favour of the home-residing English, and almost totally prohibited the Americans from reaping any share of it. Men of war, forts, castles, governors, companies, and committees are employed and authorized by the English parliament to protect, regulate, and extend the slave trade. Negroes are brought by Englishmen and sold as slaves to Americans. Bristol, Liverpool, Manchester, Birmingham, etc., etc., live upon the slave trade. The British parliament now employ their men-of-war to steal those Negroes from the Americans to whom they had sold them, pretending to set the poor wretches free, but basely trepan[1] and sell them into tenfold worse slavery in the West Indies, where probably they will become the property of Englishmen again, and of some who sit in parliament. What meanness! What complicated wickedness appears in this scene! O England, how changed! How fallen!

You know, my dear son, I abhor slavery. I was born in a country where slavery had been established by British kings and parliaments, as well as by the laws of that country ages before my existence. I found the Christian religion and slavery growing under the same authority and cultivation. I nevertheless disliked it. In former days there was no combating the prejudices of men supported by interest; the day I hope is approaching when, from principles of gratitude as well as justice, every man will strive to be foremost in showing his readiness to comply with the golden rule.

Not less than twenty thousand pounds sterling would all my Negroes produce if sold at public auction tomorrow. I am not the man who enslaved them; they are indebted to Englishmen for that favour; nevertheless I am devising means for manumitting many of them, and for cutting off the entail of slavery. Great powers oppose me — the laws and customs of my country, my own and the avarice of my countrymen. What will my children say if I deprive them of so much estate? These are difficulties, but not insuperable. I will do as much as I can in my time, and leave the rest to a better hand.

---

[1]**trepan:** entrap, lure.

The Spirit of 'Seventy-six: The Story of the American Revolution as Told by Participants, ed. Henry Steele Commager and Richard B. Morris, Bicentennial ed. (New York: Harper and Row, 1975), 405.

John Laurens to Henry Laurens

Headquarters, Valley Forge,
January 14, 1778

I barely hinted to you my dearest Father my desire to augment the Continental Forces from an untried Source. I wish I had any foundation to ask for an extraordinary addition to those favors which I have already received from you. I would sollicit you to cede me a number of your able bodied men Slaves, instead of leaving me a fortune. I would bring about a twofold good, first I would advance those who are unjustly deprived of the Rights of Mankind to a State which would be a proper Gradation between abject Slavery and perfect Liberty, and besides I would reinforce the Defenders of Liberty with a number of gallant Soldiers. Men who have the habit of Subordination almost indelibly impress'd on them, would have one very essential qualification of Soldiers. I am persuaded that if I could obtain authority for the purpose I would have a Corps of such men trained, uniformly clad, equip'd, and ready in every respect to act at the opening of the next Campaign. The Ridicule that may be thrown on the Colour I . . . despise, because I am sure of rendering essential Service to my Country. I am tired of the Languor with which so sacred a War as this, is carried on. My circumstances prevent me from writing so long a Letter as I expected and wish'd to have done on a subject which I have much at heart. I entreat you to give a favorable Answer to

Your most affectionate
John Laurens.

The Papers of Henry Laurens, ed. David R. Chestnutt et al., vol. 12, *November 1, 1777–March 15, 1778* (Columbia: University of South Carolina Press, 1990), 305, 367–69, 390–92, 412–13, 429–31, 446–47, 491–95, 530–35. (Some spelling and punctuation has been modernized.)

Henry Laurens to John Laurens

York, January 28, 1778

My Dear Son,
I Received yours of 23d & of 26th Inst.[1] last Night by Colonel Duplesis. When you transmit me your plan for the measure of raising a Black Regiment I may be better able to judge & finally determine than I am at present. I have been cautious of speaking openly of the project, but hitherto I have not heard one person approbate the Idea from the hints which I dropped in order to gain opinions, & yet I will not say that the design might not be beneficially improved provided there could be found twenty more Men to share the reproach of Quixotism & to carry it into respectable execution. Your Regiment if you trusted to your own resources would not consist of more than forty Men perhaps not so many; in 300 Ne-

---

[1] **Inst.:** "instant" means the current month; in this case, January.

groes there is a great proportion of Women & Children & if you have any dependence upon free Negroes *depend* upon it you will be deceived. If a Man had a *Bird* Plantation[2] of 1,200 & upwards he might venture a bold Stroke, have you consulted your General on this head? Have you considered that your kind intentions towards your Negroes would be deemed by them the highest cruelty, & that to escape from it they would flee into the Woods, that they would interpret your humanity to be an Exchange of Slavery, a State & circumstances not only tolerable but comfortable from habit, for an intolerable, taken from their Wives & Children & their little Plantations to the Field of Battle where Loss of Life & Loss of Limbs must be expected by every one every day.

I could offer a Thousand other things for your consideration but they are not necessary at this time nor indeed will the time allow me. You shall have my honest Sentiments & then do as you please. . . .

Adieu my Dear Friend. May God keep your heart pure etc.

[2]*Bird* **Plantation:** probably means a large plantation with numerous slaves such as those owned by the Byrds of Virginia.

JOHN LAURENS TO HENRY LAURENS

Headquarters, Valley Forge,
February 2, 1778

My dear Father,

The more I reflect upon the difficulties and delays which are likely to attend the completing our Continental Regiments, the more anxiously is my mind bent upon the Scheme which I lately communicated to you. The obstacles to the execution of it had presented themselves to me, but by no means appeared insurmountable. I was aware of having that monster popular Prejudice open-mouthed against me, of undertaking to transform beings almost irrational into well disciplined Soldiers, of being obliged to combat the arguments and perhaps the intrigues of interested persons, but zeal for the public Service and an ardent desire to assert the rights of humanity determined me to engage in this arduous business, with the sanction of your Consent. My own perseverance aided by the Countenance of a few virtuous men will I hope enable me to accomplish it.

You seem to think my dear Father, that men reconciled by long habit to the miseries of their Condition, would prefer their ignominious bonds to the untasted Sweets of Liberty, especially when offer'd upon the terms which I propose. I confess indeed that the minds of this unhappy species must be debased by a Servitude from which they can hope for no Relief but Death, and that every motive to action but Fear, must be . . . nearly extinguished in them. But do you think they are so perfectly moulded to their State as to be insensible that a better exists? Will the galling comparison between themselves and their masters leave them unenlighten'd in this respect? Can their Self-Love be so totally annihilated as not frequently to induce ardent wishes for a change?

You will accuse me [word illegible] perhaps my dearest friend of consulting my own feelings too much, but I am tempted to believe that this trampled people have so much human left in them, as to be capable of aspiring to the rights of men by noble exertions, if some friend to mankind would point the Road, and give them a prospect of Success. If I am mistaken in this, I would avail myself even of their weakness, and conquering one fear by another, produce equal good to the Public. You will ask in this view how do you consult the benefit of the Slaves? I answer that like other men, they are the Creatures of habit, their Cowardly Ideas will be gradually effaced, and they will be modified anew, their being rescued from a State of perpetual humiliation, and being advanced as it were in the Scale of being will compensate the dangers incident to their new State. The hope that will spring in each man's mind respecting his own escape will prevent his being miserable. Those who fall in battle will not lose much; those who survive will obtain their Reward.

Habits of Subordination, Patience under fatigues, Sufferings and Privations of every kind, are soldierly qualifications which these men possess in an eminent degree.

Upon the whole my dearest friend and father, I hope that my plan for serving my Country and the oppressed Negro race will not appear to you the Chimera of a young mind deceived by a false appearance of moral beauty, but a laudable sacrifice of private Interest to Justice and the Public good.

You say that my own resources would be small, on account of the proportion of women and children. I do not know whether I am right for I speak from impulse and have not reasoned upon the matter. I say although my plan is at once to give freedom to the Negroes and gain Soldiers to the States, in case of concurrence I should sacrifice the former interest, and therefore would change the Women and Children for able bodied men. The more of these I could obtain the better but 40 might be a good foundation to begin upon.

It is a pity that some such plan as I propose could not be more extensively executed by public Authority. A well chosen body of 5,000 black men properly officer'd to act as light Troops in addition to our present establishment, might give us decisive Success in the next Campaign.

I have long deplored the wretched State of these men and considered in their history, the bloody wars excited in Africa to furnish America with Slaves, the Groans of despairing multitudes toiling for the Luxuries of Merciless Tyrants. I have had the pleasure of conversing with you sometimes upon the means of restoring them to their rights. When can it be better done, than when their enfranchisement . . . may be made conducive to the Public Good, and be so modified as not to overpower their weak minds?

You ask what is the General's opinion upon this subject. He is convinced that the numerous tribes of blacks in the Southern parts of the Continent offer a resource to us that should not be neglected. With respect to my particular Plan, he only objects to it with the arguments of Pity, for a man who would be less rich than he might be.

I am obliged my dearest Friend and Father to take my leave for the present, you will excuse whatever exceptionable may have escaped in the course of my Letter, and accept the assurances of filial Love and Respect of

Your
John Laurens.

HENRY LAURENS TO JOHN LAURENS

York, February 6, 1778

My Dear Son,

Your favor of the 2d Inst. came to hand late last Night. As you have filled six Pages on the Negro scheme without approaching towards a Plan & Estimate, & as you have totally overlooked every other subject on which I have addressed you in several late Letters, the conclusion that your whole mind is enveloped in the Cloud of that project, is unavoidable. If any good shall arise from a prosecution of it, the merit will be solely yours. For now, I will undertake to say there is not a Man in America of your opinion.

Nay you will not be of your own opinion after a little reflection. 'Tis evident you want to raise a Regiment, as evident you have not digested a Plan. Admitting, which I admit only for argument, you have a right to remove a Man from one state of Slavery into another, or if you please into a state of servitude which will be esteemed by him infinitely worse than Slavery, what right have you to exchange & Barter "Women & Children" in whom you pretend to say you have no property?

The very same observation may be made with respect to the Men, for you have either property in them, or you have not. Admitting the latter which you seem to acknowledge, upon what ground of justice will you insist upon their enlisting for Soldiers, as the condition of their enfranchisement. If they are free, tell them so: Set them at full liberty, & then address them in the Language of a recruiting Officer to any other free Men, & if four in forty take your enlisting bounty, it will be very extraordinary; this small number will . . . do it through ignorance & three of the four be returned as Deserters in a very short time.

All this by no means intimates that I am an Advocate for Slavery. You know I am not, therefore it is unnecessary to attempt a vindication.

The more I think of & the more I have consulted on your scheme, the less I approve of it. Wisdom dictates that I should rather oppose than barely not consent to it, but Indulgence & friendship warranted by Wisdom, bids me let you take your own course & draw self-conviction. Therefore come forward Young Colonel, proceed to South Carolina; you shall have as full authority over all my Negroes as justice to your Brother & Sisters & a very little consideration for my self will permit you to exercise, & so far do what you please & as you please without regard to St. Mary Axe.

You want a Regiment that's certain, go to Carolina & I'll warrant you will soon get one. I Will venture to say, sooner than any other Man of my acquaintance, you will have many advantages in raising a Regiment of White Men.

On the Journey you may think . . . fully, & converse with many worthy sensible Men, on your favorite Idea. When you arrive in Charles Town you will have further advantages, if you are disposed to receive them, from the sentiments of your most judicious friends. Your own good sense will direct you to proceed warily in opposing the opinions of whole Nations, lest *without effecting any good*, you become a bye word, & be so transmitted, to Your Children's Children.

Give me a day's Notice previous to your appearance here in order that an apartment may be provided for you if possible, for it is barely possible to obtain one.

My Dear Son, I pray God protect you & add to your knowledge & learning, if it be necessary, discretion.

Henry Laurens.

JOHN LAURENS TO HENRY LAURENS

Headquarters, Valley Forge,
February 9, 1778

I have to thank you, my dear Father, for two Shirts and a piece of Scarlet Cloth. I wrote to James for some Hair Powder, & Pomatum but received only the latter with a Comb. As I am upon the subject of dress, it will not be premature to inform you, that if you should command me to remain in my present Station, blue and buff Cloth, Linding, Twist, yellow flat double gilt Buttons sufficient to make me a Uniform Suit will be wanted, besides corded Dimitty for Waistcoats and Breeches against the opening of the Campaign, and I must beg the favor of you to write to some Friend in South Carolina to procure me these Articles. A pair of gold Epaulettes and a Saddle Cloth may be added if not too expensive. If you should give me leave to execute my black project, my uniform will be a white field (faced with red), a Color which is easiest kept clean and will form a good Contrast with the Complexion of the Soldier. . . .

Your most affectionate
John Lau[rens]

Headquarters, Valley Forge,
February 15, 1778

Dear Father,

I am to thank you for your kind Letter of the 6th Inst. and the two Camp Shirts which accompanied it. The presumption which would lead me to pursue my project after what you have said upon it, would be unpardonable, praying your forgiveness therefore my dear Friend for the trouble which I have given you on this excentric Scheme I renounce it as a thing which cannot be sanctified by your approbation. At the same time I must confess to you that I am very sensibly affected by your imputing my Plan in so large a degree to Ambition. I declare upon my honor that I would not have desired any other than my present Rank, and that I would even have taken the Title of Captain of an independent Corps for the pleasure of serving my Country so usefully as I fondly hoped I should have been able to do, had my Scheme been carried into execution.

The Scarlet Cloth, four Camp Shirts (in all), a Roll of Pomatum, a hair Comb, two Shirts for Berry, and a Hunting Shirt have been received at different times, and I am exceedingly obliged to you for them. In future I will be more careful to thank you for such articles immediately after the receipt of them.

The Express is waiting only for my Letter, which circumstance has obliged me to write in haste, and forces me to take leave.

I am Your most affectionate and dutiful
John Laurens.

Henry Laurens to John Laurens

York, March 1, 1778

My Dear Son,

I believe I have not writ you a line since that by Baron Stuben,[1] to which I have received your answer under the 24th. I am anxious to know whether he will find amusement & employment in your Camp & whether he is likely to be a valuable addition to the Main Army. It is remarkable that your General has kept a profound silence on that Officer's name although I have had occasion to announce it to His Excellency in three several Letters. . . .

An Officer who came in here a few minutes ago gives me hopes of procuring buff Cloth for your present necessity. You see how I patch a Letter together, exposed to continual interruptions & diverted from the most important & serious subjects to Buff Cloth & Breeches.

I had intended to have spoken to you again on the subject of your black Regiment but I have not time at present, however let me tell you you mistook my meaning in some parts of the last Letter on that affair. I did not even intend to insinuate that you were possessed by illaudable ambition. It is evident you wished for a Command; speaking of you honestly as a fellow Citizen, & you know partial[ity] is not to be found in the Catalogue of my vices, I think you would not, young as you are, disgrace a Regiment. I intended to have recommended you to a practicable Road & to draw you off from a pursuit which in the opinion of every

---

[1]**Baron Stuben:** Baron Frederick William Augustus von Steuben, a Prussian military officer who became a general in the American army.

body would prove fruitless & which I exceedingly feared mig[ht] soil your excellent character with a charge of singularity, whimsicality, & Caprice. This however I have ever taught you to despise when se[t] in competition with Duty & with honourable Acts.

Your scheme, with respect to your own progress in [it] would have ended in essay, but you would not have heard the last jeer till the end of your life, meaning if you had gone precipitately into the prosecution. An attempt of that magnitude may originate with an Individual but must be extended after very mature deliberation by the Collective Wisdom of States. I wish for an hour's serious conversation with you on these points.

I suppose you to be strongly attached to General Washington & I do not wonder you are so. Every Gentleman loves & Esteems that great & good Man but when the proper time shall come that you feel an inclination to retire from that Army & turn your attention to your own Country I hold it probable that you may obtain a Commission & soon raise a respectable Regiment. From such Ideas & reflections I was led to write in the terms which I perceive you misapprehended. But we will postpone the subject for discussion on some future day.

I know not what my Country Men are about nor why they have so shamefully neglected to fill their Representation in Congress. I have been long striving to shame them into the performance of their duty. As the Assembly met at Charles Town on the 5 January I hold it probable that Delegates were chosen among their earliest Acts & that the Men [word illegible] whoever they are, will soon be at York & bring me permission to return, which I am determined to do immediately after I can meet & take leave of you. You will make such use of this intimation as you shall judge necessary.

I feel a strong inclination to send into Philadelphia & New York about an hundred Guineas to be applied to the relief of some of the most necessitous of our Soldiers who are Prisoners there. Tell me your thoughts. If Rich Men would open their hearts & their purses freely what infinite advantages would be gained to our Army & to our cause in general.

My best Respects to Monsieur le Baron Stüben.

My Dear son Adieu.

Henry Laurens.

JOHN LAURENS TO HENRY LAURENS

Headquarters, Valley Forge,
March 9, 1778

My dear Father,

. . . I am truly sensible of your kindness on the subject of my black Batallion; nothing would tempt me to quit my present Station, but a prospect of being more useful in another. The ambition of serving my Country and desire of gaining Fame, leads me to wish for the command of men. I would cherish those dear ragged Continentals, whose patience will be the admiration of future ages, and glory in bleeding with them. . . .

> I am ever your most affectionate
> John Laurens.

21. Extreme Measures
for Difficult Times

ALEXANDER HAMILTON, HENRY LAURENS, GEORGE WASHINGTON, CHRISTOPHER GADSDEN, JOHN LAURENS, AND DAVID RAMSAY
Letters
1779

As American leaders prepared for the impending attack on the poorly defended southern colonies, the buildup of British forces led many of them to conclude that the creation of slave battalions was more "rational" than risky. The letters reprinted here make it clear that there was a strong difference of opinion between the national leaders and most South Carolina politicians on the question of arming slaves. The issue was discussed at length; participants in the debate included Alexander Hamilton, an aide to General Washington and John Laurens's best friend; Henry Laurens, still a member of the Continental Congress and now an advocate of his son's scheme; General George Washington, commander of the American army; Christopher Gadsden, one of South Carolina's leading patriots and military leaders; John Laurens; and David Ramsay, a patriot and member of the South Carolina legislature.

ALEXANDER HAMILTON TO JOHN JAY

Middlebrook, New Jersey, March 14, 1779

Dear Sir,

Colonel Laurens, who will have the honor of delivering you this letter, is on his way to South Carolina, on a project, which I think, in the present situation of

The Papers of Alexander Hamilton, ed. Harold C. Syrett and Jacob E. Cooke, vol. 2, *1779–1781* (New York: Columbia University Press, 1961), 17–19.

affairs there, is a very good one and deserves every kind of support and encouragement. This is to raise two three or four batalions of negroes; with the assistance of the government of that state, by contributions from the owners in proportion to the number they possess. If you should think proper to enter upon the subject with him, he will give you a detail of his plan. He wishes to have it recommended by Congress to the state; and, as an inducement, that they would engage to take those batalions into Continental pay.

It appears to me, that an expedient of this kind, in the present state of Southern affairs, is the most rational, that can be adopted, and promises very important advantages. Indeed, I hardly see how a sufficient force can be collected in that quarter without it; and the enemy's operations there are growing infinitely serious and formidable. I have not the least doubt, that the negroes will make very excellent soldiers, with proper management; and I will venture to pronounce, that they cannot be put in better hands than those of Mr. Laurens. He has all the zeal, intelligence, enterprise, and every other qualification requisite to succeed in such an undertaking. It is a maxim with some great military judges, that with sensible officers soldiers can hardly be too stupid; and on this principle it is thought that the Russians would make the best troops in the world, if they were under other officers than their own. The King of Prussia is among the number who maintain this doctrine and has a very emphatical saying on the occasion, which I do not exactly recollect. I mention this, because I frequently hear it objected to the scheme of embodying negroes that they are too stupid to make soldiers. This is so far from appearing to me a valid objection that I think their want of cultivation (for their natural faculties are probably as good as ours) joined to that habit of subordination which they acquire from a life of servitude, will make them sooner became soldiers than our White inhabitants. Let officers be men of sense and sentiment, and the nearer the soldiers approach to machines perhaps the better.

I foresee that this project will have to combat much opposition from prejudice and self-interest. The contempt we have been taught to entertain for the blacks, makes us fancy many things that are founded neither in reason nor experience; and an unwillingness to part with property of so valuable a kind will furnish a thousand arguments to show the impracticability or pernicious tendency of a scheme which requires such a sacrifice. But it should be considered, that if we do not make use of them in this way, the enemy probably will; and that the best way to counteract the temptations they will hold out will be to offer them ourselves. An essential part of the plan is to give them their freedom with their muskets. This will secure their fidelity, animate their courage, and I believe will have a good influence upon those who remain, by opening a door to their emancipation. This circumstance, I confess, has no small weight in inducing me to wish the success of the project; for the dictates of humanity and true policy equally interest me in favour of this unfortunate class of men.

When I am on the subject of Southern affairs, you will excuse the liberty I take, in saying, that I do not think measures sufficiently vigorous are persuing for our defence in that quarter. Except the few regular troops of South Carolina, we seem to be relying wholly on the militia of that and the two neighbouring states.

These will soon grow impatient of service and leave our affairs in a very miserable situation. No considerable force can be uniformly kept up by militia — to say nothing of many obvious and well known inconveniences, that attend this kind of troops. I would beg leave to suggest, Sir, that no time ought to be lost in making a draft of militia to serve a twelve month from the States of North and South Carolina and Virginia. But South Carolina being very weak in her population of whites may be excused from the draft on condition of furnishing the black batalions. The two others may furnish about 3,500 men and be exempted on that account from sending any succours to this army. The states to the Northward of Virginia will be fully able to give competent supplies to the army here; and it will require all the force and exertions of the three states I have mentioned to withstand the storm which has arisen and is increasing in the South.

The troops drafted must be thrown into batalions and officered in the best manner we can. The supernumerary officers may be made use of as far as they will go.

If arms are wanted for these troops and no better way of supplying them is to be found, we should endeavour to levy a contribution of arms upon the militia at large. Extraordinary exigencies demand extraordinary means. I fear this Southern business will become a very *grave* one.

With the truest respect & esteem
I am Sir
Your most Obedient servant
Alex Hamilton

Want of time to copy it, will apologise for sending this letter in its present state. Head Quarters   March 14th. [17]79

Henry Laurens to George Washington

Philadelphia 16th March 1779.

Sir,

I had the honor of addressing Your Excellency under the 2d Inst.[1] this is chiefly intended to convey extracts of Letters which I received last night from Charles Town. These show our affairs in the Southern department in a more favorable light, than we had viewed them in, some few days ago — nevertheless the Country is greatly distressed and will be more so unless further reinforcements are sent to its relief. Had we Arms for 3,000 such black Men as I could select in Carolina I should have no doubt of success in driving the British out of Georgia and subduing East Florida before the end of July. . . .

---

[1]**Inst.:** "instant" means the current month; in this case, March.

Library of Congress, Letters to Washington, 30. 387, in *Letters of Members of the Continental Congress,* ed. Edmund C. Burnett, vol. 4, *January 1 to December 31, 1779* (Washington, D.C.: Carnegie Institution of Washington, 1928; reprint, Gloucester, Mass.: Peter Smith, 1963). (Some spelling and punctuation has been modernized.)

GEORGE WASHINGTON TO HENRY LAURENS

Middle brook, March 20, 1779.

Dear Sir: I have to thank you, and I do it very sincerely, for your obliging favors of the 2d and 16th Inst.; and for their several inclosures, containing articles of intelligence.

The policy of our arming Slaves is, in my opinion, a moot point, unless the enemy set the example;[1] for should we begin to form Battalions of them, I have not the smallest doubt (if the War is to be prosecuted) of their following us in it, and justifying the measure upon our own ground; the upshot then must be, who can arm fastest, and where are our Arms? Besides, I am not clear that a discrimination will not render Slavery more irksome to those who remain in it; most of the good and evil things of this life are judged of by comparison; and I fear a comparison in this case will be productive of much discontent in those who are held in servitude; but as this is a subject that has never employed much of my thoughts, these are no more than the first crude Ideas that have struck me upon the occasion. . . .

Mrs. Washington joins me in respectful compliments to you, and with every sentiment of regard and attachment. I am etc.

[1]This comment is perplexing, as Washington certainly knew about Dunmore's precedent and had tacitly approved the arming of slaves in Rhode Island.

The Writings of George Washington, from the Original Manuscript Sources, 1745–1799, ed. John C. Fitzpatrick, vol. 14, *January 12, 1779–May 5, 1779*, prepared under the direction of the United States George Washington Bicentennial Commission and published by authority of Congress (Washington, D.C.: United States Government Printing Office, 1936), 266–67. (Some spelling and punctuation has been modernized.)

CHRISTOPHER GADSDEN TO SAMUEL ADAMS

Charles Town 6th July 1779

Dear Sir:

In the Overflowings of an anxious Heart on Account of the Situation of Public Affairs, I let my pen run away with me the 4th of April last and then wrote you a long Letter so scribbl'd that I question whether you were able to make out what I would be at. Tho' I have received no answer not yet the friendly Letter you mention'd in yours by Colonel Ternant[1] that you intended to write me, I cannot forbear troubling you with a few Lines by him on his return. Pray let me hear from you, it will always give me great pleasure, and make my compliments to our worthy Friend Mr. John Adams who I hear is on his passage back to you; let me know as far as you can how our public matters stand. As to Charles Town we have had

[1]**Colonel Ternant:** Jean Baptiste de Ternant was a Frenchman who came to America to join the patriot forces. He became a lieutenant colonel in September 1778.

The Writings of Christopher Gadsden, 1746–1805, ed. Richard Walsh (Columbia: University of South Carolina Press, 1966), 165–66. (Some spelling and punctuation has been modernized.)

a narrow, very narrow, escape indeed, more from the treacherous Whispers and Insinuations of *internal* Enemies than from what our external and open Foes were able to do against us here. They are still hovering about us, at present at Port Royal Island, about 60 miles from hence, and not exceeding two thousand in number at most, protected by only three men of war of any consequence. Were our Frigates but ordered here, they would not only rid us of the Enemy entirely, but do the general Cause immense Service, but why do I say *our* Frigates, when by the Whole proceedings of the Congress, we begin to think, they imagine We have no right or pretentions to any share in them; a few Frigates four or five would now (it indeed always would) do us more service than as many Thousand Troops, their Business would soon be done, I am confident, if they came, and they might return to the Northward, again very speedily. As to any other assistance of that Sort from elsewhere it seems to be a *Vox et Praeterea Nihil*.[2] The Enemy are within a few days March of the Town and if not sooner, when the sickly Months are over I make no Doubt they will be at us again, if you do not make use of the most probable Means to deliver us, that is by Frigates. They expect reinforcements 'tis said but when, or from wherever uncertain.

As no one can give you a better Detail of the Occurrences here worth your Notice than Colonel Ternant give me leave to refer you altogether to him on that Score.

We are much disgusted here at the Congress recommending us to arm our Slaves, it was received with great resentment, as a very dangerous and impolitic Step. I am Dear Sir Your most humble Servant.

Christ Gadsden

[2]***Vox et Praeterea Nihil:*** empty promises (literally, "voice and nothing more").

JOHN LAURENS TO ALEXANDER HAMILTON

Charles Town. 14th July [17]79

Ternant will relate to you how many violent struggles I have had between duty and inclination — how much my heart was with you, while I appeared to be most actively employed here — but it appears to me that I should be inexcusable in the light of a Citizen if I did not continue my utmost efforts for carrying the plan of black levies into execution, while there remains the smallest hope of success. Our army is reduced to nothing almost by the departure of the Virginians; Scot's arrival[1] will scarcely restore us to our ancient number; if the Enemy destine the Reinforcements from G. B.[2] for this quarter, as in policy they ought to do, that

[1]**Scot's arrival:** Washington had ordered Brigadier General Charles Scott, the commander of American troops in Virginia, to reinforce the American forces in the Carolinas.
[2]**G. B.:** Great Britain.

The Papers of Alexander Hamilton, ed. Harold C. Syrett and Jacob E. Cooke, vol. 2, *1779–1781* (New York: Columbia University Press, 1961), 102–3. (Some spelling and punctuation has been modernized.)

number will be insufficient for the security of our country. The Governor among other matters to be laid before the House of Assembly under the head of preparations for the ensuing Campaign, intends to propose the completing our Continental battalions by drafts from the militia; this measure I am told is so exceedingly unpopular that there is no hope of succeeding in it — either this must be adopted, or the black levies, or the state may fall a victim to the supineness and improvidence of its inhabitants. The house of Representatives have had a longer recess than usual occasioned by the number of members in the field — it will be convened however in a few days — I intend to qualify — and make a final effort. Oh that I were a Demosthenes[3]—the Athenians never deserved more bitter exprobration than my Countrymen. General Moultrie who commands our Remains of an army at Stono and has a Corps of observation at Beaufort ferry informs us in his last letter, that the Enemy are preparing the Court House and Jail at Beaufort for the reception of their sick — which indicates a design to establish themselves in quarters of refreshment there. Clinton's movement and your march in consequence, made me wish to be with you; if any thing important should be done in your quarter while I am doing daily penance here, and making successless harangues, I shall execrate my Stars — & be out of humour with the world. I entreat you my dear friend write me as frequently as circumstances will permit, and enlighten me upon what is going forward — adieu — my love to our dear Colleagues. I am afraid I was so thoughtless as to omit my remembrances to Gibbes in the last Letter. Tell him that I am always his sincere well wisher and hope to laugh with him again before long. Adieu again — yours ever

John Laurens

[3]**Demosthenes:** the fourth-century B.C. Greek orator and statesman.

DAVID RAMSAY TO WILLIAM HENRY DRAYTON

Charlestown, September 1, 1779

Dear Sir:

Your favor of July 18th, came safe to hand on the 16th of August. A hurry of business prevented my acknowledging the receipt of it sooner.

Our Assembly is now drawing near to the close of a long session. Little business is yet completed. A tax bill of twenty-one dollars a head has been read twice. A bill for filling our regiments by giving a negro bounty to every volunteer recruit, has also been read twice. This measure is now our *ultima spes*.[1] Money will not procure soldiers. The militia will not submit to a draft; it has been once carried in the House to put them under Continental articles; but the friends of this measure,

[1]*ultima spes:* last hope.

Documentary History of the American Revolution, Consisting of Letters and Papers Relating to the Contest for Liberty Chiefly in South Carolina, ed. Robert W. Gibbes, vol. 2, Eyewitness Accounts of the American Revolution Series, no. 1 (North Stratford, N.H.: Ayer Company, 1971). (Some spelling and punctuation has been modernized.)

fear that it will be lost on the next reading. The patriotism of many people is *vox et praeterea nihil*. The measure for embodying the negroes had about twelve votes; it was received with horror by the planters, who figured to themselves terrible consequences. Next Friday is set apart to choose a new delegate in the room of Mr. Lowndes, when it is probably that Mr. E. Rutledge will be chosen. Mr. A. Middleton will set out in a few weeks. Most people expect the enemy here in October or November, and yet we are half asleep. When the campaign closes to the northward, it will be easy for them to send a few thousands of a reinforcement to their troops in Savannah. Our back country is much disaffected especially at the high price of salt, which is 60 dollars a bushel. We mean to solicit aid from the grand army. I wish you would send us two thousand Continentals immediately. You know the importance of Charlestown; it is the *vinculum*[2] that binds three states to the authority of Congress. If the enemy posses themselves of this town, there will be no living for honest whigs to the southward of Santee; at present, nothing is wanting to put them in possession of it, but vigor and activity on their part. A spirit of money-making has eaten up our patriotism. Our morals are more depreciated than our currency. It is with great pleasure I receive your letters, and I shall be always ready to acknowledge them.

Yours,
David Ramsay

[2]*vinculum*: tie.

22. Defeated by a "Triple-Headed Monster"

JOHN LAURENS AND GEORGE WASHINGTON *Correspondence* 1782

John Laurens's last attempt at shoring up American defenses in the South by establishing slave battalions was defeated in 1782. By this time even General Nathanael Greene of Rhode Island, who had headed the Continental troops in the South since 1780, was unsuccessfully pressing South Carolina to approve plans for raising black regiments. Once again defeated by what he called the "triple-headed monster" of "prejudice, Avarice, and pusillanimity," Laurens concluded that, for the majority of South Carolina leaders, belief in black inferiority and a desire to keep possession of their human property were stronger than any humanitarian sentiments or willingness to sacrifice for the common good.

JOHN LAURENS TO GEORGE WASHINGTON

Bacon's Bridge, S. Carolina
19th May [17]82

My dear General,

I am much obliged to you for honoring my bill in favor of General Lincoln — it includes the whole sum expended on your account in France. The plan which brought me to this country was urged with all the zeal which the subject inspired, both in our privy council and the Assembly, but the single voice of reason was drowned by the howlings of a triple-headed monster in which prejudice, Avarice, and pusillanimity were united. It was some degree of consolation to me however to perceive that Truth and Philosophy had gained some ground, the suffrage in favor of the measure being twice as numerous as on a former occasion. Some hopes have been lately given me from Georgia, but I fear when the question is put we shall be out-voted there with as much disparity as we have been in this country.

The reports of the prompt evacuation of Charles Town, I always thought groundless, and should have much sooner inferred the probability of such an event from the language of the debates in the British parliament than from the conduct and arrangements of General Leslie.[1] The late disaster of the Count de Grafe[2] in the West Indies makes me more incredulous on the subject than ever. General Leslie confines himself to the most circumspect defensive, a conduct which he is not likely to change as he recently detached the 19th and 20th regiments to Jamaica. This renders the campaign perfectly inactive here and above all inspires to the light troops which I at present command.

I presume your excellency has not yet determined for the ensuing campaign and that it must depend upon the cooperation of our Allies. I earnestly desire to be where any active plans are likely to be executed and to be near your excellency on all occasions in which any services can be acceptable. The pursuit of an object which I confess is a favorite one with me because I always regarded interests of this country and those of the union as intimately connected with it, has detached me more than once from your family, but those sentiments of veneration and attachment with which your excellency has inspired me keep me always near

---

[1]**General Leslie:** Alexander Leslie, commander of British troops in Charleston in 1782.
[2]**Count de Grafe:** Comte François de Grasse, admiral in charge of the French navy aiding the Americans.

The George Washington Papers, Series 4. The Library of Congress. (Some spelling and punctuation has been modernized.)

you with the sincerest and most zealous wishes for a continuance of your happiness and glory. Give me leave to say that I am ever [yours] my Dear General,

Your Excellency's
Faithful Aid
John Laurens

His Excellency General Washington

GEORGE WASHINGTON TO JOHN LAURENS

Head Quarters, July 10, 1782.

My Dr. Sir: The last Post brought me your Letter of the 19 May. I must confess that I am not at all astonished at the failure of your Plan. That spirit of freedom which at the commencement of this contest would have gladly sacrificed every thing to the attainment of its object has long since subsided, and every selfish Passion has taken its place; it is not the public but the private Interest which influences the generality of Mankind nor can the Americans any longer boast an exception; under these circumstances it would rather have been surprizing if you had succeeded nor will you I fear succeed better in Georgia.

In the present moment there is very little prospect of the Campaign being much more Active in this quarter than in yours; however little can be positively determined on, till we have some advices from Europe, which I am anxiously waiting for, when they arrive I shall be better able to tell you what we may expect. . . . You have my best wishes always, being sincerely. Yrs. etc.

The Writings of George Washington, from the Original Manuscript Sources, 1745–1799, ed. John C. Fitzpatrick, vol. 14, *January 12, 1779–May 5, 1779*, prepared under the direction of the United States George Washington Bicentennial Commission and published by authority of Congress (Washington, D.C.: United States Government Printing Office, 1936), 421–22.

Suggestions for Further Reading

Alden, John Richard. *The South in the Revolution, 1763–1789.* Baton Rouge: Louisiana State University Press, 1975.

Crow, Jeffrey, and Larry E. Tise, eds. *The Southern Experience in the American Revolution.* Chapel Hill: University of North Carolina Press, 1978.

Foner, Philip S. *Blacks in the American Revolution.* Westport, Conn.: Greenwood Press, 1976.

Frey, Sylvia. *Water from the Rock: Black Resistance in a Revolutionary Age.* Princeton: Princeton University Press, 1991.

Higgins, W. Roberts, ed. *The Revolutionary War in the South: Power, Conflict, and Leadership. Essays in Honor of John Richard Alden.* Durham, N.C.: Duke University Press, 1979.

Massey, Gregory D. "The Limits of Antislavery Thought in the Revolutionary Lower South: John Laurens and Henry Laurens." *Journal of Southern History* 63, no. 3 (August 1997): 495–530.

Quarles, Benjamin. *The Negro in the American Revolution.* Chapel Hill: University of North Carolina Press, 1961.

CHAPTER SEVEN

THE CREATION OF
THE AMERICAN REPUBLIC

Slavery and the Constitution

I n the late eighteenth century, slavery occupied an ambiguous position in American political life. On the one hand, it played an integral part in the economies of five southern states, where six hundred thousand slaves lived (two for every four free persons). Profits from the slave trade enriched merchants all along the Atlantic seaboard: northern farms and southern plantations offered a lucrative market. Because of this, slavery figured prominently in the organization of constitutional government well before 1787. As part of its boycott of Britain, for example, the First Continental Congress banned the importation of slaves from Africa in October 1774; the trade resumed when peace came in 1783. Later, the Confederation tried to assess state financial contributions by population — and to count slaves in their calculations. Southern slaveholders resisted, and the government compromised by using a formula that counted a slave as three-fifths of a person.

On the other hand, the Revolution had espoused an ideology of liberty at odds with the concept of one person owning another. During the 1780s, there was some discussion about limiting or even abolishing slavery, and a number of northern states began programs of gradual emancipation. Even some southern slaveholders considered the possibility of ending the institution: in 1782, the Virginia legislature for the first time enabled slaveholders to manumit, or legally free, their slaves. Virginians also agreed to the Northwest Ordinance of 1787, which ceded much of the commonwealth's western lands to the federal government and explicitly prohibited slavery from spreading to any territories and states formed out of it.

The writing of the federal constitution at the 1787 Philadelphia convention — along with the ratification debates that followed it — revealed a diversity of opinion about the role slavery should play in the political system. Although abolition was never formally addressed, the convention's delegates raised some basic questions: How much and to what extent would the federal system protect — and limit — slaveholders' rights? And how much power should slaveholders — as property holders — exercise within the constitutional system? The answers to these questions did not come easily. Indeed, James Madison observed that the tension underlying the convention was not between large and small states — a description adopted by many constitutional historians — but between slaveholding and non-slaveholding ones.

Although the word *slavery* is never mentioned in the federal constitution, the convention focused on several crucial issues, especially how the Constitution would protect "minority" — meaning the South and slaveholders — rights. The debate, which first focused on the question of how Americans should be represented in Congress, began as a disagreement between small and large states: the former favored the old "one state–one vote" principle, while the latter wanted the new Congress to represent the people more directly. In June and July 1787, the discussion also involved the critical issue of how slaves — or, more properly, slaveholders — would be represented. After considerable debate, the three-fifths clause of the Constitution resolved the matter in a compromise that conceded special rights to slave states. The prohibition of the African slave trade into the United States also engendered considerable argument. Ultimately, the Constitution specified that Congress could not prohibit the external slave trade before 1808.

That the Philadelphia convention had slaveholders in mind is apparent in other respects as well. Delegates grappled with the matter of runaway slaves: because they were well aware that every northern state that ended slavery would become a haven for fleeing slaves, southern slaveholders were determined that the Constitution provide for the legal return of runaways. The Constitution also created a lengthy amendment system that required the assent of more than three-quarters of the states, ensuring that the South wouldn't be politically crippled by its "minority" status. It limited national protections of civil liberties and civil rights to "citizens," a category that explicitly excluded slaves. Finally, the Constitution empowered Congress to provide for armed force to suppress rebellions, implicitly including slave insurrections.

For two years after the Philadelphia convention adjourned, slavery remained an important issue as state conventions considered whether to ratify the Constitution. Its opponents, known as Antifederalists, objected to the strengthened national government it proposed and, in southern ratifying conventions, pointed to what they said were inadequate protections for slaveholders. Supporters, known as Federalists, argued that a stronger national government would provide more security for the slave system. Even after the ratification debate ended, the discussion about the place of slavery in the Constitution continued — up to the outbreak of the Civil War in 1861.

The documents in this chapter reflect the controversy over slavery as the Constitution was being written and ratified. The first reading provides excerpts of the Philadelphia convention's consideration of the three-fifths clause. The second, also from excerpts of convention proceedings, shows the convention debating the troublesome matter of the African slave trade in August 1787. The slavery issue was further invoked in the ratification debate that followed the Philadelphia convention: Luther Martin's newspaper article provides an example of how one Maryland Antifederalist opposed what he believed was the deliberate overrepresentation of slaveholders. Subsequent excerpts of the ratification debates in South Carolina, Virginia, and North Carolina illustrate that slavery continued to be central to American politics.

As you read, think about the following questions. What justifications did Southerners put forth for counting slaves in their representation in Congress and for protecting the African slave trade? To what extent did Southerners differ among each other in their attitudes toward slavery? Why did northern delegates disagree with their southern counterparts? What reasons did Antifederalists provide in opposing the Constitution? How much did the Constitution actually protect slaveholders, and how much did it limit them?

23. Slavery and Representation

JAMES MADISON
Debates in the Federal Convention
June 11–July 12, 1787

Among the most important of the issues considered by the Philadelphia constitutional convention was the way slaves should be counted in congressional apportionment. Northern delegates believed that they should not be counted at all; southern slaveholders favored including them. The Continental Congress in the 1780s

James Madison, *The Debates in the Federal Convention of 1787 which Framed the Constitution of the United States of America*, International ed., ed. Gaillard Hunt and James Brown Scott (New York: Oxford University Press, 1920), 84–88, 194–95, 225, 227, 233–40, 242–43. (Some spelling and punctuation has been modernized.)

had contemplated taxing southern slaveholders by counting slaves as three-fifths of a person, so slaveholders proposed this as a standard for representation.

These debates were meticulously recorded by Virginian James Madison, in many ways the convention's guiding spirit, who was later secretary of state and the fourth president of the United States. The following excerpts from Madison's account indicate the extent to which delegates were divided on the issue. Ultimately, the three-fifths principle — incorporated into Article 1, Section 2, of the Constitution — gave the South a regional advantage in the House of Representatives.

June 11

The clause concerning the rule of suffrage in the national Legislature postponed on Saturday was resumed.

MR. SHERMAN[1] proposed that the proportion of suffrage in the first branch should be according to the respective numbers of free inhabitants; and that in the second branch or Senate, each State should have one vote and no more. He said as the States would remain possessed of certain individual rights, each State ought to be able to protect itself: otherwise a few large States will rule the rest. The House of Lords in England he observed had certain particular rights under the Constitution, and hence they have an equal vote with the House of Commons that they may be able to defend their rights.

MR. RUTLEDGE[2] proposed that the proportion of suffrage in the first branch should be according to the quotas of contribution. The justice of this rule he said could not be contested. MR. BUTLER[3] urged the same idea: adding that money was power; and that the States ought to have weight in the Government in proportion to their wealth.

MR. KING[4] and MR. WILSON,[5] in order to bring the question to a point, moved "that the right of suffrage in the first branch of the national Legislature ought not to be according [to] the rule established in the articles of Confederation, but according to some equitable ratio of representation." . . .

It was then moved by MR. RUTLEDGE seconded by MR. BUTLER to add to the words "equitable ratio of representation" at the end of the motion just agreed to, the words "according to the quotas of contribution." On motion of MR. WILSON seconded by MR. C. PINCKNEY,[6] this was postponed in order to add, after, after the words "equitable ratio of representation" the words following: "in proportion to the whole number of white & other free Citizens & inhabitants of every age, sex, & condition including those bound to servitude for a term of years and three fifths

[1]**Mr. Sherman:** Roger Sherman of Massachusetts.
[2]**Mr. Rutledge:** John Rutledge of South Carolina.
[3]**Mr. Butler:** Pierce Butler of South Carolina.
[4]**Mr. King:** Rufus King of Massachusetts.
[5]**Mr. Wilson:** James Wilson of Pennsylvania.
[6]**Mr. C. Pinckney:** Charles Cotesworth Pinckney of South Carolina.

of all other persons not comprehended in the foregoing description, except Indians not paying taxes, in each State," this being the rule in the Act of Congress agreed to by eleven States, for apportioning quotas of revenue on the States, and requiring a Census only every 5–7, or 10 years.

Mr. Gerry[7] thought property not the rule of representation. Why then should the blacks, who were property in the South, be in the rule of representation more than the Cattle & horses of the North. . . .

June 30

. . . [Mr. Madison] contended that the States were divided into different interests not by their difference of size, but by other circumstances; the most material of which resulted partly from climate, but principally from the effects of their having or not having slaves. These two causes concurred in forming the great division of interests in the United States. It did not lie between the large & small States: It lay between the Northern & Southern, and if any defensive power were necessary, it ought to be mutually given to these two interests. He was so strongly impressed with this important truth that he had been casting about in his mind for some expedient that would answer the purpose. The one which had occurred was that instead of proportioning the votes of the States in both branches, to their respective numbers of inhabitants computing the slaves in the ratio of 5 to 3, they should be represented in one branch according to the number of free inhabitants only; and in the other according to the whole number counting the slaves as if free. By this arrangement the Southern Scale would have the advantage in one House, and the Northern in the other. He had been restrained from proposing this expedient by two considerations: one was his unwillingness to urge any diversity of interests on an occasion where it is but too apt to arise of itself — the other was, the inequality of powers that must be vested in the two branches, and which would destroy the equilibrium of interests. . . .

July 9

Mr. Patterson[8] considered the proposed estimate for the future according to the Combined rule of numbers and wealth, as too vague. For this reason New Jersey was against it. He could regard negroes slaves in no light but as property. They are no free agents, have no personal liberty, no faculty of acquiring property, but on the contrary are themselves property, & like other property entirely at the will of the Master. Has a man in Virginia a number of votes in proportion to the number of his slaves? And if Negroes are not represented in the States to which they belong, why should they be represented in the General Government? What is the true principle of Representation? It is an expedient by which an assembly

---

[7]**Mr. Gerry:** Elbridge Gerry of Massachusetts.
[8]**Mr. Patterson:** William Patterson of New Jersey.

of certain individuals chosen by the people is substituted in place of the inconvenient meeting of the people themselves. If such a meeting of the people was actually to take place, would the slaves vote? They would not. Why then should they be represented? He was also against such an indirect encouragement of the slave trade; observing that Congress in their act relating to the change of the eighth article of Confederation had been ashamed to use the term "slaves" & had substituted a description. . . .

July 10

GENERAL PINCKNEY. The Report before it was committed was more favorable to the Southern States than as it now stands. If they are to form so considerable a minority, and the regulation of trade is to be given to the General Government, they will be nothing more than overseers for the Northern States. He did not expect the Southern States to be raised to a majority of representatives, but wished them to have something like an equality. At present by the alterations of the Committee in favor of the Northern States they are removed farther from it than they were before. One member had indeed been added to Virginia which he was glad of as he considered her as a Southern State. He was glad also that the members of Georgia were increased. . . .

July 11

MR. BUTLER & GENERAL PINCKNEY insisted that blacks be included in the rule of Representation, *equally* with the Whites: and for that purpose moved that the words "three fifths" be struck out.

MR. GERRY thought that ⅗ of them was to say the least the full proportion that could be admitted.

MR. GHORUM.[9] This ratio was fixed by Congress as a rule of taxation. Then it was urged by the Delegates representing the States having slaves that the blacks were still more inferior to freemen. At present when the ratio of representation is to be established, we are assured that they are equal to freemen. The arguments on the former occasion had convinced him that ⅗ was pretty near the just proportion and he should vote according to the same opinion now.

MR. BUTLER insisted that the labour of a slave in South Carolina was as productive & valuable as that of a freeman in Massachusetts, that as wealth was the great means of defence and utility to the Nation they were equally valuable to it with freemen; and that consequently an equal representation ought to be allowed for them in a Government which was instituted principally for the protection of property, and was itself to be supported by property.

MR. MASON,[10] could not agree to the motion, notwithstand it was favorable to Virginia because he thought it unjust. It was certain that the slaves were valu-

---

[9]**Mr. Ghorum:** Nathaniel Gorham of Massachusetts.
[10]**Mr. Mason:** George Mason of Virginia.

able, as they raised the value of land, increased the exports & imports, and of course the revenue, would supply the means of feeding & supporting an army, and might in cases of emergency become themselves soldiers. As in these important respects they were useful to the community at large, they ought not to be excluded from the estimate of Representation. He could not however regard them as equal to freemen and could not vote for them as such. He added as worthy of remark, that the Southern States have this peculiar species of property, over & above the other species of property common to all the States.

Mr. WILLIAMSON[11] reminded Mr. Ghorum that if the Southern States contended for the inferiority of blacks to whites when taxation was in view, the Eastern States on the same occasion contended for their equality. He did not however either then or now, concur in either extreme, but approved of the ratio of ⅗.

On Mr. Butler's motion for considering blacks as equal to Whites in the apportionment of Representation:

Massachusetts: no. Connecticut: no. New Jersey: no. Pennsylvania: no. Delaware: ay. Maryland: no. Virginia: no. North Carolina: no. South Carolina: ay. Georgia: ay. . . .

Mr. KING being much opposed to fixing numbers as the rule of representation, was particularly so on account of the blacks. He thought the admission of them along with Whites at all, would excite great discontents among the States having no slaves. He had never said as to any particular point that he would in no event acquiesce in & support it; but he would say that if in any case such a declaration was to be made by him, it would be in this. He remarked that in the temporary allotment of Representatives made by the Committee, the Southern States had received more than the number of their white & three fifths of their black inhabitants entitled them to.

Mr. SHERMAN. South Carolina had not more beyond her proportion than New York & New Hampshire, nor either of them more than was necessary in order to avoid fractions or reducing them below their proportion. Georgia had more; but the rapid growth of that State seemed to justify it. In general the allotment might not be just, but considering all circumstances, he was satisfied with it.

Mr. GHORUM supported the propriety of establishing numbers as the rule. He said that in Massachusetts estimates had been taken in the different towns, and that persons had been curious enough to compare these estimates with the respective numbers of people; and it had been found even including Boston, that the most exact proportion prevailed between numbers & property. He was aware that there might be some weight in what had fallen from his colleague, as to the umbrage which might be taken by the people of the Eastern States. But he recollected that when the proposition of Congress for changing the eighth article of Confederation was before the Legislature of Massachusetts the only difficulty then was to satisfy them that the negroes ought not to have been counted equally with whites instead of being counted in the ratio of three fifths only.

[11]**Mr. Williamson:** Hugh Williamson of North Carolina.

Mr. Wilson did not well see on what principle the admission of blacks in the proportion of three fifths could be explained. Are they admitted as Citizens? then why are they not admitted on an equality with White Citizens? are they admitted as property? then why is not other property admitted into the computation? These were difficulties however which he thought must be overruled by the necessity of compromise. He had some apprehensions also from the tendency of the blending of the blacks with the whites, to give disgust to the people of Pennsylvania as had been intimated by his Colleague.[12] But he differed from him in thinking numbers of inhabitants so incorrect a measure of wealth. He had seen the Western settlements of Pennsylvania and on a comparison of them with the City of Philadelphia could discover little other difference, than that property was more unequally divided among individuals here than there. Taking the same number in the aggregate in the two situations he believed there would be little difference in their wealth and ability to contribute to the public wants.

Mr. Gouverneur Morris was compelled to declare himself reduced to the dilemma of doing injustice to the Southern States or to human nature, and he must therefore do it to the former. For he could never agree to give such encouragement to the slave trade as would be given by allowing them a representation for their negroes, and he did not believe those States would ever confederate on terms that would deprive them of that trade.

On Question for agreeing to include ⅗ of the blacks:

Massachusetts: no. Connecticut: ay. New Jersey: no. Pennsylvania: no. Delaware: no. Maryland: no. Virginia: ay. North Carolina: ay. South Carolina: no. Georgia: ay. . . .

July 12

Mr. Davie,[13] said it was high time now to speak out. He saw that it was meant by some gentlemen to deprive the Southern States of any share of Representation for their blacks. He was sure that North Carolina would never confederate on any terms that did not rate them at least as ⅗. If the Eastern States meant therefore to exclude them altogether the business was at an end.

Dr. Johnson,[14] thought that wealth and population were the true, equitable rule of representation; but he conceived that these two principles resolved themselves into one, population being the best measure of wealth. He concluded therefore that the number of people ought to be established as the rule, and that all descriptions including blacks *equally* with the whites, ought to fall within the computation. As various opinions had been expressed on the subject, he would move that a Committee might be appointed to take them into consideration and report thereon.

---

[12]**his Colleague:** Gouverneur Morris of Pennsylvania.
[13]**Mr. Davie:** William R. Davie of North Carolina.
[14]**Dr. Johnson:** William Samuel Johnson of Connecticut.

MR. GOUVERNEUR MORRIS. It has been said that it is high time to speak out, as one member, he would candidly do so. He came here to form a compact for the good of America. He was ready to do so with all the States. He hoped & believed that all would enter into such a Compact. If they would not he was ready to join with any States that would. But as the Compact was to be voluntary, it is in vain for the Eastern States to insist on what the Southern States will never agree to. It is equally vain for the latter to require what the other States can never admit; and he verily believed the people of Pennsylvania will never agree to a representation of Negroes. What can be desired by these States more than has been already proposed; that the Legislature shall from time to time regulate Representation according to population & wealth.

GENERAL PINCKNEY desired that the rule of wealth should be ascertained and not left to the pleasure of the Legislature; and that property in slaves should not be exposed to danger under a Government instituted for the protection of property.

The first clause in the Report of the first Grand Committee was postponed.

MR. ELSEWORTH.[15] In order to carry into effect the principle established, moved to add to the last clause adopted by the House the words following: "and that the rule of contribution by direct taxation for the support of the Government of the United States shall be the number of white inhabitants, and three fifths of every other description in the several States, until some other rule that shall more accurately ascertain the wealth of the several States can be devised and adopted by the Legislature."

MR. BUTLER seconded the motion in order that it might be committed.

MR. RANDOLPH[16] was not satisfied with the motion. The danger will be revived that the ingenuity of the Legislature may evade or pervert the rule so as to perpetuate the power where it shall be lodged in the first instance. He proposed in lieu of Mr. Elseworth's motion, "that in order to ascertain the alterations in Representation that may be required from time to time by changes in the relative circumstances of the States, a census shall be taken within two years from the first meeting of the General Legislature of the U. S., and once within the term of every [——] year afterwards, of all the inhabitants in the manner & according to the ratio recommended by Congress in their resolution of the 18th day of April 1783; [rating the blacks at ⅗ of their number] and, that the Legislature of the U. S. shall arrange the Representation accordingly." He urged strenuously that express security ought to be provided for including slaves in the ratio of Representation. He lamented that such a species of property existed. But as it did exist the holders of it would require this security. It was perceived that the design was entertained by some of excluding slaves altogether; the Legislature therefore ought not to be left at liberty.

[15]**Mr. Elseworth:** Oliver Ellsworth of Connecticut.
[16]**Mr. Randolph:** Edmund Randolph of Virginia.

24. The African Slave Trade

JAMES MADISON
Debates in the Federal Convention
August 21–25, 1787

Toward the close of the convention in August 1787, delegate Luther Martin of Mary-land proposed adding a constitutional provision empowering Congress to limit or ban the importation of African slaves. As Madison's account of the ensuing debate shows, Martin's motion provoked considerable discussion and substantial southern opposition, especially from South Carolina. But northern delegates resented con-cessions to slaveholding states — including the three-fifths clause and Article 4, Sec-tion 2, which obligated states to return fugitive slaves to their masters in other states. In the end, the convention adopted a compromise — embodied in Article 1, Section 9 — that permitted but did not require Congress to impose restrictions. Deliberately avoiding the use of the term slave, *this provision empowered Congress eventually to end the external slave trade. Significantly, no restrictions could be put into effect for twenty years.*

August 21

MR. L. MARTIN proposed to vary the Sect: 4. art VII. so as to allow a prohibi-tion or tax on the importation of slaves. 1. as five slaves are to be counted as 3 free men in the apportionment of Representatives; such a clause would leave an en-couragement to this traffic. 2. slaves weakened one part of the Union which the other parts were bound to protect: the privilege of importing them was therefore unreasonable. 3. it was inconsistent with the principles of the revolution and dis-honorable to the American character to have such a feature in the Constitution.

MR. RUTLEDGE did not see how the importation of slaves could be encour-aged by this Section. He was not apprehensive of insurrections and would read-ily exempt the other States from the obligation to protect the Southern against them. Religion & humanity had nothing to do with this question. Interest alone is the governing principle with nations. The true question at present is whether the Southern States shall or shall not be parties to the Union. If the Northern States consult their interest, they will not oppose the increase of Slaves which will in-crease the commodities of which they will become the carriers.

James Madison, *The Debates in the Federal Convention of 1787 which Framed the Constitution of the United States of America,* international ed., ed. Gaillard Hunt and James Brown Scott (New York: Ox-ford University Press, 1920), 442–43, 443–45, 467–69. (Some spelling and punctuation has been modernized.)

MR. ELSEWORTH was for leaving the clause as it stands. Let every State import what it pleases. The morality or wisdom of slavery are considerations belonging to the States themselves. What enriches a part enriches the whole, and the States are the best judges of their particular interest. The old confederation had not meddled with this point, and he did not see any greater necessity for bringing it within the policy of the new one.

MR. PINCKNEY. South Carolina can never receive the plan if it prohibits the slave trade. In every proposed extension of the powers of the Congress, that State has expressly & watchfully excepted that of meddling with the importation of negroes. If the States be all left at liberty on this subject, South Carolina may perhaps by degrees do of herself what is wished, as Virginia & Maryland have already done.

August 22

COLONEL MASON. This infernal traffic originated in the avarice of British Merchants. The British Government constantly checked the attempts of Virginia to put a stop to it. The present question concerns not the importing States alone but the whole Union. The evil of having slaves was experienced during the late war. Had slaves been treated as they might have been by the Enemy, they would have proved dangerous instruments in their hands. But their folly dealt by the slaves, as it did by the Tories. He mentioned the dangerous insurrections of the slaves in Greece and Sicily; and the instructions given by Cromwell to the Commissioners sent to Virginia, to arm the servants & slaves, in case other means of obtaining its submission should fail. Maryland & Virginia he said had already prohibited the importation of slaves expressly. North Carolina had done the same in substance. All this would be in vain if South Carolina & Georgia be at liberty to import. The Western people are already calling out for slaves for their new lands, and will fill that Country with slaves if they can be got through South Carolina & Georgia. Slavery discourages arts & manufactures. The poor despise labor when performed by slaves. They prevent the immigration of Whites, who really enrich & strengthen a Country. They produce the most pernicious effect on manners. Every master of slaves is born a petty tyrant. They bring the judgment of heaven on a Country. As nations can not be rewarded or punished in the next world they must be in this. By an inevitable chain of causes & effects providence punishes national sins, by national calamities. He lamented that some of our Eastern brethren had from a lust of gain embarked in this nefarious traffic. As to the States being in possession of the Right to import, this was the case with many other rights, now to be properly given up. He held it essential in every point of view that the General Government should have power to prevent the increase of slavery.

MR. ELSEWORTH. As he had never owned a slave could not judge of the effects of slavery on character: He said however that if it was to be considered in a moral light we ought to go farther and free those already in the Country. As slaves also multiply so fast in Virginia & Maryland that it is cheaper to raise than import them, whilst in the sickly rice swamps foreign supplies are necessary, if we go no farther than is urged, we shall be unjust towards South Carolina & Georgia. Let us not intermeddle. As population increases poor laborers will be so plenty as to render slaves useless. Slavery in time will not be a speck in our Country. Provision is already made in Connecticut for abolishing it. And the abolition has already taken place in Massachusetts. As to the danger of insurrections from foreign influence, that will become a motive to kind treatment of the slaves.

MR. PINCKNEY. If slavery be wrong, it is justified by the example of all the world. He cited the case of Greece, Rome, & other ancient States; the sanction given by France, England, Holland, & other modern States. In all ages one half of mankind have been slaves. If the Southern States were let alone they will probably of themselves stop importations. He would himself as a Citizen of South Carolina vote for it. An attempt to take away the right as proposed will produce serious objections to the Constitution which he wished to see adopted.

GENERAL PINCKNEY declared it to be his firm opinion that if himself & all his colleagues were to sign the Constitution & use their personal influence, it would be of no avail towards obtaining the assent of their Constituents. South Carolina & Georgia cannot do without slaves. As to Virginia she will gain by stopping the importations. Her slaves will rise in value, & she has more than she wants. It would be unequal to require South Carolina & Georgia to confederate on such unequal terms. He said the Royal assent before the Revolution had never been refused to South Carolina as to Virginia. He contended that the importation of slaves would be for the interest of the whole Union. The more slaves, the more produce to employ the carrying trade; The more consumption also, and the more of this, the more of revenue for the common treasury. He admitted it to be reasonable that slaves should be dutied like other imports, but should consider a rejection of the clause as an exclusion of South Carolina from the Union. . . .

August 25

The Report of the Committee of eleven being taken up,

GENERAL PINCKNEY moved to strike out the words "the year eighteen hundred" as the year limiting the importation of slaves, and to insert the words "the year eighteen hundred and eight."

MR. GHORUM seconded the motion.

MR. MADISON. Twenty years will produce all the mischief that can be apprehended from the liberty to import slaves. So long a term will be more dishonorable to the National character than to say nothing about it in the Constitution.

On the motion, which passed in the affirmative:

New Hampshire: ay. Massachusetts: ay. Connecticut: ay. New Jersey: no. Pennsylvania: no. Delaware: no. Maryland: ay. Virginia: no. North Carolina: ay. South Carolina: ay. Georgia: ay.

MR. GOUVERNEUR MORRIS was for making the clause read at once, "importation of slaves into North Carolina, South Carolina, & Georgia shall not be prohibited etc." This he said would be most fair and would avoid the ambiguity by which, under the power with regard to naturalization, the liberty reserved to the States might be defeated. He wished it to be known also that this part of the Constitution was a compliance with those States. If the change of language however should be objected to by the members from those States, he should not urge it.

COLONEL MASON was not against using the term "slaves" but against naming North Carolina, South Carolina, & Georgia, lest it should give offence to the people of those States.

MR. SHERMAN liked a description better than the terms proposed, which had been declined by the old Congress & were not pleasing to some people. MR. CLYMER[1] concurred with Mr. Sherman.

MR. WILLIAMSON said that both in opinion & practice he was, against slavery; but thought it more in favor of humanity, from a view of all circumstances, to let in South Carolina & Georgia on those terms, than to exclude them from the Union.

MR. GOUVERNEUR MORRIS withdrew his motion.

MR. DICKENSON[2] wished the clause to be confined to the States which had not themselves prohibited the importation of slaves, and for that purpose moved to amend the clause so as to read "The importation of slaves into such of the States as shall permit the same shall not be prohibited by the Legislature of the United States until the year 1808" — which was disagreed to nem. cont.[3]

The first part of the report was then agreed to, amended as follows.

"The migration or importation of such persons as the several States now existing shall think proper to admit, shall not be prohibited by the Legislature prior to the year 1808."

New Hampshire, Massachusetts, Connecticut, Maryland, North Carolina, South Carolina, Georgia: ay.

New Jersey, Pennsylvania, Delaware, Virginia: no.

MR. BALDWIN[4] in order to restrain & more explicitly define "the average duty" moved to strike out of the second part the words "average of the duties laid on imports" and insert "common impost on articles not enumerated" which was agreed to nem. cont.

MR. SHERMAN was against this second part, as acknowledging men to be property, by taxing them as such under the character of slaves.

MR. KING & MR. LANGDON[5] considered this as the price of the first part.

GENERAL PINCKNEY admitted that it was so.

COLONEL MASON. Not to tax, will be equivalent to a bounty on the importation of slaves.

MR. GHORUM thought that Mr. Sherman should consider the duty, not as implying that slaves are property, but as a discouragement to the importation of them.

MR. GOUVERNEUR MORRIS remarked that as the clause now stands it implies that the Legislature may tax freemen imported.

---

[1]**Mr. Clymer:** George Clymer of Pennsylvania.
[2]**Mr. Dickenson:** John Dickinson of Delaware.
[3]**nem. cont.:** *nemine contradicente* (Latin for "no one contradicting").
[4]**Mr. Baldwin:** Abraham Baldwin of Georgia.
[5]**Mr. Langdon:** John Langdon of New Hampshire.

Mr. Sherman in answer to Mr. Ghorum observed that the smallness of the duty shewed revenue to be the object, not the discouragement of the importation.

Mr. Madison thought it wrong to admit in the Constitution the idea that there could be property in men. The reason of duties did not hold, as slaves are not like merchandize, consumed, etc. . . .

25. A Southerner Opposes the Three-Fifths Clause

Luther Martin
"Genuine Information"
1788

Southerners were far from unanimous about the status of slavery in the Constitution. In general, "Upper South" states such as Maryland and Virginia were more willing to consider some modification of the absolute power of slaveholders, while "Deep South" states such as South Carolina ardently advocated special protections for them. Some even opposed the three-fifths clause. Luther Martin, a resident of Baltimore and a delegate to the Philadelphia convention, served as attorney general for Maryland during the Revolution and, in 1785, was elected to the Continental Congress. Martin became a vigorous opponent of a strong national government; indeed, he was so displeased with the results of the convention that he walked out before it adjourned and refused to sign the Constitution. Thereafter, he became one of Maryland's leading Antifederalists.

During and after the convention, Martin was deeply suspicious of constitutional protections for slaveholders. In this article, part of an Antifederalist newspaper attack he composed in early 1788, Martin criticizes the three-fifths clause and the "infamous traffic" in slaves that it appeared to encourage.

Maryland Gazette (Baltimore), 11 January 1788. Reprinted in *A Necessary Evil?: Slavery and the Debate over the Constitution*, ed. John P. Kaminski, Constitutional Heritage Series, vol. 2 (Madison, Wis.: Madison House, Center for the Study of the American Constitution, 1995), 166–67.

January 11, 1788

With respect to *that part* of the *second* section of the *first* article, which relates to the *apportionment of representation* and *direct taxation*, there were considerable objections made to it, besides the great objection of *inequality* — It was urged, that no principle could justify taking *slaves* into computation in *apportioning* the number of *representatives* a State should have in the government — that it involved the absurdity of *increasing* the power of a State in making laws for *free men* in *proportion* as that State *violated* the *rights of freedom* — That it might be proper to take slaves into consideration, when *taxes* were to be apportioned, because it had a tendency to *discourage slavery*; but to take them into account in *giving representation* tended to *encourage* the *slave trade*, and to make it the *interest* of the States to *continue* that *infamous traffic* — That slaves could not be taken into account as *men*, or *citizens*, because they were not admitted to the *rights of citizens* in the States which adopted or continued slavery — If they were to be taken into account as *property*, it was asked, what peculiar circumstance should render this property (of *all others* the most *odious* in its nature) entitled to the *high privilege* of conferring *consequence* and *power* in the *government* to its possessors, rather than *any other* property — and why *slaves* should, as property, be taken into account rather than *horses, cattle, mules,* or any *other species* — and it was observed by an honorable member from Massachusetts, that he considered it as dishonorable and humiliating to enter into compact with the *slaves* of the *southern States*, as it would be with the *horses* and *mules* of the *eastern.* It was also objected, that the *numbers* of representatives appointed by this section to be sent by the particular States to compose the *first* legislature, were not precisely *agreeable* to the *rule* of representation adopted by this system, and that the numbers in this section are *artfully lessened* for the *large* States, while the *smaller* States have their *full proportion* in order to prevent the *undue influence* which the *large* States will have in the government from being *too apparent*; and I think, Mr. Speaker, that this objection is *well founded.*—I have taken some pains to obtain information of the numbers of free men and slaves in the different States, and I have reason to believe, that if the estimate was *now* taken, which is directed, and one delegate to be sent for every thirty thousand inhabitants, that Virginia would have at least *twelve* delegates, Massachusetts *eleven*, and Pennsylvania *ten*, instead of the numbers stated in *this section*; whereas the *other* States, I believe, would not have more than the numbers there allowed them, nor would Georgia, most probably at present, send more than *two* — If I am right, Mr. Speaker, upon the enumeration being made, and the representation being apportioned according to the rule prescribed, the *whole number* of delegates would be *seventy-one, thirty-six* of which would be a *quorum* to do business; the delegates of Virginia, Massachusetts, and Pennsylvania, would amount to *thirty-three* of that quorum — Those three States will, therefore, have *much more* than *equal* power and influence in *making* the laws and regulations, which are to affect this continent, and will have a *moral certainty* of *preventing* any laws or regulations which *they disapprove*, although they might be thought ever so *necessary* by a *great majority* of the States.

26. Ratification

Debates in South Carolina, Virginia, and North Carolina

1788

After the Philadelphia convention adjourned, the Constitution's advocates and opponents fastened on to a number of issues in their arguments. But much of the debate concerned slavery. In the North, especially in New England, Antifederalists objected to the three-fifths clause; many others were unhappy about the Constitution's approach to the slave trade because although Congress was banned from limiting the slave trade for twenty years, the states themselves were under no constitutional limits.

In the South, Antifederalists suggested that the Constitution placed too much power in the hands of a national government that might eventually come under the domination of nonslaveholders. They feared that the protections provided in the Constitution were insufficient to protect the slavocracy. In speeches delivered at state conventions in South Carolina, Virginia, and North Carolina, Federalists made their case, detailing the ways in which the Constitution protected slavery.

SOUTH CAROLINA

January 17, 1788

. . . [C. C. PINCKNEY.] Every member who attended the Convention, was, from the beginning, sensible of the necessity of giving greater powers to the federal government. This was the very purpose for which they were convened. The delegations of Jersey and Delaware were, at first, averse to this organization; but they afterwards acquiesced in it; and the conduct of their delegates has been so very agreeable to the people of these states, that their respective conventions have unanimously adopted the Constitution. As we have found it necessary to give very extensive powers to the federal government both over the persons and estates of the citizens, we thought it right to draw one branch of the legislature immediately from the people, and that both wealth and numbers should be considered in the representation. We were at a loss, for some time, for a rule to ascertain the proportionate wealth of the states. At last we thought that the productive labor of the inhabitants was the best rule for ascertaining their wealth. In conformity to this rule, joined to a spirit of concession, we determined that representatives should be apportioned among the several states, by adding to the whole number of free

The Records of the Federal Convention of 1787, ed. Max Ferrand, vol. 3 (New Haven: Yale University Press, 1911), 253–54.

persons three fifths of the slaves. We thus obtained a representation for our property; and I confess I did not expect that we had conceded too much to the Eastern States, when they allowed us a representation for a species of property which they have not among them.

The numbers in the different states, according to the most accurate accounts we could obtain, were —

In New Hampshire,	102,000
Massachusetts,	360,000
Rhode Island,	58,000
Connecticut,	202,000
New York,	233,000
New Jersey,	138,000
Pennsylvania,	360,000
Delaware,	37,000
Maryland, (including three-fifths of 80,000 negroes,)	218,000
Virginia, (including three-fifths of 280,000 negroes,)	420,000
N. Carolina, (including three-fifths of 60,000 negroes,)	200,000
S. Carolina, (including three-fifths of 80,000 negroes,)	150,000
Georgia, (including three-fifths of 20,000 negroes,)	90,000

. . . The general then said he would make a few observations on the objections which the gentleman had thrown out on the restrictions that might be laid on the African trade after the year 1808. On this point your delegates had to contend with the religious and political prejudices of the Eastern and Middle States, and with the interested and inconsistent opinion of Virginia, who was warmly opposed to our importing more slaves. I am of the same opinion now as I was two years ago, when I used the expressions the gentleman has quoted — that, while there remained one acre of swampland uncleared of South Carolina, I would raise my voice against restricting the importation of negroes. I am as thoroughly convinced as that gentleman is, that the nature of our climate, and the flat, swampy situation of our country, obliges us to cultivate our lands with negroes, and that without them South Carolina would soon be a desert waste.

You have so frequently heard my sentiments on this subject, that I need not now repeat them. It was alleged, by some of the members who opposed an unlimited importation, that slaves increased the weakness of any state who admitted them; that they were a dangerous species of property, which an invading enemy could easily turn against ourselves and the neighboring states; and that, as we were allowed a representation for them in the House of Representatives, our influence in government would be increased in proportion as we were less able to defend ourselves. "Show some period," said the members from the Eastern States, "when it may be in our power to put a stop, if we please, to the importation of this weakness, and we will endeavor, for your convenience, to restrain the religious and political prejudices of our people on this subject." The Middle States and Virginia made us no such proposition; they were for an immediate and total prohibition. We endeavored to obviate the objections that were made in the best manner we could, and assigned reasons for our insisting on the importation, which there is no occasion to repeat, as they must occur to every gentleman in the house: a committee of the states was appointed in order to accommodate this matter, and, after a great deal of difficulty, it was settled on the footing recited in the Constitution.

By this settlement we have secured an unlimited importation of negroes for twenty years. Nor is it declared that the importation shall be then stopped; it may be continued. We have a security that the general government can never emancipate them, for no such authority is granted; and it is admitted, on all hands, that the general government has no powers but what are expressly granted by the Constitution, and that all rights not expressed were reserved by the several states. We have obtained a right to recover our slaves in whatever part of America they may take refuge, which is a right we had not before. In short, considering all circumstances, we have made the best terms for the security of this species of property. . . .

VIRGINIA

June 17, 1788

(The first clause, of the ninth section, read.)

. . . MR. MADISON. — Mr. Chairman — I should conceive this clause to be impolitic, if it were one of those things which could be excluded without encountering greater evils. — The southern states would not have entered into the union of America, without the temporary permission of that trade. And if they were excluded from the union, the consequences might be dreadful to them and to us. We are not in a worse situation than before. That traffic is prohibited by our laws, and we may continue the prohibition. The union in general is not in a worse situation. Under the articles of confederation, it might be continued forever: But by this clause an end may be put to it after twenty years. There is therefore an amelioration of our circumstances. A tax may be laid in the mean time; but it is limited, otherwise congress might lay such a tax as would amount to a prohibition. From the mode of representation and taxation, congress cannot lay such a tax on slaves as will amount to manumission. Another clause secures us that property which we now possess. At present, if any slave elopes to any of those states where slaves are free, he becomes emancipated by their laws. For the laws of the states are uncharitable to one another in this respect. But in this constitution, "no person held to service, or labor, in one state, under the laws thereof, escaping into another, shall in consequence of any law or regulation therein, be discharged from such service or labor; but shall be delivered up on claim of the party to whom such service or labor may be due." — This clause was expressly inserted to enable owners of slaves to reclaim them. This is a better security than any that now exists. No power is given to the general government to interpose with respect to the property in slaves now held by the states. The taxation of this state being equal only to its representation, such a tax cannot be laid as he supposes. They cannot prevent the

The Records of the Federal Convention of 1787, ed. Max Farrand, vol. 3 (New Haven, Conn.: Yale University Press, 1911), 324–26.

importation of slaves for twenty years; but after that period they can. The gentle-men from South-Carolina and Georgia argued in this manner: — "We have now liberty to import this species of property, and much of the property now possessed, has been purchased, or otherwise acquired, in contemplation of improving it by the assistance of imported slaves. What would be the consequence of hindering us from it? The slaves of Virginia would rise in value, and we would be obliged to go to your markets." I need not expatiate on this subject. Great as the evil is, a dis-memberment of the union would be worse. If those states should disunite from the other states, for not indulging them in the temporary continuance of this traffic, they might solicit and obtain aid from foreign powers. . . .

(The 2d, 3d, and 4th clauses read.)

. . . Mr. MADISON replied, that even the southern states, who were most affected, were perfectly satisfied with this provision, and dreaded no danger to the property they now hold. It appeared to him, that the general government would not inter-meddle with that property for twenty years, but to lay a tax on every slave imported, not exceeding ten dollars; and that after the expiration of that period they might pro-hibit the traffic altogether. The census in the constitution was intended to introduce equality in the burdens to be laid on the community.—No gentleman objected to laying duties, imposts, and excises, uniformly. But uniformity of taxes would be sub-versive of the principles of equality: For that it was not possible to select any article which would be easy for one state, but what would be heavy for another. . . .

NORTH CAROLINA

July 24, 1788

Mr. GOUDY.[1] Mr. Chairman, this clause of taxation will give an advantage to some states over the others. It will be oppressive to the Southern States. Taxes are equal to our representation. To augment our taxes, and increase our burdens, our negroes are to be represented. If a state has fifty thousand *negroes*, she is to send one representative for them. I wish not to be represented with negroes, especially if it increases my burdens.

Mr. DAVIE. Mr. Chairman, I will endeavor to obviate what the gentleman last up said. I wonder to see gentlemen so precipitate and hasty on a subject of such awful importance. It ought to be considered, that some of us are slow of appre-hension, or not having those quick conceptions, and luminous understandings, of which other gentlemen may be possessed. The gentleman "does not wish to be represented with negroes." This, sir, is an unhappy species of population; but we cannot at present alter their situation. The Eastern States had great jealousies on

---

[1]**Mr. Goudy:** William Goudy.

The Debates in the Several State Conventions on the Adoption of the Federal Constitution, as Recom-mended by the General Convention at Philadelphia, in 1787 . . . , ed. Jonathan Elliot, 2d ed., vol. 4 (Philadelphia: J. B. Lippincott Co., 1836–45), 30–32, 100–1.

this subject. They insisted that their cows and horses were equally entitled to representation; that the one was property as well as the other. It became our duty, on the other hand, to acquire as much weight as possible in the legislation of the Union; and, as the Northern States were more populous in whites, this only could be done by insisting that a certain proportion of our slaves should make a part of the computed population. It was attempted to form a rule of representation from a compound ratio of wealth and population; but, on consideration, it was found impracticable to determine the comparative value of lands, and other property, in so extensive a territory, with any degree of accuracy; and population alone was adopted as the only practicable rule or criterion of representation. It was urged by the deputies of the Eastern States, that a representation of two fifths would be of little utility, and that their entire representation would be unequal and burdensome — that, in a time of war, slaves rendered a country more vulnerable, while its defence devolved upon its free inhabitants. On the other hand, we insisted that, in time of peace, they contributed, by their labor, to the general wealth, as well as other members of the community — that, as rational beings, they had a right of representation, and, in some instances, might be highly useful in war. On these principles the Eastern States gave the matter up, and consented to the regulation as it has been read. I hope these reasons will appear satisfactory. It is the same rule or principle which was proposed some years ago by Congress, and assented to by twelve of the states. It may wound the delicacy of the gentleman from Guilford, (Mr. Goudy,) but I hope he will endeavor to accommodate his feelings to the interest and circumstances of his country.

Mr. James Galloway said, that he did not object to the representation of negroes, so much as he did to the fewness of the number of representatives. He was surprised how we came to have but five, including those intended to represent negroes. That, in his humble opinion, North Carolina was entitled to that number independent of the negroes.

Mr. Spaight[2] endeavored to satisfy him, that the Convention had no rule to go by in this case — that they could not proceed upon the ratio mentioned in the Constitution till the enumeration of the people was made — that some states had made a return to Congress of their numbers, and others had not — that it was mentioned that we had had time, but made no return — that the present number was only temporary — that in three years the actual census would be taken, and our number of representatives regulated accordingly.

July 26, 1788

1st clause of the 9th section read.

Mr. J. M'Dowall[3] wished to hear the reasons of this restriction.

Mr. Spaight answered, that there was a contest between the Northern and Southern States; that the Southern States, whose principal support depended on

---

[2]**Mr. Spaight:** Richard Dobbs Spaight.
[3]**Mr. M'Dowall:** Joseph McDowell.

the labor of slaves, would not consent to the desire of the Northern States to exclude the importation of slaves absolutely; that South Carolina and Georgia insisted on this clause, as they were now in want of hands to cultivate their lands; that in the course of twenty years they would be fully supplied; that the trade would be abolished then, and that, in the mean time, some tax or duty might be laid on.

Mr. M'DOWALL replied, that the explanation was just such as he expected, and by no means satisfactory to him, and that he looked upon it as a very objectionable part of the system.

Mr. IREDELL.[4] Mr. Chairman, I rise to express sentiments similar to those of the gentleman from Craven. For my part, were it practicable to put an end to the importation of slaves immediately, it would give me the greatest pleasure; for it certainly is a trade utterly inconsistent with the rights of humanity, and under which great cruelties have been exercised. When the entire abolition of slavery takes place, it will be an event which must be pleasing to every generous mind, and every friend of human nature; but we often wish for things which are not attainable. It was the wish of a great majority of the Convention to put an end to the trade immediately; but the states of South Carolina and Georgia would not agree to it. Consider, then, what would be the difference between our present situation in this respect, if we do not agree to the Constitution, and what it will be if we do agree to it. If we do not agree to it, do we remedy the evil? No, sir, we do not. For if the Constitution be not adopted, it will be in the power of every state to continue it forever. They may or may not abolish it, at their discretion. But if we adopt the Constitution, the trade must cease after twenty years, if Congress declare so, whether particular states please so or not; surely, then, we can gain by it. This was the utmost that could be obtained. I heartily wish more could have been done. But as it is, this government is nobly distinguished above others by that very provision. Where is there another country in which such a restriction prevails? We, therefore, sir, set an example of humanity, by providing for the abolition of this inhuman traffic, though at a distant period. I hope, therefore, that this part of the Constitution will not be condemned because it has not stipulated for what was impracticable to obtain.

Mr. SPAIGHT further explained the clause. That the limitation of this trade to the term of twenty years was a compromise between the Eastern States and the Southern States. South Carolina and Georgia wished to extend the term. The Eastern States insisted on the entire abolition of the trade. That the state of North Carolina had not thought proper to pass any law prohibiting the importation of slaves, and therefore its delegation in the Convention did not think themselves authorized to contend for an immediate prohibition of it.

Mr. IREDELL added to what he had said before, that the states of Georgia and South Carolina had lost a great many slaves during the war, and that they wished to supply the loss.

Mr. GALLOWAY. Mr. Chairman, the explanation given to this clause does not satisfy my mind. I wish to see this abominable trade put an end to. But in case it

[4]**Mr. Iredell:** James Iredell.

be thought proper to continue this abominable traffic for twenty years, yet I do not wish to see the tax on the importation extended to all persons whatsoever. Our situation is different from the people to the north. We want citizens; they do not. Instead of laying a tax, we ought to give a bounty to encourage foreigners to come among us. With respect to the abolition of slavery, it requires the utmost consideration. The property of the Southern States consists principally of slaves. If they mean to do away slavery altogether, this property will be destroyed. I apprehend it means to bring forward manumission. If we must manumit our slaves, what country shall we send them to? It is impossible for us to be happy, if, after manumission, they are to stay among us.

MR. IREDELL. Mr. Chairman, the worthy gentleman, I believe, has misunderstood this clause, which runs in the following words: "The migration or importation of such persons as any of the states now existing shall think proper to admit, shall not be prohibited by the Congress prior to the year 1808; but a tax or duty may be imposed on such importation, not exceeding ten dollars for each person." Now, sir, observe that the Eastern States, who long ago have abolished slaves, did not approve of the expression *slaves*; they therefore used another, that answered the same purpose. The committee will observe the distinction between the two words *migration* and *importation*. The first part of the clause will extend to persons who come into this country as free people, or are brought as slaves. But the last part extends to slaves only. The word *migration* refers to free persons; but the word *importation* refers to slaves, because free people cannot be said to be imported. The tax, therefore, is only to be laid on slaves who are imported, and not on free persons who migrate. I further beg leave to say that the gentleman is mistaken in another thing. He seems to say that this extends to the abolition of slavery. Is there any thing in this Constitution which says that Congress shall have it in their power to abolish the slavery of those slaves who are now in the country? Is it not the plain meaning of it, that after twenty years they may prevent the future importation of slaves? It does not extend to those now in the country. There is another circumstance to be observed. There is no authority vested in Congress to restrain the states, in the interval of twenty years, from doing what they please. If they wish to prohibit such importation, they may do so. Our next Assembly may put an entire end to the importation of slaves.

Suggestions for Further Reading

Faber, Doris, and Harold Faber. *We the People: The Story of the United States Constitution since 1787.* New York: Charles Scribner's Sons, 1987.

Fehrenbacher, Don E. "Slavery, the Framers, and the Living Constitution." In *Slavery and Its Consequences: The Constitution, Equality, and Race,* ed. Robert A. Goldwin and Art Kaufman (Washington, D.C.: American Enterprise Institute, 1988), 1–22.

Finkelman, Paul. *An Imperfect Union: Slavery, Federalism, and Comity.* Chapel Hill: University of North Carolina Press, 1981.

Lively, Donald E. *The Constitution and Race.* New York: Praeger, 1992.

Rakove, Jack N. *Original Meanings: Politics and Ideas in the Making of the Constitution.* 1947. Reprint, New York: Alfred A. Knopf, 1996.

CHAPTER EIGHT

THE NEW REPUBLIC

The Americanization of New Orleans?

O ne of the most important events in the history of the new American republic and a crowning achievement of Thomas Jefferson's presidency
was the Louisiana Purchase in 1803. For a bargain fifteen million dollars,
the new nation gained 828,000 square miles of territory, including the city of New
Orleans. "Americanizing" this proud city with its rich and distinctly French culture, however, would prove to be difficult and — fortunately for America's cultural
heritage — never fully accomplished.

France sold Louisiana to the United States soon after reacquiring it from
Spain, which had held it since 1763. After forty years of Spanish rule, the New Orleans of 1803 was still in most respects a French colonial city. Few Spaniards had
immigrated to Louisiana, and the arrival of Acadians from the 1760s to the 1790s
and of French-speaking immigrants from St. Domingue (Haiti) after the successful slave revolt that began there in 1791 further entrenched French culture. Perhaps the most enduring contribution of the Spanish was the establishment of
their version of European civil law, which differed from French law principally in
that it facilitated the manumission of slaves, thus helping to create in New Orleans
a large black population with a unique social standing midway between free and
slave.

By the time the United States acquired New Orleans, the city had attracted
a multicultural population of 8,000 that included, in addition to people of French,
Spanish, and African backgrounds, smaller numbers from Germany, Scotland, Ireland, England, and America. New Orleans was clearly dominated by the white
Creole (native-born) elite of French or Spanish descent. Fewer than two hundred
of its residents were American.

Thomas Jefferson and other American officials recognized the need for good relations with the local population. The Spanish still controlled vast expanses on either side of the city, and American military presence in the area was slight. The territory's first American governor would face the task of firmly establishing American authority while winning the cooperation and allegiance of the Louisianians. Jefferson tried to please the locals as well as his fellow Americans by appointing the Marquis de Lafayette, French hero of the American Revolution, but he declined the governorship. The man who ended up with the job was W. C. C. Claiborne, only twenty-eight years old and unable to speak French.

As Claiborne quickly discovered, his mission would not be an easy one. In announcing France's cession of Louisiana, the French colonial prefect, Pierre Clément Laussat, had urged the populace to view the transfer to this promising young nation as a stroke of good fortune. But the people of New Orleans were unconvinced. As a worried Claiborne reported to Jefferson only days after taking office, ethnic tensions erupted at the midwinter balls: American and French officers came to blows over whose music and dances would take precedence on the dance floor and engaged in a singing duel in which the newly minted French national anthem, "La Marseillaise," competed with America's "Hail Columbia." (The "Star-Spangled Banner" had yet to be written.)

On a far more significant level, American laws and customs clashed with those of New Orleans, intensifying the conflict between Americans and Creoles. The Americans who poured into New Orleans after the cession were generally Protestant, distrustful of Catholics, and often offended by the cosmopolitan ways of a city many viewed as corrupt and decadent. Many were well educated and had ample capital resources that allowed them to quickly dominate the city's mercantile economy. The Americans made English the legal language and intended to replace the existing civil law with the Anglo-American common law, which they regarded as the essential bulwark of American liberty. The Creoles, on the other hand, bristled at any suggestion of cultural inferiority and resolved to defend their religion and other cherished institutions including the civil law which was clearly in jeopardy.

The Creoles were particularly indignant that they were not to have immediate self-government — as the 1803 American treaty with the French had suggested — but a legislative council composed of thirteen members appointed by the president. Jefferson and Claiborne were careful to select bilingual Louisianians, and appointed six Creoles along with seven Americans. The Creoles, however, were quite unhappy with the American majority on the council. Though Claiborne was of the opinion that the people of Louisiana were not yet capable of self-government (an opinion that Jefferson's Federalist critics in Washington leaked to the press to Claiborne's detriment), Congress soon yielded to Louisianians' demand for representative government. In 1805, it gave citizens of the territory the right to elect their own House of Representatives and established an upper house, the Legislative Council, whose five members would be appointed by the president from a list of ten names submitted by the House of Representatives. In October 1805, elections for the House of Representatives yielded a resounding victory for the Creoles, who then submitted a predominantly Creole list of candidates for the Legislative Council. The native-born Louisianians thus gained control of the political machinery and significant power in the cultural conflicts that would continue for decades.

As time passed and the proportion of Americans in the population increased, these two dominant groups continued to sort out their differences, each coming to accept some aspects of the other's culture. Many prominent Americans (including Governor Claiborne) married into Creole families, and intermarriage helped to calm the culture wars. Though New Orleans remained an American city, American culture would be only one of several that contributed to its unique character.

In this chapter, the French colonial prefect's announcement explains to its inhabitants the cession of New Orleans; correspondence between President Jefferson and Governor Claiborne illustrates their efforts to establish a successful territorial government; the Louisianians' desire to retain cherished religious and legal institutions is evident in the correspondence between the Ursuline order of nuns and the president, as well as in the Legislative Council's resolution on the law; and the 1818 diary entries of Benjamin Latrobe reflect the gradual changes that were taking place in New Orleans society and culture as the cultures intermingled.

As you read, consider these questions: What does the French proclamation reveal about relations between France and the United States in 1803 and French attitudes toward its former colony? What challenges faced American officials as they set up the territorial government, and what prejudices or preconceptions does their correspondence reveal? Did Catholic leaders have cause for concern regarding their rights? How persuasive were the arguments presented for the retention of civil law? What changes in New Orleans culture were visible to a visitor to the city by 1819?

27. Explaining the French Decision

PIERRE CLÉMENT LAUSSAT
Proclamation in the Name of the French Republic, to the Louisianians
1803

Pierre Laussat, colonial prefect and commissioner of the French Republic, issued this proclamation to the people of Louisiana on November 30, 1803, the day the French Republic formally took possession of the territory. Earlier in the year, the Spanish had traded Louisiana to Napoleon for a duchy in Italy. Now at war, Napoleon recognized the difficulties of defending his new possession and seized the opportunity to gain badly needed funds and enhance French relations with the United States. Only twenty days later, on December 20, 1803, Laussat delivered Louisiana to American ownership. By issuing this proclamation, Laussat may have hoped to prevent a recurrence of the bloody revolt of Louisianians that took place after the French surrendered the colony to the Spanish in 1763.

Louisianians: The mission which brought me across 2,500 leagues of sea to your midst, that mission in which I have for a long time placed so many honorable hopes & so many wishes for your happiness, is changed today: that of which I am at this time the minister & the executer, less pleasing, though equally flattering to me, offers me one consolation, that is, that in general it is much more advantageous to you.

In virtue of the powers & the respective orders, the Commissioners of H.C.M.[1] have just turned the country over to me, & you see the standards of the French Republic floating & you hear the repeated sound of its cannons announce to you on all sides on this day the return of its sovereignty over these shores: it will be, Louisianians, only for a short time, & I am on the eve of transferring them to the United States Commissioners charged with taking possession of them, in the name of their Federal Government: they are about to arrive; I am awaiting them.

The approach of a war[2] begun under bloody & terrible auspices & threatening the four quarters of the globe has led the French Government to turn its attention and its thoughts to these regions: views of prudence & humanity, allied with views of a broader and firmer policy, worthy, in brief, of the genius who at this very hour is swaying such great destinies among the Nations, have then given a

---

[1] **H.C.M.:** His Catholic Majesty (the king of Spain).
[2] **approach of a war:** Laussat refers to renewed hostilities between France and other major European powers, especially Britain.

The Territorial Papers of the United States, ed. Clarence Edwin Carter, vol. 9, *The Territory of New Orleans, 1803–1812* (Washington, D.C.: United States Government Printing Office, 1940), 129–32.

new turn to France's beneficent intentions toward Louisiana: she has ceded it to the United States of America.

Thus you become, Louisianians, the cherished pledge of a friendship between these two Republics that can not fail to keep on getting stronger from day to day & that must contribute so strongly towards their common tranquillity and their common prosperity.

Article III of the Treaty will not escape you: "The inhabitants," it is said in that article, "of the ceded territories shall be incorporated into the union of the United States, & admitted, as soon as possible, according to the principles of the Federal Constitution, to the enjoyment of all the rights, advantages & immunities of Citizens of the United States; &, while waiting, they shall be maintained & protected in the enjoyment [of] their liberties and possessions & in the practice of the religions that they profess."

Thus, Louisianians, you are at one stroke invested with an acquired right to the prerogatives of a constitution & of a free government, erected by might, cemented by treaties, & tested by experience & years.

You are going to form part of a People already numerous & powerful, renowned also for its activity, its industry, its patriotism and its enlightenment, & which, in its rapid advance, promises to fill one of the most splendid places that a people has ever occupied on the face of the globe.

Its position is, at the same time, so fortunate, that neither its successes nor its splendor can for long detract from its felicity.

However benevolent and pure the wishes of a mother country may have been (you understand, do you not?), an immense distance is an impregnable rampart favoring oppression, exactions & abuses: frequently the very facility & certainty of covering them up will corrupt a man who first viewed them with the greatest hate & fear.

From this time on you cease to be exposed to that fatal and disheartening drawback.

By the nature of the government of the United States & the guaranties into the enjoyment of which you enter immediately, you will have, even under a provisional system, popular leaders, subject with impunity to your protests and your censure, & who will have permanent need of your esteem, your votes & your affections.

Public affairs & interests, far from being prohibited to you, will be your own affairs & interests, over which wise & impartial opinions will be sure to obtain preponderant influence in the long run, & to which even you could not remain indifferent without experiencing bitter repentance.

The time will soon come when you will give yourselves a special form of government which, while respecting the sacred maxims recorded in the constitution of the federal union, will be adapted to your manners, your usages, your climate, your soil, and your location.

But in particular you will not be long in experiencing the precious benefits of full, impartial and incorruptible justice, where uniform procedure, publicity, and the restrictions carefully placed on injustice in the application of the laws will contribute, with the high & national character of the judges & juries, toward effectively being responsible to the citizens for their safety and their property; for that is one of the attributes peculiarly characteristic of the government under which you are passing.

Its principles, its legislation, its conduct, its care, its vigilance, its encouragement, to the interests of agriculture & commerce, & the progress which they have made are well known to you, Louisianians, by the very share you have derived from them with so much profit during these last few years.

There is not & can not be a mother country without a more or less exclusive colonial monopoly: on the contrary, you have to expect from the United States only unbounded freedom of exportation, & import duties devised solely to suit your public needs or your domestic industry: through unlimited competition, you can buy cheaply, you will sell at high prices and will also receive the benefits of an immense market: the Nile of America, this Mississippi, which bathes, not deserts of burning sand, but the most extensive, the most fertile, the most fortunately situated plains in the New World, will shortly be seen to be covered, along the wharves of this other Alexandria, with thousands of vessels of all nations.

Among them your glances, Louisianians, will, I hope, always pick out with gratification the French flag, & the sight of it will not fail to rejoice your hearts: such is our firm hope; I profess it formally here in the name of my country & my Government.

Bonaparte, in stipulating by Article VII of the treaty that Frenchmen should be permitted for twelve years to trade on your shores under the same conditions as & without paying other charges than the citizens of the United States themselves, had as one of his principal aims that of giving opportunity and time for the old ties between the French people of Louisiana and the French people of Europe to be renewed, reenforced, perpetuated. A new correspondence of relations is going to be established between us, from one continent to the other, all the more satisfactory and lasting as it will be based purely on constant reciprocity of feelings, services & advantage. Your children, Louisianians, will be our children, & our children will become yours: you will see them perfecting their knowledge & their talents amongst us, & we shall see them amongst you increasing your powers, your labor, your industry, & wresting with you their tribute from a still unconquered Nature.

I am pleased, Louisianians, to contrast rather fully this picture with the touching reproaches of abandonment & the tender regrets which the ineffaceable attachment of a multitude among you to the country of their ancestors has made them breathe forth under these circumstances: France and her Government will listen to the recital of them with love & gratitude; but you will do them before long, from your own experience, this justice that they have distinguished themselves with respect to you by the most eminent & the most memorable of benefits.

The French Republic in this event, the first in modern times, traces the example of a colony which she herself voluntarily emancipates, the example of one of those colonies the image of which we discover with charm in the fine ages of antiquity: so in our days & in the future may a Louisianian and a Frenchman never meet, anywhere in the world, without feeling affected and giving each other the sweet name of brother; may that title alone be capable of representing from this time on the idea of their eternal attachments & their free dependence!

New Orleans, Frimaire 8, Year XII[3] of the French Republic & November 30, 1803.

Signed Laussat

By the Colonial Prefect, Commissioner of the French Government, Signed Daugerot. Secretary of the Commission

[3]**Frimaire 8, Year XII:** the designation for November 30, 1803, in the French Republican calendar.

28. Establishing a Government for Orleans Territory

THOMAS JEFFERSON AND WILLIAM C. C. CLAIBORNE
Correspondence
1804

Written on the same day, August 30, 1804, these letters between President Jefferson and Governor Claiborne illustrate their approach to establishing an American government in Orleans Territory. (Congress divided the ceded territory into the Orleans Territory and the District of Louisiana.) Aware that the people of Louisiana had had no experience with self-government under the Spanish or the French, both were convinced that Louisianians must make a gradual transition to republicanism under political appointees.

Jefferson was severely criticized by both Federalists and Republicans for denying self-government to Louisiana and for allowing the youthful Claiborne to retain the governorship. Yet Claiborne had considerable political experience, having served as a judge, a U.S. congressman from Tennessee, and governor of the Mississippi Territory. The highest-ranking American official in the area at the time of the cession,

The Territorial Papers of the United States, ed. Clarence Edwin Carter, vol. 9, *The Territory of New Orleans, 1803–1812* (Washington, D.C.: United States Government Printing Office, 1940), 281–84. (Some spelling and punctuation has been modernized.)

Claiborne was asked initially only to go to New Orleans to receive Louisiana from France. As he wrote this letter, his wife was dying from an illness that nearly killed him as well — an 1803 epidemic of yellow fever that many Creoles blamed on the American newcomers. The correspondence between Claiborne and the president not only illustrates the difficulties facing these American leaders but also reveals their attitudes toward the people of Louisiana.

President Jefferson to Governor Claiborne

August 30. 1804

Dear Sir   Various circumstances of delay have prevented my forwarding till now the general arrangements for the government of the territory of Orleans. Enclosed herewith you will receive the commissions. Among these is one for yourself as Governor. With respect to this I will enter into frank explanations. This office was originally destined for a person whose great services and established fame would have rendered him peculiarly acceptable to the nation at large. Circumstances however exist which do not now permit his nomination, & perhaps may not at any time hereafter. That therefore being suspended, and entirely contingent, your services have been so much approved as to leave no desire to look elsewhere to fill the office. Should the doubts which you have sometimes expressed, whether it would be eligible for you to continue, still exist in your mind, the acceptance of the commission gives you time to satisfy yourself by further experience, and to make the time and manner of withdrawing, should you ultimately determine on that, agreeable to yourself. Be assured that whether you continue or retire, it will be with every disposition on my part to be just & friendly to you.

James Brown of Kentucky is appointed Secretary for the territory. His distinguished understanding, his legal knowledge, & his possession of the languages, will, I trust, render him a useful aid. Dominic A. Hall, late a district judge of South Carolina, accepts the office of judge of the district of Orleans: as does Mahlone Dickerson of Pennsylvania, that of Attorney of the district. Commissions for Colonel Kirby of Connecticut & Mr. Prevost of New York as judges of the Superior court are also sent. The other commission for that bench cannot go at this time, because its acceptance is not known. The office of Marshal being one which could probably be discharged by a native Creole, I should like to avail ourselves of it to show my desire that they should have a fair participation of office in all cases where their education & line of life qualifies them. The character given me of a Mr. Clouet & a Mr. Guillot, had suggested one of them to my mind for the office: a Mr. Urquhart is represented as still more fit. Whether his long standing in the place would be equivalent to his being a native in the view of the inhabitants may be doubted. I leave to you therefore to select which of the three you think best.

In the legislative council I think it necessary to place a majority of Americans, say 7 Americans and 6 French, or persons of such long standing as to be considered as French; that there should be some mixture of the mercantile with the planting interest; and a representation of the different settlements in the country, justly proportioned, as far as they can furnish proper materials, to that of the city. On this account I was particularly anxious to get your information & recommendation, & wrote to you for it at a very early period. As soon as I had reason to fear that that letter had miscarried, I wrote a second, in time, I hoped, still to obtain your information. But it is not arrived, & I am obliged to proceed without it. Mr. Boré's protest,[1] against an act of the legislature, is such a proceeding as our law would deem more than disrespectful. Yet knowing that it is not so viewed by a Frenchman, considering his integrity, his agricultural merits, the interests he has at stake, & his zeal for liberty, I consider it proper to name him absolutely as a member, as I also do Mr. Poydras of Point Coupée, & Mr. Bellechasse, whom you recommended. I wish you also to select three others out of the 5 following names, to wit, Derbigné, Detrehan, Dubuys, Cantarelle of the Acadian coast, & Sauvé. Proceeding then to the Americans, I name Messieurs[2] Benjamin Morgan, Daniel Clarke, Dr. Watkins, Evan Jones, Roman (said to be of the Attacapas), and Wikoff (said to be of the Appelousas) absolutely, and propose George Pollock & Dr. Dow, out of whom you will select one to make the 7th and with the 6 preceding, to make up 13. In choosing these characters it has been an object of considerable attention to choose French who speak the American language, & Americans who speak the French. Yet I have not made the want of the two languages an absolute exclusion. But it should be earnestly recommended to all persons concerned in the business of the government, to acquire the other language, & generally to inculcate the advantage of every person's possessing both, and of regarding both equally as the language of the territory. Another object still more important is that every officer of the government make it his peculiar object to root out that abominable venality,[3] which is said to have been practised so generally there heretofore. Every connivance at it should be branded with indelible infamy, and would be regarded by the General government with distinguished severity. I have not filled up the blanks for the names in the commissions, because the Christian names are for the most part unknown to me, and the orthography of the French names not ascertained. . . . On the subject of the Marshal, I will add that if you know any person whom it would be more advantageous to appoint than either of the three whom I have named, you are free to make the substitution. Be pleased immediately after filling up the blanks to return to the Secretary of state's office a correct list of all the names, as the commissions are recorded in his office, where the blanks must be filled; and in order that I may be able correctly to renew the nominations to the Senate. I salute you with friendship & respect.

Th. Jefferson

---

[1]**Mr. Boré's protest:** Etienne Boré had been appointed mayor of New Orleans by Claiborne, but he resigned his post in protest, saying that the newly formed government denied Louisianians their rights. Boré also refused appointment to the Legislative Council.
[2]**Messieurs:** French equivalent of "Misters."
[3]**venality:** bribery and corrupton.

GOVERNOR CLAIBORNE TO PRESIDENT JEFFERSON

New-Orleans *August* 30th 1804

Dear Sir, During my late Illness, I had the pleasure to receive your esteem'd favours of the 7th, 12th, and 17th of July. But being then unable to write, I requested my private Secretary Mr. Briggs to inform you of their receipt, and to forward to you the names of several Gentlemen as suitable characters for the Legislative Council.—I regret exceedingly the miscarriage of your Letter to me of the 17th of April. Had I received that communication, I should have had more time to investigate Characters, & might have made a more general & perhaps better recommendation.—On the List however forwarded by Mr. Briggs (by my direction) will be found the names of our most respectable Citizens.—

Mr. Julien Poidrass of Point Coupee, is among the most influential Men in the Province; he possesses a large Estate & is a Man of good Information.—There was another Gentleman (Mr. Samuel Young) mentioned as residing at Point Coupee; he also is a man of fortune; But I do not think his Appointment would be pleasing; Mr. Young is much disliked in this City, & I have *lately* learned that he considers himself a Citizen of the Mississippi Territory, where he has a large Estate, & on which he now does, or will shortly reside.

Messieurs Morgan, Watkins, Kenner & Donelson of New-Orleans are Men of sense and property; — The first & second are decidedly attached to Republican principles; — of the sentiments of the latter, I am not so well advised; — But they are moderate, prudent Men: — The three last are said to be in a small degree interested in the Florida purchases, and indeed unless it be Mr. Benjamin Morgan, there *are few Americans of fortune* who resided in New Orleans previous to the Treaty, but were more or less engaged in that speculation.

Messieurs Pitot, Petit, and Duplessis are all wealthy Merchants & held in high estimation; Doctor Dow is also highly esteemed, and I believe deservedly so.—

Messieurs Bellechasse, Le Briton D'Orgenoi, & Mather are all Farmers, residing on the Coast between the City and Manshac'; The two first are Creoles of the Province, and amiable Men; the third is a Native of Scotland, & a man of great Information & Integrity of Character: His Affairs are said to be embarrassed;[1] But he has in possession a handsome estate. Mr. Mather, next to the British, is most partial to the American Government, and I believe he would execute with fidelity any Trust committed to him.

William Wikoff Junior opposite Batton Rouge, William Wykoff Senior, and Theophilus Collins of Opelousas are Native Americans,[2] Men of clear property, sense, and Integrity; — of their political sentiments I have no knowledge.

---

[1]**embarrassed:** in financial difficulties.
[2]**Native Americans:** born in the United States (Claiborne is not referring to American Indians).

The Territorial Papers of the United States, ed. Clarence Edwin Carter, vol. 9, *The Territory of New Orleans, 1803–1812* (Washington, D.C.: United States Government Printing Office, 1940), 284–89. (Some spelling and punctuation has been modernized.)

Monsieur Loviell, Dubuche, Fontenet, and Durall of Attackapus, I have no personal acquaintance with; But fame represents them all, as Men of Sense, fortune, and probity.—

Doctor Sibley of Nachitoches, is a Man of Science and a true Republican; I have understood that previous to his leaving the United States his Affairs were much embarrassed; — But during his residence at Nachitoches, he is said to have acquired some valuable landed property.—

I have heard Mr. Benjamin Morgan express his disapprobation of the Slave Trade, But the sentiment here is so general in favor of that Inhuman Traffic, that I am enclined to think most of the other Gentlemen above named are advocates for it; at least for a few years.—

The confidence with which you honor me by the Blank Commissions you transmit for a Revenue Officer at the Bayou St. John, I feel as a flattering compliment; and shall endeavour as soon as possible to name such Person for those Offices as your Letter contemplates, and the situation of Revenue affairs in that quarter requires. . . .

. . . It has been my misfortune, ever since I have had the honor to represent the General Government in the Western Country, to have found the weight of at least professional Talents on the federal side.—When I arrived in the Mississippi Territory, it was impossible to fill the Offices under the Government, with Justice to the Country, without borrowing assistance from a Sect whom I had no satisfaction in employing, and who conscious of the necessity that gave them consequence, affected to despise the favours they enjoyed; My situation in that respect, was afterwards somewhat bettered.—But now again at the commencement of this Government, I look around in vain for Men capable of holding offices with Credit to themselves and the State, and in the purity of whose political sentiments I can place entire reliance. Among the Lawyers (amounting to near thirty) there are but three whom I knew to be Republicans.—One was Mr. Lewis Kerr (from the State of Ohio, & lately of Natchez) and I appointed him Sheriff of the City; conceiving that in the incipiency of the operation of American Law, that important office should be filled by one who personally enjoyed my confidence, & was himself possessed of legal Information; — the second was Mr. Edward Nichols (late of Maryland) whom I appointed Clerk of my Court, and with this appointment, I am not as satisfied as I could wish; — and the third was Mr. Henry Brown (late of the City of Washington) and him I have made a Notary Public, which in this City is a lucrative office.—

As federal Influence declines in the States, the remote Territories will naturally become Asylums for that Party; and particularly for those young Men whose politicks expose them to embarrassment at Home; they will either calculate on strengthening their Party in a more promising quarter, or indulge a prudent hope of political oblivion.—

There can be no doubt, but this City is much exposed to the Yellow Fever; — this Disease is now raging, and altho' the Physicians pronounce it not contagious, yet seven or eight die of a Day, and new cases are hour'ly occuring.—My late Indisposition, was a violent attack of the yellow Fever, and I am represented as the only American who has yet recovered.—I should most certainly remove my family in the Country, if Mrs. Claiborne's situation would permit; but she continues dangerously ill; her Fever has been constant for three Weeks, & her consequent Debility is very great, but the Physicians still entertain *hopes* of her recovery, *which* I pray God may be realised. . . .

From every thing I can learn, the Indians on the West side of the River are well disposed to the United States; — A Chief and some Warriors of the Caddoe' nation, lately visited our Commandant at Nachitoches; and were at first displeased to find that they received no presents, as was usual under the Spanish Government; — But upon the Commandants informing them that the United States would probably establish a Trading House for the purpose of supplying their wants on moderate Terms, and protecting them against the impositions of private Traders, it is reported to me, they expressed much satisfaction; and after having received their Rations retired from the Post well pleased. . . .

Under the former Government, of this Province, Smuggling was carried on to a great extent, and the facility with which the Revenue Officers could be bribed was no less disgraceful than notorious. That like fraudulent attempts will often be made under our Government, I consider as highly probable; — But I persuade myself that the vigilance and inflexible Integrity of our Officers will in a year or two put down this species of Corruption.—There is however, one great evil existing in this Province, a remedy for which I fear cannot easily be devised. It is the little regard which is paid to Oaths, particularly among the lower class of Citizens; — The moral Obligation seems to have but little Influence, which may perhaps in some degree be attributed to their Religion, for I believe it is understood among the ignorant, that a confession to the Priest wipes away all Sin. . . .

I have recently read my Letter of the 2d of January, and my residence here, has tended to confirm me in the sentiments there delivered.—The fact is, that the people of Louisiana, are not prepared for a Representative Government, and the experiment would be hazardous; But perhaps policy might justify the Introduction of the second Grade of Territorial Government.—In New-Orleans and its vicinity, the Society may be considered as tolerably well informed; But in the other parts of the Province, the great Bulk of the Inhabitants are in a State of wretched Ignorance, and very much under the Influence of their Priests.—

As soon as my state of health will permit, I will examine the Land adjoining the Canal of Carondulet, and will give you an accurate account of its situation, relative value et cetera.—I should feel happy in promoting the Interest of General La Fayette, and I do really think his residence in Louisiana would be a great public Benefit.

The family of my departed friend Mr. Trist, have not yet recovered of their distress, and the Indisposition of Mr. Henry Brown, who is now confined to his Bed, increases their uneasiness; His Physicians however, I learn, do not consider him dangerous.—

I pray you to excuse this incorrect Scrawl; — My late Disease has left me in a state of great feebleness both of mind & Body — so much so, that I fear my Health will not be entirely restored for some time.

Will you accept my best wishes for a Continuance of your health & happiness, and believe me to be — With the greatest respect! Your faithful friend.

William C. C. Claiborne

Thomas Jefferson, President of the United States.
[*Endorsed*] Claiborne Govr N. O. Aug. 30. 04. recd Oct. 9.

29. Fears for the Church in a Secular Republic

THE URSULINES OF NEW ORLEANS AND THOMAS JEFFERSON
Correspondence
1804

The Ursuline order of nuns came to New Orleans from France in 1727. Their long tenure of service included operating a hospital, maintaining an orphanage, and educating poor and enslaved women as well as more affluent women and girls. As a result, by the late 1700s, the women of New Orleans had a literacy rate of 72 percent compared to a rate of 40 percent for women and 80 percent for men in the American colonies. The news that Spain intended to turn Louisiana over to France rocked the well-established convent. Well aware that the revolutionary regime had confiscated the property of monasteries and guillotined nuns unwilling to return to secular life in France, nearly half of the Ursulines fled to Cuba. Suddenly faced with the uncertainties of American control, Sister Marie Therese Farjon of St. Xavier sought the assurances of President Jefferson himself. Jefferson's reply reflects the new republican ideals concerning women and their role as educators of future citizens in a republic.

The Ursulines of New Orleans to Thomas Jefferson

To Thomas Jefferson
President of the United States of America

Dear Sir:

The Ursuline Religious of New Orleans, encouraged by the honorable mention which you so kindly made of their order, take the liberty of having recourse to you in regard to some business which is of great concern to their Institute.

Although no express mention has been made of it, they think that the Treaty of Cession, and still more the spirit of justice which characterizes the United States of America, will certainly guarantee to those seeking your help the continued enjoyment of their present property. But, keeping in mind that this same property is a sacred trust which has been confided to them, they believe that they would certainly fail in one of their principal obligations were they to neglect to see to it that this right to their property be put officially in writing, confirming their rights to this property not only for themselves but also for those of their Sisters who will succeed them; and, for this reason, to beg you, dear Sir, to present our petition to the Congress in the manner and form which you will judge the most suitable.

This request of the Ursulines of New Orleans is not dictated by personal interest nor ambitious aims. Separated from the world and its pomps and vanities, and, in a word, from all that is called its advantages, they have scarcely any ambition for earthly goods; but, bound by a solemn vow to use their time in the formation of youth, they cannot help but be anxious to know if they will be able with certainty to count on the continued enjoyment of their revenues which will enable them to fulfill their obligations. It is, then, less their own interests which they plead than it is that of the public good. In reality, it is the cause of the orphan and the abandoned child, of unfortunates brought up in the midst of the horrors of vice and infamy who come to be reared by us in the ways of Religion and virtue, and be given a formation which will enable them one day to become happy and useful citizens. Finally, it is in the interest of this country which can but reap for itself honor and glory in encouraging and protecting an establishment as useful, and, we might even say, as necessary as ours. Dear Sir, we who seek your help dare to believe that these considerations will make an impression on you. Even more, we dare to count in advance on your protection.

We end by begging Heaven most fervently for your personal prosperity and for the happiness of the country whose great interests have been confided to you.

The Archives of the Ursuline Convent of New Orleans, La. Courtesy of archivist Sr. Joan Marie Aycock, O.S.U. [Special thanks to Emily Clark for bringing this correspondence to our attention and securing permission for its use. —Editors' note.]

With the most profound respect, "Monsieur le President," we have the honor of being

> Your very humble and very obedient servants
> The Ursulines of New Orleans
> Sr. Marie Therese Farjon of St. Xavier
> Superior

March 21, 1804

THOMAS JEFFERSON TO THE URSULINES OF NEW ORLEANS

Washington May the 15, 1804

To the Soeur Therese de St. Xavier Farjon Superior, and the Nuns of the order of St. Ursula at New Orleans.

I have received, holy sisters, the letter you have written me wherein you express anxiety for the property vested in your institution by the former governments of Louisiana. The principles of the constitution and government of the United States are a sure guarantee to you that it will be preserved to you sacred and inviolate, and that your institution will be permitted to govern itself according to its own voluntary rules, without interference from the civil authority. Whatever diversity of shade may appear in the religious opinions of our fellow citizens, the charitable objects of your institution cannot be indifferent to any; and its furtherance of the wholesome purposes of society, by training up its younger members in the way they should go, cannot fail to ensure it the patronage of the government it is under. Be assured it will meet all the protection which my office can give it.

I salute you, holy sisters, with friendship and respect.

> Thomas Jefferson

30. Creoles Demand the Civil Law

LEGISLATIVE COUNCIL OF THE TERRITORY OF ORLEANS
Resolution
1806

After Louisiana was turned over to France and then to America, the city's native-born population remained fiercely committed to the civil law. After winning political control of the territory in the elections of 1805, the Creoles were determined to reestablish their own civil law — enhanced by the Anglo-American provisions of habeas corpus *and trial by jury, which they admired — as the basis of law in the territory. The Legislative Council explained its passionate defense of the civil law in this resolution, which was published in the New Orleans newspaper* Le Telegraphe. *Instead of disbanding (as they threatened in this document), the council appointed a committee that produced the famous* Digest of the Civil Laws Now in Force in the Territory of New Orleans. *It was accepted by the legislature and the governor in 1808.*

May 28, 1806

"Whereas the most essential and salutary measures taken by this Legislature have been successively rejected by the Governor of the Territory, and whereas this Legislature, whose members had accepted their office only in the hope of being useful to their fellow-citizens, must be convinced today that it can do nothing except cause them considerable expense;

"*Resolved*, that the General Assembly be immediately dissolved."

The Legislative Council believes that it owes to its fellow-citizens a statement of the motives which have determined it to propose the resolution copied above, and which have caused it to consider the act which confirmed it, and to which the Governor has refused his sanction, as that on which the happiness and future tranquillity of this country depended most essentially. It is for the public to judge whether these motives were pure and free from any kind of private passion.

The most inestimable benefit for a people is the preservation of its laws, usages, and habits. It is only such preservation that can soften the sudden transition from one government to another and it is by having consideration for that natural attachment that even the heaviest yoke becomes endurable. The Congress of the

Le Telegraphe (New Orleans), 3 June 1806. Reprinted in *The Territorial Papers of the United States*, ed. Clarence Edwin Carter, vol. 9, *The Territory of New Orleans, 1803–1812* (Washington, D.C.: United States Government Printing Office, 1940), 650–57.

United States apparently wished to reflect these sacred principles and render its domination still easier for the inhabitants of the Territory of Orleans by preserving to them their former laws: such at least is the natural and reasonable sense of Article 4 of the act of March 2, 1805, which provides further for the government of the Territory of Orleans, and which is expressed in these terms: "The laws which shall be in force in the said Territory at the commencement of this act, and not inconsistant with the provisions thereof, shall continue in force, until altered, modified or repealed by the Legislature."

Now, what are the laws which Congress intended to preserve to us by this provision? What are the laws which must be subject to review and rectification by the Legislatures of this Territory? The question is not a doubtful one. It is evident that they are the old laws which were in use in this country before its cession to the United States of America. For Congress took care to apply to us all of the common law which it considered indispensable to prescribe for us to the end that our régime might not conflict with that which is in force in all the States of the Union, that is to say, the right to be judged by one's peers and the *writ of habeas corpus*,[1] the two great *palladiums*[2] of civil liberty. In this regard we cannot change anything of what Congress has thus, constitutionally, determined; but it is clear that regarding all the rest we are free to adopt or to reject any of the common law which shall appear proper to us.

Now, since we have the power to keep our old laws in so far as they do not conflict with the Constitution of the United States and the special acts passed for our provisional government, no one can deny the advantage to us of remaining under a system to which we are accustomed and which has nothing contrary to the affection which we owe to our Government. For it is necessary to distinguish, among the laws which govern a state, those which depend on its constitution and its government from those which only regulate contracts and agreements between private persons. The former must necessarily be common to all parts of the Republic, but the latter may differ without disadvantages. Thus the Constitution of the United States and the other Federal laws being general for the whole Union, it would be absurd to claim that this Territory ought not to be subject to them: but as to the laws regarding contracts, wills, and successions, what difference does it make that here such acts should be governed by the civil law while in the other States of the Union they are governed by the common law? How is it that the multiplicity of customs which is noticed in England is not prejudicial to the general harmony? Do those differences in local law prevent an Englishman from being just as good a citizen and just as loyal to the Constitution of his country? On the contrary, and it would be exposing his affection to the danger of being alienated and exciting disorder and general discontent to disturb those customs to which each province is attached by the bonds of experience and long habit.

---

[1] *habeas corpus:* literally, "you should have the body"; a writ of *habeas corpus* is an order to present a party before a court or a judge. The right to obtain a writ of *habeas corpus* is a citizen's basic protection against illegal imprisonment.
[2] *palladiums:* safeguards.

In the United States itself there is no general civil code: the common law of England is not adopted here as an article of the Constitution — Ever since the original establishment of the New England colonies that common law has been received, in each province, only with modifications and alterations, which bring it about that the common law of Virginia is no more like that in use in South Carolina than the latter is like the common law adopted in the State of New York. At the time of the general confederation and after the war of the American Revolution, Congress had the wisdom not to do violence to those differences by laying down a general and uniform common law for all the States of the Union, and it left to each State the right to preserve or to modify that which it had seen fit to adopt of the common law and even to replace it with other laws according as it might judge to be most suitable to its special situation.

There is no doubt that it is as a consequence of this prudent and judicious policy that Congress desired to grant to this Territory the privilege of keeping its old laws or of changing or modifying them according as its legislatures might find it necessary. Now, every one knows that those old laws are nothing but the civil or Roman law modified by the laws of the government under which this region existed before the latter's cession to the United States. If the title of the books in which those laws are contained is unknown, if those titles appear barbarous or ridiculous, those very circumstances are the most to their credit because they prove, by the ignorance of those who have obeyed them until now without knowing that they were doing so, how great is their mildness and their wisdom and how small is the number of disadvantages resulting from their execution. In any case it is no less true that the Roman law which formed the basis of the civil and political laws of all the civilized nations of Europe presents an ensemble of greatness and prudence which is above all criticism. What purity there is in those decisions based on natural equity; what clearness there is in the wording which is the work of the greatest jurists, encouraged by the wisest emperors; what simplicity there is in the form of those contracts and what sure and quick means there are for obtaining the remedies prescribed by the law, for the reparation of all kinds of civil wrongs.

We certainly do not attempt to draw any parallel between the civil law and the common law; but, in short, the wisdom of the civil law is recognized by all Europe; and this law is the one which nineteen-twentieths of the population of Louisiana know and are accustomed to from childhood, of which law they would not see themselves deprived without falling into despair. If the inhabitants of this Territory had never known any laws, if they had lived down to the present time without making agreements or contracts, it would perhaps be a matter of indifference to them whether to adopt one system or another system, and it is even probable that their attachment to their new mother country would cause them to prefer that system which would bring them nearest to their new fellow-citizens. But it is a question here of overthrowing received and generally known usages and the uncertainty with which they would be replaced would be as unjust as disheartening. Every one knows today and from a long experience how successions are transferred, what is the power of parents over their children and the amount of property of which they can dispose to their prejudice, what are the rights which result from marriages effected with or without contract, the manner in which one can dispose by will, the manner of selling, of exchanging or alienating one's properties with sureness and the remedies which the law accords in the case of default of payment. Each of the inhabitants dispersed over the vast expanse of this Territory, however little educated he may be, has a tincture of this general and familiar jurisprudence, necessary to the conduct of the smallest affairs, which assures the tranquility of families; he has sucked this knowledge at his mother's breast, he has received it by the tradition of his forefathers and he has perfected it by the experience of a long and laborious life. Overthrow this system all at once. Substitute new laws for the old laws; what a tremendous upset you cause! What becomes of the experience of an old man and what becomes of the facility and sureness of transfers? Who will dare to sign a contract under a new régime the effects of which will not be known to him? What will be the lot of the inhabitant who is so unfortunate as not to have received sufficient education to learn these new laws at least by reading them, even supposing that his understanding of them is facilitated by transmitting the new laws to him in his own language? Will he not shudder every time that he wishes to dispose of his properties? Will he not then be afraid lest he be throwing himself into a bottomless pit without outlet and of bringing about his total ruin? Or must he always have recourse to the knowledge of a jurist regarding the most ordinary transactions of civil law? . . .

Those are the real reasons which attach us to our old legislation and not any other and political reasons which may falsely be attributed to the good inhabitants of Louisiana; and those are the reasons which could not but lead this Legislature to see to it that so precious a deposit should not be touched by an imprudent hand. . . .

. . . Other members have been heard to claim that by keeping the civil law we are adopting everything that is most revolting and contrary to the Republican régime, when the provision of the act of Congress cited in the declaratory act, as forming the basis thereof, states that nothing is retained of that law except what will not be contrary to the Constitution of the United States, which expressly proscribes anything which may be contrary to the form of a free and republican government.

When such great uncertainty and such mistakes have appeared among those very persons whose opinion ought to serve as a torch for the people, we have been all the more justified in congratulating ourselves for having proposed a law capable of dissipating all doubts and of reassuring all classes of citizens. The majority of the Chamber of Representatives has had the same opinion as ourselves, as was shown in approving the declaratory act; nothing more was lacking to the act than the approval of the Governor in order to give the act the force of law, but such approval was refused! . . .

Under these circumstances, the Legislative Council, being strongly persuaded that it could not by any means hope to do good and that its present condition was only an expense for its fellow-citizens since the measures which were of the greatest importance for the happiness of the Territory were thus rejected, has in a unanimous and spontaneous movement resolved that the Legislature should be immediately dissolved. For it must not be thought that it is only the refusal to sanction the declaratory law, however salutary it appeared to the Legislative Council, which caused the Council to decide thus to bring its functions to a stop; it is because it has seen rejected, one after the other, other measures of no less importance. . . .

[List of laws given.]

Finally an act *declaratory of the laws which continue to be in force in the Territory* was proposed as a measure to preserve our present laws in so far as the latter are not contrary to the Constitution of the United States. The Legislature attached great importance to this bill for the purpose of clarifying our present judicial system and doing away with its uncertainty, until it should have time to draw up a civil code. The Legislature considered this provision as a safeguard against dangerous innovations, and a measure necessary to the tranquillity of the citizens. This bill also has been rejected and we have returned to confusion.

Under this state of things, the Legislative Council had to consider it wise to think of putting an end to an expensive and useless session. Without doubt the executive holds his absolute *veto* from the special Constitution applied to this Territory, but if by means of that *veto* his will and nothing but his will is to constitute the supreme rule, if he is to reign alone, and openly, the Legislature ought not to be willing to serve as a plaything to amuse people. What difference does it make to the Territory that the executive should sanction laws regarding the Protestant Church, regarding hired persons and apprentices, and regarding drinking places if he stops by his *veto* the execution of a single law favorable to the happiness of the Territory? Was it necessary to cause the expenditure of twenty or thirty thousand dollars in the Territory for the purpose of presenting to it the spectacle of a scandalous struggle in which the minority finds means to mock the desires of the majority, in which struggle it has as its last resort the *veto* of the executive for the purpose of proscribing whatever it has not approved? . . .

We do not know the sentiments which reading this will cause to be felt in the hearts of our fellow-citizens, but being strong in the witness of our conscience we are persuaded that if they do not approve entirely of the warmth which has dictated our conduct, our motives at least will preserve their esteem for us. We are, finally, persuaded that in spite of the odious views which some ill-disposed persons have seen fit to attribute to us, the general and local government, and even our antagonists, cannot but do us justice.

New Orleans, *May* 28, 1806, and the thirtieth year of the independence of the United States.

31. Changes in New Orleans Society

BENJAMIN LATROBE
Entries from His Diary
1819

Benjamin Henry Boneval Latrobe, one of America's most distinguished architects of the early national period, sailed from Baltimore to New Orleans in 1818. The journals he kept during his voyage and residence there provide a fascinating glimpse of the social and cultural life of this exciting and rapidly changing city.

Latrobe, born in England to American parents, was educated in Germany and in England. He came to the United States in 1796. Thomas Jefferson appointed Latrobe "Surveyor of the Public Buildings of the United States" in 1803 and charged him with completing the Capitol. Latrobe and his son Henry, also an architect, designed many of the buildings constructed in New Orleans in the early nineteenth century, as well as the monuments of the first two wives of Governor Claiborne. Both father and son died in New Orleans of yellow fever. Benjamin Latrobe's diaries cover nearly every aspect of life in New Orleans — religion, Afro-Creole culture, cemeteries, crawfish, and, of course, American-Creole relations.

The State of Society in New Orleans

New Orleans, January 22d, 1819.   What is the state of society in New Orleans? is one of many questions which I am required to answer by a friend who seems not to be aware that this question is equivalent to that of Hamlet to Polonius. He might as well ask, What is the shape of a cloud? The state of society at any time *here* is puzzling. There are in fact three societies here: 1. the French, 2. the American, & 3. the mixed. The French society is not exactly what it was at the change of government, & the American is not strictly what it is in the Atlantic cities. The opportunities of growing rich by more active, extensive, & intelligent modes of agriculture & commerce has diminished the hospitality, destroyed the leisure, & added more selfishness to the character of the Creoles. The Americans, coming hither to make money, & considering their residence as temporary, are doubly active in availing themselves of the enlarged opportunities of becoming wealthy which the place offers. On the whole, the state of society is similar to that of every city rapidly rising into wealth, & doing so much & such fast-increasing business that no man can be said to have a moment's leisure. Their business is to make money. They are in an eternal bustle. Their limbs, their heads, & their

Benjamin Henry Boneval Latrobe, *Impressions Respecting New Orleans: Diary and Sketches, 1818–1820,* ed. Samuel Wilson Jr. (New York: Columbia University Press, 1951), 32–36, 58–62, 82–84. (Some spelling and punctuation has been modernized.)

hearts move to that sole object. Cotton & tobacco, buying & selling, and all the rest of the occupation of a money-making community fills their time, & gives the habit of their minds. The post, which comes in & goes out three times a week, renders those days, more than the others, days of oppressive exertion. I have been received with great hospitality, have dined out almost every day, but the time of a late dinner and a short sitting after it have been the only periods during which I could make any acquaintance with the Gentlemen of the place. As it is now the Carnival, every evening is closed with a ball, or a play, or a concert. I have been to two of each. . . .

January 25th, 1819.   The French population in Louisiana is said to be only 20,000; in the city not above 5 or 6,000. The increase is of Americans. Some French have come hither since the return of the Bourbons; but they did not find themselves at home; some joined General Lallemand in his settlement on Trinity river, & a few remained so as sensibly to increase the French population. The accession, if worth mentioning, did not exceed the emigration which has taken place of those who did not like the American Government, or had amassed fortunes, & have returned to France or settled in the West India Islands. Since the breaking up of Lallemand's colony, a few have returned to New Orleans, but so few that they are not a perceptible quantity, even in the comparatively small French community.

On the other hand, Americans are pouring in daily, not in families, but in large bodies. In a few years therefore, this will be an American town. What is good & bad in the French manners, & opinions must give way, & the American notions of right & wrong, of convenience & inconvenience will take their place.

When this period arrives, it would be folly to say that things are better or worse than they now are. They will be changed, but they will be changed into that which is more agreeable to the new population than what now exists. But a man who fancies that he has seen the world on more sides than one cannot help wishing that a *mean*, an *average* character, of society may grow out of the intermixture of the French & American manners. . . .

At present, the most prominent, & to the Americans, the most offensive feature of French habits, is the manner in which they spend Sunday. . . .

Sunday in New Orleans is distinguished only, 1., by the flags that are hoisted on all the ships, 2., by the attendance at Church (the Cathedral) of all the beautiful girls in the place, & of 2 or 300 quateroons, negroes, and mulattoes, & perhaps of 100 white males to hear high Mass, during which the two bells of the Cathedral are jingling, 3., by the shutting up of the majority of the shops & warehouses kept by the Americans, & 4., by the firing of the guns of most of the young gentlemen in the neighboring swamps, to whom Sunday affords leisure for field sports. 5. The Presbyterian, Episcopal, & Methodist churches are also open on that day, & are attended by a large majority of the ladies of their respective congregations.

In other respects no difference between Sunday & any other day exists. The shops are open, as well as the theater & the ball room, & in the city at least, *"Sunday shines no holiday"* to slaves & hirelings.

In how far the intermarriage of Americans with French girls will produce a less rigid observance of the gloom of an English Sunday it is impossible to foresee. . . .

Change of Character Which Is Gradually Taking Place in New Orleans in Manners and Religious Ceremonies

Feb'y 26th, 1819.   The change which is gradually taking place in the character of this city is not very rapid compared with the march of society on the continent generally. But to the old inhabitants it must appear extraordinary enough. Much of what was daily practice has entirely disappeared never to return: for instance, the military parade of the Intendant, and all the ceremony that belonged to the Government of a city in which the people were only an appendage to the Magistracy. The Governor of the State is certainly the head of a much more important & powerful community than the Spanish authority ever reigned over. But the difference of respect with which the former is treated compared with the submission shown to the latter whenever he appeared, is in an inverse ratio entirely. I observed a remarkable instance of the democratic character of the citizens at the magnificent ball given at Davis's, on Washington's birthday. There were about 300 Gentlemen present, & probably 400 Ladies. When supper was ready, . . . the Governor Villeré, the Chief Judge U.S. Circuit Court, *Hall*, a General Officer whom I do not know, Commodore Patterson, & the Mayor of Orleans were shown to the head of the table by the managers. But all the places were occupied by young men, not one of whom would give way. I happened to be amongst them & immediately rose, offering my place to the Governor & giving a hint to my neighbors. They looked round, but not a man of them followed my example, & as I vacated only one place & did not sit down again, it was soon filled by somebody else.

The Catholic religion formerly was the only one permitted, and was carried on with all the pomp and ceremony of a Spanish establishment. The host was carried to the sick in great parade, & all those whom it encountered knelt devoutly till it had passed. All that is now over; & I understand that the procession of the host through the streets has not been seen here for several years. . . .

Although the procession of the host no longer parades the streets, the parade of funerals is still a thing which is peculiar to New Orleans alone among all the American cities. I have twice met, accidentally, a funeral. They were both of colored people, for the coffin was carried by men of that race, & none but negroes & quateroons followed it. First marched a man in a military uniform with a drawn sword. Then came three boys in surplusses,[1] with pointed caps, two carrying staves with candelabras in the form of urns on the top, & the third in the center a large silver Cross. At some distance behind came Father Anthony & another priest, who seemed very merry at the ceremony of yesterday & were engaged in loud & cheerful conversation. At some distance further came the coffin. It was carried by

---

[1]**surplusses:** surplices.

four well dressed black men, & to it were attached 6 white ribbands about 2 yards in length, the ends of which were held by 6 colored girls very well dressed in white, with long veils. A crowd of colored people followed confusedly, filling the street across, many of whom carried candles lighted. I stood upon a step till the whole had passed & counted 69 candles.

About a month ago I attended high Mass at the Cathedral. All the usual motions were made, I think, in greater profusion, indeed, than ordinary, & the common service performed in the common way. But what was unusual was the procession of the host round the Church; the *Mostranza* (literally the showbox, Latin pix, from which the exclamation *please the pigs* [pix] is derived) was a very fine affair indeed, and an embroidered Canopy was carried over it upon 6 silver staves, held by 6 very respectable looking men. . . .

The congregation consisted of at least 4/5th women, of which number one half at least were colored. For many years I have not seen candles offered at the Altars, but at each of the side Altars there were half a dozen candles stuck upon the steps by old colored women, who seemed exceedingly devout.

At Baltimore, the metropolis of American Catholicism, the stage of the Mass performing within the church is no longer announced to those who do not attend there. But here the pious Catholic confined to his bed at home can follow the congregation in the church through the whole exhibition. The bell is kept at work, as a Signal, & when the host is elevated, it rings a peal that is heard all over the city. . . .

Cemeteries

New Orleans, March 8th 1819. I walked today to the burial grounds on the Northwest side of the town. There is an enclosure — for the Catholic Church — of about 300 feet square; & immediately adjoining is the burial place of the Protestants, of about equal dimensions. The Catholic tombs are of a very different character from those of our Eastern & Northern cities. They are of bricks, much larger than necessary to enclose a single coffin, & plaistered over, so as to have a very solid & permanent appearance. . . .

The Protestant burying ground has tombs of much the same construction, but a little varied in character, and they are all ranged parallel to the sides of the enclosure. The monument of the wife, child, & brother-in-law of Governor Claiborne is the most conspicuous, & has a panel enriched with very good sculpture. A female lies on a bed with her child lying across her body, both apparently just departed. A winged figure, pointing upward, holds over her head the crown of immortality. At the foot of the bed kneels the husband in an attitude of extreme grief. . . .

There were two or three graves opened & expecting their tenants: 8 or 9 inches below the surface they were filled with water, & were not three feet deep. Thus, all persons are here buried in the water. The surface of the burying ground must now be 7 or 8 feet below the level of the Mississippi, which has still 5 or 6 feet to rise before it attains its usual highest level. The ground was everywhere perforated by the crawfish — the amphibious lobster (écrevisse). I have, indeed, seen them in their usual attitude of defiance in the gutters of the streets. The French are fond of them, & make excellent and *handsome* soup[2] of them, their scarlet shells being filled with forced meat & served up in the tureen. But the Americans, with true English Antigallican prejudice, disdain this species of the Cancer, although we delight in crabs & lobsters, the food of which we all know to be in the last degree disgusting. They pretend that the sellers of this fish collect them principally in the Church Yards, which is not, I believe, true — and in fact impossible, considering the quantity that are sold.

We are all slaves, nationally & individually, of habit. Our minds & our bodies are equally fashioned by education, and although the original dispositions of individuals give specific variety to character, the general sentiment, like the general manners, modes of living & cooking, of sitting & standing & walking can only be slowly changed, by the gradual substitution of a new habit for the old. . . .

[2]**soup:** crawfish bisque, still a popular Creole dish.

Suggestions for Further Reading

Bell, Caryn Cossé. *Revolution, Romanticism, and the Afro-Creole Protest Tradition in Louisiana, 1718–1868.* Baton Rouge: Louisiana State University Press, 1997.

Brasseaux, Carl A. *Acadian to Cajun: Transformation of a People, 1803–1877.* Jackson: University Press of Mississippi, 1992.

Clark, Emily. "A New World Community: The New Orleans Ursulines and Colonial Society, 1727–1803." Ph.D. Dissertation, Tulane University, 1998.

Dargo, George. *Jefferson's Louisiana: Politics and the Clash of Legal Traditions.* Cambridge: Harvard University Press, 1975.

Hirsch, Arnold R., and Joseph Logsdon, eds. *Creole New Orleans: Race and Americanization.* Baton Rouge: Louisiana State University Press, 1992. See especially Joseph G. Tregle Jr., "Creoles and Americans," pp. 131–85.

Peterson, Merrill D. *Thomas Jefferson and the New Nation: A Biography.* New York: Oxford University Press, 1970.

Schafer, Judith Kelleher. *Slavery, the Civil Law, and the Supreme Court of Louisiana.* Baton Rouge: Louisiana State University Press, 1994.

CHAPTER NINE

THE AGE OF JACKSON

The Removal of the Cherokees

The presidency of Andrew Jackson (from 1828 to 1836) was, for white men, an era of great opportunity, increased political power, and economic expansion. Jackson was wildly popular among white Southerners as an advocate for "the common man." But for the Indians of the South — the Creek, Chickasaw, Choctaw, Seminole, and Cherokee tribes — Jackson's presidency was a disaster. Under federal policy adopted during his administration, they were forcibly removed to land in present-day Oklahoma. Many perished in the process — including one-fourth of the Cherokees, who died on what became known as the "Trail of Tears."

The Cherokees' fight against removal is a dramatic saga that began with the Revolution. Viewing the Americans who encroached upon their land as enemies, the Cherokees allied themselves with the British and attacked frontier settlements in Georgia, South Carolina, North Carolina, and Virginia. In response, these colonies joined forces and crushed the Cherokees, causing them to suffer many casualties and lose thousands of miles of territory. And international law dictated that the Indians had lost still more: by right of conquest, the United States gained sovereignty over all the land and people that had been claimed by the British — including Indian territory.

Nevertheless, George Washington and his secretary of war, Henry Knox, developed a clear policy of treating the tribes as independent sovereign nations with the right to self-government within their borders. When North Carolina and Georgia claimed large tracts of Cherokee territory under the "conquered nations" concept in the 1780s, Congress tried to settle matters by treaty, hoping that restraining the states would prevent warfare and also protect the Indians from extinction.

Washington and Knox were also convinced that to survive, Indians must become "civilized" by fully adopting American ways of working, dressing, speaking, and worshiping. They negotiated a new treaty with the Cherokees in which the government paid for land already seized by white settlers, banned further incursions, and stated that the U.S. government would "furnish gratuitously . . . useful implements of husbandry" in order that the Cherokees would "be led to a greater degree of civilization" as "herdsmen and cultivators" rather than remain hunters. In addition, they accepted the aid of missionaries eager to convert the Cherokees to American culture as well as to Christianity.

Between the 1790s and 1830s the Cherokees made drastic changes in their economy and culture. Mixed-race Cherokees seemed the most eager to assimilate, but full-blooded Cherokees who recognized that the old way of life based on hunting and subsistence farming was dying out were also eager for their children to participate in the mission schools' "civilization" programs. A new Cherokee elite even adopted Anglo-American ways to the point of establishing cotton plantations worked by slaves and indulging in all of the amenities of Anglo-American domestic life.

One emblem of assimilated Cherokee civilization was the adoption of written laws and a republican form of government. Their 1827 constitution established a bicameral legislature, a judicial system, and an executive branch soon headed by Chief John Ross. The Cherokee nation chose New Echota as its capital, created a written Cherokee language, and established a newspaper, the *Cherokee Phoenix*, edited by John Ridge's cousin Elias Boudinot and printed in English and Cherokee. The Cherokee government, however, was intent on strengthening tribal power against those who would seize its land. In 1829 the Cherokee council adopted a law making it a capital offense to sell land without the council's approval. Thus the establishment of an Americanized Cherokee government served to increase rather than diminish the hostility of the white Southerners who were increasingly intent on acquiring valuable Indian lands.

Developments in the 1820s and 1830s, including population growth and an agricultural boom, heightened pressure on politicians to remove the Cherokees. Many of those clamoring for Indian land also held racial views that questioned Indian potential for civilization and insisted that government policies based on the ideal of assimilation only encouraged false hopes and interfered with the adoption of more "realistic" plans. Leaders in Georgia, whose boundaries included most of the Cherokee territory, were particularly eager for a change in federal policy.

Soon after Jackson's election, impatient Georgia officials claimed the right to govern all lands within its borders. The new president refused to intervene. Although the Constitution explicitly assigned authority for negotiations with the Indians to the federal government rather than the states, Jackson declared that he had no power to protect Indians from the actions of state governments and that Indian interests were best served by relocation in the West, where he said Indians would be safe from inevitable conflict with white Americans. Indeed, his 1830 Indian Removal Act included $500,000 to relocate one hundred thousand Indians, including sixteen thousand Cherokees, to lands west of the Mississippi River. Jackson and the act were severely criticized by people in the Northeast who had supported the missionaries, as well as by well-known Southerners including Davy Crockett, Henry Clay, and Sam Houston, but Congress voted to adopt it.

Removal was delayed as the Cherokees, led by Chief John Ross, defended their rights and their territory all the way to the Supreme Court. The court ruled in their favor in the celebrated *Worcester v. Georgia* of 1832, declaring that Georgia laws had no authority within Cherokee territory. With President Jackson's backing, however, Georgia ignored the decision.

Chief Ross remained determined to resist removal at all costs, and the vast majority of Cherokees supported him. But in 1835 a splinter group of Cherokee leaders came to the conclusion that the Cherokees would have no peace if they stayed in Georgia. They signed the Treaty of New Echota, which ceded all tribal lands to Georgia in exchange for five million dollars plus land in the western Indian territory and gave the Cherokees two years to prepare to move. Chief Ross and other Cherokee officials denounced the treaty as fraudulent; nonetheless, the U.S. Senate ratified it by a slight margin.

Determined to remain, the Cherokees were unprepared when the May 1838 deadline for evacuation came and federal troops under General Winfield Scott arrived to enforce the removal policy. The Cherokees were rounded up and placed in stockades, where many died from unhealthy conditions and lack of provisions. The first group to set out on the twelve-hundred-mile Trail of Tears left during that hot, dry summer, and many perished en route. Seeing the suffering, Chief Ross obtained permission for the Cherokees to organize their own emigration, but even then exhaustion, exposure, and hunger during the forced march took a heavy toll.

In this chapter, John Ridge's letter to Albert Gallatin and Chief John Ross's 1828 message to his nation describe the changes taking place in Cherokee society and refute white claims on Indian land. Speeches by Wilson Lumpkin of Georgia and President Jackson advocate removal of the Indians. Finally, letters from Evan Jones, a white missionary who accompanied the Cherokees on the Trail of Tears, provide an account of their hardships.

As you read, contemplate these questions. What was the attitude of Cherokee leaders regarding Indian adoption of American ways? What basic changes in Indian ways of life, including the division of work between men and women, were required for Americans to view them as "civilized"? What were the arguments for and against removal, and how did the actual process differ from what was promised?

32. The Civilized State of the Cherokees

John Ridge
Letter to Albert Gallatin
1826

A full-blooded Cherokee, John Ridge was educated, affluent, and part of the gener-
ation whose parents had made the conversion from traditional ways to the Anglo-
American world. His father, Kahmungdaclageh (known as "Major Ridge"), had
been a warrior and an ally of Andrew Jackson in the Creek wars before becoming a
landowner and slaveholder in northern Georgia. John Ridge attended a mission
school, a Tennessee academy, and the American Board's Foreign Mission School in
Connecticut before working for the Creek Indians in negotiations with the federal
government.

Ridge wrote this description of the Cherokee nation in response to questions
from Albert Gallatin, formerly an official in the Jefferson administration, who was
conducting research on Indian languages and customs. Nine years later, John Ridge,
Ridge's father, and Elias Boudinot led the group that signed the Treaty of New
Echota. After making the long journey west, the three paid for their decision with
their lives; although their killers were never identified, historians assume the assas-
sinations were an act of revenge for their roles in the despised treaty and the infamous
Trail of Tears.

February 27, 1826

The Cherokee Nation is bounded on the North by east Tennessee & North
Carolina, east by Georgia, south by the Creek Nation & state of Alabama, & west
by west Tennessee. The extreme length of the Nation must be upwards of 200
miles & extreme breadth about 150. At a rough conjecture, it has been supposed
to contain about 10,000,000 of acres of land. It is divided into eight districts or
Counties by a special act of the National Council, & their boundaries are distinctly designated and defined. A census of the Nation was taken last year (1825)
by order of the Council to ascertain the amount of property and Taxable persons
within the Nation. The correctness of this may be relied on, and the population
proved to be 13,583 native citizens, 147 white men married in the Nation, 73
white women, and 1,277 African slaves, to which if we add 400 cherokees who
took reservations in North Carolina & who are not included in the census & who
have since merged again among us, the Cherokee Nation will contain 15,480 in-

Payne Papers, Newberry Library. Reprinted in *The Cherokee Removal: A Brief History with Docu-*
ments, ed. Theda Perdue and Michael D. Green (Boston: Bedford/St. Martin's, 1995), 34–43. (Some
spelling and punctuation has been modernized.)

habitants. There is a scanty instance of African mixture with the Cherokee blood, but that of the white may be as 1 to 4, occasioned by intermarriages which has been increasing in proportion to the march of civilization. The above population is dispersed over the face of the Country on separate farms; villages, or a community, having a common enclosure to protect their hutches, have disappeared long since, & to my knowledge, there is but one of this character at Coosawattee, the inhabitants of which are gradually diminishing by emigration to the woods, where they prefer to clear the forest & govern their own individual plantations. In this view of their location, it really appears that they are farmers and herdsmen, which is their real character. It is true that there are distinctions now existing & increasingly so in the value of property possessed by individuals, but this only answers a good purpose, as a stimulus to those in the rear to equal their neighbors who have taken the lead. Their principal dependence for [subsistence] is on the production of their own farms. Indian corn is a staple production and is the most essential article of food in use. Wheat, rye & oats grow very well & some families have commenced to introduce them on their farms. Cotton is generally raised for domestic consumption and a few have grown it for market & have realized very good profits. I take pleasure to state, tho' cautiously, that there is not to my knowledge a solitary Cherokee to be found that depends upon the chase for subsistence and every head of a family has his house & farm. The hardest portion of manual labor is performed by the men, & the women occasionally lend a hand to the field, more by choice and necessity than any thing else. This is applicable to the poorer class, and I can do them the justice to say, they very contentedly perform the duties of the kitchen and that they are the most valuable portion of our Citizens. They sew, they weave, they spin, they cook our meals and act well the duties assigned them by Nature as mothers as far as they are able & improved. The African slaves are generally mostly held by Half breeds and full Indians of distinguished talents. In this class the principal value of property is retained and their farms are conducted in the same style with the southern white farmers of equal ability in point of property. Their houses are usually of hewed logs, with brick chimneys & shingled roofs, there are also a few excellent Brick houses & frames. Their furniture is better than the exterior appearance of their houses would incline a stranger to suppose. They have their regular meals as the whites, Servants to attend them in their repasts, and the tables are usually covered with a clean cloth & furnished with the usual plates, knives & forks &c. Every family more or less possess hogs, Cattle & horses and a number have commenced to pay attention to the introduction of sheep, which are increasing very fast. The horse is in general use for purposes of riding, drawing the plough or wagon.

Domestic manufactures is still confined to women who were first prevailed to undertake it. These consist of white or striped homespun, coarse woolen Blankets & in many instances very valuable & comfortable, twilled & figured coverlets. Woolen & cotton Stockings are mostly manufactured for domestic use within the Nation. I can only say that these domestic cloths are preferred by us to those brought from the New England. Domestic plaids our people are most generally clothed with them, but calicoes, silks, cambricks, &c. Handkerchiefs & shawls &c.

are introduced by Native merchants, who generally trade to Augusta in Georgia. The only trade carried on by the Cherokees with the adjoining States, is in hogs & horned Cattle. Skins formerly were sold in respectable quantities but that kind of trade is fast declining & getting less reputable. Cherokees on the Tennessee river have already commenced to trade in cotton & grow the article in large plantations and they have realized very handsome profit. All those who have it in their power, are making preparations to grow it for market & it will soon be the staple commodity of traffic for the Nation.

You will be able more fully to ascertain their state of improvement by giving the out lines of their Government. Having been honored with a seat in its National Councils, I have better acquaintance with this branch of your enquiry, than any other. All Indian Nations are either divided into tribes, distinguished by different names & these are subdivided into Towns. In each of these tribes or Towns are of course some men, prominent for valor, humanity & wisdom. The Assemblage of such men forms their Council fire. They are a standing body, & indefinitely so in number of warriors. They possess within themselves Legislation, Judicial & Executive powers. . . . A Treasurer was appointed & a National seat for their future Government was selected. In short, these Chiefs organized themselves into Standing body of Legislators who meet in October annually at New Town [New Echota], their seat of Government.

They are composed of two departments, the National Committee & the Representative Council. The former consist of 13 members including their President & have a Clerk to record their proceedings. They control & regulate their monied concerns: powers to inspect the Books of the Treasury, & acknowledge claims, power to Legislate & Negative the sets of the other Branch of the Legislative Council. The Representatives have also their Secretary, consist of 45 members including their Speaker. They have power to Legislate & Negative the proceedings of the National committee, fill their own vacancies & the vacancies in the Committee, to elect the two head chiefs, or their executive in conjunction with the National Committee. All laws of course are passed with the concurrences of these two departments & approved of by the head Chiefs. Their laws at present are written in the English Language and commence in the words, to wit. "Be it Resolved by the National Committee & Council" &c. and are signed by the speaker of the Representatives, the President of the Committee, and when approved, by the first head Chief & attested by the Clerks. These Branches of our Legislature are composed of men chosen from the eight districts heretofore mentioned in as satisfactory proportion as circumstances will allow. The Judiciary of our Nation is more perfect than the Legislature, having less obstacles to make it so than the latter. It is independent [with] Power to bring any Chief before it of any grade, to pass sentence & put it in execution. There is a Court of Justice in every district & its district Judge, who presides over two Districts. Every Court has a Jury and its district officers, Sheriff constables &c. to attend it. . . . I am assured of the loyalty of our Citizens to their Government and their laws and [am] determined to secure these blessings to their descendants yet unborn as an inheritance.

Property belonging to the wife is not exclusively at the control & disposal of the husband, and in many respects she has exclusive & distinct control over her own, particularly among the less civilized & in fact in every class & grade of intelligence, the law is in favor of the females in this respect. Rules & customs in the transfer of property are adopted & respected from the adjoining states in the absence of any law to regulate this branch of our trade. Property descends from parents, equally to the children; if none, to the next relatives &c. But if a will is made, it is respected to the fullest extent & every person, possessed of property, is entitled to dispose of his or her property in this way.

Superstition is the portion of all uncivilized Nations and Idolatry is only engendered in the Brain of rudeness. The Cherokees in their most savage state, never worshipped the work of their own hands — neither fire or water nor any one or portion of splendid fires that adorn heaven's Canopy above. They believed in a great first cause or Spirit of all Good & in a great being the author of all evil. These [were] at variance and at war with each other, but the good Spirit was supposed to be superior to the bad one. These immortal beings had on both sides numerous intelligent beings of analogous dispositions to their chieftains. They had a heaven, which consisted of a visible world to those who had undergone a change by death. This heaven was adorned with all the beauties which a savage imagination could conceive: An open forest, yet various, giving shade & fruit of every kind; Flowers of various hues & pleasant to the Smell; Game of all kinds in great abundance, enough of feasts & plenty of dances, & to crown the whole, the most beautiful women, prepared & adorned by the great Spirit, for every individual Indian that by wisdom, hospitality & Bravery was introduced to this happy & immortal region. The Bad place was the reverse of this & in the vicinity of the good place, where the wretched, compelled to live in hunger, hostility & darkness, could hear the rejoicings of the happy, without the possibility of reaching its shores.

Witches or wizards were in existence and pretended to possess Supernatural powers & intercourse with the Devil or bad Spirit. . . . There [are] yet among us [some] who pretend to possess powers of milder character, Such as making rain, allaying a storm or whirlwinds, playing with thunder & foretelling future events with many other trifling conjurations not worth mentioning, but they are generally living monuments of fun to the young and grave Ridicule for those in maturer years. There [are] about 8 churches, where the gospel is preached on sabbath days with in the Nation. They are missionary stations supported by moravians, Presbyterians, Baptists and methodists and each of these churches have a goodly number of pious & exemplary members and others, not professors, attend to preaching with respectable deportment. I am not able to say the precise number of actual christians, but they are respectable in point of number & character. And many a drunken, idle & good for nothing Indian has been converted from error & have become useful Citizens: Portions of Scripture & sacred hymns are translated and I have frequently heard with astonishment a Cherokee, unacquainted with the English take his text & preach, read his hymn & sing it, Joined by his audience, and pray to his heavenly father with great propriety & devotion. The influence of Religion on the life of the Indians is powerful & lasting. I have an uncle, who was given to all the vices of savagism in drunkenness, fornication and roguery & he is now tho' poorer in this world's goods but rich in goodness & makes his living by hard labor & is in every respect an honest praying christian.

In respect to marriage, we have no law regulating it & polygamy is still allowed to Native Cherokees. Increase of morality among the men, the same among the women & a respect for their characters & matrimonial happiness is fast consuming this last vestige of our ignorance. We attempted to pass a law regulating marriage, but as nearly all the members of our Legislature, tho' convinced of the propriety, had been married under the old existing ceremony, [and] were afraid it would reflect dishonor on them, it failed. Time will effect the desired change in this system & it is worthy of mention, even now, that the most respectable portion of our females prefer, tho' not required by law to be united in marriage attended by the solemnities of the Christian mode. Indians, tho' naturally high-minded, are not addicted to as much revenge as they have been represented, and I can say this, much it is paid for them to endure an intended Insult but they are ready to forgive if they discover marks of repentance in the countenance of an enemy. In regard to Intemperance, we are still as a nation grossly degraded. We are however on the improve. Five years ago our best chiefs during their official labors would get drunk & continue so for two or three days. It is now not the case & any member who should thus depart from duty would now be expelled from the Council. Among the younger class, a large number are of fine habits, temperate & genteel in their deportment. The females aspire to gain the affection of such men & to the females we may always ascribe the honor of effecting the civilization of man. There are about 13 Schools established by missionaries in the Nation and may contain 250 students. They are entirely supported by the humane Societies in different parts of the United States. The Nation has not as yet contributed to the support of these Schools. Besides this, some of our most respectable people have their children educated at the academies in the adjoining states. Two Cherokee females have recently completed their Education, at the expense of their father, at a celebrated female Academy in Salem, North Carolina. They are highly accomplished & in point of appearance & deportment; they would pass for the genteel & wellbred ladies in any Country.

I know of some others who are preparing for an admission in the same institution. I suppose that there are one third of our Citizens, that can read & write in the English Language. George Guess a Cherokee who is unacquainted with the English has invented 86 characters, in which the Cherokees read & write in their own Language and regularly correspond with their Arkansas friends. This mode of writing is most extensively adopted by our people particularly by those who are ignorant of the English Language. A National Academy of a high order is to be soon established by law at our seat of Government. The edifice will be of Brick & will be supported by the Nation. It is also in contemplation to establish an English & Cherokee printing press & a paper edited in both languages at our seat of Government. In our last Session, $1500 was appropriated to purchase the press and regulations adopted to carry the object into effect. We have also a Society organized called the "Moral & Literary Society of the Cherokee Nation." A library is attached to this Institution. . . .

Having given a view of the present of civilization of the Cherokee Nation, it may not be amiss to relate the time & manner when it was first introduced. About the year 1795 Missionaries were sent by the United Abraham Or Moravians to the Cherokees & established a Station called Spring place in the center of [the] Nation. At or about that time, Colonel Silas Dinsmore was appointed by General Washington as Agent of the Nation, who from the Indian Testimony itself, labored indefatigably in Teaching the Cherokees the art of agriculture by distributing hoes & ploughs & giving to the women Spinning wheels, cards & Looms. It appears when this change of Hunter life to a civilized one was proposed by the Agent to the Chiefs in Council, that he was unanimously laughed at by the Council for attempting [to] introduce white peoples' habits among the Indians, who were created to pursue the chase. Not discouraged here, the Agent turned to Individuals & succeeded to gain some to pay their attention to his plan by way of experiment, which succeeded. An anecdote is related of a Chief who was heartily opposed to the Agent's view. He came to Colonel Dinsmore & said, "I don't want you to recommend these things to my people. They may suit white people, but will do [nothing] for the Indians. I am now going to hunt & shall be gone six moons & when I return, I shall expect to hear nothing of your talks made in [my] absence to induce my people to take hold of your plan." But in his absence the Agent induced his wife & daughters to Spin & weave with so much assiduity as to make more cloth in value, than the Chief's Hunt of six months amounted to. He was astonished & came to the Agent with a smile, accusing him for making his wife & daughters better hunters than he & requested to be furnished a plough & went to work on his farm.

In the meantime, the Moravians opened their School for the Indians, cleared a farm, cultivated a garden & planted an orchard. The Venerable Reverend John Gambold & his amiable Lady were a standing monument of Industry, Goodness & friendship. As far as they had means, they converted the "Wilderness to blossom as the Rose." There the boys & girls were taught to read & write, & occasionally labor in the Garden & in the field. There they were first taught to sing & pray to their Creator, & here Gospel Worship was first Established. Never shall I forget father Gambold & mother Mrs. Gambold. By them the clouds of ignorance which surrounded me on all sides were dispersed. My heart received the rays of civilization & my intellect expanded & took a wider range. My superstition vanished & I began to reason correctly

> "Curious to view the Kings of ancient days,"
> "The mighty dead that live in endless praise."

I draw to a close. Solemn & gloomy is the thought that all the Indian nations who once occupied America are nearly Gone! Powerful in War & Sage in peace, the Chiefs now sleep with their heroic deeds silent, in the bosom of the Earth! It was not their destiny to become great. Their Council fires could not be united into one, as the Seat of a great empire. It was for strangers to effect this, and necessity now compels the last Remnants to look to it for protection. It is true we Govern ourselves, but yet we live in fear. We are urged by these strangers to make room for their settlements & go farther west. Our National existence is suspended on the faith & honor of the United States, alone. Their convenience may cut this asunder, & with a little faint struggle we may cease to be. All Nations have had their rises & their falls. This has been the case with us. Within the orbit the United States move the States & within these we move in a little circle, dependent on the great center. We may live in this way fifty years & then we shall by Natural causes merge in & mingle with the United States. Cherokee blood, if not destroyed, will wind its courses in beings of fair complexions, who will read that their ancestors became civilized under the frowns of misfortunes & causes of their enemies.

33. Disputing Georgia's Claim

CHIEF JOHN ROSS
Annual Message to the Cherokee Nation
1828

John Ross, formerly a trader with the Indians, gave up that occupation to devote his life to living as a Cherokee. He settled in Rome, Georgia, where he operated a ferry and a plantation. Although Ross was only one-eighth Cherokee (he was otherwise of Scottish ancestry) and had been educated at a white academy in Tennessee, he fully identified with the tribe and served as its chief from 1828 until his death in 1866.

Despite his vigorous attempts to overturn the Indian Removal Act, Ross and his wife, Quatie, were forced to embark on the Trail of Tears in 1838–39; his wife was one of the many who perished. Chief Ross continued to head the Cherokees in the West. In this speech delivered to the Cherokee nation in 1828, he denies that Georgia has any rightful claim to Cherokee land.

Fellow Citizens:

New Echota C.N. Oct. 13, 1828

In addressing you on this momentous occasion, we cannot, in justice to our feelings, forbear a solemn pause, and with grateful feelings meditate on the many

Chief John Ross, *The Papers of Chief John Ross*, ed. Gary E. Moulton, 2 vols. (Norman: University of Oklahoma Press, 1985). Reprinted in *Cornerstones of Georgia History: Documents That Formed the State*, ed. Thomas A. Scott (Athens: University of Georgia Press, 1995), 58–62.

blessings which a kind Providence has conferred on us as a people. Although we have had trials and tribulations to encounter, and in some instances, the sad effects of intemperance have been experienced within the circle of our citizens, yet, there is every reason to flatter us in the hope, that under wise and wholesome laws, the preponderating influence of civilization, morality and religion will secure to us and our posterity, an ample share of prosperity and happiness.

Occupying your seats by the free suffrage of the people, under the privileges guaranteed by the Constitution, the various subjects requiring your deliberation [on] the present session, will, necessarily be important. The organization of the new Government, the revision and amendments of the old laws, so as to make them in unison with the principles of the Constitution, will require your attention; and it cannot escape your wisdom, that the laws should be short, plain, and suitable to the condition of the people, and to be well executed. The Judiciary system demands your serious deliberation, and the mode for conducting suits in courts should be free from all complicated formalities, and no other *form* should be required than, to let both parties know distinctly, what is alleged, that a fair trial may be had. . . .

The circumstances of our Government assuming a new character under a constitutional form, and on the principles of republicanism, has, in some degree, excited the sensations of the public characters of Georgia, and it is sincerely to be regretted that this excitement should have been manifested by such glaring expressions of hostility to our true interests. By the adoption of the Constitution, our relation to the United States, as recognized by existing Treaties, is not in the least degree affected, but on the contrary, this improvement in our government, is strictly in accordance with the recommendations, views and wishes of the Great Washington under whose auspicious administration our Treaties of peace, Friendship and protection, were made and whose policy in regard to Indian civilization has been strictly pursued by the subsequent administrations.

The pretended claim of Georgia to a portion of our lands, is alleged on the following principles. First, by discovery. Secondly, by conquest. Thirdly, by compact.

We shall endeavor briefly to elucidate the character of this claim. In the first place, the Europeans by the skill and enterprise of their Navigators, discovered this vast Continent, and found it inhabited exclusively by Indians of various Tribes, and by a pacific courtesy and designing stratagems, the aboriginal proprietors were induced to permit a people from a foreign clime to plant colonies, and without the consent or knowledge of the native Lords, a potentate of England, whose eyes never saw, whose purse never purchased, and whose sword never conquered the soil we inhabit, presumed to issue a parchment, called a "Charter," to the Colony of Georgia, in which its boundary was set forth, including a great extend of country inhabited by the Cherokee and other Indian Nations.

Secondly, after a lapse of many years when the population of their Colonies had become strong, they revolted against their sovereign, and by success of Arm, established an Independent Government, under the name of "the United States." It is further alleged that the Cherokee Nation prosecuted a war at the same time against the Colonies.

3dly. Several years after the Treaties of peace, friendship and protection, which took place between the U.S. & Cherokee Nation, and by which the faith of the United States was solemnly pledged to guarantee to the Cherokee Nation forever, their title to their lands, a Compact was entered into between the United States and the State of Georgia, by which the United States promised to purchase for the use of Georgia certain lands belonging to the Cherokee Nation so soon as it could be done on *reasonable* and *peaceable terms.*

Thus stands the naked claim of Georgia to a portion of our lands. The claim advanced under the plea of discovery, is preposterous. Our ancestors from time immemorial possessed this country, not by a "Charter" from the hand of a mortal King, who had no right to grant it, but by the Will of the King of Kings, who created all things and liveth for ever & ever.

The claim advanced on the second head, on the ground of conquest, is no less futile than the first, even admitting that the Cherokees waged a war with the Colonies, at the time they fought for their independence. The Cherokees took part in the war, *only* as the allies of Great Britain, and not as her subjects, being an independent Nation, over whose lands she exercised no rights of jurisdiction; therefore, nothing could be claimed from them, in regard to their lands by the conqueror over the rights of Great Britain. At the termination of the war, the United States negotiated with the Cherokees on the terms of peace as an Independent Nation, and since the close of that war, other wars took place, and at their terminations, other treaties were made, and in no one stipulation can there be found a single idea that our title to the soil has been forfeited, or claimed as the terms of peace; but, to the contrary, we discover that the United States solemnly pledged their faith that our title should be guaranteed to our Nation forever.

The third pretension is extremely lame. The United States enters into a compact with Georgia that they will purchase certain lands, which belong to us, for Georgia, so soon as they can do it on *peaceable* and *reasonable terms.* This promise was made on the part of the United States without knowing whether this nation would ever consent to dispose of those lands on any terms whatever; and the Cherokees not being a part in the compact, their title cannot be affected in the slightest degree. It appears astonishingly unreasonable, that all those hard expressions of denunciation which have been unsparingly lavished against our sacred rights and interests, by interested politicians, have arose from no other circumstance than our honest refusal to sell to the United States lands, for the fulfillment of their Compact with Georgia. Although our views & condition may be misrepresented — although we may be stigmatized with the appellation of *"nabobs,"* and should be represented as ruling with an *"Iron rod"* and *"grinding down into dust the wretched* and *abject mass"* of our citizens; and although we may be called *avaricious* for *refusing to sell our lands,* we should not be diverted from the path of rectitude. In all our intercourse with our neighboring white brethren, we should endeavor to cultivate the utmost harmony and good understanding, by strictly observing the relations which we sustain to the United States.

Owing to the various representations respecting us, we have been frequently called upon to make a treaty of cession. . . . We would recommend you as the immediate representatives of the people, to submit a respectful memorial to the Congress of the United States, expressive of the true sentiments of the people respecting their situation, and praying that measures may be adopted on the part of the United States for the adjustment of their Compact with the State of Georgia, otherwise than to anticipate any further cession of land from this nation.

William Hicks
John Ross

34. Justifying Removal

WILSON LUMPKIN AND ANDREW JACKSON
Arguments for Removal
1830

Wilson Lumpkin, a Georgia congressman, and his political ally, President Andrew Jackson, gave these speeches to support what would become the Indian Removal Act of 1830. Despite the changes in Cherokee life and culture, both men insisted that efforts to civilize the Indians had failed and that removal was the best alternative for them.

A lawyer from northeast Georgia, Lumpkin went on to serve as its governor from 1831 to 1835; under his administration, the state defied the Supreme Court's Worcester v. Georgia *decision. Lumpkin later served as the federal commissioner charged with enforcing the Treaty of New Echota and in 1837 was elected to the U.S. Senate, where he helped prevent the overturn of the treaty.*

WILSON LUMPKIN

Speech to Congress
1830

Mr. Chairman: My life has never been free from care and responsibility; but, on no former occasion, have I ever felt more deeply impressed with a sense of that responsibility to *God and my country*, than I do at the present moment. The obli-

Wilson Lumpkin, *The Removal of the Cherokee Indians from Georgia, 1827–1841*, 2 vols. in 1 (New York: Dodd, Mead, 1907; reprint, New York: Augustus M. Kelley, 1971). Reprinted in *Cornerstones of Georgia History: Documents That Formed the State*, ed. Thomas A. Scott (Athens: University of Georgia Press, 1995), 53–57.

gations which rest on me are common to every member of this House. The great importance which I attach to the decisions of this House upon the bill now under consideration, does not arise from any apprehension of material effects being produced in relation to any one of the states who are interested. It is true, your decision will have a strong bearing on their interest; but they have the capacity to some extent to take care of themselves. But to those remnant tribes of Indians whose good we seek, the subject before you is of vital importance. It is a measure of life and death. Pass the bill on your table, and you save them; reject it, and you leave them to perish. Reject this bill, and you thereby encourage delusory hopes in the Indians which their professed friends and allies well know will never be realized. The rejection of this bill will encourage and invite the Indians to acts of indiscretion and assumptions which will necessarily bring upon them chastisement and injury, which will be deplored by every friend of virtue and humanity. I therefore call upon you to avoid these evil consequences while you may. Delay is pregnant with great danger to the Indians; what you do, do quickly, before the evil day approaches.

I differ with my friend from Tennessee (Mr. Bell) in regard to Indian civilization. I entertain no doubt that a remnant of these people may be entirely reclaimed from their native savage habits, and be brought to enter into the full enjoyment of all the blessings of civilized society. It appears to me we have too many instances of individual improvement amongst the various native tribes of America to hesitate any longer in determining whether the Indians are susceptible of civilization. Use the proper means, and success will crown your efforts. The means hitherto resorted to by the Government, as well as by individuals, to improve the condition of the Indians, must, from the present state of things, very soon be withheld from these unfortunate people, if they remain in their present abodes, for they will every day be brought into closer contact and conflict with the white population, and this circumstance will diminish the spirit of benevolence and philanthropy towards them which now exists. . . .

Sir, before I pursue the course of the opposition any further, I will remark that I have so far confined myself principally to that part of the subject which relates to the interest of the Indians; but there are other interests which are entitled to a share of your considerations. The State of Georgia, one of whose Representatives I am, has, from my infancy till this day, been struggling with perplexing difficulties, strifes, and heart-burnings, upon the subject of her Indian relations.

Yes, sir, amongst my earliest recollections are the walls of an old fort, which gave protection to the women and children from the tomahawk and scalping knife of the Indians. And let me inform you that, while the Indians have receded thousands of miles before the civilized population, in other sections of the Union, the frontier of Georgia has comparatively remained stationary.

My present residence is not more than one day's travel from the place of the old fort to which I alluded. It is but part of a day's travel from my residence to the line of the Cherokee country.

In entering upon this branch of my subject, I find it necessary to summon up all the powers of philosophy to restrain feelings of indignation and contempt for those who are at this time straining every nerve and using every effort to perpetuate on the people whom I represent the evils which they have borne for so many years; and, whatever has or may be said of this Union, would have submitted, with equal patriotism, to the many ills and wrongs which we have received at the hands of those who were bound by the strongest human obligations to aid in relieving us from Indian perplexities, give us justice, and assist in the advancement of our peace, happiness, and prosperity.

Georgia, sir, is one of the good old thirteen States; she entered the Union upon an equal footing with any of her sisters. She claims no superiority, but contends for equality. That sovereignty which she concedes to all the rest, and would at any time unite with them in defending from all encroachment, she will maintain for herself. Our social compact, upon which we stand as a state, gives you the metes and bounds of our sovereignty; and within the limits therein defined and pointed out our state authorities claim entire and complete jurisdiction over soil and population, regardless of complexion.

The boundaries of Georgia have been defined, recognized, and admitted, by circumstances of a peculiar kind. Her litigations in relation to boundary and title to her soil may justly be considered as having been settled "according to law." Her boundaries are not only admitted by her sister states, but by this General Government, and every individual who administered any part of it, Executive or Legislative, must recollect that the faith of this Government has stood pledged for twenty-eight years past to relieve Georgia from the embarrassment of Indian population. It is known to every member of this Congress that this pledge was no gratuity to Georgia. No, sir, it was for and in consideration of the two entire states of Alabama and Mississippi.

I feel disposed to pity those who make the weak and false plea of inability, founded on the words *"reasonable and peaceable,"* whenever I hear it made.

Such pettifogging quibbles deserve the contempt of a statesman. No man is fit to be a Congressman who does not know that the General Government might many years ago, upon both reasonable and peaceable terms, have removed every Indian from Georgia.

But, sir, upon this subject this Government has been wanting in good faith to Georgia. It has, by its own acts and policy, forced the Indians to remain in Georgia, by the purchase of their lands in the adjoining states and by holding out to the Indians strong inducements to remain where they are, by the expenditures of vast sums of money, spent in changing the habits of the savage for those of civilized life. All this was in itself right and proper; it has my hearty approbation; but it should not have been done at the expense of Georgia. The Government, long after it was bound to extinguish the title of the Indians to all the lands in Georgia, has actually forced the Cherokees from their lands in other states, settled them upon Georgia lands, and aided in furnishing the means to create the Cherokee aristocracy.

Sir, I blame not the Indians; I commiserate their case. I have considerable acquaintance with the Cherokees, and amongst them I have seen much to admire. To me, they are in many respects an interesting people. If the wicked influence of designing men, veiled in the garb of philanthropy and Christian benevolence, should excite the Cherokees to a course that will end in their speedy destruction, I now call upon this Congress, and the whole American people, not to charge the Georgians with this sin; but let it be remembered that it is the fruit of cant and fanaticism, emanating from the land of steady habits; from the boasted progeny of the Pilgrims and Puritans.

Sir, my State stands charged before this House, before the Nation, and before the whole world, with cruelty and oppression towards the Indian. I deny the charge and demand proof from those who made it.

I have labored, as one of your Committee, day and night, in examining everything which has any connection with the history of this subject. Amongst other duties, we have examined all the various laws of the colonial and state governments in relation to the Indians. The selection made and submitted has long since been in the hands of every gentleman of this House. Let the laws of other states be compared with those which are the subject of complaint, and it must be admitted by every candid man that the states complained of stand pre-eminent in humanity, mildness, and generosity towards the Indians.

Georgia, it is true, has slaves; but she did not make them such; she found them upon her hands when she became a sovereign state. She never has, by her legislation, changed the state of freedom to slavery. If she has ever owned an Indian slave, it has never come to my knowledge; but more than one of the other states of this Union have not only treated them as brutes, destitute of any human rights — depriving them of their own modes of worshipping Deity — hunting them as wild beasts for slaughter — holding out rewards for their scalps, and even giving premiums for the raising of a certain breed of dogs, called bloodhounds, to hunt savages, that they might procure their scalps, and obtain the reward offered by Government for them. Sir, compare this legislation with that of Georgia, and let the guilty be put to shame. . . .

. . . I admit we do find in the Cherokee country many families enjoying all the common comforts of civil and domestic life, and possessing the necessary means to secure these enjoyments. Moreover, we find a number of schools and houses built for religious worship. Many of these comfortable families, too, are composed of natives born in the Cherokee country. But the principal part of these enjoyments are confined to the blood of the white man, either in whole or in part. But few, very few, of the real Indians participate largely in these blessings. A large portion of the full-blooded Cherokees still remain a poor degraded race of human beings. As to the proportion that are comfortable, or otherwise, I cannot speak from my own personal knowledge with any degree of certainty; but from what I have seen, I can readily conclude that but a very small portion of the real Indians are in a state of improvement, whilst their lords and rulers are white men and descendants of white men, enjoying the fat of the land, and enjoying exclusively the Government annuities upon which they foster, feed, and clothe the most violent and dangerous enemies of our civil institutions.

Whilst the smallest intrusion (as it is called) by the frontier citizens of Georgia on the lands occupied by the Cherokees excites the fiery indignation of the fanatics, from one end of the *chain of concert and coalition* to the other, do we not find an annual increase of intruders, from these philanthropic ranks, flocking in upon the poor Cherokees, like the caterpillars and locusts of Egypt, leaving a barren waste behind them? Yes, sir, these are the intruders who devour the substance which of right belongs to the poor, perishing part of the Cherokees.

They divide the spoil with the Cherokee rulers and leave the common Indians to struggle with want and misery, without hope of bettering their condition by any change but that of joining their brethren West of the Mississippi.

The inhumanity of Georgia, so much complained of, is nothing more nor less than the extension of her laws and jurisdiction over this mingled and misguided population who are found within her acknowledged limits.

And what, I would ask, is to be found in all this that is so very alarming? Sir, I have endeavored to tear the mask from this subject, that the character and complexion of this opposition might be seen and known. The absolute rulers of the Cherokee country, like other men, love office, distinction, and power.

They are enjoying great and peculiar benefits. They do not like the idea of becoming private citizens. It is with great reluctance they yield up their stewardship. They know they have not been faithful to the interest of the poor degraded Indians. They know the great mass of their people have been left to suffer in want and ignorance, whilst they have spent their substance in forming foreign alliances with an enthusiastic, selfish and money-loving people. These men, when incorporated into the political family of Georgia, cannot calculate on becoming at once the Randolphs of the State. And if they join the Western Cherokees they cannot carry with them their present assumed sovereignty and rule.

They will there find equals in many of their pioneer brethren. The Cadmus of the Cherokees, George Guess, and many others, are already there. Yes, sir, these Western Cherokees are in the full enjoyment of all the blessings of their emigrating enterprise, and there is but one opinion among them in regard to their relative comfort and prospect of future blessings. All the various emigrants to the West so far agree as to authorize the assurance that no inducement could be offered to them strong enough to bring them back again.

The Cherokees and Creeks are charmed with their country, and to the many things which attach to their comfort in it. The New England farmers who have emigrated to the fertile valleys of the West would as soon consent to return to the barren sand and sterile rocks of their native land as a Western Cherokee or Creek would return to the sepulchre of his forefathers.

Pages may be filled with the sublimated *cant* of the day, and in wailing over the departure of the Cherokees from the *bones* of their forefathers. But if the heads of these pretended mourners were waters, and their eyes were a fountain of tears, and they were to spend days and years in weeping over the departure of the Cherokees from Georgia, yet they will go. The tide of emigration, with the Indians as well as the whites, directs its course westwardly. . . .

ANDREW JACKSON

State of the Union Address
December 6, 1830

It gives me pleasure to announce to Congress that the benevolent policy of the Government, steadily pursued for nearly thirty years, in relation to the removal of the Indians beyond the white settlements is approaching to a happy consummation. . . .

Humanity has often wept over the fate of the aborigines of this country, and Philanthropy has been long busily employed in devising means to avert it, but its progress has never for a moment been arrested, and one by one have many powerful tribes disappeared from the earth. To follow to the tomb the last of his race and to tread on the graves of extinct nations excite melancholy reflections. But true philanthropy reconciles the mind to these vicissitudes as it does to the extinction of one generation to make room for another. In the monuments and fortresses of an unknown people, spread over the extensive regions of the West, we behold the memorials of a once powerful race, which was exterminated or has disappeared to make room for the existing savage tribes. Nor is there anything in this which, upon a comprehensive view of the general interests of the human race, is to be regretted. Philanthropy could not wish to see this continent restored to the condition in which it was found by our forefathers. What good man would prefer a country covered with forests and ranged by a few thousand savages to our extensive Republic, studded with cities, towns, and prosperous farms, embellished with all the improvements which art can devise or industry execute, occupied by more than 12,000,000 happy people, and filled with all the blessings of liberty, civilization, and religion?

The present policy of the Government is but a continuation of the same progressive change by a milder process. The tribes which occupied the countries now constituting the Eastern States were annihilated or have melted away to make room for the whites. The waves of population and civilization are rolling to the westward, and we now propose to acquire the countries occupied by the red men of the South and West by a fair exchange, and, at the expense of the United States, to send them to a land where their existence may be prolonged and perhaps made perpetual. Doubtless it will be painful to leave the graves of their fathers; but what do they more than our ancestors did or than our children are now doing? To better their condition in an unknown land our forefathers left all that was dear in earthly objects. Our children by thousands yearly leave the land of their birth to seek new homes in distant regions. Does Humanity weep at these painful separations from everything, animate and inanimate, with which the young heart has become entwined? Far from it. It is rather a source of joy that our country affords scope where our young population may range unconstrained in body or in mind,

The Messages and Papers of the Presidents, comp. James D. Richardson (New York: Bureau of National Literature, 1897). Reprinted in *The Cherokee Removal: A Brief History with Documents*, ed. Theda Perdue and Michael D. Green (Boston: Bedford/St. Martin's, 1995), 119–20.

developing the power and faculties of man in their highest perfection. These remove hundreds and almost thousands of miles at their own expense, purchase the lands they occupy, and support themselves at their new homes from the moment of their arrival. Can it be cruel in this Government when, by events which it can not control, the Indian is made discontented in his ancient home to purchase his lands, to give him a new and extensive territory, to pay the expense of his removal, and support him a year in his new abode? How many thousands of our own people would gladly embrace the opportunity of removing to the West on such conditions! If the offers made to the Indians were extended to them, they would be hailed with gratitude and joy.

And is it supposed that the wandering savage has a stronger attachment to his home than the settled, civilized Christian? Is it more afflicting to him to leave the graves of his fathers than it is to our brothers and children? Rightly considered, the policy of the General Government toward the red man is not only liberal, but generous. He is unwilling to submit to the laws of the States and mingle with their population. To save him from this alternative, or perhaps utter annihilation, the General Government kindly offers him a new home, and proposes to pay the whole expense of his removal and settlement.

35. The Trail of Tears

Evan Jones
Letters
1838

Evan Jones was a Baptist minister who started working among the Cherokees in North Carolina in 1822. Though eager to convert the Cherokees to Christianity, Jones was somewhat unusual among missionaries in that he appreciated the Indians' traditional culture and was in turn admired by them for his dedication to their cause and for his courage.

Jones was one of three white missionaries who accompanied the Cherokees on their forced march west; Chief John Ross chose him to be one of the leaders during the journey. His group of 1,250 left in October and arrived three and one-half

Baptist Missionary Magazine, September 1838 and April 1839, American Periodical Series, Microfilm. Reprinted in *The Cherokee Removal: A Brief History with Documents*, ed. Theda Perdue and Michael D. Green (Boston: Bedford/St. Martin's, 1995), 164–68.

months later, having lost seventy-one members along the way. Jones and other missionaries won valuable support for the Indians by keeping their denominations informed about the Indians' plight. He sent these letters describing the experience of the Trail of Tears to the Baptist Missionary Magazine, *which printed excerpts for its readers.*

May 21.   Our minds have, of late, been in a state of intense anxiety and agitation. The 24th of May is rapidly approaching. The major-general has arrived, and issued his summons, declaring that every man, woman and child of the Cherokees must be on their way to the west before another moon shall pass. The troops, by thousands, are assembling around the devoted victims. The Cherokees, in the mean time, apprized of all that is doing, wait the result of these terrific preparations; with feelings not to be described. Wednesday, the 16th inst.,[1] was appointed as a day of solemn prayer.

Camp Hetzel, near Cleveland, June 16.   The Cherokees are nearly all prisoners. They have been dragged from their houses, and encamped at the forts and military posts, all over the nation. In Georgia, especially, multitudes were allowed no time to take any thing with them, except the clothes they had on. Well-furnished houses were left a prey to plunderers, who, like hungry wolves, follow in the train of the captors. These wretches rifle the houses, and strip the helpless, unoffending owners of all they have on earth. Females, who have been habituated to comforts and comparative affluence, are driven on foot before the bayonets of brutal men. Their feelings are mortified by vulgar and profane vociferations. It is a painful sight. The property of many has been taken, and sold before their eyes for almost nothing — the sellers and buyers, in many cases, being combined to cheat the poor Indians. These things are done at the instant of arrest and consternation; the soldiers standing by, with their arms in hand, impatient to go on with their work, could give little time to transact business. The poor captive, in a state of distressing agitation, his weeping wife almost frantic with terror, surrounded by a group of crying, terrified children, without a friend to speak a consoling word, is in a poor condition to make a good disposition of his property and is in most cases stripped of the whole, at one blow. Many of the Cherokees, who, a few days ago, were in comfortable circumstances, are now victims of abject poverty. Some, who have been allowed to return home, under passport, to inquire after their property, have found their cattle, horses, swine, farming-tools, and house-furniture all gone. And this is not a description of extreme cases. It is altogether a faint representation of the work which has been perpetrated on the unoffending, unarmed and unresisting Cherokees.

---

[1]**inst.:** instant, that is, the current month.

Our brother Bushyhead and his family, Rev. Stephen Foreman, native missionary of the American Board, the speaker of the national council, and several men of character and respectability, with their families, are here prisoners.

It is due to justice to say, that, at this station (and I learn the same is true of some others), the officer in command treats his prisoners with great respect and indulgence. But fault rests somewhere. They are prisoners, without a crime to justify the fact.

These *savages*, prisoners of *Christians*, are now all hands busy, some cutting and some carrying posts, and plates, and rafters — some digging holes for posts, and some preparing seats, for a temporary place for preaching tomorrow. There will also be preaching at another camp, eight miles distant. We have not heard from our brethren in the mountains since their capture. I have no doubt, however, but the grace of God will be sufficient for them, and that their confidence is reposed in the God of their salvation. My last accounts from them were truly cheering. In a few days they expected the victorious army, to sweep them into their forts, but they were going on steadily in their labors of love to dying sinners. Brother O-ga-na-ya wrote me, May 27, that seven, (four males and three females,) were baptized at Taquohee on that day. He says, "If it shall be peace, we intend to meet at this place on the second Saturday. We are in great trouble. It is said, that on Monday next we are to be arrested, and I suppose it to be true. Many are greatly terrified."

The principal Cherokees have sent a petition to General Scott, begging most earnestly that they may not be sent off to the west till the sickly season is over. They have not received any answer yet. The agent is shipping them by multitudes from Ross's Landing. Nine hundred in one detachment, and seven hundred in another, were driven into boats, and it will be a miracle of mercy if one-fourth escape the exposure to that sickly climate. They were exceedingly depressed, and almost in despair.

July 10.   The work of war in time of peace, is commenced in the Georgia part of the Cherokee nation, and is carried on, in most cases, in the most unfeeling and brutal manner; no regard being paid to the orders of the commanding General, in regard to humane treatment of the Indians. I have heard of only one officer in Georgia (I hope there are more), who manifests any thing like humanity, in his treatment of this persecuted people. . . .

The work of capturing being completed, and about 3,000 sent off, the General has agreed to suspend the further transportation of the captives till the first of September. This arrangement, though but a small favor, diffused universal joy through the camps of the prisoners. . . .

July 11.   Brethren Wickliffe and O-ga-na-ya, and a great number of members of the church at Valley Towns, fell into Fort Butler, seven miles from the mission. They never relaxed their evangelical labors, but preached constantly in the fort. They held church meetings, received ten members, and on Sabbath, June 17, by permission of the officer in command, went down to the river and baptized them (five males and five females). They were guarded to the river and back. Some whites present, affirm it to have been the most solemn and impressive religious service they ever witnessed.

I have omitted till now to say that as soon as General Scott agreed to suspend the transportation of the prisoners till autumn, I accompanied brother Bushyhead, who, by permission of the General, carried a message from the chiefs to those Cherokees who had evaded the troops by flight to the mountains. We had no difficulty in finding them. They all agreed to come in, on our advice, and surrender themselves to the forces of the United States; though, with the whole nation, they are still as strenuously opposed to the treaty as ever. Their submission, therefore, is not to be viewed as an acquiescence in the principles or the terms of the treaty; but merely as yielding to the physical force of the United States.

On our way, we met a detachment of 1,300 prisoners. As I took some of them by the hand, the tears gushed from their eyes. Their hearts, however, were cheered to see us, and to hear a word of consolation. Many members of the church were among them. At Fort Butler, we found a company of 300, just arrived from the mountains, on their way to the general depot, at the Agency. Several of our members were among these also. I believe the Christians, the salt of the earth, are pretty generally distributed among the several detachments of prisoners, and these Christians maintain among themselves the stated worship of God, in the sight of their pagan brethren, and of the white heathens who guard them.

We had a very laborious journey through the mountains, which we extended to the Cherokee settlement in North Carolina. Here we had several meetings with whites and Indians, and on Sabbath, the 1st inst., had the pleasure to baptize, on profession of their faith, three Cherokee females, who had previously been examined and approved.

December 30. We have now been on our road to Arkansas seventy-five days, and have travelled five hundred and twenty-nine miles. We are still nearly three hundred miles short of our destination. We have been greatly favored by the kind providence of our heavenly Father. We have as yet met with no serious accident, and have been detained only two days by bad weather. It has, however, been exceedingly cold for some time past, which renders the condition of those who are but thinly clad, very uncomfortable. In order, however, to counteract the effects of the severity of the weather in some degree, we have, since the cold set in so severely, sent on a company every morning, to make fires along the road, at short intervals. This we have found a great alleviation to the sufferings of the people.

At the Mississippi river, we were stopped from crossing, by the ice running so that boats could not pass, for several days. Here brother Bushyhead's detachment came up with us, and we had the pleasure of having our tents in the same encampment; and before our detachment was all over, Rev. Stephen Foreman's detachment came up, and encamped along side of us. I am sorry to say, however, that both their detachments have not been able to cross.

The members of the church, generally, maintain consistency of conduct, and many of them are very useful. Our native preachers are assiduous in their labors, seizing all favorable opportunities to cherish a devotional spirit among the brethren. Their influence is very salutary.

I am afraid that, with all the care that can be exercised with the various detachments, there will be an immense amount of suffering, and loss of life attending the removal. Great numbers of the old, the young, and the infirm, will inevitably be sacrificed. And the fact that the removal is effected by coercion, makes it the more galling to the feelings of the survivers.

Suggestions for Further Reading

Anderson, William L., ed. *Cherokee Removal: Before and After.* Athens: University of Georgia Press, 1991.

McLoughlin, William G. *Champions of the Cherokees: Evan and John B. Jones.* Princeton: Princeton University Press, 1990.

———. *Cherokee Renascence in the New Republic.* Princeton: Princeton University Press, 1986.

Perdue, Thea, et al. *The Cherokee.* Indians of North America Series. Broomall, Pa.: Chelsea House, 1989.

Perdue, Theda, and Michael D. Green, eds. *The Cherokee Removal: A Brief History with Documents.* Boston: Bedford/St. Martin's, 1995.

Wallace, Anthony F. C. *The Long, Bitter Trail: Andrew Jackson and the Indians.* New York: Hill & Wang, 1993.

CHAPTER TEN

ANTEBELLUM REFORM

Religion and Morality in the Debate over Slavery

Between 1815 and the Civil War, the United States experienced a surge of reform activity that reached its peak in the 1830s. One of the most important contributing factors was the Second Great Awakening, a wave of religious enthusiasm that spurred the growth of evangelical Protestantism and encouraged Americans to strive not only for individual salvation but for the perfection of society.

In the North, religious enthusiasm combined with economic developments to produce a growing consensus against slavery. Although the vast majority of Northerners believed in white supremacy, most viewed the South's slave-based economy as an anachronism, a relic of barbarism, while seeing their own region — in which free men competed in an economy that combined commerce, farming, and industry — as progressive, egalitarian, and moral. Some became active in the antislavery movement, speaking, writing, and petitioning the government for gradual and peaceful emancipation. A minority of antislavery advocates, the abolitionists (considered radical in the North as well as the South), favored an immediate and uncompensated end to slavery. The most radical among them called for slave revolts.

Northern opponents of slavery, a highly vocal and visible minority within their own region, gradually won converts with their courage and their persuasive arguments based largely on religion. Although they generally operated outside the religious establishment, they launched an impassioned attack on slavery as something contrary to Christian precepts. The slave South, they insisted, was evil in every way — morally debasing to both slave and slaveholder.

In the South, the congressional debate leading up to the Missouri Compromise of 1820 produced a growing awareness that slavery was embattled just as the expanding slave-based economy made the region increasingly dependent on it. In addition, slave revolts (or the threat of them) in Charleston in 1820 and in Virginia in 1831 prompted the South to tighten restrictions on slaves and on the distribution of antislavery literature in the region. Increased economic dependence, fear, and a growing resentment of northern attacks on southern society and culture fueled southern defensiveness about the region's "peculiar institution." Dissenting opinions were no longer tolerated.

Southern churches came down squarely on the side of slavery. Even southern evangelicals, once quite critical of the institution, changed their stance as their ranks expanded to include wealthy slaveholders. By the mid-1820s, Baptists, Methodists, and Presbyterians had joined Episcopalians as defenders of slavery. In fact, southern evangelicals became staunch defenders of the social order and came into conflict with northern members of their denominations over the slavery issue: the Presbyterians in 1837, then the Methodists in 1844, and finally the Baptists in 1845 divided along sectional lines.

By the 1830s, a proslavery movement had emerged in which southern ministers joined other intellectual and political leaders in urging fellow Southerners to stop defending slavery as a "necessary evil" and instead affirm it as a positive good. Religious and moral arguments augmented proslavery arguments based on the classics, on economics, and on "science" asserting that slavery was not only sanctioned by Christianity but created a more just and moral society than did free labor. Southerners contrasted the South — which they considered paternalistic, harmonious, and God-fearing — with the North — which they portrayed as materialistic, competitive, and immoral. The images the two regions were creating of themselves and of one another would later cause each to believe that God was on its side in the fratricidal conflict of the 1860s.

The documents in this chapter clearly demonstrate religion's centrality in the debate over slavery. The authors of the first two documents use religious and moral arguments as justification: Richard Furman, an influential Baptist minister, explains to the governor of South Carolina why Christianity supports rather than condemns slaveholding; and George Fitzhugh, a leading writer in the proslavery movement, insists that a slave society is more conducive to Christian virtue than a free society. In the second two documents, a white Southerner and a black Southerner insist that slavery is in violent conflict with Christian doctrine. Both were writing from the safety of the North: Angelina Grimké, a woman from a South Carolina slaveholding family, became famous — indeed notorious — as an antislavery agent and advocate for women's rights; Frederick Douglass escaped from slavery in Maryland and became a leading abolitionist and one of the most important African American leaders of the nineteenth century. Each assumes that religion is such a powerful force in both South and North that slavery would come to an end if Christians would only demand it.

As you read, consider these questions: How do defenders and opponents of slavery invoke the Bible and Christianity to support their arguments? What do they say about the moral effects of slavery on slaves and slaveholders? What do proslavery and antislavery writers say about the arguments of their opponents? What do the opponents of slavery want religious people and the churches to do?

36. A Minister Defends Slavery

RICHARD FURMAN
The Biblical Justification for Slavery
1822

Richard Furman was a leading Baptist minister in South Carolina. This address, prepared for presentation to Governor Thomas Bennett and endorsed by the Baptist State Convention, provides a concrete example of the church supporting the state on the slavery issue. It was published the year after South Carolina narrowly escaped a bloody insurrection: Denmark Vesey, a free black man of Charleston whose wife and children were slaves, planned a slave revolt, which was betrayed by one of the conspirators. Vesey was a literate and highly religious man; Furman's exposition suggests the degree to which he and other South Carolinians were concerned about the potential impact of antislavery literature on their slaves.

On the lawfulness of holding slaves, considering it in a moral and religious view, the convention think it their duty to exhibit their sentiments on the present occasion before Your Excellency, because they consider their duty to God, the peace of the state, the satisfaction of scrupulous consciences, and the welfare of the slaves themselves as intimately connected with a right view of the subject. The

Richard Furman, Rev. Dr. Richard Furman's Exposition of the Views of the Baptists, Relative to the Coloured Population of the United States, in a Communication to the Governor of South-Carolina (Charleston, 1823). Reprinted in American Social Thought: Sources and Interpretations since the Civil War, ed. Michael McGiffert and Robert Allen Skotheim (Reading, Mass.: Addison-Wesley, 1972), 352–55.

rather, because certain writers on politics, morals, and religion, and some of them highly respectable, have advanced positions and inculcated sentiments very unfriendly to the principle and practice of holding slaves; and, by some, these sentiments have been advanced among us, tending in their nature *directly* to disturb the domestic peace of the state, to produce insubordination and rebellion among the slaves, and to infringe the rights of our citizens; and *indirectly* to deprive the slaves of religious privileges by awakening in the minds of their masters a fear that acquaintance with the Scriptures and the enjoyment of these privileges would naturally produce the aforementioned effects; because the sentiments in opposition to the holding of slaves have been attributed by their advocates to the Holy Scriptures and to the genius of Christianity.

These sentiments, the convention, on whose behalf I address Your Excellency, cannot think just or well-founded; for the right of holding slaves is clearly established in the Holy Scriptures, both by precept and example. In the Old Testament, the Israelites were directed to purchase their bondmen and bondmaids of the heathen nations; except they were of the Canaanites, for these were to be destroyed. And it is declared that the persons purchased were to be their "bondmen forever," and an "inheritance for them and their children." They were not to go out free in the year of jubilee, as the Hebrews, who had been purchased, were; the line being clearly drawn between them. . . .

Had the holding of slaves been a moral evil, it cannot be supposed that the inspired apostles, who feared not the faces of men and were ready to lay down their lives in the cause of their God, would have tolerated it for a moment in the Christian Church. If they had done so on a principle of accommodation, in cases where the masters remained heathen, to avoid offenses and civil commotion, yet, surely, where both master and servant were Christian, as in the case before us, they would have enforced the law of Christ and required that the master should liberate his slave in the first instance. But, instead of this, they let the relationship remain untouched as being lawful and right, and insist on the relative duties.

In proving this subject justifiable by scriptural authority, its morality is also proved; for the Divine Law never sanctions immoral actions.

The Christian Golden Rule of doing to others as we would they should do to us has been urged as an unanswerable argument against holding slaves. But surely this rule is never to be urged against that order of things which the Divine Government has established; nor do our desires become a standard to us, under this rule, unless they have a due regard to justice, propriety, and the general good. . . .

If the holding of slaves is lawful, or according to the Scriptures, then this scriptural rule can be considered as requiring no more of the master, in respect of justice (whatever it may do in point of generosity) than what he, if a slave, could consistently wish to be done to himself, while the relationship between master and servant should be still continued.

In this argument, the advocates for emancipation blend the ideas of injustice and cruelty with those which respect the existence of slavery, and consider them as inseparable. But, surely, they may be separated. A bond-servant may be treated with justice and humanity as a servant; and a master may, in an important sense, be the guardian and even father of his slaves. . . .

That Christian nations have not done all they might, or should have done, on a principle of Christian benevolence for the civilization and conversion of the Africans; that much cruelty has been practised in the slave trade, as the benevolent Wilberforce and others have shown; that much tyranny has been exercised by individuals, as masters over their slaves, and that the religious interests of the latter have been too much neglected by many cannot, will not be denied. But the fullest proof of these facts will not also prove that the holding [of] men in subjection, as slaves, is a moral evil and inconsistent with Christianity. Magistrates, husbands, and fathers have proved tyrants. This does not prove that magistracy, the husband's right to govern, and parental authority are unlawful and wicked. The individual who abuses his authority and acts with cruelty must answer for it at the Divine Tribunal, and civil authority should interpose to prevent or punish it; but neither civil nor ecclesiastical authority can consistently interfere with the possession and legitimate exercise of a right given by the Divine Law. . . .

It appears to be equally clear that those, who by reasoning on abstract principles, are induced to favor the scheme of general emancipation, and who ascribe their sentiments to Christianity, should be particularly careful, however benevolent their intentions may be, that they do not by a perversion of the scriptural doctrine, through their wrong views of it, not only invade the domestic and religious peace and rights of our citizens on this subject but, also by an intemperate zeal, prevent indirectly the religious improvement of the people they design, professedly, to benefit; and, perhaps, become, evidently, the means of producing in our country scenes of anarchy and blood. And all this in a vain attempt to bring about a state of things which, if arrived at, would not probably better the state of that people; which is thought by men of observation to be generally true of the Negroes in the Northern states who have been liberated.

To pious minds it has given pain to hear men, respectable for intelligence and morals, sometimes say that holding slaves is indeed indefensible, but that to us it is necessary and must be supported. On this principle, mere politicians, unmindful of morals, may act. But surely, in a moral and religious view of the subject, this principle is inadmissible. It cannot be said that theft, falsehood, adultery, and murder are become necessary and must be supported. Yet there is reason to believe that some of honest and pious intentions have found their minds embarrassed, if not perverted, on this subject by this plausible but unsound argument. From such embarrassment the view exhibited above affords relief.

The convention, sir, are far from thinking that Christianity fails to inspire the minds of its subjects with benevolent and generous sentiments; or that liberty, rightly understood or enjoyed, is a blessing of little moment. The contrary of these positions they maintain. But they also consider benevolence as consulting the truest and best interests of its objects; and view the happiness of liberty as well as of religion as consisting not in the name or form but in the reality. While men remain in the chains of ignorance and error, and under the dominion of tyrant lusts and passions, they cannot be free. And the more freedom of action they have in this state, they are but the more qualified by it to do injury both to themselves and others. It is, therefore, firmly believed that general emancipation to the Negroes in this country would not, in present circumstances, be for their own happiness, as a body; while it would be extremely injurious to the community at large in various ways; and, if so, then it is not required even by benevolence. . . .

Should, however, a time arrive when the Africans in our country might be found qualified to enjoy freedom, and, when they might obtain it in a manner consistent with the interest and peace of the community at large, the convention would be happy in seeing them free. And so they would, in seeing the state of the poor, the ignorant, and the oppressed of every description and of every country meliorated; so that the reputed free might be free, indeed, and happy. But there seems to be just reason to conclude that a considerable part of the human race, whether they bear openly the character of slaves or are reputed freemen, will continue in such circumstances, with mere shades of variation, while the world continues. . . .

And here I am brought to a part of the general subject which I confess to Your Excellency, the convention, from a sense of their duty as a body of men to whom important concerns of religion are confided, have particularly at heart, and wish it may be seriously considered by all our citizens: This is the religious interests of the Negroes. For though they are slaves, they are also men; and are with ourselves accountable creatures, having immortal souls and being destined to future eternal award. Their religious interests claim a regard from their masters of the most serious nature; and it is indispensable. Nor can the community at large, in a right estimate of their duty and happiness, be indifferent on this subject. To the truly benevolent it must be pleasing to know that a number of masters, as well as ministers and pious individuals of various Christian denominations among us, do conscientiously regard this duty; but there is great reason to believe that it is neglected and disregarded by many.

The convention are particularly unhappy in considering that an idea of the Bible's teaching the doctrine of emancipation as necessary, and, tending to make servants insubordinate to proper authority, has obtained access to any mind; both on account of its direct influence on those who admit it, and the fear it excites in others, producing the effects before noticed. But it is hoped it has been evinced that the idea is an erroneous one, and that it will be seen that the influence of a right acquaintance with that Holy Book tends directly and powerfully, by promoting the fear and love of God, together with just and peaceful sentiments toward men, to produce one of the best securities to the public for the internal and domestic peace of the state. . . .

37. Slavery Defended as Moral and Beneficial

George Fitzhugh
"Slavery Justified, by a Southerner"
1850

George Fitzhugh, a well-known proslavery writer, was a self-educated lawyer-journalist from Port Royal, Virginia. Like other authors in the proslavery genre, Fitzhugh wrote not only to counter the attacks of antislavery writers but also to awaken fellow white Southerners to the virtues of their society and give them the tools with which "to promote [their] peculiar interests." According to Fitzhugh, slavery produced a civilization superior to all others and far better than the exploitative society of the North, in which free laborers were essentially "slaves without masters." In other writings, Fitzhugh shocked even his fellow Southerners by insisting that slavery should be adopted in the North and in Europe, and that if people really believed in the beneficence of slavery and in human inequality, they should enslave inferior whites as well as blacks.

. . . The moral effect of free society is to banish Christian virtue, that virtue which bids us love our neighbor as ourself, and to substitute the very equivocal virtues proceeding from mere selfishness. The intense struggle to better each one's pecuniary condition, the rivalries, the jealousies, the hostilities which it begets, leave neither time nor inclination to cultivate the heart or the head. Every finer feeling of our nature is chilled and benumbed by its selfish atmosphere; affection is under the ban, because affection makes us less regardful of mere self; hospitality is considered criminal waste, chivalry a stumbling-block, and the code of honor foolishness; taste, sentiment, imagination, are forbidden ground, because no money is to be made by them. Gorgeous pageantry and sensual luxury are the only pleasures indulged in, because they alone are understood and appreciated, and they are appreciated just for what they cost in dollars and cents. What makes money, and what costs money, are alone desired. Temperance, frugality, thrift, attention to business, industry, and skill in making bargains are virtues in high repute, because they enable us to supplant others and increase our own wealth. The character of our Northern brethren, and of the Dutch, is proof enough of the justice of these reflections. The Puritan fathers had

George Fitzhugh, "Slavery Justified, by a Southerner" (Fredericksburg: Recorder Printing Office, 1850), later included in *Sociology for the South, or the Failure of Free Society* (Richmond: A. Morris, 1854), 226–58 passim. Reprinted in *Slavery Defended: The Views of the Old South*, ed. Eric L. McKitrick (Englewood Cliffs, N.J.: Prentice Hall, 1963), 40–41, 44–50.

lived in Holland, and probably imported Norway rats and Dutch morality in the Mayflower.

Liberty and equality are not only destructive to the morals, but to the happiness of society. Foreigners have all remarked on the care-worn, thoughtful, unhappy countenances of our people, and the remark only applies to the North, for travellers see little of us at the South, who live far from highways and cities, in contentment on our farms.

The facility with which men may improve their condition would, indeed, be a consideration much in favor of free society, if it did not involve as a necessary consequence the equal facility and liability to lose grade and fortune. As many fall as rise. The wealth of society hardly keeps pace with its numbers. All cannot be rich. The rich and the poor change places oftener than where there are fixed hereditary distinctions; so often, that the sense of insecurity makes every one unhappy. . . .

. . . Those who rise, pull down a class as numerous, and often more worthy than themselves, to the abyss of misery and penury. Painful as it may be, the reader shall look with us at this dark side of the picture; he shall view the vanquished as well as the victors on this battle-ground of competition; he shall see those who were delicately reared, taught no tricks of trade, no shifts of thrifty avarice, spurned, insulted, down-trodden by the coarse and vulgar, whose wits and whose appetites had been sharpened by necessity. If he can sympathize with fallen virtue or detest successful vice, he will see nothing in this picture to admire. . . .

In Boston, a city famed for its wealth and the prudence of its inhabitants, nine-tenths of the men in business fail. In the slaveholding South, except in new settlements, failures are extremely rare; small properties descend from generation to generation in the same family; there is as much stability and permanency of property as is compatible with energy and activity in society; fortunes are made rather by virtuous industry than by tricks, cunning, and speculation. . . .

Domestic slavery in the Southern States has produced the same results in elevating the character of the master that it did in Greece and Rome. He is lofty and independent in his sentiments, generous, affectionate, brave, and eloquent; he is superior to the Northerner in every thing but the arts of thrift. History proves this. . . . Scipio and Aristides, Calhoun and Washington, are the noble results of domestic slavery. Like Egyptian obelisks 'mid the waste of time — simple, severe, sublime, — they point ever heavenward, and lift the soul by their examples. . . .

But the chief and far most important enquiry is, how does slavery affect the condition of the slave? One of the wildest sects of Communists in France proposes not only to hold all property in common, but to divide the profits, not according to each man's input and labor, but according to each man's wants. Now this is precisely the system of domestic slavery with us. We provide for each slave, in old age and in infancy, in sickness and in health, not according to his labor, but according to his wants. The master's wants are more costly and refined, and he therefore gets a larger share of the profits. A Southern farm is the beau ideal of Communism; it is a joint concern, in which the slave consumes more than the master, of the coarse products, and is far happier, because although the concern may fail, he is always sure of a support; he is only transferred to another master to participate in the profits of another concern; he marries when he pleases, because he knows he will have to work no more with a family than without one, and whether he live or die, that family will be taken care of; he exhibits all the pride of ownership, despises a partner in a smaller concern, "a poor man's negro," boasts of "our crops, horses, fields and cattle"; and is as happy as a human being can be. And why should he not?—he enjoys as much of the fruits of the farm as he is capable of doing, and the wealthiest can do no more. Great wealth brings many additional cares, but few additional enjoyments. Our stomachs do not increase in capacity with our fortunes. We want no more clothing to keep us warm. We may create new wants, but we cannot create new pleasures. The intellectual enjoyments which wealth affords are probably balanced by the new cares it brings along with it.

There is no rivalry, no competition to get employment among slaves, as among free laborers. Nor is there a war between master and slave. The master's interest prevents his reducing the slave's allowance or wages in infancy or sickness, for he might lose the slave by so doing. His feeling for his slave never permits him to stint him in old age. The slaves are all well fed, well clad, have plenty of fuel, and are happy. They have no dread of the future — no fear of want. A state of dependence is the only condition in which reciprocal affection can exist among human beings — the only situation in which the war of competition ceases, and peace, amity and good will arise. A state of independence always begets more or less of jealous, rivalry, and hostility. A man loves his children because they are weak, helpless, and dependent. He loves his wife for similar reasons. When his children grow up and assert their independence, he is apt to transfer his affection to his grandchildren. He ceases to love his wife when she becomes masculine or rebellious; but slaves are always dependent, never the rivals of their master. Hence, though men are often found at variance with wife or children, we never saw one who did not like his slaves, and rarely a slave who was not devoted to his master. "I am thy servant!" disarms me of the power of master. Every man feels the beauty, force and truth of this sentiment of Sterne. But he who acknowledges its truth, tacitly admits that dependence is a tie of affection, that the relation of master and slave is one of mutual good will. Volumes written on the subject would not prove as much as this single sentiment. It has found its way to the heart of every reader, and carried conviction along with it. The slaveholder is like other men; he will not tread on the worm nor break the bruised reed. The ready submission of the slave, nine times out of ten, disarms his wrath even when the slave has offended. The habit of command may make him imperious and fit him for rule; but he is only imperious when thwarted or crossed by his equals; he would scorn to put on airs of command among blacks, whether slaves or free; he always speaks to them in a kind and subdued tone. We go farther, and say the slaveholder is better than others — because he has greater occasion for the exercise of the affections. His whole life is spent in providing for the minutest wants of others, in taking care of them in sickness and in health. Hence he is the least selfish of men. Is not the old bachelor who retires to seclusion always selfish? Is not the head of a large family almost always kind and benevolent? And is not the slaveholder the head of the largest family? Nature compels master and slave to be friends; nature makes employers and free laborers enemies.

The institution of slavery gives full development and full play to the affections. Free society chills, stints, and eradicates them. In a homely way the farm will support all, and we are not in a hurry to send our children into the world, to push their way and make their fortunes, with a capital of knavish maxims. We are better husbands, better fathers, better friends, and better neighbors than our Northern brethren. The tie of kindred to the fifth degree is often a tie of affection with us. First cousins are scarcely acknowledged at the North, and even children are prematurely pushed off into the world. Love for others is the organic law of our society, as self-love is of theirs.

Every social structure must have its substratum. In free society this substratum, the weak, poor, and ignorant, is borne down upon and oppressed with continually increasing weight by all above. We have solved the problem of relieving this substratum from the pressure from above. The slaves are the substratum, and the master's feelings and interests alike prevent him from bearing down upon and oppressing them. With us the pressure on society is like that of air or water, so equally diffused as not any where to be felt. With them it is the pressure of the enormous screw, never yielding, continually increasing. Free laborers are little better than trespassers on this earth given by God to all mankind. The birds of the air have nests, and the foxes have holes, but they have not where to lay their heads. They are driven to cities to dwell in damp and crowded cellars, and thousands are even forced to lie in the open air. This accounts for the rapid growth of Northern cities. The feudal Barons were more generous and hospitable and less tyrannical than the petty land-holders of modern times. Besides, each inhabitant of the barony was considered as having some right of residence, some claim to protection from the Lord of the Manor. A few of them escaped to the municipalities for purposes of trade, and to enjoy a larger liberty. Now penury and the want of a home drive thousands to towns. The slave always has a home, always an interest in the proceeds of the soil. . . .

At the slaveholding South all is peace, quiet, plenty, and contentment. We have no mobs, no trades unions, no strikes for higher wages, no armed resistance to the law, but little jealousy of the rich by the poor. We have but few in our jails, and fewer in our poor houses. We produce enough of the comforts and necessaries of life for a population three or four times as numerous as ours. We are wholly exempt from the torrent of pauperism, crime, agrarianism, and infidelity which Europe is pouring from her jails and alms houses on the already crowded North. Population increases slowly, wealth rapidly. . . . Wealth is more equally distributed than at the North, where a few millionaires own most of the property of the country. (These millionaires are men of cold hearts and weak minds; they know how to make money, but not how to use it, either for the benefit of themselves or of others.) High intellectual and moral attainments, refinement of head and heart, give standing to a man in the South, however poor he may be. Money is, with few exceptions, the only thing that ennobles at the North. We have poor among us, but none who are over-worked and under-fed. We do not crowd cities because lands are abundant and their owners kind, merciful and hospitable. The poor are as hospitable as the rich, the negro as the white man. Nobody dreams of turning a friend, a relative, or a stranger from his door. The very negro who deems it no crime to steal, would scorn to sell his hospitality. We have no loafers, because the poor relative or friend who borrows our horse, or spends a week under our roof, is a welcome guest. The loose economy, the wasteful mode of living at the South, is a blessing when rightly considered; it keeps want, scarcity, and famine at a distance, because it leaves room for retrenchment. The nice, accurate economy of France, England, and New England, keeps society always on the verge of famine, because it leaves no room to retrench, that is to live on a part only of what they now consume. Our society exhibits no appearance of precocity, no symptoms of decay. A long course of continuing improvement is in prospect before us, with no limits which human foresight can descry. Actual liberty and equality with our white population has been approached much nearer than in the free States. Few of our whites ever work as day laborers, none as cooks, scullions, ostlers, body servants, or in other menial capacities. One free citizen does not lord it over another; hence that feeling of independence and equality that distinguishes us; hence that pride of character, that self-respect, that gives us ascendancy when we come in contact with Northerners. It is a distinction to be a Southerner, as it was once to be a Roman citizen.

. . . Until the last fifteen years, our great error was to imitate Northern habits, customs, and institutions. Our circumstances are so opposite to theirs, that whatever suits them is almost sure not to suit us. Until that time, in truth, we distrusted our social system. We thought slavery morally wrong, we thought it would not last, we thought it unprofitable. The Abolitionists assailed us; we looked more closely into our circumstances; became satisfied that slavery was morally right, that it would continue ever to exist, that it was as profitable as it was humane. This begat self-confidence, self-reliance. Since then our improvement has been rapid. Now we may safely say, that we are the happiest, most contented and prosperous people on earth. The intermeddling of foreign pseudo-philanthropists in our affairs, though it has occasioned great irritation and indignation, has been of inestimable advantage in teaching us to form a right estimate of our condition. This intermeddling will soon cease; the poor at home in thunder tones demand their whole attention and all their charity. Self-preservation will compel them to listen to their demands. . . .

In conclusion, we will repeat the propositions, in somewhat different phraseology, with which we set out. First — That Liberty and Equality, with their concomitant Free Competition, beget a war in society that is as destructive to its weaker members as the custom of exposing the deformed and crippled children. Secondly — That slavery protects the weaker members of society just as do the relations of parent, guardian, and husband, and is as necessary, as natural, and almost as universal as those relations. Is our demonstration imperfect? Does universal experience sustain our theory? Should the conclusions to which we have arrived appear strange and startling, let them therefore not be rejected without examination. The world has had but little opportunity to contrast the working of Liberty and Equality with the old order of things, which always partook more or less of the character of domestic slavery. The strong prepossession in the public mind in favor of the new system, makes it reluctant to attribute the evil phenomena which it exhibits, to defects inherent in the system itself. That these defects should not have been foreseen and pointed out by any process of *a priori*[1] reasoning, is but another proof of the fallibility of human sagacity and foresight when attempting to foretell the operation of new institutions. It is as much as human reason can do, when examining the complex frame of society, to trace effects back to their causes — much more than it can do, to foresee what effects new causes will produce. We invite investigation.

[1] *a priori*: based on theory rather than experience or experiment.

38. An Expatriate Urges Southern Women to Oppose Slavery

Angelina Grimké
From "Appeal to the Christian Women of the South"
1836

Angelina Grimké was the youngest of fourteen children in a socially and politically prominent slaveholding family in Charleston. Intensely opposed to slavery, both she and her sister Sarah left the South; they became famous for their work in the North against slavery and for women's rights. Angelina's "Appeal," published by the American Antislavery Society and widely read in the United States and in England, was unique in abolitionist literature as the only appeal by a southern abolitionist woman to other southern women. In writing it, she hoped to reach Southerners who discounted Northerners' arguments on the assumption that they did not understand southern life and were prejudiced against the South. She also believed that an address written to men would not reach women, whereas one written to women could influence the whole community. The "Appeal," like other abolitionist literature, was burned publicly in Charleston, and Grimké's mother was warned that Angelina would be arrested if she ever attempted to visit the city.

Then Mordecai commanded to answer Esther, Think not within thyself that thou shalt escape in the king's house more than all the Jews. For if thou altogether holdest thy peace at this time, then shall there enlargement and deliverance arise to the

Angelina Grimké, "Appeal to the Christian Women of the South" (1836). Reprinted in *American Political Thought: Four Hundred Years of Ideas and Ideologies*, ed. Sue Davis (Englewood Cliffs, N.J.: Prentice Hall, 1995), 228–34.

*Jews from another place: but thou and thy father's house shall be destroyed; and
who knoweth whether thou art come to the kingdom for such a time as this. And
Esther bade them return Mordecai this answer: — and so will I go in unto the
king, which is not according to law, and if I perish, I perish.*

Esther IV. 13–16.

Respected Friends,

It is because I feel a deep and tender interest in your present and eternal welfare that I am willing thus publicly to address you. Some of you have loved me as
a relative, and some have felt bound to me in Christian sympathy, and Gospel fel-
lowship; and even when compelled by a strong sense of duty, to break those outward bonds of union which bound us together as members of the same community, and members of the same religious denomination, you were generous
enough to give me credit, for sincerity as a Christian, though you believed I had
been most strangely deceived. . . .

But there are other Christian women scattered over the Southern States, a
very large number of whom have never seen me, and never heard my name, and
who feel *no* interest whatever in *me*. But I feel an interest in *you*, as branches of
the same vine from whose root I daily draw the principle of spiritual vitality — Yes!
Sisters in Christ I feel an interest in *you*, and often has the secret prayer arisen on
your behalf, Lord "open thou their eyes that they may see wondrous things out of
thy Law" — It is then, because I *do feel* and *do pray* for you, that I thus address you
upon a subject about which of all others, perhaps you would rather not hear any
thing; but, "would to God ye could bear with me a little in my folly, and indeed
bear with me, for I am jealous over you with godly jealousy." Be not afraid then
to read my appeal; it is *not* written in the heat of passion or prejudice, but in that
solemn calmness which is the result of conviction and duty. It is true. I am going
to tell you unwelcome truths, but I mean to speak those *truths in love*, and remember Solomon says, "faithful are the *wounds* of a friend." I do not believe the
time has yet come when *Christian women* "will not endure sound doctrine," even
on the subject of Slavery, if it is spoken to them in tenderness and love, therefore
I now address *you*. . . .

I have thus, I think, clearly proved to you seven propositions. viz.: First, that
slavery is contrary to the declaration of our independence. Second, that it is contrary to the first charter of human rights given to Adam, and renewed to Noah.
Third, that the fact of slavery having been the subject of prophecy, furnishes *no*
excuse whatever to slavedealers. Fourth, that no such system existed under the pa-
triarchal dispensation. Fifth, that *slavery never* existed under the Jewish dispensation; but so far otherwise, that every servant was placed under the *protection of law*,
and care taken not only to prevent all *involuntary* servitude, but all *voluntary perpetual* bondage. Sixth, that slavery in America reduces a *man* to a *thing*, a "chattel personal," *robs him* of *all* his rights as a *human being*, fetters both his mind and
body, and protects the *master* in the most unnatural and unreasonable power,
whilst it *throws him out* of the protection of law. Seventh, that slavery is contrary
to the example and precepts of our holy and merciful Redeemer, and of his
apostles.

But perhaps you will be ready to query, why appeal to *women* on this subject? We do not make the laws which perpetuate slavery. No legislative power is vested in *us; we* can do nothing to overthrow the system, even if we wished to do so. To this I reply, I know you do not make the laws, but I also know that *you are the wives and mothers, the sisters and daughters of those who do,* and if you really suppose *you* can do nothing to overthrow slavery, you are greatly mistaken. You can do much in every way: four things I will name. 1st. You can read on this subject. 2d. You can pray over this subject. 3d. You can speak on this subject. 4th. You can *act* on this subject. I have not placed reading before praying because I regard it more important, but because, in order to pray aright, we must understand what we are praying for; it is only then we can "pray with the understanding and the spirit also."

1. Read then on the subject of slavery. Search the Scriptures daily, whether the things I have told you are true. Other books and papers might be a great help to you in this investigation, but they are not necessary, and it is hardly probable that your Committees of Vigilance will allow you to have any other. The *Bible* then is the book I want you to read in the spirit of inquiry, and the spirit of prayer. Even the enemies of Abolitionists, acknowledge that their doctrines are drawn from it. In the great mob in Boston, last autumn, when the books and papers of the Anti-Slavery Society, were thrown out of the windows of their office, one individual laid hold of the Bible and was about tossing it out to the ground, when another reminded him that it was the Bible he had in his hand. "*O! 'tis all one,*" he replied, and out went the sacred volume, along with the rest. We thank him for the acknowledgment. Yes, "*it is all one,*" for our books and papers are mostly commentaries on the Bible, and the Declaration. Read the *Bible* then, it contains the words of Jesus, and they are spirit and life. Judge for yourselves whether *he sanctioned* such a system of oppression and crime.

2. Pray over this subject. When you have entered into your closets, and shut to the doors, then pray to your father, who seeth in secret, that he would open your eyes to see whether slavery is *sinful,* and if it is, that he would enable you to bear a faithful, open and unshrinking testimony against it, and to do whatsoever your hands find to do, leaving the consequences entirely to him, who still says to us whenever we try to reason away duty from the fear of consequences, "*What is that to thee, follow thou me.*" Pray also for that poor slave, that he may be kept patient and submissive under his hard lot, until God is pleased to open the door of freedom to him without violence or bloodshed. Pray too for the master that his heart may be softened, and he made willing to acknowledge, as Joseph's brethren did, "Verily we are guilty concerning our brother," before he will be compelled to add in consequence of Divine judgment, "therefore is all this evil come upon us." Pray also for all your brethren and sisters who are laboring in the righteous cause of Emancipation in the Northern States, England and the world. There is great encouragement for prayer in these words of our Lord. "Whatsoever ye shall ask the Father *in my name,* he *will give* it to you" — Pray then without ceasing, in the closet and the social circle.

3. Speak on this subject. It is through the tongue, the pen, and the press, that truth is principally propagated. Speak then to your relatives, your friends, your ac-

quaintances on the subject of slavery; be not afraid if you are conscientiously convinced it is *sinful,* to say so openly, but calmly, and to let your sentiments be known. If you are served by the slaves of others, try to ameliorate their condition as much as possible; never aggravate their faults, and thus add fuel to the fire of anger already kindled, in a master and mistress's bosom; remember their extreme ignorance, and consider them as your Heavenly Father does the *less* culpable on this account, even when they do wrong things. Discountenance *all* cruelty to them, all starvation, all corporal chastisement; these may brutalize and *break* their spirits, but will never bend them to willing, cheerful obedience. If possible, see that they are comfortably and *seasonably* fed, whether in the house or the field; it is unreasonable and cruel to expect slaves to wait for their breakfast until eleven o'clock, when they rise at five or six. Do all you can, to induce their owners to clothe them well, and to allow them many little indulgences which would contribute to their comfort. Above all, try to persuade your husband, father, brothers, and sons, that *slavery is a crime against God and man,* and that it is a great sin to keep *human beings* in such abject ignorance; to deny them the privilege of learning to read and write. The Catholics are universally condemned, for denying the Bible to the common people, but, *slaveholders must not* blame them, for *they* are doing the *very same thing,* and for the very same reason, neither of these systems can bear the light which bursts from the pages of that Holy Book. And lastly, endeavour to inculcate submission on the part of the slaves, but whilst doing this be faithful in pleading the cause of the oppressed.

> "Will *you* behold unheeding,
> Life's holiest feelings crushed,
> Where *woman's* heart is bleeding,
> Shall *woman's* voice be hushed?"

4. Act on this subject. Some of you *own* slaves yourselves. If you believe slavery is *sinful,* set them at liberty, "undo the heavy burdens and let the oppressed go free." If they wish to remain with you, pay them wages, if not let them leave you. Should they remain teach them, and have them taught the common branches of an English education; they have minds and those minds, *ought to be improved.* So precious a talent as intellect, never was given to be wrapt in a napkin and buried in the earth. It is the *duty* of all, as far as they can, to improve their own mental faculties, because we are commanded to love God with *all our minds,* as well as with all our hearts, and we commit a great sin, if we *forbid or prevent* that cultivation of the mind in others, which would enable them to perform this duty. Teach your servants then to read &c, and encourage them to believe it is their *duty* to learn, if it were only that they might read the Bible.

But some of you will say, we can neither free our slaves nor teach them to read, for the laws of our state forbid it. Be not surprised when I say such wicked laws *ought to be no barrier* in the way of your duty, and I appeal to the Bible to prove this position. What was the conduct of Shiphrah and Puah, when the king of Egypt issued his cruel mandate, with regard to the Hebrew children? *"They* feared *God*, and did *not* as the King of Egypt commanded them, but saved the men children alive." Did these *women* do right in disobeying that monarch? "*Therefore* (says the sacred text,) *God dealt well* with them, and made them houses" Ex. i. . . . .

But some of you may say, if we do free our slaves, they will be taken up and sold, therefore there will be no use in doing it. Peter and John might just as well have said, we will not preach the gospel, for if we do, we shall be taken up and put in prison, therefore there will be no use in our preaching. *Consequences*, my friends, belong no more to *you*, than they did to these apostles. . . .

I know that this doctrine of obeying *God*, rather than man, will be considered as dangerous, and heretical by many, but I am not afraid openly to avow it, because it is the doctrine of the Bible; but I would not be understood to advocate resistance to any law however oppressive, if, in obeying it, I was not obliged to commit *sin*. If for instance, there was a law, which imposed imprisonment or a fine upon me if I manumitted a slave, I would on no account resist that law, I would set the slave free, and then go to prison or pay the fine. If a law commands me to *sin I will break it*; if it calls me to *suffer*, I will let it take its course *unresistingly*. The doctrine of blind obedience and unqualified submission to *any human* power, whether civil or ecclesiastical, is the doctrine of despotism, and ought to have no place among Republicans and Christians. . . .

But you may say we are *women*, how can *our* hearts endure persecution? And why not? Have not *women* stood up in all the dignity and strength of moral courage to be the leaders of the people, and to bear a faithful testimony for the truth whenever the providence of God has called them to do so? Are there no *women* in that noble army of martyrs who are now singing the song of Moses and the Lamb? Who led out the women of Israel from the house of bondage, striking the timbrel, and singing the song of deliverance on the banks of that sea whose waters stood up like walls of crystal to open a passage for their escape? It was a *woman*; Miriam, the prophetess, the sister of Moses and Aaron. Who went up with Barak to Kadesh to fight against Jabin, King of Canaan, into whose hand Israel had been sold because of their iniquities? It was a *woman*! Deborah the wife of Lapidoth, the judge, as well as the prophetess of that backsliding people; Judges iv, 9. Into whose hands was Sisera, the captain of Jabin's host delivered? Into the hand of a *woman*. Jael the wife of Heber! Judges vi, 21. . . .

To whom did he *first* appear after his resurrection? It was to a *woman*! Mary Magdalene; Mark xvi, 9. Who gathered with the apostles to wait at Jerusalem, in prayer and supplication, for "the promise of the Father"; the spiritual blessing of the Great High Priest of his Church, who had entered, *not* into the splendid temple of Solomon, there to offer the blood of bulls, and of goats, and the smoking censer upon the golden altar, but into Heaven itself, there to present his intercessions, after having "given himself for us, an offering and a sacrifice to God for a sweet smelling savor?" *Women* were among that holy company; Acts i, 14. And did *women* wait in vain? Did those who had ministered to his necessities, followed in his train, and wept at his crucifixion, wait in vain? No! No! Did the cloven tongues of fire descend upon the heads of *women* as well as men? Yes, my friends, "it sat upon *each one of them*"; Acts ii, 3. *Women* as well as men were to be living stones in the temple of grace, and therefore *their* heads were consecrated by the descent of the Holy Ghost as well as those of men. Were *women* recognized as fellow laborers in the gospel field? They were! Paul says in his epistle to the Philippians, "help those *women* who labored with me, in the gospel"; Phil. iv, 3. . . .

And what, I would ask in conclusion, have *women* done for the great and glorious cause of Emancipation? Who wrote that pamphlet which moved the heart of Wilberforce to pray over the wrongs, and his tongue to plead the cause of the oppressed African? It was a *woman*, Elizabeth Heyrick. Who labored assiduously to keep the sufferings of the slave continually before the British public? They were *women*. And how did they do it? By their needles, paint brushes and pens, by speaking the truth, and petitioning Parliament for the abolition of slavery. And what was the effect of their labors? Read it in the Emancipation bill of Great Britain. Read it, in the present state of her West India Colonies. Read it, in the impulse which has been given to the cause of freedom, in the United States of America. Have English women then done so much for the negro, and shall American women do nothing? Oh no! Already are there sixty female Anti-Slavery Societies in operation. These are doing just what the English women did, telling the story of the colored man's wrongs, praying for his deliverance, and presenting his kneeling image constantly before the public eye on bags and needle-books, card-racks, pen-wipers, pin-cushions, &c. Even the children of the north are inscribing on their handy work, "May the points of our needles prick the slaveholder's conscience." Some of the reports of these Societies exhibit not only considerable talent, but a deep sense of religious duty, and a determination to persevere through evil as well as good report, until every scourge, and every shackle, is buried under the feet of the manumitted slave.

The Ladies' Anti-Slavery Society of Boston was called last fall, to a severe trial of their faith and constancy. They were mobbed by "the gentlemen of property and standing," in that city at their anniversary meeting, and their lives were jeoparded by an infuriated crowd; but their conduct on that occasion did credit to our sex, and affords a full assurance that they will *never* abandon the cause of the slave. . . . The Northern women may labor to produce a correct public opinion at the North, but if Southern women sit down in listless indifference and criminal idleness, public opinion cannot be rectified and purified at the South. It is manifest to every reflecting mind, that slavery must be abolished; the era in which we live, and the light which is overspreading the whole world on this subject, clearly show that the time cannot be distant when it will be done. Now there are only two ways in which it can be effected, by moral power or physical force, and it is for *you* to choose which of these you prefer. Slavery always has, and always will produce insurrections wherever it exists, because it is a violation of the natural order of things, and no human power can much longer perpetuate it. . . .

. . . Can you not, my friends, understand the signs of the times; do you not see the sword of retributive justice hanging over the South, or are you still slumbering at your posts?—Are there no Shiphrahs, no Puahs among you, who will dare in Christian firmness and Christian meekness, to refuse to obey the *wicked laws* which require *woman to enslave, to degrade and to brutalize woman?* Are there no Miriams, who would rejoice to lead out the captive daughters of the Southern States to liberty and light? Are there no Huldahs there who will dare to *speak the truth* concerning the sins of the people and those judgments, which it requires no prophet's eye to see, must follow if repentance is not speedily sought? Is there no Esther among you who will plead for the poor devoted slave? . . . Yes! if there were but *one* Esther at the South, she *might* save her country from ruin; but let the Christian women there arise, as the Christian women of Great Britain did, in the majesty of moral power, and that salvation is certain. Let them embody themselves in societies, and send petitions up to their different legislatures, entreating their husbands, fathers, brothers, and sons, to abolish the institution of slavery; no longer to subject *woman* to the scourge and the chain, to mental darkness and moral degradation; no longer to tear husbands from their wives, and children from their parents; no longer to make men, women, and children, work *without wages*; no longer to make their lives bitter in hard bondage; no longer to reduce *American citizens* to the abject condition of *slaves*, of "chattels personal"; no longer to barter the *image of God* in human shambles for corruptible things such as silver and gold.

The *women of the South can overthrow* this horrible system of oppression and cruelty, licentiousness and wrong. Such appeals to your legislatures would be irresistible, for there is something in the heart of man which *will bend under moral suasion.* There is a swift witness for truth in his bosom, which *will respond to truth* when it is uttered with calmness and dignity. If you could obtain but six signatures to such a petition in only one state, I would say, send up that petition, and be not in the least discouraged by the scoffs and jeers of the heartless, or the resolution of the house to lay it on the table. It will be a great thing if the subject can be introduced into your legislatures in any way, even by *women*, and *they* will be the most likely to introduce it there in the best possible manner, as a matter of *morals* and *religion*, not of expediency or politics. You may petition, too, the different ecclesiastical bodies of the slave states. Slavery must be attacked with the whole power of truth and the sword of the spirit. You must take it up on *Christian* ground, and fight against it with Christian weapons, whilst your feet are shod with the preparation of the gospel of peace. And *you are now* loudly called upon by the cries of the widow and the orphan, to arise and gird yourselves for this great moral conflict, with the whole armour of righteousness upon the right hand and on the left. . . .

Sisters in Christ, I have done. As a Southerner, I have felt it was my duty to address you. I have endeavoured to set before you the exceeding sinfulness of slavery, and to point you to the example of those noble women who have been raised up in the church to effect great revolutions, and to suffer for the truth's sake. I have appealed to your sympathies as women, to your sense of duty as *Christian women.* I have attempted to vindicate the Abolitionists, to prove the entire safety of immediate Emancipation, and to plead the cause of the poor and oppressed. I have done — I have sowed the seeds of truth, but I well know, that even if an

Apollos were to follow in my steps to water them, *"God only* can give the in-crease." To Him then who is able to prosper the work of his servant's hand, I com-mend this Appeal in fervent prayer, that as he "hath *chosen the weak things of the world,* to confound the things which are mighty," so He may cause His blessing, to descend and carry conviction to the hearts of many Lydias through these speak-ing pages. Farewell — Count me not your "enemy because I have told you the truth," but believe me in unfeigned affection,

Your sympathizing Friend,
Angelina E. Grimké
1836

39. A Former Slave Exposes Hypocrisy

FREDERICK DOUGLASS
"What to the Slave Is the Fourth of July?"
1852

Frederick Douglass was one of the most famous of the escaped slaves who partici-pated in the antislavery movement in the North. His oratorical skills and his first-hand knowledge of slavery made him an impassioned, effective, and much-sought-after speaker. Douglass also generated support for the antislavery cause through his abolitionist newspaper, the North Star, *and his moving autobiography,* Narrative of the Life of Frederick Douglass, An American Slave, Written by Himself *(1845). Like the Grimkés, Douglass combined his antislavery efforts with work for women's rights (he was one of the earliest advocates of woman suffrage). A staunch supporter of the Republican Party, Douglass was appointed ambassador to Haiti in 1889.*

In this powerful address, delivered in Rochester, New York, in 1852, Douglass attacks the hypocrisy of a nation that celebrates freedom while tolerating the en-slavement of millions, as well as the Christian Church, which has failed to take a united stand against an "un-Christian" institution.

———————

The Frederick Douglass Papers, Series One: Speeches, Debates, and Interviews, ed. John W. Blassingame et al. (New Haven, Conn.: Yale University Press, 1982), 2: 359, 360, 363–88. Reprinted in *The Amer-ican Intellectual Tradition: A Sourcebook,* ed. David A. Hollinger and Charles H. Capper, vol. 1, *1630–1865,* 2d ed. (New York: Oxford University Press, 1993), 400–10.

Mr. President, Friends and Fellow Citizens:

He who could address this audience without a quailing sensation, has stronger nerves than I have. . . .

The papers and placards say, that I am to deliver a 4th [of] July oration. This certainly sounds large, and out of the common way, for me. It is true that I have often had the privilege to speak in this beautiful Hall, and to address many who now honor me with their presence. But neither their familiar faces, nor the perfect gage I think I have of Corinthian Hall, seems to free me from embarrassment.

The fact is, ladies and gentlemen, the distance between this platform and the slave plantation, from which I escaped, is considerable — and the difficulties to be overcome in getting from the latter to the former, are by no means slight. That I am here to-day is, to me, a matter of astonishment as well as of gratitude. . . .

The Present

. . . Fellow-citizens, pardon me, allow me to ask, why am I called upon to speak here to-day? What have I, or those I represent, to do with your national independence? Are the great principles of political freedom and of natural justice, embodied in that Declaration of Independence, extended to us? and am I, therefore, called upon to bring our humble offering to the national altar, and to confess the benefits and express devout gratitude for the blessings resulting from your independence to us?

Would to God, both for your sakes and ours, than an affirmative answer could be truthfully returned to these questions! Then would my task be light, and my burden easy and delightful. For *who* is there so cold, that a nation's sympathy could not warm him? Who so obdurate and dead to the claims of gratitude, that would not thankfully acknowledge such priceless benefits? Who so stolid and selfish, that would not give his voice to swell the hallelujahs of a nation's jubilee, when the chains of servitude had been torn from his limbs? I am not that man. In a case like that, the dumb might eloquently speak, and the "lame man leap as an hart."

But, such is not the state of the case. I say it with a sad sense of the disparity between us. I am not included within the pale of this glorious anniversary! Your high independence only reveals the immeasurable distance between us. The blessings in which you, this day, rejoice, are not enjoyed in common. The rich inheritance of justice, liberty, prosperity and independence, bequeathed by your fathers, is shared by you, not by me. The sunlight that brought life and healing to you, has brought stripes and death to me. This Fourth [of] July is *yours*, not *mine.* *You* may rejoice, *I* must mourn. To drag a man in fetters into the grand illuminated temple of liberty, and call upon him to join you in joyous anthems, were inhuman mockery and sacrilegious irony. Do you mean, citizens, to mock me, by asking me to speak to-day? . . .

Fellow-citizens; above your national, tumultous joy, I hear the mournful wail of millions! whose chains, heavy and grievous yesterday, are, to-day, rendered more intolerable by the jubilee shouts that reach them. If I do forget, if I do not faithfully remember those bleeding children of sorrow this day, "may my right hand forget her cunning, and may my tongue cleave to the roof of my mouth!" To forget them, to pass lightly over their wrongs, and to chime in with the popular theme, would be treason most scandalous and shocking, and would make me a reproach before God and the world. My subject, then fellow-citizens, is AMERICAN SLAVERY. I shall see, this day, and its popular characteristics, from the slave's point of view. Standing, there, identified with the American bondman, making his wrongs mine, I do not hesitate to declare, with all my soul, that the character and conduct of this nation never looked blacker to me than on this 4th of July! Whether we turn to the declarations of the past, or to the professions of the present, the conduct of the nation seems equally hideous and revolting. America is false to the past, false to the present, and solemnly binds herself to be false to the future. Standing with God and the crushed and bleeding slave on this occasion, I will, in the name of humanity which is outraged, in the name of liberty which is fettered, in the name of the constitution and the Bible, which are disregarded and trampled upon, dare to call in question and to denounce, with all the emphasis I can command, everything that serves to perpetuate slavery — the great sin and shame of America! "I will not equivocate; I will not excuse"; I will use the severest language I can command; and yet not one word shall escape me that any man, whose judgement is not blinded by prejudice, or who is not at heart a slaveholder, shall not confess to be right and just.

But I fancy I hear some one of my audience say, it is just in this circumstance that you and your brother abolitionists fail to make a favorable impression on the public mind. Would you argue more, and denounce less, would you persuade more, and rebuke less, your cause would be much more likely to succeed. But, I submit, where all is plain there is nothing to be argued. What point in the anti-slavery creed would you have me argue? . . .

Would you have me argue that man is entitled to liberty? that he is the rightful owner of his own body? You have already declared it. Must I argue the wrongfulness of slavery? Is that a question for Republicans? Is it to be settled by the rules of logic and argumentation, as a matter beset with great difficulty, involving a doubtful application of the principle of justice, hard to be understood? How should I look to-day, in the presence of Americans, dividing, and subdividing a discourse, to show that men have a natural right to freedom? speaking of it relatively, and positively, negatively, and affirmatively. To do so, would be to make myself ridiculous, and to offer an insult to your understanding. There is not a man beneath the canopy of heaven, that does not know that slavery is wrong *for him.*

What, am I to argue that it is wrong to make men brutes, to rob them of their liberty, to work them without wages, to keep them ignorant of their relations to their fellow men, to beat them with sticks, to flay their flesh with the lash, to load their limbs with irons, to hunt them with dogs, to sell them at auction, to sunder their families, to knock out their teeth, to burn their flesh, to starve them into obedience and submission to their masters? Must I argue that a system thus marked with blood, and stained with pollution, is *wrong?* No! I will not. I have better employments for my time and strength, than such arguments would imply.

What, then, remains to be argued? Is it that slavery is not divine; that God did not establish it; that our doctors of divinity are mistaken? There is blasphemy in the thought. That which is inhuman, cannot be divine! *Who* can reason on such a proposition? They that can, may; I cannot. The time for such argument is past.

At a time like this, scorching irony, not convincing argument, is needed. O! had I the ability, and could I reach the nation's ear, I would, to-day, pour out a fiery stream of biting ridicule, blasting reproach, withering sarcasm, and stern rebuke. For it is not light that is needed, but fire; it is not the gentle shower, but thunder. We need the storm, the whirlwind, and the earthquake. The feeling of the nation must be quickened; the conscience of the nation must be roused; the propriety of the nation must be startled; the hypocrisy of the nation must be exposed; and its crimes against God and man must be proclaimed and denounced.

What, to the American slave, is your 4th of July? I answer; a day that reveals to him, more than all other days in the year, the gross injustice and cruelty to which he is the constant victim. To him, your celebration is a sham; your boasted liberty, an unholy license; your national greatness, swelling vanity; your sounds of rejoicing are empty and heartless; your denunciations of tyrants, brass fronted impudence; your shouts of liberty and equality, hollow mockery; your prayers and hymns, your sermons and thanksgivings, with all your religious parade, and solemnity, are, to him, mere bombast, fraud, deception, impiety, and hypocrisy — a thin veil to cover up crimes which would disgrace a nation of savages. There is not a nation on the earth guilty of practices, more shocking and bloody, than are the people of these United States, at this very hour. . . .

Religious Liberty

I take this law to be one of the grossest infringements of Christian Liberty, and, if the churches and ministers of our country were not stupidly blind, or most wickedly indifferent, they, too, would so regard it.

At the very moment that they are thanking God for the enjoyment of civil and religious liberty, and for the right to worship God according to the dictates of their own consciences, they are utterly silent in respect to a law which robs religion of its chief significance, and makes it utterly worthless to a world lying in wickedness. . . . The fact that the church of our country, (with fractional exceptions), does not esteem "the Fugitive Slave Law" as a declaration of war against religious liberty, implies that that church regards religion simply as a form of worship, an empty ceremony, and *not* a vital principle, requiring active benevolence, justice, love and good will towards man. It esteems sacrifice above mercy; psalm-singing above right doing; solemn meetings above practical righteousness. A worship that can be conducted by persons who refuse to give shelter to the houseless, to give bread to the hungry, clothing to the naked, and who enjoin obedience to a law forbidding these acts of mercy, is a curse, not a blessing to mankind. The Bible addresses all such persons as "scribes, pharisees, hypocrites, who pay tithe of *mint, anise,* and *cummin,* and have omitted the weightier matters of the law, judgement, mercy and faith."

The Church Responsible

But the church of this country is not only indifferent to the wrongs of the slave, it actually takes sides with the oppressors. It has made itself the bulwark of American slavery, and the shield of American slave-hunters. Many of its most eloquent Divines, who stand as the very lights of the church, have shamelessly given the sanction of religion and the Bible to the whole slave system. They have taught that man may, properly, be a slave; that the relation of master and slave is ordained of God; that to send back an escaped bondman to his master is clearly the duty of all the followers of the Lord Jesus Christ; and this horrible blasphemy is palmed off upon the world for Christianity.

For my part, I would say, welcome infidelity! welcome atheism! welcome anything! in preference to the gospel, *as preached by those Divines!* They convert the very name of religion into an engine of tyranny, and barbarous cruelty, and serve to confirm more infidels, in this age, than all the infidel writings of Thomas Paine, Voltaire, and Bolingbroke, put together, have done! These ministers make religion a cold and flinty-hearted thing, having neither principles of right action, nor bowels of compassion. They strip the love of God of its beauty, and leave the throne of religion a huge, horrible, repulsive form. It is a religion for oppressors, tyrants, man-stealers, and *thugs*. It is not that *"pure and undefiled religion"* which is from above, and which is *"first pure, then peaceable, easy to be entreated,* full of mercy and good fruits, *without partiality, and without hypocrisy."* But a religion which favors the rich against the poor; which exalts the proud above the humble; which divides mankind into two classes, tyrants and slaves; which says to the man in chains, *stay there*; and to the oppressor, *oppress on*; it is a religion which may be professed and enjoyed by all the robbers and enslavers of mankind; it makes God a respecter of persons, denies his fatherhood of the race, and tramples in the dust the great truth of the brotherhood of man. All this we affirm to be true of the popular church, and the popular worship of our land and nation — a religion, a church, and a worship which, on the authority of inspired wisdom, we pronounce to be an abomination in the sight of God. In the language of Isaiah, the American church might be well addressed. "Bring no more vain oblations; incense is an abomination unto me: the new moons and Sabbaths, the calling of assemblies, I cannot away with; it is iniquity, even the solemn meeting. Your new moons and your appointed feasts my soul hateth. They are a trouble to me; I am weary to bear them; and when ye spread forth your hands I will hide mine eyes from you. Yea! when ye make many prayers, I will not hear. YOUR HANDS ARE FULL OF BLOOD; cease to do evil, learn to do well; seek judgement; relieve the oppressed; judge for the fatherless; plead for the widow."

The American church is guilty, when viewed in connection with what it is doing to uphold slavery; but it is superlatively guilty when viewed in connection with its ability to abolish slavery.

The sin of which it is guilty is one of omission as well as of commission. Albert Barnes but uttered what the common sense of every man at all observant of the actual state of the case will receive as truth, when he declared that "There is no power out of the church that could sustain slavery an hour, if it were not sustained in it."

Let the religious press, the pulpit, the Sunday school, the conference meeting, the great ecclesiastical, missionary, Bible and tract associations of the land array their immense powers against slavery and slave-holding; and the whole system of crime and blood would be scattered to the winds; and that they do not do this involves them in the most awful responsibility of which the mind can conceive.

In prosecuting the anti-slavery enterprise, we have been asked to spare the church, to spare the ministry; but *how*, we ask, could such a thing be done? We are met on the threshold of our efforts for the redemption of the slave, by the church and ministry of the country, in battle arrayed against us; and we are compelled to fight or flee. From what *quarter*, I beg to know, has proceeded a fire so deadly upon our ranks, during the last two years, as from the Northern pulpit? As the champions of oppressors, the chosen men of American theology have appeared — men, honored for their so-called piety, and their real learning. The LORDS of Buffalo, the SPRINGS of New York, the LATHROPS of Auburn, the COXES and SPENCERS of Brooklyn, the GANNETS and SHARPS of Boston, the DEWEYS of Washington, and other great religious lights of the land, have, in utter denial of the authority of *Him*, by whom they professed to be called to the ministry, deliberately taught us, against the example of the Hebrews and against the remonstrance of the Apostles, they teach *"that we ought to obey man's law before the law of God."*

My spirit wearies of such blasphemy; and how such men can be supported, as the "standing types and representatives of Jesus Christ," is a mystery which I leave others to penetrate. In speaking of the American church, however, let it be distinctly understood that I mean the *great mass* of the religious organizations of our land. There are exceptions, and I thank God that there are. Noble men may be found scattered all over these Northern States, of whom Henry Ward Beecher of Brooklyn, Samuel J. May of Syracuse, and my esteemed friend[1] on the platform, are shining examples; and let me say further, that upon these men lies the duty to inspire our ranks with high religious faith and zeal, and to cheer us on in the great mission of the slave's redemption from his chains. . . .

[1] **my esteemed friend:** Rev. R. R. Raymond.

Suggestions for Further Reading

Faust, Drew Gilpin. *A Sacred Circle: The Dilemma of the Intellectual in the Old South, 1840–1860.* Baltimore: Johns Hopkins University Press, 1977. Reprint, 1986.

Genovese, Eugene D., and Elizabeth Fox-Genovese. "The Religious Ideals of Southern Slave Society." *Georgia Historical Quarterly* 70, no. 1 (spring 1986): 1–16.

Lerner, Gerda. *The Grimké Sisters from South Carolina: Pioneers for Women's Rights and Abolition.* Boston: Houghton Mifflin, 1967.

Loveland, Anne C. *Southern Evangelicals and the Social Order, 1800–1860.* Baton Rouge: Louisiana State University Press, 1980.

Martin, Waldo E., Jr. *The Mind of Frederick Douglass.* Chapel Hill: University of North Carolina Press, 1984.

Tise, Larry E. *Proslavery: A History of the Defense of Slavery in America, 1701–1840.* Athens: University of Georgia Press, 1987.

CHAPTER ELEVEN

WESTWARD EXPANSION

The Texas Frontier

Nineteenth-century Americans were a people on the move, and in ever-increasing numbers they moved west. The addition of new territories occurred rapidly: Florida was acquired from Spain in 1819 and, more important, the vast trans-Mississippi territories of the Louisiana Purchase were obtained from France in 1803. By 1860, the nation's boundaries stretched across the continent to encompass the older coastal Atlantic states, the Pacific coastal state of California, and the states newly organized out of the Old Northwest (Ohio, Indiana, Illinois, and Wisconsin) and the Old Southwest (Alabama, Tennessee, and Mississippi). Almost inevitably, Americans also relocated to the sparsely populated lands of northern Mexico; this region—soon known as "Texas"—came to attract much of the westward migration of Southerners.

American migration to Texas began in the 1820s when Moses Austin, a merchandiser, miner, and land speculator, and his son Stephen negotiated terms with Mexican officials by which several hundred American families were permitted to settle the area. But tensions between the Anglo-Americans and Mexicans appeared at once. Certainly, there were cultural clashes — not only over language, but also as a result of differences between the Roman Catholic Mexicans and the mostly Protestant Anglo-Americans. There was also a conflict between the two on the issue of slavery: although Mexico had ended the practice, most of the immigrants to Texas were southern slaveholders. They soon bridled at Mexican control of Texan affairs, while Mexicans resented the expanding Anglo presence.

Texas's population continued to swell — from 7,000 in the mid-1820s to 52,000 in 1836, and about 60 percent of the burgeoning population was Anglo-American. In 1830, concerned about the looming possibility of American annexation, the Mexican government tried to stem the flow by prohibiting settlers from the United States. But as Mexico sought greater control over its northern province, Texans sought greater autonomy. In October 1832, they held a convention protesting the ban against American immigration; a year later, they drafted their first constitution. Stephen Austin visited Mexico to seek a solution but was imprisoned for nearly a year. By 1835, the Texas Revolution had begun, and at the Battle of San Jacinto in the spring of 1836, Texans triumphed over (and captured) the Mexican president Santa Anna. The Lone Star Republic, established by force of arms, elected Sam Houston as its first president in the fall of 1836.

Over the next decade Texas existed as a separate nation, but its connection with the United States remained powerful. The new republic continued to fear Mexico, which refused to recognize its boundaries. In the United States, Texas became a cause for leading southern politicians, who enthusiastically promoted its annexation in order to provide a westward path for the expanding slave system. The Mexican War of 1846–48, fought primarily over Texas, resulted in a decisive American victory: not only was Texas incorporated into the United States, but also a large portion of northern Mexico. Migration accelerated, about 90 percent of the new immigrants being native-born Southerners lured there because of available — often free — land. The state grew rapidly: by 1860, its total population stood at more than six hundred thousand.

Eastern Texas, the state's most rapidly expanding region, was closely identified with the cotton-growing South. During the antebellum period over half of the white immigrants to Texas came from Alabama and Tennessee, most of the rest from Georgia and Mississippi. Many of these immigrants were cotton farmers moving from the exhausted soils of their home states. As a result, cotton plantations spread rapidly into eastern Texas and with them the institution of slavery. The number of slaves brought in corresponded closely with the boom in the state's economy: during the 1850s, for example, the slave population increased by about 214 percent as the white population was increasing by 177 percent. In some of the major plantation counties of east Texas, the Civil War slaves outnumbered whites — much as they did in the plantation counties of the South.

During the 1840s and 1850s, Texans became a distinctive people. They inhabited a frontier society, to be sure, but, unlike other parts of the American West, Texas melded together sharply different cultural and regional traditions. Land developers' promises of prime land available for the taking drew a combination of frontiersmen, land speculators, cotton planters, and other people on the make — the phrase "Gone to Texas" was commonly used to refer to Southerners who had left home to escape their bad debts, petty crimes, felonies, or other brushes with the law. The largest non-English-speaking group, the Germans, began arriving in the 1840s and numbered more than thirty thousand by 1860. The diversity of Texas was further augmented by the continued immigration of Mexicans, who preserved a powerful culture, despite the border wars that raged within the state and across the Rio Grande. But conflict between whites and Native Americans continued, and between 1836 and 1860 an average of two hundred white Texans were killed or captured in Indian wars every year. This continuous race war with Native Americans united Texas's mixture of other races and cultures.

As the readings in this chapter show, Texas illustrates the divergent tendencies involved in westward expansion, and also how that phenomenon affected Americans' view of themselves. Explaining why Texans sought independence in 1836, Stephen F. Austin argues that the values of the Texas Revolution closely resembled those of the American Revolution. Nonetheless, antebellum Texas was indisputably a frontier society, as Ann Raney Thomas Coleman shows in her description of the experiences of one woman living on the early Texas frontier. That society was changing and complex, as Frederick Law Olmsted shows in his portrayal of Texas during the 1850s as a society of frontiersmen, slaveholders, and ambitious men — perhaps the nation's best example of the social mix that accompanied the great rush across the Mississippi near the middle of the nineteenth century.

As you read, pay attention to the similarities and differences in the way Texas is portrayed in these documents. What perspectives do Austin, Coleman, and Olmsted bring to their accounts, and how do their perspectives affect their descriptions? What were antebellum Texas's most important social and political values, and how had they changed by 1860?

40. Texas and the Union

STEPHEN F. AUSTIN
Address Delivered at Louisville, Kentucky
1836

Widely regarded as the founding father of Texas, Stephen F. Austin was born in 1793 in southwest Virginia. At an early age, he moved west with his parents to the Missouri territory, and, in 1820, to Arkansas. After his father, Moses Austin, obtained Mexico's consent to settle three hundred Anglo families in Texas, Stephen led the first

William C. Fray and Lisa A. Spar, dirs., *The Avalon Project* <http://www.yale.edu/lawweb/avalon /texind01.htm> (21 May 1998).

settlement of Anglos in January 1822. He continued to enjoy broad powers as the de facto head of local government until the early 1830s. Although he had worked well with Mexican officials in the 1820s, relations deteriorated in the 1830s, and Austin became a leader of the Texas independence movement.

Austin delivered this speech on March 7 as part of his efforts to promote American support for the Texas cause in early 1836. Negotiations with Andrew Jackson's government for loans, financial support, recognition, and even annexation were unsuccessful, and Austin eventually returned home empty-handed. His speech, directed to an audience of Kentuckians (many of whom emigrated to Texas), suggests the political values that Texans associated with their revolution.

. . . When a people consider themselves compelled by circumstances or by oppression, to appeal to arms and resort to their natural rights, they necessarily submit their cause to the great tribunal of public opinion. The people of Texas, confident in the justice of their cause, fearlessly and cheerfully appeal to this tribunal. In doing this the first step is to show, as I trust I shall be able to do by a succinct statement of facts, that our cause is just, and is the cause of light and liberty: — the same holy cause for which our forefathers fought and bled: — the same that has an advocate in the bosom of every freeman, no matter in what country, or by what people it may be contended for.

But a few years back Texas was a wilderness, the home of the uncivilized and wandering Comanche and other tribes of Indians, who waged a constant warfare against the Spanish settlements. These settlements at that time were limited to the small towns of Bexar (commonly called San Antonio) and Goliad, situated on the western limits. The incursions of the Indians also extended beyond the Rio Bravo del Norta, and desolated that part of the country. . . .

The question here naturally occurs, what inducements, what prospects, what hopes could have stimulated us, the pioneers and settlers of Texas, to remove from the midst of civilized society, to expatriate ourselves from this land of liberty, from this our native country, endeared to us as it was, and still is, and ever will be, by the ties of nativity, the reminiscences of childhood and youth and local attachments, of friendship and kindred? Can it for a moment be supposed that we severed all these ties — the ties of nature and of education, and went to Texas to grapple with the wilderness and with savage foes, merely from a spirit of wild and visionary adventure, without guarantees of protection for our persons and property and political rights? No, it cannot be believed. No American, no Englishman, no one of any nation who has a knowledge of the people of the United States, or of the prominent characteristics of the Anglo-Saxon race to which we belong — a race that in all ages and in all countries wherever it has appeared has been marked for a jealous and tenacious watchfulness of its liberties, and for a cautious and calculating view of the probable events of the future — no one who has a knowledge of this race can or will believe that we removed to Texas without such guarantees, as free born, and, enterprising men naturally expect and require. The fact is, we had such guarantees; for, in the first place the government bound itself to protect us by the mere act of admitting us as citizens, on the general and long established principle, even in the dark ages, that protection and allegiance are reciprocal — a principle which in this enlightened age has been extended much further; for its received interpretation now is, that the object of government is the well being, security, and happiness of the governed, and that allegiance ceases whenever it is clear, evident, and palpable, that this object is in no respect effected. . . .

Without exhausting the patience by a detail of numerous other vexatious circumstances, and violations of our rights, I trust that what I have said on this point, is sufficient to show that the federal social compact of Mexico is dissolved; that we have just and sufficient cause to take arms against the revolutionary government which has been established; that we have forborne until the cup was full to overflowing; and that further forbearance or submission on our part would have been both ruinous and degrading; and that it was due to the great cause of liberty, to ourselves, to our posterity, and to the free blood which I am proud to say, fills our veins, to resist and proclaim war against such acts of usurpation and oppression.

The justice of our cause being clearly shown, the next important question that naturally presents itself to the intelligent and inquiring mind, is, what are the objects and intentions of the people of Texas?

To this we reply, that our object is freedom — civil and religious freedom — emancipation from that government, and that people, who, after fifteen years experiment, since they have been separated from Spain, have shown that they are incapable of self-government, and that all hopes of any thing like stability or rational liberty in their political institutions, at least for many years, are vain and fallacious.

This object we expect to obtain, by a total separation from Mexico, as an independent community, a new republic, or by becoming a state of the United States. Texas would have been satisfied to have been a state of the Mexican Confederation, and she made every constitutional effort in her power to become one. But that is no longer practicable, for that confederation no longer exists. One of the two alternatives above mentioned, therefore, is the only recourse which the revolutionary government of Mexico has left her. Either will secure the liberties and prosperity of Texas, for either will secure to us the right of self-government over a country which we have redeemed from the wilderness, and conquered without any aid or protection whatever from the Mexican government (for we never received any) and which is clearly ours. Ours, by every principle on which original titles to countries are, and ever have been founded. We have explored and pioneered it, developed its resources, made it known to the world, and given to it a high and rapidly increasing value. The federal republic of Mexico had a constitutional right to participate generally in this value, but it had not, and cannot have any other; and this one has evidently been forfeited and destroyed by unconstitutional acts and usurpation, and by the total dissolution of the social compact. Consequently, the true and legal owners of Texas, the only legitimate sovereigns of that country, are the people of Texas.

It is also asked, what is the present situation of Texas, and what are our resources to effect our objects, and defend our rights? The present position of Texas
is an absolute Declaration of Independence — a total separation from Mexico.
This declaration was made on the 7th of November last. . . .

It is worthy of particular attention that this declaration affords another and
unanswerable proof of the forbearance of the Texans, and of their firm adher-
ence, even to the last moment, to the constitution which they had sworn to support, and to their political obligations as Mexican citizens. For, although at this
very time the federal system and constitution of 1824, had been overturned and
trampled under foot by military usurpation, in all other parts of the republic, and
although our country was actually invaded by the usurpers for the purpose of sub-
jecting us to the military rule, the people of Texas still said to the Mexican nation — "restore the federal constitution and govern in conformity to the social
compact, which we are all bound by our oaths to sustain, and we will continue to
be a member of the Mexican Confederation." This noble and generous act, for
such it certainly was, under the circumstances, is of itself sufficient to repel and
silence the false charges which the priests and despots of Mexico have made of the
ingratitude of the Texans. In what does this ingratitude consist? I cannot see, unless it be in our enterprise and perseverance, in giving value to a country that the
Mexicans considered valueless, and thus exciting their jealousy and cupidity. . . .

The true interpretation of this charge of ingratitude is as follows: — The Mexican government have at last discovered that the enterprising people who were induced to remove to Texas by certain promises and guaranties, have by their labours
given value to Texas and its lands. An attempt is therefore now made to take them
from us and to annul all those guaranties, and we are ungrateful because we are
not sufficiently "docile" to submit to this usurpation and injustice as the "docile"
Mexicans have in other parts of the nation.

To close this matter about ingratitude, I will ask — if it was not ingratitude in
the people of the United States to resist the "theory of oppression" and separate
from England? — can it be ingratitude in the people of Texas to resist oppression
and usurpation by separating from Mexico?

To return to the declaration of the 7th of November last, it will be observed
that it is a total separation from Mexico — an absolute declaration of independence — in the event of the destruction of the federal compact or system, and the
establishment of centralism. This event has taken place. The federal compact is
dissolved, and a central or consolidated government is established. I therefore repeat that the present position of Texas is absolute independence: — a position in
which we have been placed by the unconstitutional and revolutionary acts of the
Mexican government. The people of Texas firmly adhered to the last moment, to
the constitution which they and the whole nation had sworn to support. The government of Mexico have not — the party now in power have overturned the constitutional government and violated their oaths — they have separated from their
obligations, from their duty and from the people of Texas; and, consequently,
they are the true rebels. So far from being grateful, as they ought to be, to the
people of Texas for having given value to that country, and for having adhered to

their duty and constitutional obligations, the Mexicans charge us with these very acts as evidence of ingratitude. Men of judgment and impartiality must decide this point, and determine who has been, and now is ungrateful, and who are the true rebels.

In order to make the position of Texas more clear to the world, a convention has been called to meet the first of March, and is no doubt, now in session, for the express purpose of publishing a positive and unqualified declaration of independence, and organizing a permanent government.

Under the declaration of 7th November, a provisional government has been organized, composed of an executive head or governor, a legislative council and a judiciary. A regular army has been formed, which is now on the western frontiers prepared to repel an invasion, should one be attempted. A naval force has been fitted out, which is sufficient to protect our coast. We have met the invading force that entered Texas in October, under General Cos, and beaten him in every contest and skirmish, and driven every hostile soldier out of Texas. In San Antonio de Bexar, he was entrenched in strong fortifications, defended by heavy cannon, and a strong force of regular troops, greatly superior to ours in number, which was of undisciplined militia without any experienced officer. This place was besieged by the militia of Texas. The enemy was driven into his works; his provisions cut off, and the spirits and energies of his soldiers worn down, with the loss of only one man to the Texans, and the place was then taken by storm. A son of Kentucky, a noble and brave spirit from this land of liberty and of chivalry, led the storm. He conquered, and died, as such a spirit wished to die, in the cause of liberty, and in the arms of victory. Texas weeps for her Milam; Kentucky has cause to be proud of her son. His free spirit appeals to his countrymen to embark in the holy cause of liberty for which he died, and to avenge his death.

I pass to an examination of the resources of Texas. We consider them sufficient to effect and sustain our independence. We have one of the finest countries in the world, a soil surpassed by none for agriculture and pasturage, not even by the fairest portions of Kentucky — a climate that may be compared to Italy; within the cotton or sugar region, intersected by navigable rivers, and bounded by the Gulf of Mexico, on which there are several fine bays and harbors suitable for all the purposes of commerce — a population of about seventy thousand, which is rapidly increasing, and is composed of men of very reputable education and property, enterprising, bold and energetic, devotedly attached to liberty and their country, inured to the exercise of arms, and at all times ready to use them, and defend their homes inch by inch if necessary. The exportations of cotton are large. Cattle, sheep, and hogs are very abundant and cheap. The revenue from importations and direct taxes will be considerable, and rapidly increasing; the vacant lands are very extensive and valuable, and may be safely relied upon as a great source of revenue and as bounties to emigrants.

The credit of Texas is good, as is proven by the extensive loans already negotiated. The country and army are generally well supplied with arms and ammunition, and the organized force in February last in the field exceeded two thousand, and is rapidly increasing. But besides these resources, we have one which ought not, and certainly will not fail us — it is our cause — the cause of light and liberty, of religious toleration and pure religion. To suppose that such a cause will fail, when defended by Anglo-Saxon blood, by Americans, and on the limits, and at the very door of this free and philanthropic and magnanimous nation, would be calumny against republicanism and freedom, against a noble race, and against the philanthropic principles of the people of the United States. I therefore repeat that we consider our resources sufficient to effect our independence against the Mexicans, who are disorganized and enfeebled by revolutions, and almost destitute of funds or credit.

Another interesting question which naturally occurs to every one is, what great benefits and advantages are to result to philanthropy and religion, or to the people of these United States from the emancipation of Texas? To this we reply, that ours is most truly and emphatically the cause of liberty, which is the cause of philanthropy, of religion, of mankind; for in its train follow freedom of conscience, pure morality, enterprise, the arts and sciences, all that is dear to the noble minded and the free, all that renders life precious. On this principle, the Greeks and the Poles, and all others who have struggled for liberty, have received the sympathies or aid of the people of the United States; on this principle the liberal party in priest-ridden Spain, is now receiving the aid of high-minded and free born Englishmen; on this same principle Texas expects to receive the sympathies and aid of their brethren, the people of the United States, and of the freemen of all nations. But the Greeks and the Poles are not . . . the sons and daughters of Anglo-Americans. We are. We look to this happy land as to a fond mother from whose bosom we have imbibed those great principles of liberty which are now nerving us, although comparatively few in numbers and weak in resources, to contend against the whole Mexican nation in defence of our rights.

The emancipation of Texas will extend the principles of self-government, over a rich and neighbouring country, and open a vast field there for enterprise, wealth, and happiness, and for those who wish to escape from the frozen blasts of a northern climate, by removing to a more congenial one. It will promote and accelerate the march of the present age, for it will open a door through which a bright and constant stream of light and intelligence will flow from this great northern fountain over the benighted regions of Mexico.

That nation of our continent will be regenerated; freedom of conscience and rational liberty will take root in that distant and, by nature, much favoured land, where for ages past the banner of the inquisition, of intolerance, and of despotism has paralized, and sickened, and deadened every effort in favour of civil and religious liberty.

But apart from these great principles of philanthropy, and narrowing down this question to the contracted limits of cold and prudent political calculation, a view may be taken of it, which doubtless has not escaped the penetration of the sagacious and cautious politicians of the United States. It is the great importance of Americanizing Texas, by filling it with a population from this country, who will harmonize in language, in political education, in common origin, in every thing, with their neighbours to the east and north. By this means, Texas will become a great outwork on the west, to protect the outlet of this western world, the mouths of the Mississippi, as Alabama and Florida are on the east; and to keep far away from the southwestern frontier — the weakest and most vulnerable in the nation — all enemies who might make Texas a door for invasion, or use it as a theatre from which mistaken philanthropists and wild fanatics, might attempt a system of intervention in the domestic concerns of the south, which might lead to a servile war, or at least jeopardize the tranquility of Louisiana and the neighbouring states.

This view of the subject is a very important one, so much so that a bare allusion to it is sufficient to direct the mind to the various interests and results, immediate and remote, that are involved.

To conclude, I have shown that our cause is just and righteous, that it is the great cause of mankind, and as such merits the approbation and moral support of this magnanimous and free people. That our object is independence, as a new republic, or to become a state of these United States; that our resources are sufficient to sustain the principles we are defending; that the results will be the promotion of the great cause of liberty, of philanthropy, and religion, and the protection of a great and important interest to the people of the United States.

With these claims to the approbation and moral support of the free of all nations, the people of Texas have taken up arms in self-defence, and they submit their cause to the judgement of an impartial world, and to the protection of a just and omnipotent God.

41. Going to Texas

ANN RANEY THOMAS COLEMAN
A Frontier Marriage
1830s

Among the immigrants to Texas during the 1830s was a young woman, Ann Raney, who emigrated from England with her parents in 1832. They settled in Brazoria, in the new plantation district of eastern Texas. Soon after their arrival, both of Raney's parents died of fever, and she had to make her own way; for most young women, that meant marriage. Like other frontier societies, eastern Texas had a shortage of women:

Ann Raney Thomas Coleman, *Victorian Lady on the Frontier: The Journal of Ann Raney Coleman*, ed. C. Richard King (Norman: University of Oklahoma Press, 1971). Reprinted in *Texas Tears and Texas Sunshine: Voices of Frontier Women*, ed. J. Ella Powell Exley (College Station: Texas A&M University Press, 1985), 38–44.

Ann immediately was courted by suitors. The first one was interested in marriage, but his father opposed the match because of Ann's limited wealth. Then she met John Thomas, a respected and wealthy planter. The following excerpt from her memoir — published in 1971, long after her death in 1897 — describes their courtship and marriage and Ann's early experiences of moving to Texas's new frontier society.

Before we had finished breakfast . . . , in walked Mr. Thomas. I was again caught for another day's courtship. I tried to excuse myself by saying I had to go and meet a friend, but he would not let me off and made himself as agreeable as possible. When evening came I could hardly believe I had been sitting all day in his company. Next day I was in hopes he would go home, but I was disappointed. He stayed this day also. He had been three days in town, notwithstanding he came in such a hurry and said he must leave the next day. He had appointed to return in one week from the time he left. I thought I would be absent, but he came in before breakfast and left me no chance to escape. It was during those visits he had been seen by Mr. McNeel coming to the house. Now Mr. Thomas had proposed marriage to me and waited my answer. . . .

After many a debate in my own mind I determined to accept Mr. Thomas's proposal. He had visited me about half a dozen times; he was well known in the country; everyone spoke well of him. This was satisfactory to me. He had given me several references as to his standing as a man in society. . . .

It was on returning from seeing [a friend] and his family one evening, I was called in the street by someone. On looking around I saw Mrs. Smith who was now keeping the same hotel as Mrs. Long used to keep, Mrs. Long having retired into private life with her daughter into the country. Mrs. Smith said, "I wish to see you a little while." I went in, took off my bonnet when Mrs. Smith remarked, "I hear you are going to be married to Mr. Thomas." "Who told you so?" I replied. "Mr. Thomas himself." "He is rather too communicative," I said. She replied, "You need not be ashamed of him. He is one of the finest men in the country. He will make you a good husband." She then went on to tell all his good qualities and said nothing about the bad ones. I came out of her house to go home when I was met by Mrs. A, another friend of Mr. Thomas and one of mine also. She got hold of my arm and said, "Come take a walk with me up the street." I complied. She commenced with, "I hear you are going to be married to Mr. Thomas. Is it so?" I was silent. "If you marry him you will get a close stingy husband; and he has got a woman at home, one of his servants that will turn you out of doors before you have been home a month. He has lived a bachelor so long, he knows every grain of coffee that goes into his pot."

I listened patiently to this unpleasant news and said little in return. We did not stay long; or rather, I made my walk as short as possible without seeming rude, and bid her good evening. I was determined to tell Mr. Thomas of what his friend Mrs. A had said the next time we met, for he was a constant visitor at their house. I was looking for him to come in town daily. Had my death knell going to be sounded, I could not have dreaded it more. I was trying to summon up all my fortitude for the occasion when in walked Mr. Thomas. He came up to myself first and shook my hand and then passed on to the rest of the family. As soon as breakfast was finished Mr. Thomas and myself were left alone in the breakfast room.

He first broke the silence by saying, "I hope, Miss Ann, you have made up your answer to make me happy. It is to receive your answer I came to town today. I came near getting drowned crossing Linnville's Bayou, but I shall be repaid for the dangers I have passed if you consent to be my wife." My silence seemed to give consent, and he took my hand in his and pressed it warmly, while I burst into an agony of tears. "You shall never have cause to repent being my wife. I will do everything in my power to make you happy." I now told him what his friend Mrs. A had said. He seemed surprised and said, "Everyone is jealous of my expected happiness. You may pay no attention to anything you may hear against me. If you do not find strict obedience from every servant I have got, I will sell the first one that dares to insult or disobey you. I have a woman called Minerva who I raised from a child. She is a smart field hand and in cotton picking time she picks 300 pounds a day. In my absence she is my overseer, and though she is sometimes saucy she knows better than to give my wife any insolence." I told him I should expect perfect obedience from every one of his servants, and should they prove otherwise, he must sell them, which he said he would do. I told him I wished my sister to live with us. He said it would give him great pleasure to offer her a home.

He then went into town to make arrangements for our wedding. He was determined that no expense should be spared to make a handsome supper, which was to be provided at the hotel, Doctor Counsel's house not being large enough to entertain all that were being invited. Mr. Thomas left for home next day, and a week from that day was the one appointed for our wedding day. Mr. Thomas gave me an order on Mr. Mill's store to get anything I wanted for the occasion. I was now as busy as a bee making up my wedding suit, which was of rich white satin with blond lace, white silver artificial flowers, silver tinsel belt, black kid shoes with white satin rosettes and a gold bracelet, gold chain and no veil. This was all of my wedding dress. I had been in a fever of excitement all week, and with no appetite.

The day arrived. It rained in the morning so hard the streets were one sheet of water. Mr. Thomas arrived early in the morning bringing the girl Minerva, who I understood was such a high minded piece of humanity. He brought a boy to wait upon himself. At three o'clock in the evening I left Dr. Counsel's house for the hotel on horseback with Mr. Thomas. The streets were muddy from the recent rain. The sun shone out with all its brightness. There was a possibility that before night the water would dry up sufficiently to admit of visitors to attend our marriage. The amphibious race, the frogs, were silenced by the subduing melody of the winged tribes; all nature was bespangled with smiles. I alone seemed sad. Everyone else seemed cheerful. My intended tried to cheer me, as he saw me look thoughtful, and never left my side only when obliged to. We had a private room to ourselves, and when it was time to dress he left me and went to dress also. Crowds of persons began to flock in from the country, and by seven o'clock in the evening the hotel was filled to overflowing by two hundred persons.

Ours was the first public wedding given at the town of Brazoria. At eight o'clock my bridesmaids arrived, one a Miss Anderson, the other a Miss Bailey with whom we found our father on our arrival in Texas. Mr. Thomas had two grooms-men, one Mr. Edmond St. J. Hawkins, the other a gentleman whose name I have forgotten. At eight o'clock we entered the ball room to be married, it being the largest room in the house. The bridesmaids and groomsmen went first into the room, myself and Mr. Thomas last. I felt much abashed at the presence of so many people, and my eyes which on first entering had been cast to the ground were now raised to the face of Mr. Smith, the presiding alcalde,[1] who was going to perform the marriage ceremony. A breathless silence pervaded the room whilst the ceremony was performed. The alcalde himself was so much excited that he paused once or twice while performing the ritual. I looked at the bridesmaids who were tastefully dressed. They looked like marble statues. As for myself, I trembled from head to foot, and when the ceremony was finished and the alcalde told Mr. Thomas to salute his bride, I saw no motion made by him to do it. At last, feeling for his embarrassment, I turned my cheek to his so that he might more easily salute me, which he did. The same was done by the bridesmaids and groomsmen, the groomsmen kissing me first, then the bridesmaids. We then went out as we came in until tea and coffee were ready. Then we all assembled in the dining room where tea, coffee and cakes were handed around.

I saw a multitude of people, half of whom I was unacquainted with. The ladies were dressed very gay and in good taste and might have vied with city belles. After tea our congratulations commenced. I stood up with my husband until I was nearly exhausted, receiving one after another. At last a chair was brought me, and I sat down and only rose when obliged to. The dance had commenced and not more than half of the company had been presented to us. About ten o'clock that night I got liberty to dance for a short time. My engagements were too many to fill, so I danced but a little that I might give offense to none. About twelve o'clock at night supper was announced by our hostess, Mrs. Smith, and we retired to the sup-per room. Everything was tastefully arranged and the table laden with every del-icacy that could be procured. Fruit from Orleans was in abundance, the cake de-licious, fowl and meats plentiful, plenty of wine, also coffee. All eyes were on my husband and myself, so I ate but little; a cup of coffee was grateful to me, as it had always been my favorite beverage.

I hurried to retire where I would not be so closely observed. Everyone praised my dress, which I made myself, and said I looked charming but sad. This was a truth. I masked the feeling of my heart on this night that I might make him who I had chosen for my husband feel happy. At one o'clock I went up to my room with my servant Minerva, who, I had forgotten to state, was all obedience. I dismissed her shortly afterwards and I was left alone. My bridesmaids insisted on waiting upon me to disrobe me and see me in bed, but I would not permit them to and told them to go and enjoy themselves in the ball room. I had been sitting in one position half an hour before a looking glass that reflected my form to my view, when I thought, "I am dressed and adorned for a sacrifice." I had been sitting in

---

[1] **alcalde:** the designation in Spanish for the chief administrative and judicial officer of a town.

one position without a motion to undress. My thoughts were on my native land with my dear brother and Henry, who I never expected to forget; my love was still his, and parted only by force of circumstances. I was disappointed in not seeing that beloved face, my sister, at my wedding.

In the midst of these reflections, someone opened the door and the alcalde put in his head. "My dear, are you not in bed? Your husband wishes to retire for the night, and it is my business, according to the Spanish law, to see you both in bed." I felt indignant to this method of the Spanish law and promised to go to bed directly. With that promise he closed the door. My face, if anyone could have seen it, was crimson with blushes. And my husband came in and I was still sitting there with all my clothes on. He was surprised at seeing me still up, and taking my hand and kissing it, he said, "My child, I will be a father as well as a husband. Do not sit there, but go to bed and take some rest, for you have need of it. Tomorrow you have a long and tiresome journey to take. The roads are bad, and without rest, you will be unfit for it. I want to start as soon as we get breakfast."

I hid my face in my handkerchief and wept bitter tears. Would he fulfill all he had promised? I had need of a father's and a husband's care. I was fifteen years younger than Mr. Thomas and a child in appearance to himself. Without saying any more he went to the other end of the room, my back being turned to him, and in a few minutes he was in bed. I slipped off my dress and all my ornaments, blew out the light, and in a few minutes I was also in bed. Shortly afterwards in came my evil genius with a light in his hand, opened a part of the [mosquito] bar and looked at us both the space of a minute and was gone without speaking. My husband laughed and so did I, though no one saw me do so for I hid my face with the cover.

Mr. Thomas was up before day, and Mrs. Smith and many of the gentlemen who had never gone to bed went to the horse lot to joke him for being up so early, and he wished himself away from Brazoria and in his quiet home. In an hour from the time he got up, breakfast was ready. I was in hopes it was too early for anyone to be up, only those laid down, but when I went to the table it was crowded. As breakfast was over, I put on my riding skirt, which was the same one I had when thrown from Mr. Sterling McNeel's horse in the pond. I had a black silk basque, green broadcloth riding cap, with a plume of black ostrich feathers, white satin rosette on one side. A great many bouquets hung in a small basket on the horn on my saddle presented me by my friends. When ready to start, everyone grasped my hand to bid me adieu until it was sore from shaking hands with so many friends. On leaving the hotel three cheers went up for us, and three more for the Caney boys, in compliment to Mr. Thomas's taking the only Belle in Brazos.

I had a nice pony of iron gray bought by Mr. Thomas expressly for me, and a natural pacer. We found the roads bad, and it was night before we reached Mr. Hensley's on Cedar Creek or Lake. They were old people, had one son, who like the Dutchman's pig, little but old. We were entertained kindly, and as we were tired, went to bed early. After supper, Mrs. Smith had put no small quantity of cake and other nice things for our lunch on the road. I slept from fatigue, the first sleep that did me any good in a week.

In the morning, we started early again. It was but thirty miles, but the roads being so bad, it took us two days to reach home. I inquired many times of Mr. Thomas if this or that place was his, being impatient to arrive at home. He replied, "No, but we will soon reach there now. We are but a few miles from my plantation." Presently we came to Caney Creek, which seemed full of water. After stopping a few minutes on the brink, Mr. Thomas observed to me, "I think Caney is swimming, but don't be afraid. It is not far across. Follow me; it has a hard bottom. There is no danger of our horses bogging down." I looked after as he went into the creek with his horse, frequently saw him swimming with him. I felt afraid and told him so. After some encouraging words from him, I whipped my horse into the creek. I was soon wet over the knees, my horse swimming but a short distance. The banks of the creek were steep and our horses found difficulty in getting up them. We were now on the opposite bank. On looking up I saw a little log cabin, a beautiful orchard of peach trees, a fine vegetable garden and lawn in front of the house. "Whose place is this?" "This is my place," said Mr. Thomas. "How glad I am," I replied. "I have got home."

On entering the enclosure, a nice, tidy mulatto woman met us at the door. She helped me off my horse and said with a polite curtsy, "I am glad, Mr., you have come home." I went into the house and as I was entering the passage through the middle of the cabin, I hit my head against the roof. I remarked to Mr. Thomas, "I think you will have to raise the roof of your house or build a new one." "Oh, my child," he replied, "I had no one to fix for when I built this house. Now I have got a wife, I will build a better one." Every place was the essence of cleanness, and although a puncheon floor, it was clean enough to eat off. The furniture was all hand made, chairs with deerskin bottoms, tables and bedstead fixtures. Dinner was prepared and we, being very hungry, did honor to the table, which was filled with vegetables of all kinds, milk and butter, and the best kind of corn bread, which my husband observing, asked me if I liked it. On replying I was not fond of it, he said he would get some flour for me shortly. "At present, we are out."

After dinner he asked me to take a walk with him in the field, "where my negroes are at work. I want to see how they have got along in my absence." On coming near enough for the hands to see us, they cheered us once or twice, and when they came up to us each one congratulated us on our happiness with a shake of the hand. They all appeared glad to see us, and Mr. Thomas was satisfied with the work they had done in his absence. . . .

42. Life in Texas

FREDERICK LAW OLMSTED
"Route across Eastern Texas"
1857

Frederick Law Olmsted, one of the most versatile Americans of the nineteenth century, is best known as the leading landscape architect of his time. But Olmsted was also an acute social commentator, and his travel narratives survive as classic sources. After publishing an account of a visit to rural England in 1852, he was commissioned by Henry J. Raymond, editor of the New York Times, *to conduct an intensive study of the slaveholding South. On the heels of the widely read* Journey in the Seaboard Slave States *(1856), Olmsted published* A Journey through Texas *(1857), which was followed by* A Journey in the Back Country *(1860) and* The Cotton Kingdom *(1861). In this selection, he describes some fundamental characteristics of Texas society on the eve of the Civil War.*

Emigrant Trains

We overtook, several times in the course of each day, the slow emigrant trains, for which this road, though less frequented than years ago, is still a chief thoroughfare. Inexorable destiny it seems that drags or drives on, always Westward, these toil-worn people. Several families were frequently moving together, coming from the same district, or chance met and joined, for company, on the long road from Alabama, Georgia, or the Carolinas. Before you come upon them you hear, ringing through the woods, the fierce cries and blows with which they urge on their jaded cattle. Then the stragglers appear, lean dogs or fainting negroes, ragged and spiritless. An old granny, hauling on, by the hand, a weak boy — too old to ride and too young to keep up. An old man, heavily loaded, with a rifle. Then the white covers of the wagons, jerking up and down as they mount over a root or plunge into a rut, disappearing, one after another, where the road descends. Then the active and cheery prime negroes, not yet exhausted, with a joke and a suggestion about tobacco. Then the black pickininnies, staring, in a confused heap, out at the back of the wagon, more and more of their eyes to be made out among the table legs and bedding as you get near; behind them, further in, the old people and young mothers, whose turn it is to ride. As you get by, the white mother and babies, and the tall, frequently ill-humored master, on horseback, or walking with his gun, urging up the black driver and his oxen. As a scout ahead is a brother, or

Frederick Law Olmsted, A *Journey through Texas; or, a Saddle-trip on the Southwestern Frontier: With a Statistical Appendix* (New York: Dix, Edwards & Co., 1857), 55–57, 100–3, 123–28.

an intelligent slave, with the best gun, on the look-out for a deer or a turkey. We passed in the day perhaps one hundred persons attached to these trains, probably an unusual number; but the immigration this year had been retarded and condensed by the fear of yellow fever, the last case of which, at Natchitoches, had indeed begun only the night before our arrival. Our chances of danger were considered small, however, as the hard frosts had already come. One of these trains was made up of three large wagons, loaded with furniture, babies, and invalids, two or three light wagons, and a gang of twenty able field hands. They travel ten or fifteen miles a day, stopping wherever night overtakes them. The masters are plainly dressed, often in home-spun, keeping their eyes about them, noticing the soil, sometimes making a remark on the crops by the roadside; but, generally, dogged, surly, and silent. The women are silent, too, frequently walking, to relieve the teams, and weary, haggard, mud be-draggled, forlorn, and disconsolate, yet hopeful and careful. The negroes, mud-incrusted, wrapped in old blankets or gunny-bags, suffering from cold, plod on, aimless, hopeless, thoughtless, more indifferent than the oxen to all about them.

A Yellow Gentleman

At noon, when we had stopped in the woods for a lunch, at a roadside fire, left well piled for the next comer, as is the pleasant custom, by some one in advance, a handsome mulatto young man rode up, and bowing, joined us at this open hearth. He proved a pleasant fellow, genial and quite intelligent. He accepted a share of our eatables, and told us he had been sent back to look for a lost dog. "His master, and a little boy, and two nigger women, and another yellow fellow, were on ahead." When we had finished, he said — "Perhaps youm (you and he) 'll wait a spell longer."

"Yes."

"Well, then, I'll go along, my master 'll be looking for me," and he rode off, lifting his hat like a Parisian. . . .

A Grazier's Farm

It was a log cabin, of one room, fourteen feet by fourteen, with another small room in a "lean-to" of boards on the windward side. There was no window, but there were three doors, and openings between the logs in all quarters. The door of the "lean-to" was barricaded, but this erection was very open; and as the inner door, from sagging on its wooden hinges, could not be closed at all, the norther had nearly free course through the cabin. A strong fire was roaring in the great chimney at the end of the room, and we all clustered closely around it, "the woman" alone passing through our semicircle, as she prepared the "pone" and "fry," and coffee for supper.

Our host seemed a man of thirty, and had lived in Texas through all the "trouble times." His father had moved his family here when Texas was still Mexican territory; and for years of the young man's life, Indians were guarded against and hunted just as wolves now are by the shepherd. They had always held their ground against them, however, and had constantly increased in wealth, but had retired for a few weeks before the Mexican invasion. His father had no property when he came here, but the wagon and horses, and the few household effects he brought with him. "Now," said the son, "he raises fifty bales of cotton" — equivalent to informing us that he owned twenty or thirty negroes, and his income was from two to three thousand dollars a year. The young man himself owned probably many hundred acres of the prairie and woodland range about him, and a large herd of cattle. He did not fancy taking care of a plantation. It was too much trouble. He was a regular Texan, he boasted, and was not going to slave himself looking after niggers. Any man who had been brought up in Texas, he said, could live as well as he wanted to, without working more than one month in the year. For about a month in the year he had to work hard, driving his cattle into the pen, and roping and marking the calves; this was always done in a kind of frolic in the spring — the neighboring herdsmen assisting each other. During the rest of the year he hadn't anything to do. When he felt like it he got on to a horse and rode around, and looked after his cattle; but that wasn't work, he said — 'twas only play. He raised a little corn; sometimes he got more than he needed, and sometimes not as much; he didn't care whether it was enough or not — he could always buy meal, only bought meal wasn't so sweet as that was which they ground fresh in their own steel mill. When he wanted to buy anything, he could always sell some cattle and raise the money; it did not take much to supply them with all they wanted.

This was very evident. The room was, as I said, fourteen feet square, with battens of split boards tacked on between the broader openings of the logs. Above, it was open to the rafters, and in many places the sky could be seen between the shingles of the roof. A rough board box, three feet square, with a shelf in it, contained the crockery-ware of the establishment; another similar box held the store of meal, coffee, sugar, and salt, a log crib at the horse-pen held the corn, from which the meal was daily ground, and a log smoke or store-house contained the store of pork. A canopy-bed filled one quarter of the room; a cradle, four chairs seated with untanned deer-hide, a table, a skillet or bake-kettle, a coffee-kettle, a frying-pan, and a rifle laid across two wooden pegs on the chimney, with a string of patches, powder-horn, pouch, and hunting-knife, completed the furniture of the house. We all sat with hats and overcoats on, and the woman cooked in bonnet and shawl. As I sat in the chimney-corner I could put both my hands out, one laid on the other, between the stones of the fire-place and the logs of the wall.

A pallet of quilts and blankets was spread for us in the lean-to, just between the two doors. We slept in all our clothes, including overcoats, hats, and boots, and covered entirely with blankets. At seven in the morning, when we threw them off, the mercury in the thermometer in our saddle-bags, which we had used for a pillow, stood at 25 deg. Fahrenheit.

We contrived to make cloaks and hoods from our blankets, and after going through with the fry, coffee and pone again, and paying one dollar each for the entertainment of ourselves and horses, we continued our journey.

The norther was stronger and the cold greater than the day before; but as we took it on our quarter in the course we were going during most of the day, we did not suffer.

Harbor in an Inn

Late in the same evening we reached the town of Caldwell, the "seat of justice" of Burleson County. We were obliged to leave our horses in a stable, made up of a roof, in which was a loft for the storage of provender, set upon posts, without side-boarding, so that the norther met with no obstruction. It was filled with horses, and ours alone were blanketed for the night. The mangers were very shallow and narrow, and as the corn was fed on the cob, a considerable proportion of it was thrown out by the horses in their efforts to detach the edible portion. With laudable economy, our landlord had twenty-five or thirty pigs running at large in the stable, to prevent this overflow from being wasted.

The hotel building was an unusually large and fine one; the principal room had glass windows. Several panes of these were, however, broken, and the outside door could not be closed from without; and when closed, was generally pried open with a pocket-knife by those who wished to go out. A great part of the time it was left open. Supper was served in another room, in which there was no fire, and the outside door was left open for the convenience of the servants in passing to and from the kitchen, which, as usual here at large houses, was in a detached building. Supper was, however, eaten with such rapidity that nothing had time to freeze on the table. . . .

Slavery with a Will

We were several times struck, in Eastern Texas, with a peculiarity in the tone of the relation between master and slave. Elsewhere at the South, slavery had seemed to be accepted generally, as a natural, hereditary, established state of things, and the right and wrong of it, or the how of it, never to be discussed or thought of any more than that of feudal tenures elsewhere. But in Texas, the state of war in which slavery arises, seems to continue in undertone to the present.

"Damn 'em, give 'em hell," frequent expressions of the ruder planters towards their negroes, appeared to be used as if with a meaning — a threat to make their life infernal if they do not submit abjectly and constantly. There seemed to be the consciousness of a wrong relation and a determination to face conscience down, and continue it; to work up the "damned niggers," with a sole eye to selfish profit, cash down, in this world. As to "treasures in Heaven," their life is a constant sneer at the belief in them.

Texas as It Used to Be

I will add no further details upon the moral and social aspect of Eastern Texas. Cheap as such privileges may be considered, old Texans express, in speaking of them, great admiration and satisfaction. Society has certainly made a great advance there in becoming even what it is. The present generation has, peculiarly, but the faults founded upon laziness. The past, if we may believe report, had something worse. In fact, in the rapid settlement of the country, many an adventurer crossed the border, spurred by a love of life or liberty, forfeited at home, rather than drawn by the love of adventure or of rich soil. Probably a more reckless and vicious crew was seldom gathered than that which peopled some parts of Eastern Texas at the time of its first resistance to the Mexican government.

"G. T. T." (gone to Texas) was the slang appendage, within the reader's recollection, to every man's name who had disappeared before the discovery of some rascality. Did a man emigrate thither, every one was on the watch for the discreditable reason to turn up.

Mr. Dewees, in his naive "Letters from Texas," thus describes (1831):

"It would amuse you very much, could you hear the manner in which people of this new country address each other. It is nothing uncommon of us to inquire of a man why he ran away from the States! but few persons feel insulted by such a question. They generally answer for some crime or other which they have committed; if they deny having committed any crime, or say they did not run away, they are generally looked upon rather suspiciously. Those who come into the country at the present time, frequently tell us rough, ragged, old settlers, who have worn out our clothes and our constitutions in the service of the country, that they have a great deal of wealth in the States which they are going after, as soon as they can find a situation to suit them. But we, not relishing this would-be aristocracy, generally manage to play some good joke upon them in return.

"One day, there were quite a number of these aristocrats, who seemed to think themselves better than those who were worn out by toil and hardships, seated at the dinner table, in a sort of tavern kept by a man named William Pettis, or Buck Pettis, as he was always called at San Felipe; these persons were boasting largely of their wealth, their land, their negroes, the ships they had at sea, etc. There was at the table an old man by the name of Macfarlane, a don't care sort of a fellow, who had married a Mexican wife, and was living on the Brazos when we first came to the country. He listened to them quietly for a while, at length he could restrain himself no longer. 'Well, gentlemen,' he said, 'I, too, once commenced telling that I had left a large property in the States, and, in fact, gentlemen, I told the story so often, that at length I really believed it true, and eventually started to go for it. Well, I traveled on very happily till I reached the Sabine river which separates this country from the United States. On its bank I paused, and now for the first time, began to ask myself seriously, What am I doing? Why am I here? I have no property in the States, and if I had, if I cross the river, 'tis at the risk of my life; for I was obliged to flee to this country to escape the punishment of the laws. I had better return, and live in safety as I have done. I did so, gentlemen, and since then have been contented without telling of the wealth I left in the States.' The relation of this story so exasperated those for whose benefit it was told, that they fell upon the old gentleman, and would have done him injury, had it not been for the interference of his friends. This, however, put a stop to long yarns."

If your life, in those times, an old settler told us, would be of the slightest use to any one, you might be sure he would take it, and it was safe only as you were in constant readiness to defend it. Horses and wives were of as little account as umbrellas in more advanced States. Everybody appropriated everything that suited him, running his own risk of a penalty. Justice descended into the body of Judge Lynch, sleeping when he slept, and when he woke hewing down right and left for exercise and pastime.

Out of this has come, with as much rapidity as could be expected, by a process of gradual fermentation and admixture, the present society.

Law and Gospel

We picked up one incident oddly illustrating the transition state:

We were speaking of the probability of a further annexation of Mexican territory, with a road companion, upon a prairie near the Brazos. He was an old ranger, had made one of the Mier expedition,[1] and had the fortune to draw a white bean on the occasion of the decimation. He had afterwards spent two years in Mexico, as prisoner.

"Mexico!" said he, "what the hell do we want of it? It isn't worth a cuss. The people are as bigoted and ignorant as the devil's grandchildren. They haven't even the capacities of my black boy. Why, they're most as black as niggers any way, and ten times as treacherous. How would you like to be tried by a jury of Mexicans? You see it an't like it was with Texas. You go any further into Mexico with your surveyor's chains, and you'll get Mexicans along with your territory; and a dam'd lot of 'em, too. What are you going to do with 'em? You can't drive 'em out, because there an't nowhere to drive 'em. No, *sir!* There they've got to stay, and it'll be fifty year before you can outvote 'em. Well, they'll elect the judges, or they'll elect the legislature, and that'll appoint their judges — same thing. And their judges an't a going to disqualify them, you may be dam sure of that. But how many of 'em would pass muster for a jury? The whole of 'em ought to be disqualified. Just think of going before a jury of them. How could they understand evidence? They don't know the first difference between right and wrong, any way."

We asked an explanation of the "disqualifying." It appeared that the Texan county courts had the power to disqualify citizens from serving upon juries for bad moral character, gross ignorance, or mental incapacity. In further explanation, he gave us the incident:

The decision as to moral character, of course, rests with the judges. A few years ago, it happened that the bench in —— County was filled entirely by ministers of the gospel, and men of bigoted piety. The court, during a night session, ruled that no man should be considered as of good moral character, who was

---

[1] **Mier expedition:** In 1842, a group of Texans crossed into Mexico to pursue raiders. After capturing Laredo and Guerrero, their commander, Alexander Somervell, ordered them home. Part of this group refused to leave. As a result, 176 Texans were captured in the Mexican town of Mier. Santa Anna ordered the execution of seventeen men, or a tenth of the total. The condemned were chosen by lot: a black bean meant death; a white bean, survival.

known to have drunk spirits, to have played a game of cards, or to have used profane language. Accordingly, the whole population of the county was incapacitated, except a few leading church members in good and regular standing. And though every one was glad to be rid of jury-duty, in general, no one liked to be classed in this way as unfit for it, and the indignation rose nearly to open riot. However, the matter was passed by, and nothing done until the following election, when the tables were turned by rigorously excluding all church members from the court.

The reader who has not been there, may think our social experience of this part of the state peculiar and exceptional. I can only say that we traveled on an average not more than fourteen miles a day, and so must have stopped at almost every tenth or fifteenth house on the chief emigrant and mail-road of the state. I have given our impressions as we received them, and the only advantage they now have over his own, is in the the strength which the reiteration of day after day gives over that of page after page. Had we entered Texas by the sea, stopped at the chief towns and the frequented hotels, traveled by public conveyances, and delivered letters to prominent and hospitable individuals, upon rich old coast plantations, our notes of the East might have had, perhaps, a more rosy tone.

Suggestions for Further Reading

Barr, Alwyn. *Black Texans: A History of African Americans in Texas, 1528–1995.* Norman: University of Oklahoma Press, 1996.

Campbell, Randolph. *An Empire for Slavery: The Peculiar Institution in Texas, 1821–1865.* Baton Rouge: Louisiana State University Press, 1989.

Fehrenbach, T. R. *Lone Star: A History of Texas and the Texans.* New York: Macmillan, 1968. Reprint, New York: American Legacy Press, 1983.

Lack, Paul D. *The Texas Revolutionary Experience: A Political and Social History, 1835–1836.* College Station: Texas A & M University Press, 1996.

CHAPTER TWELVE

THE SLAVE SOUTH

The Case of Jordan Hatcher

B y 1860, with some four million slaves living below the Mason-Dixon line, the South had become a thoroughly slave-based society. The entire plantation system depended on enslaved labor. Slaves were, by far, the largest single category of capital investment — by the 1850s, their value totaled in the billions of dollars. They labored in the cotton fields of the Deep South; the tobacco plantations of Virginia, Kentucky, and North Carolina; the rice plantations of South Carolina's low country; and the sugar plantations of Louisiana. But slavery was not confined to the plantation. The construction of a canal and railroad system relied heavily on slave labor, while slaves staffed hotels in the tourist areas of western North Carolina and manned the hot springs of western Virginia. Throughout the South, most slaves were manual laborers forming the base of the labor system. In the larger southern cities — Savannah, Charleston, New Orleans, Nashville, and Baltimore — many others became skilled carpenters, wheelwrights, masons, or factory workers.

In many ways, the slave South was a contradictory society. Masters often "hired out" their slaves to employers, usually in exchange for a fixed annual sum, the terms of which were specified by contract. Hired slaves were common, especially in Maryland, Virginia, and the Carolinas. But because they worked and lived largely beyond the control of slaveholders, many whites regarded them warily. Equally troublesome to white Southerners were the more than one hundred thousand free people of color dispersed throughout the South but especially concentrated in urban areas. These circumstances generated constant worry about the possibility of slave revolt. Three major aborted and actual uprisings seemed to give cause for this concern. In 1800, a plot in Richmond, Virginia, led by Gabriel Prosser, a free black, was averted only after one of the conspirators confessed.

Two decades later in Charleston, South Carolina, another free black, Denmark Vesey, was exposed in 1822 before he could lead a citywide slave revolt. The deadliest uprising of all, however, was led by Nat Turner, in Southampton County, in southeastern Virginia, in August 1831. By the time their rampage ended, Turner and his band had killed more than thirty whites.

These were, however, isolated events. More commonly, slaveholders faced subtler forms of resistance. Slaves everywhere banded together and succeeded in creating a common culture: they fashioned their own religion, music, food, and family units as ways of maintaining dignity in the midst of an oppressive, immoral system. Others resisted by stealing, by destroying property, and, above all, by running away. Still others turned to violence: Frederick Douglass, in his famous autobiography, tells of a turning point in his life as a slave in Maryland in the 1830s, when he resisted a beating by a slave "breaker" hired to bring Douglass — regarded by his overseers as a troublemaker — under control.

Slaves were regulated by a strict legal code, in existence since the colonial period, that was fundamentally ambiguous. Although it was indisputable that slaves occupied an unequal position, the law regarded them as something more than chattel and something less than fully human. It limited their ability to exercise economic rights and sought to prevent rebellious behavior. (For example, it was commonly illegal after 1830 to teach slaves to read and write.) At the same time, the law in many states granted slaves some rights and limited slaveholders' ability to discipline them brutally. A dramatic set of events in Richmond, Virginia, exposed the law's anomalies and revealed how tensely the white population anticipated acts of slave revolt and resistance.

On March 12, 1852, Jordan Hatcher — a hired slave owned by a widow in Chesterfield County — was tried for first-degree murder for killing the overseer of the tobacco factory where he worked. Although it was one of many cases in which slaves violently resisted the authority of slaveholders and their overseers, the Hatcher trial drew widespread attention and tested the political system's willingness to protect the established slave system. In Virginia, the governor reviewed all slave cases and possessed the right to veto death sentences: immediately following Hatcher's conviction and sentencing, a group of whites from Richmond signed a petition asking Governor Joseph Johnson to commute the slave's death sentence to the more lenient sentence of "transportation," or exile from the state. A rival group immediately petitioned Johnson to uphold and impose the death penalty. On April 22, the day before the scheduled execution, Johnson postponed it for two weeks to give himself time to make up his mind; on May 6, he commuted Hatcher's sentence.

Although the law in Virginia had provided for the option of transportation since 1801 — and although about thirty slaves per year were transported to unknown fates in the early 1850s — Johnson's decision proved to be wildly controversial. Soon after news of it spread, a citywide protest erupted. The legislature took up a vigorous debate, with Johnson's supporters demanding that the capital be relocated out of Richmond and his opponents demanding that the legislature censure the governor. And despite the explanations Johnson provided for his actions, some citizens were so enraged that they encircled his mansion in an "indignation" meeting. Others questioned the implications of Johnson's decision, suggesting that his willingness to apply constitutional protections to a slave threatened the stability of southern society.

The readings in this chapter trace the course of the Hatcher saga. The trial record presents the complete testimony from the case; the petitions for and against Hatcher's pardon reveal the arguments and attitudes on both sides of the controversy that ensued. Governor Johnson's May 11 and May 19 messages to the legislature outline the logic behind his decision, and selected articles from Richmond newspapers narrate some of the uproar that followed it.

As you read, try to answer the following questions. Based on the events of the Hatcher case, what is the meaning of justice in a slave society? How fairly was Hatcher judged in his trial? What was the basis of his conviction on the murder charge? Why did supporters and opponents of commuting his sentence disagree? What were the reasons for Johnson's decision, and why were Virginians so outraged?

43. Trial and Conviction

Trial Record from the Case of Jordan Hatcher
1852

Jordan Hatcher was a seventeen-year-old hired slave in Richmond, Virginia, the South's leading manufacturing center in the 1850s. He worked in a tobacco factory, where he converted cured tobacco to plugs of chew. He was accused of killing William P. Jackson, his white overseer, in March of 1852. The case was heard by the hustings court, which served as the primary court for major crimes — including capital crimes by slaves — in Richmond. The court was composed of twelve elected aldermen, the mayor, and the city recorder. In a unanimous vote, it convicted and sen-

Record of the Court, Virginia House of Delegates Documents, no. 78, 1852.

tenced Hatcher to death, ordering that he be hanged on April 23 of that year. As was the custom in capital slave crimes, the court assessed Hatcher's value and instructed the state auditor to provide six hundred dollars as compensation to his owner. As was also the custom, the trial record was then immediately forwarded to Governor Joseph Johnson for review.

In Richmond Hustings Court, March 12th, 1852: Present — SAMUEL T. PULLIAM, *Recorder,* JAS. K. CASKIE, JOSEPH C. WINGFIELD, EDWIN FARRAR *and* JAMES BRAY, *Aldermen:*

Jordan Hatcher, a slave, who stands charged with a felony by him committed, in this, that he did on the 25th day of February 1852, in the city of Richmond, feloniously and of his malice, kill and murder William P. Jackson — was this day led to the bar in custody of the sergeant; and William W. Day being assigned his counsel, he was arraigned and pleaded not guilty to the charge; and the court having heard the evidence, are unanimously of opinion that the said Jordan Hatcher is guilty of the crime with which he stands charged. And it being demanded of the said Jordan Hatcher if he had anything to say why the court should not now proceed to pronounce judgment on him according to law, and nothing being offered in arrest or delay of judgment, it is considered by the court that the said Jordan Hatcher be hanged by the neck until he be dead. And it is ordered that execution of this sentence be done upon the said Jordan Hatcher by the sergeant of this city, on Friday the 23d day of April 1852, between the hours of 10 o'clock in the forenoon and 2 o'clock in the afternoon of that day, at the usual place of execution. And the said Jordan Hatcher is remanded to jail.

The court affix the value of the said slave Jordan Hatcher, who is proved to the satisfaction of the court to be the property of Mrs. P. O. Godsey of the county of Chesterfield, at six hundred dollars, it being the opinion of the court that he would sell for that sum, if sold publicly, under a knowledge of his condemnation.

The following is a copy of the certificate of the mayor of this city, under which this trial was had, viz:

"City of Richmond, to wit:

To the Clerk of the Hustings Court of said City:

I, William Lambert, mayor of the said city, do hereby certify, that I have by my warrant this day committed Jordan Hatcher, a slave, to the jail of this city, that he may be tried before the hustings court of said city, for a felony by him committed, in this, that he did on the 25th day of February 1852, in said city, feloniously and of his malice, kill and murder one William P. Jackson. Given under my hand this 28th day of February 1852.

WILLIAM LAMBERT, *Mayor.*"

The following are copies of the depositions of the witnesses for the commonwealth, taken down in court and filed, viz:

Robert Jones, a slave, being charged and sworn, deposed, that the affair commenced by Mr. Jackson speaking to the prisoner about some inferior stems which prisoner had on his bench in Walker and Harris's factory. Mr. Jackson was overseer in the factory, and called the prisoner from his bench up near the stove to chastise the prisoner about his work; prisoner caught hold of the cowhide. Mr. Jackson told him to let go the cowhide, but the prisoner did not let go. Mr. Jackson kicked the prisoner, and prisoner caught hold of Mr. Jackson and threw Mr. Jackson off, and picked up an iron poker which lies generally at the stove and struck Mr. Jackson a blow with it on the fore part of the head, which caused Mr. Jackson to fall. The iron poker produced in court was here shewn to the witness, who stated that it was the same poker with which prisoner struck Mr. Jackson. A few minutes passed before Mr. Jackson got up, and then the prisoner was not in the room — witness did not see prisoner when he left the room. This occurred about 9 or 10 o'clock in the morning, as witness thinks.

Dr. John A. Cunningham, being sworn, deposed, that he was called, on Wednesday, the 25th February last, about 8 o'clock in the morning, to see Mr. William P. Jackson, whom he found with a slight wound or cut on his forehead, and which he had been bathing with cold water: witness saw no evidence of any serious injury, and Mr. Jackson not complaining of any pain or sickness of stomach, witness told him he supposed that what he had been doing was all required; and witness left him and did not see him again until next day, when he was again sent for, and at a glance he saw that Mr. Jackson was suffering from a very severe injury to the brain. Witness having a particular reason for not having anything to do with the case, and knowing that what he would think necessary was directly at variance with the opinions of the father of Mr. Jackson on the subject, told the mother of Mr. Jackson what the injury was, and stated that he could not have anything to do with the case, unless in company with another physician. Some time afterwards witness received another urgent message to come and see Mr. Jackson in company with another physician. Witness immediately went, and met Dr. Deane there, and they examined the wound, and thinking that an operation was necessary, urged that another physician should instantly be sent for, and Dr. Bolton was sent for, and when he came, an investigation of the case was made, and it was found that the skull had been broken and portions of it forced in upon the brain. An operation was performed upon Mr. Jackson, and portions of the broken skull bone were removed. Witness again saw Mr. Jackson about 10 o'clock at night, when the symptoms of his case were still worse and more alarming; and on next day witness saw him again about 10 o'clock, when he was evidently dying. Witness is perfectly satisfied that the death of Mr. Jackson was attributable directly to the blow inflicted on his forehead.

Dr. James Bolton, being sworn, deposed, that he was requested to meet Dr. Cunningham, about 4 o'clock of the day after the wound was inflicted, at the house of Mr. Jackson. Witness did go, and on examining the wound, saw that it seemed to be a very slight wound; but on a more minute examination, found that Mr. Jackson's skull was fractured, and portions of the skull were forced into the opening and upon the brain. Witness operated upon Mr. Jackson's skull and found that the brain was very seriously injured. The substance of the brain itself was injured by the weapon which had broken the skull bone, and a puncture of the brain was observed immediately under the fracture of the skull. Witness put his little finger carefully into the puncture in the brain, to see if any fragment of the skull had been driven into the brain: witness found no portion of the skull in this puncture. After the operation, Mr. Jackson seemed to be somewhat better, and was roused up and said he felt better; but shortly after he relapsed into a state of insensibility. Next morning about 10 o'clock witness saw Mr. Jackson again, when he was evidently dying. Witness has no doubt that the death of Mr. Jackson was owing entirely to the puncture made into the substance of the brain by the instrument which was used in inflicting the wound. Witness thinks that the fatal termination of the case would not have been in any way changed by performing any surgical operation at an earlier period after the infliction of the injury. No post mortem examination was made, as far as witness is aware, of this injury to Mr. Jackson's brain, the mother of Mr. Jackson refusing to allow any such examination to be made.

Daniel Walthall, a slave, being charged and sworn, deposed, that he saw Mr. Jackson strike Jordan Hatcher with a cowhide, and Jordan Hatcher took up the iron poker and struck Mr. Jackson with it. Mr. Jackson fell on receiving the blow, and Jordan Hatcher ran off out of the room, and Mr. Jackson got up immediately and followed Jordan Hatcher out of the room. Witness thinks this occurred about 8 o'clock in the morning. Witness was going from his work place to the scales to weigh a box, when he saw Mr. Jackson strike Jordan with a cowhide. Witness went to the scales, about 20 feet off, and weighed the box, and as he was returning to his work place, he saw Jordan strike Mr. Jackson on the head with the iron poker.

Alonzo Heath, a slave, being charged and sworn, deposed, that the first commencement of the fray between Mr. Jackson and Jordan was about some dirty stems Jordan had on his bench. Mr. Jackson attempted to whip Jordan, and did give Jordan several blows with the cowhide, when Jordan caught hold of the cowhide. Mr. Jackson told Jordan to let go the cowhide, but Jordan would not let go; and Mr. Jackson kicked Jordan, and they had a tussle, and Jordan pushed Mr. Jackson off, and picked up the iron poker and struck Mr. Jackson a blow with it on the forehead. Mr. Jackson fell on the floor when he received the blow, and Jordan immediately ran out of the room down the steps, dropping the poker on the floor. Mr. Jackson got up almost immediately, and ran down stairs after Jordan. The iron poker in court being shewn to witness, he identified it as the same poker with which Jordan struck Mr. Jackson.

William Barkus, a slave, a witness introduced and examined on behalf of the prisoner, being charged and sworn, deposed, that he was at his bench, in Walker and Harris's factory, when the fray commenced between Mr. Jackson and Jordan Hatcher. Mr. Jackson looked at Jordan's stems, and found fault with him about them, and asked Jordan if he had not told him not to have dirty stems on his bench; and said he would whip him; Jordan said that he had told him so, and that he would try to do better if he would not whip him. Mr. Jackson said that he would whip him about it first, and make him do it. Mr. Jackson did cut Jordan several times with the cowhide, and Jordan caught hold of the cowhide and asked Mr.

Jackson not to whip him any more. Mr. Jackson told him to let go the cowhide, and to come out by the stove, and Jackson did so. Witness saw no more of the matter, but shortly after he heard a sort of cry, and saw Jordan run down stairs, and Mr. Jackson ran down after him directly afterwards, with his forehead bleeding.

A Transcript of the Record.
Teste,
Ch[arle]s Howard

44. Pleading for Justice

Petitions for and against Commutation
1852

Soon after Hatcher's conviction, a group of nearly sixty prominent Richmond citizens petitioned the governor to commute the death sentence. The motives behind the petition remain unclear. That so many prominent citizens were willing to support Hatcher's case suggests a softening of attitudes among a portion of Richmond whites toward the city's slave population, but the impulses behind the petition were not all humanitarian. There was already substantial evidence of growing tensions between the relatively new tobacco manufacturers and the city's older and more established mercantile, trade, and transportation classes. The second petition, which vigorously opposed the commutation of Hatcher's sentence, represented the views of the tobacco manufacturers — and of a significant portion of Richmond whites as well.

Petition for Commutation

To his Excellency Joseph Johnson, Esq.
Governor of Virginia.

The petition of the undersigned respectfully represents, that a negro slave named Jordan Hatcher, aged about seventeen years, was, on Friday, the 12th day of the present month (March), tried by the hustings court of the city of Richmond, charged with killing one [William] Jackson, found guilty, and sentenced to be hung on the 23d day of April 1852. Your petitioners represent that the fol-

Petition, Virginia House of Delegates Documents, no. 78, 1852.

lowing are the facts developed upon the trial: The boy Jordan was hired at a tobacco factory in the said city, and the said [William] Jackson was an overseer in said factory; that on the morning on which the fatal blow was given, Jackson came to the boy's bench where he was at work and found fault with a bundle of tobacco stems put up by the boy, stating that it was the second occasion on which he had to complain of the boy's work — the boy begged his forgiveness, and promised to endeavor to do better for the future. Jackson replied, that if he did do better it should be after he was chastised, and commenced whipping him with a cowhide. After a number of lashes had been struck, the boy caught hold of the cowhide. Jackson then ordered him to leave his bench and walk out with him into the floor near the stove. The boy immediately released his hold on the cowhide and obeyed him. Upon getting into the floor near the stove, Jackson again began to whip him; and after some lashes had been inflicted, the boy again seized the cowhide, whereupon Jackson kicked him. The boy then picked up an iron poker, which was immediately under his feet, and struck Jackson a blow on the forehead. Jackson fell to the floor — the boy dropped the poker and left the room immediately. That the boy did not attempt to repeat the blow, although he might easily have done so, as no one attempted to prevent him, many being present at the time. In a moment or two Jackson arose and pursued the boy, but did not overtake him. A physician was almost immediately called in, who found Jackson sitting up, and, for certain professional reasons, did not make any examination of the wound. The same physician was called in again the next morning, when he found his patient laboring under a compression of the brain. Other physicians were then called in by his advice, and the wound was explored. Upon an exploration, it appeared that the skull was fractured — an aperture having been made in it and the brain wounded. An operation was then deemed necessary, and was then performed, but the patient survived only a few hours. These are all of the material facts developed on the trial. But at the trial one of the eyes of the boy was exceedingly inflamed by reason, as he alleged, of a blow in the eye given by Jackson on that occasion — but of this there was no distinct proof.

Your petitioners frankly admit that there can be but little doubt but that Jackson came to his death by reason of the blow inflicted by the boy, but they submit that that consequence was neither expected nor desired by him. All of the facts of the case tend to establish that the blow was struck under circumstances tending greatly to aggravate the boy — without premeditation and with no design to kill. There is no malignant, willful or deliberate purpose developed by the proofs to commit murder. Under these circumstances, while your petitioners do not complain of the conviction as being contrary to the strict letter of the law, they are humbly of opinion that this is precisely one of those cases upon which a sound discretion would induce the exercise of some degree of executive clemency. The youthfulness of the party may also be pleaded not as an excuse but certainly in mitigation of his offence.

Your petitioners therefore pray a commutation of his punishment.

> And your petitioners will ever, &c.
> [Petition signers]

Petition against Commutation

Richmond, 26th Mar 1852
His Excellency, Joseph Johnson, Governor of the Commonwealth of Virginia

Sir

It has come to our knowledge that a petition is being circulated for signatures, the object of which is to have the sentence of Jordan (a slave) recently convicted of murder in this city, commuted to transportation for life.

Against the prayer of that petition we must most solemnly and earnestly protest. As far as we can learn nothing in his favor has been elicited, since his trial, and hence we cannot see upon what grounds, the Executive clemency is asked. We believe for the protection of our lives and property, that examples should be made of all such offenders and the change of punishment asked for in the present instance, will we are satisfied, fail to produce any satisfactory effect whatever.

A growing spirit of insubordination amongst the negroes of this city has been manifested for several years and particularly amongst those employed in the Tobacco Factories; who number some two or three thousand. This evil has become so great that the managers of those establishments can now rarely correct the negroes for the gravest offences, without hazarding their lives. In view of the possibility of your heeding the prayer of the petition referred to, we have thought it our duty to make the present request — that the Executive clemency may not be extended to slave Jordan as desired therein.

[Petition signers]

Executive Papers (Governor Joseph Johnson), Library of Virginia, Richmond, Va.

45. The Commutation

Governor Joseph Johnson
Messages to the Legislature
1852

Governor Joseph Johnson was from Harrison County, a largely nonslaveholding county of western Virginia. Elected as a Democrat in December 1851, he ran on a plank that portrayed Whigs as ineffectual protectors of slavery. His decision six months later to pardon a convicted slave's death sentence sparked considerable con-

*troversy in Richmond. This was particularly so because of the logic he used in issu-
ing the commutation. By law, governors who commuted death sentences to transportation were required to make an accounting to the General Assembly explaining
their reasons for doing so. Five days after he made his decision, Johnson sent his message to the legislature. But because that message — and the rationale he provided
in the case — seemed so controversial, Johnson took the extraordinary step of issuing
a second message, on May 19, in which he backed off considerably from his original argument.*

MESSAGE TO THE VIRGINIA LEGISLATURE

Executive Department,
May 11, 1852.

To the General Assembly of Virginia.

On the 12th day of March last, Jordan Hatcher, a slave, aged about seventeen
years, charged with having killed one William P. Jackson, was tried in the hustings
court of this city, found guilty, and sentenced to be hung on the 23d day of April
1852. Shortly after this conviction, and during my late visit to the county of Harrison, papers relating to this subject were sent to me, which failed to arrive before
my return, and were not received here until after the day upon which the execution was to have taken place. Desiring to see those papers before making a final
decision, I granted a *respite* of two weeks; and after mature and deliberate consideration, I, on the 6th instant,[1] commuted the sentence against the said Hatcher
to "sale and transportation beyond the United States." And (as it is made my duty
to do by the constitution) I herewith respectfully communicate to the legislature
my reasons for said commutation.

That Jackson's death was caused by a blow inflicted by Hatcher, there can be
no doubt; but the testimony and all the attending circumstances, so far from shewing that the unfortunate result was contemplated or desired by the slave, rather
prove that he had no intention of committing murder, or of taking the life of his
overseer, Mr. Jackson, in any way; and that the unfortunate casualty was one of
those results which, though deeply to be deplored by all, was not contemplated by
any one. The injury was inflicted by a single blow, given at a moment of great excitement and suffering; and without any effort to inflict further injury, the boy ran
from the building in a manner shewing that his object and effort was but to escape
from the chastisement he was receiving. The great and essential ingredient to constitute *murder*, to wit: *intent* or *malice prepense* was, therefore, wholly wanting.

---

[1] **instant:** of the current month.

Communication, Virginia House of Delegates Documents, no. 74, 1852.

That the penalty under such circumstances should be death, though perhaps authorized by the letter, is, I believe, against the spirit of our laws and of the age, as it is contrary to mercy and humanity, which are designed for and extended only to the unfortunate and the guilty. If Hatcher had been a white man, the utmost he could have been charged with would have been justifiable homicide or involuntary manslaughter, and in this case it was but manslaughter without intent to kill. My *right* to interpose was clear and unquestionable; and believing this to be exactly one of those cases contemplated and provided for by the constitution, I commuted the sentence as aforesaid.

The power to pardon and commute is a high and sacred trust, but it is one in the discharge of which the executive of this commonwealth is responsible only to his conscience, his God, and the *State of Virginia*. And in conclusion, I will say, that although strengthened and confirmed in my convictions by the opinions of other gentlemen, of high legal attainments and moral worth, yet my own judgment and sense of duty would have led me to the same conclusions and to the performance of the same act, in the absence of all such support.

Very respectfully,
JOS. JOHNSON.

Reasons for Commuting Jordan Hatcher's Sentence

Executive Department, May 19, 1852.

To the General Assembly of Virginia.

In the discharge of my constitutional duty, I had the honor to communicate to your body on the 11th inst. the reasons for the commutation of the sentence of the slave Jordan Hatcher. I learn that the terms in which those reasons were expressed have been misconstrued, and my views upon the delicate relations existing between master and slave misapprehended. Upon this grave subject I cannot permit a doubt to be felt of the views of the executive.

I never entertained the opinion, nor did I intend to intimate, that the slave would under any circumstances be excused or justified in resisting the legal authority of his master. The right of the master or his agent to punish the slave, whenever in his opinion he deserves it, is a legal right — results from the nature of the property itself, and is necessary for wholesome discipline and restraint. It is founded on the soundest principles of public policy, and our courts have held that the owner of a slave cannot be indicted for the cruel or excessive whipping of his own slave. If the master abuses this high power so far as to commit crime, he is responsible to the laws of the land alone: the slave has no rights adverse to those of the master or the agent to whom he has delegated his authority.

Explanation, Virginia House of Delegates Documents, no. 79, 1852.

With these views, long entertained, it is almost unnecessary to say that, in my late message, I did not intend to convey the idea that the relative positions of the white citizen and the slave to the laws of the country were the same, or that the exercise by the master or his agent of the ample power of chastisement given by the law, furnishes any excusable or justifiable reason for resistance or an exhibition of resentment upon the part of the slave.

Our laws wisely discriminate between the punishment of white men and slaves for similar offences, and in my interposition in behalf of the slave Jordan Hatcher, I did not intend to express the conviction of my mind that a slave should not suffer death for offences below the grade of murder. In many instances it is proper in the execution of the laws. Upon an examination of the record of Jordan Hatcher's trial and conviction, I came to the conclusion that it presented a case for the interference of the executive, and commuted the punishment to the only substitute for the death penalty provided by the law. In stating my reasons, if I have failed to do so in clear and distinct terms, it has resulted rather from a want of familiarity with the *technicalities* of the law, than from any disposition to misinterpret them.

I have the honor to be,
Very respectfully,
JOS. JOHNSON.

46. Virginians React

Newspaper Articles
1852

The commutation of Hatcher's death sentence set off a wide-scale debate regarding the role of the political system in protecting slavery. To a large measure, the discussions took place on the pages of the state's newspapers. These articles — published in the highly partisan, pro-Whig Richmond Republican *and the* Richmond Whig *in the days and weeks following the announcement of Governor Johnson's decision — not only report what was happening but also announce their interpretation of events, question the implications, and call their readers to action.*

"THE INDIGNATION MEETING.
GREAT EXCITEMENT! LARGE GATHERING!!"

Never, since our residence in this city, have we seen the feelings of the people so thoroughly aroused, as they were at the meeting held at the City Hall, last night. Only one day's notice of the call had been given, but that the news had spread like electricity throughout the various ramifications of the city, and all sections, classes and vocations of the people, had poured out their hundreds to express their great indignation at the course pursued by Gov. Johnson in commuting the sentence of the negro slave Jordan Hatcher, who was condemned to be hung for the murder of William P. Jackson.

By a quarter past 8 o'clock the Hall was literally packed, and an uneasy anxiety manifested itself throughout the audience to proceed to business.

About half-past 8 o'clock the meeting was called to order by Mr. George R. Peake, on whose motion William Gray, Esq., was called to the Chair; and on motion of Mr. R. R. Duval, J. W. Lowellen was requested to act as Secretary.

The Chairman, on taking his seat, briefly announced the object of the meeting; when "Mayo," "Mayo," was loudly called for.

Mr. Joseph Mayo, Esq., took the stand, and addressed the meeting briefly. He regretted exceedingly the necessity for this meeting, and hoped those present would be satisfied with the adoption of a resolution condemnatory of the course of the Executive. He thought the negro should have been executed as he had been fairly tried and condemned by an impartial Court, who had the power to commute his punishment, and would have done so had not the law, the evidence and all the circumstances of the case been directly in conflict with such a course. It was not his purpose, however, to offer any resolutions on the occasion.

"Watson," "Watson," was then called for, when Mr. Wm. F. Watson arose and enquired if any resolutions had been prepared. On being answered in the affirmative, he resumed his seat, when

Mr. George R. Peake announced that he had been requested to offer the following resolution, which, though not prepared by himself, he fully endorsed:

Resolved, That Governor Johnson, in commuting the sentence of the slave *Jordan Hatcher,* convicted of the murder of William P. Jackson, has abated the trust confided to him by the Constitution, has outraged the feelings of the community, and has given an encouragement to insubordination and crime which calls for the indignant reprobation of the people of Virginia.

Mr. Watson then arose, and after a brief address, offered the following as a substitute for the resolution:

Resolved, That the chair appoint a committee of ——, whose duty it shall be to wait upon the Governor and ascertain from him whose solicitation and upon what representations the reprieve or pardon of the slave Jordan Hatcher was granted; and if not incompatible with the public interests to obtain from the Governor a copy of the petition, if any, which was presented to him for the said pardon, and the names of the signers thereto, as well as any other papers or memorials, if any, as were laid before him in behalf of said slave Jordan Hatcher, and to report to a adjourned meeting to be held on the —— day of the present month, at this place.

A gentleman from Alexandria then obtained the floor, and offered a substitute for the substitute and resolution, which he afterwards withdrew.

Col. J. W. Spalding advocated the passage of the main resolution in a very happy and eloquent speech of ten minutes, opposing with much force the substitute of Mr. Watson.

The question was then vociferously called for, and being first taken on the substitute, it was lost by an overwhelming majority. . . .

"Scene at the Governor's House"

A great hue and cry was raised on our streets, last Saturday, at the *tremendous* indignity offered to Governor Johnson, the night before, by some hundred or so youngsters, who, after the close of the meeting at the City Hall, repaired to the grounds around the Governor's mansion, and after calling him out, and his failing to obey the call, some few of them set up a series of groans and hisses, and others approached the door and rang the bell a number of times. — This conduct, we grant, was exceedingly improper, and none can regret it more than ourselves; but we have been credibly assured that the actors in the commotion were entirely composed of young and indiscreet persons; and that, had the Governor answered to the call, no disorder would have taken place. We also learned from the Mayor of the city that he was present during the entire evening, with a posse of police, and that by mixing in the crowd and appealing to it, he succeeded eventually in getting it to disperse.

The proverbial quietness and good order of our people is too well established for us to argue it at present, and therefore it is we are satisfied no indignity was intended to the Governor's family. — Had circumstances thrown every lady attached to it into the midst of that *infuriated mob*, as it has been called, they would have been as perfectly safe from harm, as if one hundred miles from Richmond. No man who calls himself a Virginian would dare outrage the feelings of a helpless female. The great "to-do" made over the disturbance about his Excellency's mansion, is all gammon, and has been brought about with the hope of crushing the effect of the resolution, passed almost unanimously by one of the largest and most respectable meetings ever held in this city; but its originators will find themselves vastly mistaken in their efforts. — The voice of our people, condemnatory of the act of Governor Johnson, has gone forth upon the wings of the wind, and is now reverberating on every hill and in every valley of Virginia and the South. — No

Richmond Republican, 10 May 1852.

counter action can stay its effects upon those for whom it is intended; and it is use-less, therefore, to attempt to fasten upon the citizens of Richmond, or the respectable portion of them who attended that meeting, any responsibility for the acts of those hair-brained youngsters who, for sport, as much as for any other reason, sought that occasion to give the Governor a few yells and groans, for his misguided sympathy. . . .

"Higher Law!"

As the Constitution makes it the duty of the Governor to lay his reasons before the Legislature, whenever he exercises the pardoning power, we presume it is the privilege and duty of the Legislature to judge of the sufficiency of those reasons.—Governor Johnson, in his message, which we published yesterday, based his recent action substantially upon the ground, that a *negro is as good as a white man.*—We are a little curious to know what opinion this Democratic Legislature entertains on this point. Will they repudiate it, as the honor and welfare of the State demand that they should do? Or will they, by their silence, approve it?

If this latter course be pursued, in what an attitude will the slaveholding State of Virginia stand before the world? With what propriety or force can she ever again complain of the *"Higher Law"* doctrines of the Abolitionists? The equality of the races is the foundation of those doctrines. Our Governor asserts that equality; he acts upon it — it is a matter of *conscience* with him, and he proclaims his *conscience* to be paramount to all the laws of the Commonwealth! This is all that any Abolitionists have ever done. They hold that white men are no better than negroes — it's a point of *conscience* with them. And our unfortunate Governor from Goose Creek holds the same doctrine, and is afflicted with the same *conscientious* infirmity. It would be *justifiable homicide* for a white man to kill, if stricken with a cowhide — it is the same in the case of a negro; — the Governor's *conscience* says so — all laws to the contrary notwithstanding! If this be not the very quintessence of the "higher law," we know not what that doctrine is. . . .

We hold, and we believe it is the sentiment of the great mass of the Virginia people, that the African is an inferior race to the White. The thick lips, the woolly head, the oleagenous skin, the compressed cranium — the whole physical and intellectual organization — all stamp them with indelible marks of inferiority. The labours of physiologists, aided by the lights of science, have incontestibly demonstrated this inferiority. This conviction of inferiority is deeply impressed on the public mind of Virginia; and Gov. Johnson's effort to subvert it and to establish the doctrine of equality, will only result in demonstrating his unfitness to act as Chief Magistrate of a Commonwealth whose every law is based on the radical difference of races.

But we recur to the question, which cannot be too often repeated. What will the Virginia Legislature do? Will it sanction the Governor's doctrine of equality?

Richmond Whig, 14 May 1852.

Will it give its aid and countenance to the "higher law" of the Abolitionists? Its silence is acquiescence in the worst Abolition notions that have ever been preached within the limits of this Commonwealth. What are the fanatical ravings of Abby Kelly, or Joshua Giddings, or Wendell Phillips, compared with the abrogation of the laws regulating the relations of master and slave, and practically asserting the equality of whites and blacks?

And what will become of all those eloquent and indignant denunciations of the Abolitionists by infuriated Democrats, when we have the very worst sort of an Abolitionist in our very midst? Where will the *Enquirer* and other ultra-Southern Democratic papers get material for their impassioned paragraphs against the Free-Soilers? Their thunderbolts will all recoil upon themselves. The Abolitionists will tell them, and tell them truly: We have no better "higher law" man in all our ranks than your own Democratic Governor!

What will the Legislature do?

"Public Meeting in Orange"

Monday (June 28th) being Orange court day, and there being a good attendance of the citizens, it was proposed that a meeting should be held to take into consideration the recent course of the Executive in pardoning the slave Jordan Hatcher, and notice was given that such a meeting, irrespective of party, would be held at the Court House on that day.

In pursuance of that notice, the meeting took place in the afternoon, and organized by the appointment of Philip Mallory, Esq., as Chairman, and W. G. Crinshaw Secretary.

Dr. Pannill explained the object of the meeting and proposed the adoption of the following preamble and resolutions, all of which were adopted, with one or two dissenting voices, viz:

In consideration of the recent act of Executive clemency extended to the culprit, Jordan Hatcher, condemned to die after a fair and full hearing in the Hastings Court at Richmond, for the murder of his overseer, William P. Jackson,

Resolved, That Gov. Johnson in the exercise of Executive power in this case did do violence to the sentiments and judgment of the people of this county and to the spirit and purpose of our criminal laws, and did set a precedent fraught with danger to the established relations of master and slave and to the community.

Resolved, That his reasons given in his communication of 11th May, to the Legislature of Virginia, for the commutation of punishment of said Hatcher, are in our opinion not only flimsy and unsatisfactory, but are insulting to every true hearted Virginian, disorganizing and insurrectionary in their purport and operation, and call for the speedy and full condemnation of the people of the whole State.

Richmond Whig, 9 July 1852.

Resolved, That we respectfully recommend to our fellow-citizens of Virginia to hold meetings and adopt resolutions condemnatory of this act of Gov. Johnson, which tarnishes Virginia's brightest escutcheon, and to request him, as we do now request him, to resign the office he holds, that another may occupy it better informed of the relative rights of master and slave, and wiser in the performance of the high duty of administering the Government according to the wishes, safety and general welfare of the people.

After the conclusion of Dr. Pannill's remarks, and when the vote was about to be taken on the above resolutions, Col. Woolfolk proposed an amendment, which, on being read, was found so repugnant to the feelings of the whole meeting, that the Chairman refused even to entertain it, in which he was heartily supported by nearly every individual present.

On motion it was ordered, that a copy of the proceedings of this meeting be sent to the *Richmond Whig* for publication, and that the papers generally in Richmond be requested to copy them.

Philip Mallory, Chairman.
Wm. G. Crinshaw, Secretary.

Suggestions for Further Reading

Ayers, Edward L. *Vengeance and Justice: Crime and Punishment in the Nineteenth-Century American South.* New York: Oxford University Press, 1984.

Genovese, Eugene D. *From Rebellion to Revolution: Afro-American Slave Revolts in the Making of the Modern World.* Baton Rouge: Louisiana State University Press, 1979.

Goldin, Claudia Dale. *Urban Slavery in the American South, 1820–1860: A Quantitative History.* Chicago: University of Chicago Press, 1976.

Link, William A. "The Jordan Hatcher Case and Politics in Antebellum Virginia." *Journal of Southern History*, LXIV November 1998.

Schwarz, Philip J. *Twice Condemned: Slaves and the Criminal Laws of Virginia, 1705–1865.* Baton Rouge: Louisiana State University Press, 1988.

CHAPTER THIRTEEN

THE SECTIONAL CRISIS

John Brown's Raid, True Womanhood, and the Alienation of North and South

In the decade before the Civil War, the slavery issue created a growing rift between Americans of the North and the South. Sectional tensions flared as politicians fought over the extension of slavery to the territories and the party system seemed unable to resolve or contain sectional conflicts. Antislavery feeling grew in the North, and white Southerners seethed with resentment at criticism of their society. An increasing number of Americans on both sides of the issue became convinced that the nation must become all slave or all free. Then an event occurred that crystallized sectional feeling and made peaceful resolution of differences seem impossible: John Brown's 1859 attempt to launch a slave uprising at Harpers Ferry, Virginia. The stage was set for war as the people of the North and of the South began to see one another as fanatics determined to have their own way.

Sentiment against slavery had been growing in the North as the issue became less remote and abstract. The Fugitive Slave Act of 1850 brought the horrors of slavery to northern soil and made Northerners feel their complicity in maintaining the institution; antislavery leaders urged noncompliance, and dramatic scenes ensued as citizens intervened to save fugitives from recapture. At the same time, antislavery writers were struggling to make white audiences aware of their common humanity with slaves. Harriet Beecher Stowe's *Uncle Tom's Cabin*, published in 1852, was especially effective in making readers feel the human anguish of slaves, particularly slave mothers. By 1852, more than three million copies of the book had been sold.

Stowe was not alone in directing her appeal at women. Many writers did the same, hoping that "true women" would be particularly sympathetic and use their moral authority in behalf of slaves. According to prevailing ideas, a "true woman" was naturally religious and compassionate, sexually pure until marriage, and dedicated to influencing her children and husband — and thus society — to follow the path of righteousness. Antislavery writers such as Lydia Maria Child argued that true women were obligated to oppose the institution of slavery because it permitted children to be sold away from their mothers, denied marriage to slave women, and countenanced their sexual abuse. They denounced southern society for its immoral impact — ruining the lives of black women, men, and children and debasing white men who exploited slave women and then allowed their own offspring to grow up enslaved.

Southerners bitterly resented such portraits of their society, which they fervently believed was morally superior to that of the North. Slavery, they insisted, was a system of benevolent paternalism in which masters and mistresses cared for a childlike, dependent people who served them in exchange for sustenance, protection, and guidance. They insisted that slaves were generally happy and well treated, and that instances of abuse were rare and punished. The plantation mistress had a particular role to play in this defense of the slave system: she was described as the most pious and benevolent of all creatures, superior among women for her Christlike selflessness and devotion to her husband, children, and extended "family" — including slaves. Though physically weak, she ruled men indirectly through her charm and her moral example; many suggested that she was therefore the moral guardian of society. Defenders of southern civilization insisted that no society under her sway would countenance the horrors described by the antislavery authors, who simply didn't understand southern society and whose unrealistic ideas about human equality and the nature of black people led them to champion the rights of slaves rather than the rights — and safety — of their fellow (white) Americans who lived in the South.

Indeed John Brown's raid convinced many white Southerners that Northerners were willing to see them slaughtered in order to strike a blow against slavery. With twenty well-armed supporters, black and white, Brown seized the federal arsenal at Harpers Ferry. Planning to distribute weapons to slaves willing to join him, he sent out men to spread the word. The raiders, however, were quickly overcome by U.S. Marines; seventeen men were killed before Brown was captured. Virginia governor Henry Wise, hoping to avoid both southern lynch mobs and northern rescue attempts, arranged for a speedy trial. Brown was convicted of murder, treason, and conspiracy to incite insurrection, and hanged on December 2, 1859, in Charlestown, Virginia.

The raid and its aftermath inflamed the entire nation. The South seethed with rumors of impending slave revolts, and Brown's execution — at which he displayed great dignity and courage — inspired a wave of mourning throughout the North. Many of those who eulogized Brown went so far as to glorify the whole idea of slave insurrection, which especially angered white Southerners.

Lincoln and many other leading northern politicians went out of their way to reassure Southerners, saying that although Brown "agreed with us in thinking slavery wrong, that cannot excuse violence, bloodshed, and treason." But John Brown's raid caused, as historian David Potter has said, "a deep sense of alienation on the part of the South, which felt that the North was canonizing a fiend who sought to plunge the South into a blood bath."[1] Historians believe that within the six weeks after Harpers Ferry there was a virtual revolution of sentiment in the South. The governor of Florida said that after Brown's raid and the reaction of the North, he finally favored "eternal separation from those whose wickedness and fanaticism forbid us longer to live with them in peace and safety."[2]

The correspondence exchanged among abolitionist Lydia Maria Child, Governor Henry Wise, and Margaretta Mason, wife of the Virginia senator who authored the Fugitive Slave Act, demonstrates the sharp differences of opinion on the slavery issue and a true woman's proper response to it. Published in 1859 as an antislavery pamphlet that sold more than 300,000 copies, these letters helped to inflame public debate following John Brown's raid. They fully illustrate the northern "canonization" of Brown and the southern outrage at that response.

———

As you read, consider these questions. What do these letters reveal about sectional tensions? Why did the Southerners believe that Northerners like Child helped cause John Brown's attack? How do Child, Wise, and Mason agree and disagree about the proper role of a true woman? How do Child and Mason support their assertions that the women of their region — and only their region — are acting as true women should?

[1]*The Impending Crisis, 1848–1861,* 378.
[2]Qtd. in Potter, *The Impending Crisis, 1848–1861,* 384.

47. A Plea from Massachusetts

LYDIA MARIA CHILD
Letter to Governor Wise
1859

Before becoming one of the most famous women in the antislavery movement, Lydia Maria Child was a popular and noncontroversial author, who wrote historical novels, edited the first American magazine for children (she wrote the well-

known Thanksgiving poem "Over the River and Through the Woods"), and published best-selling advice literature for women and girls. After meeting William Lloyd Garrison in 1831, she and her reformer husband, David Child, joined the movement to abolish slavery. Her celebrated antislavery tract Appeal in Favor of that Class of Americans Called Africans *(1833) converted many to the antislavery cause including some of its most famous supporters. Although the furor over the Appeal caused her to be ostracized from Boston society and her magazine to collapse, Child continued to write antislavery pamphlets. She became editor of the* National Anti-Slavery Standard *in 1841 but later resigned when it was criticized as too genteel and mild.*

Deeply moved by John Brown's cause, Child wrote this letter to Virginia's governor. In it, she seeks permission to tend to Brown's physical and spiritual wounds.

Wayland, Mass., Oct. 26th, 1859

Governor Wise: I have heard that you were a man of chivalrous sentiments, and I know you were opposed to the iniquitous attempt to force upon Kansas a constitution abhorrent to the moral sense of her people. Relying upon these indications of honor and justice in your character, I venture to ask a favor of you. Enclosed is a letter to Capt. John Brown. Will you have the kindness, after reading it yourself, to transmit it to the prisoner?

I and all my large circle of abolition acquaintances were taken by surprise when news came of Capt. Brown's recent attempt; nor do I know of a single person who would have approved of it had they been apprised of his intention. But I and thousands of others feel a natural impulse of sympathy for the brave and suffering man. Perhaps God, who sees the inmost of our souls, perceives some such sentiment in your heart also. He needs a mother or sister to dress his wounds, and speak soothingly to him. Will you allow me to perform that mission of humanity? If you will, may God bless you for the generous deed!

I have been for years an uncompromising abolitionist, and I should scorn to deny it or apologize for it as much as John Brown himself would do. Believing in peace principles, I deeply regret the step that the old veteran has taken, while I honor his humanity towards those who became his prisoners. But because it is my habit to be as open as the daylight, I will also say that if I believed our religion justified men in fighting for freedom, I should consider the enslaved everywhere as best entitled to that right. Such an avowal is a simple, frank expression of my sense of natural justice.

But I should despise myself utterly if any circumstances could tempt me to seek to advance these opinions in any way, directly or indirectly, after your per-

Correspondence between Lydia Maria Child and Gov. Wise and Mrs. Mason, of Virginia (Boston: American Anti-Slavery Society, 1860), 3–4.

mission to visit Virginia has been obtained on the plea of sisterly sympathy with a brave and suffering man. I give you my word of honor, which was never broken, that I would use such permission solely and singly for the purpose of nursing your prisoner, and for no other purpose whatsoever.

Yours, respectfully,
L. Maria Child.

48. The Virginia Governor's Response

GOVERNOR HENRY A. WISE
Letter to Lydia Maria Child
1859

Governor Henry A. Wise had the difficult job of keeping order in Virginia during the imprisonment, trial, and hanging of John Brown. A veteran politician from tideland Accomac County, he had represented Virginia in the United States Congress in the 1830s and 1840s where he was a leader among the Southern Whigs and fought to preserve slavery. An admirer of Andrew Jackson and an advocate for the democratization of Virginia politics, he switched parties before becoming the state's Democratic governor.

Henry Wise was, as historian David Potter put it, "a Virginian far gone in chivalry"[1] who held very traditional ideas about woman's role in public affairs. He once wrote that his wife was "not competent to advise the statesman or the politician — her knowledge, her advice, her ministry is in a kindlier sphere."[2] Despite his disgust at John Brown's deed, Wise admitted to being captivated by Brown's courage as he awaited execution: "He is a bundle of the best nerves I ever saw, cut and thrust and bleeding and in bonds. . . . He is a man of clear head, of courage, fortitude, and simple ingeniousness . . . cool, collected, and indomitable."[3] But as this letter suggests, Wise was livid over Child's request: he did not hesitate to turn her correspondence over to the press.

---

[1] *The Impending Crisis, 1848–1861*, 375.
[2] Qtd. in Wyatt-Brown, *Southern Honor: Ethics and Behavior in the Old South*, 271.
[3] Qtd. in Potter, *The Impending Crisis, 1846–1861*, 375–76.

Correspondence between Lydia Maria Child and Gov. Wise and Mrs. Mason, of Virginia (Boston: American Anti-Slavery Society, 1860), 4–6.

Richmond, Va., Oct. 29th, 1859

Madam: Yours of the 26th was received by me yesterday, and at my earliest leisure I respectfully reply to it, that I will forward the letter for John Brown, a prisoner under our laws, arraigned at the bar of the Circuit Court for the county of Jefferson, at Charlestown, Va., for the crimes of murder, robbery and treason, which you ask me to transmit to him. I will comply with your request in the only way which seems to me proper, by enclosing it to the Commonwealth's attorney, with the request that he will ask the permission of the Court to hand it to the prisoner. Brown, the prisoner, is now in the hands of the judiciary, not of the executive of this Commonwealth.

You ask me, further, to allow you to perform the mission "of mother or sister, to dress his wounds and speak soothingly to him." By this, of course, you mean to be allowed to visit him in his cell, and to minister to him in the offices of humanity. Why should you not be so allowed, Madam? Virginia and Massachusetts are involved in no civil war, and the Constitution which unites them in one confederacy guarantees to you privileges and immunities of a citizen of the United States in the State of Virginia. That Constitution I am sworn to support, and am, therefore, bound to protect your privileges and immunities as a citizen of Massachusetts coming into Virginia for any lawful and peaceful purpose.

Coming, as you propose, to minister to the captive in prison, you will be met, doubtless, by all our people, not only in a chivalrous, but in a Christian spirit. You have the right to visit Charlestown, Va., Madam; and your mission being merciful and humane, will not only be allowed, but respected, if not welcomed. A few unenlightened and inconsiderate persons, fanatical in their modes of thought and action, to maintain justice and right, might molest you, or be disposed to do so; and this might suggest the imprudence of risking any experiment upon the peace of a society very much excited by the crimes with whose chief author you seem to sympathize so much. But still, I repeat, your motives and avowed purpose are lawful and peaceful, and I will, as far as I am concerned, do my duty in protecting your rights in our limits. Virginia and her authorities would be weak indeed — weak in point of folly, and weak in point of power — if her State faith and constitutional obligations cannot be redeemed in her own limits to the letter of morality as well as of law; and if her chivalry cannot courteously receive a lady's visit to a prisoner, every arm which guards Brown from rescue on the one hand, and from lynch law on the other, will be ready to guard your person in Virginia.

I could not permit an insult even to woman in her walk of charity among us, though it be to one who whetted knives of butchery for our mothers, sisters, daughters and babes. We have no sympathy with your sentiments of sympathy with Brown, and are surprised that you were "taken by surprise when news came of Capt. Brown's recent attempt." His attempt was a natural consequence of your sympathy, and the errors of that sympathy ought to make you doubt its virtue from the effect on his conduct. But it is not of this I should speak. When you arrive at Charlestown, if you go there, it will be for the Court and its officers, the Commonwealth's attorney, sheriff and jailer, to say whether you may see and wait on the prisoner. But, whether you are thus permitted or not (and you will be, if my advice can prevail), you may rest assured that he will be humanely, lawfully and mercifully dealt by in prison and on trial.

Respectfully,
Henry A. Wise.

49. What Is a True Woman to Do?

MARGARETTA MASON AND LYDIA MARIA CHILD
Correspondence
1859

After reading the exchange of letters between Lydia Maria Child and Governor Wise in the newspaper, M. J. C. (Margaretta) Mason wrote this indignant letter, which Child answered after Brown's execution. Mason was the wife of Virginia senator James M. Mason, the author of the Fugitive Slave Act and head of a congressional committee appointed to investigate the causes of John Brown's raid. Like her husband, she was irate over northern sympathy for a man who had plotted to murder southern slaveholders.

Child's reply summarizes biblical arguments, cites examples of southern slave policies as revealed by laws and newspapers, and includes testimony from former slaves and slaveholders — among them, Angelina and Sarah Grimké. Together the two letters constitute a fascinating debate on the proper response of a "true woman" to slavery and reveal the tremendous differences of opinion between this leading abolitionist and the wife of one of the foremost defenders of slavery.

M. J. C. MASON TO LYDIA MARIA CHILD

Alto, King George's Co., Va., Nov. 11th, 1859

Do you read your Bible, Mrs. Child? If you do, read there, "Woe unto you, hypocrites," and take to yourself with two-fold damnation that terrible sentence;

Correspondence between Lydia Maria Child and Gov. Wise and Mrs. Mason, of Virginia (Boston: American Anti-Slavery Society, 1860), 16–18, 18–28.

for, rest assured, in the day of judgment it shall be more tolerable for those thus scathed by the awful denunciation of the Son of God, than for you. *You* would soothe with sisterly and motherly care the hoary-headed murderer of Harper's Ferry! A man whose aim and intention was to incite the horrors of a servile war — to condemn women of your own race, ere death closed their eyes on their sufferings from violence and outrage, to see their husbands and fathers murdered, their children butchered, the ground strewed with the brains of their babes. The antecedents of Brown's band proved them to have been the offscourings of the earth; and what would have been our fate had they found as many sympathizers in Virginia as they seem to have in Massachusetts?

Now, compare yourself with those your "sympathy" would devote to such ruthless ruin, and say, on that "word of honor, which never has been broken," would *you* stand by the bedside of an old negro, dying of a hopeless disease, to alleviate his sufferings as far as human aid could? Have *you* ever watched the last, lingering illness of a consumptive, to soothe, as far as in you lay, the inevitable fate? Do *you* soften the pangs of maternity in those around you by all the care and comfort you can give? Do *you* grieve with those *near* you, even though their sorrows resulted from their own misconduct? Did *you* ever sit up until the "wee hours" to complete a dress for a motherless child, that she might appear on Christmas day in a new one, along with her more fortunate companions? We do these and more for our servants, and why? Because we endeavor *to do our duty in that state of life it has pleased God to place us.* In his revealed word we read our duties to them — theirs to us are there also — "Not only to the good and gentle, but to the froward." — (Peter II: 18.) Go thou and do likewise, and keep away from Charlestown. If the stories read in the public prints be true, of the sufferings of the poor of the North, you need not go far for objects of charity. "Thou hypocrite! take first the beam out of thine own eye, then shalt thou see clearly to pull the mote out of thy neighbor's." But if, indeed, you do lack objects of sympathy near you, go to Jefferson county, to the family of George Turner, a noble, true-hearted man, whose devotion to his friend (Col. Washington) causing him to risk his life, was shot down like a dog. Or to that of old Beckham, whose grief at the murder of his negro subordinate made him needlessly expose himself to the aim of the assassin Brown. And when you can equal in deeds of love and charity to those *around* you, what is shown by nine-tenths of the Virginia plantations, then by your "sympathy" whet the knives for our throats, and kindle the torch that fires our homes. You reverence Brown for his clemency to his prisoners! Prisoners! and how taken? Unsuspecting workmen, going to their daily duties; unarmed gentlemen, taken from their beds at the dead hour of the night, by six men doubly and trebly armed. Suppose he had hurt a hair of their heads, do you suppose one of the band of desperadoes would have left the engine-house alive? And did not he know that his treatment of them was his only hope of life then, or of clemency afterward? Of course he did. The United States troops could not have prevented him from being torn limb from limb.

I will add, in conclusion, no Southerner ought, after your letter to Governor Wise and to Brown, to read a line of your composition, or to touch a magazine which bears your name in its lists of contributors; and in this we hope for the "sympathy," at least of those at the North who deserve the name of woman.

M. J. C. Mason.

LYDIA MARIA CHILD TO M. J. C. MASON

Wayland, Mass., Dec. 17th, 1859

Prolonged absence from home has prevented my answering your letter so soon as I intended. I have no disposition to retort upon you the "two-fold damnation," to which you consign me. On the contrary, I sincerely wish you well, both in this world and the next. If the anathema proved a safety valve to your own boiling spirit, it did some good to you, while it fell harmless upon me. Fortunately for all of us, the Heavenly Father rules His universe by laws, which the passions or the prejudices of mortals have no power to change.

As for John Brown, his reputation may be safely trusted to the impartial pen of History; and his motives will be righteously judged by Him who knoweth the secrets of all hearts. Men, however great they may be, are of small consequence in comparison with principles; and the principle for which John Brown died is the question at issue between us.

You refer me to the Bible, from which you quote the favorite text of slaveholders: —

> "Servants, be subject to your masters with all fear; not only to the good and gentle, but also to the froward." — 1 Peter, 2: 18.

Abolitionists also have favorite texts, to some of which I would call your attention: —

> "Remember those that are in bonds as bound with them." — Heb. 13: 3.
> "Hide the outcasts. Bewray not him that wandereth. Let mine outcasts dwell with thee. Be thou a covert to them from the face of the spoiler." — Isa. 16: 3, 4.
> "Thou shalt not deliver unto his master the servant which is escaped from his master unto thee. He shall dwell with thee where it liketh him best. Thou shalt not oppress him." — Deut. 23: 15, 16.
> "Open thy mouth for the dumb, in the cause of all such as are appointed to destruction. Open thy mouth, judge righteously, and plead the cause of the poor and needy." — Prov. 29: 8, 9.
> "Cry aloud, spare not, lift up thy voice like a trumpet, and show my people their transgression, and the house of Jacob their sins." — Isa. 58: 1.

I would especially commend to slaveholders the following portions of that volume, wherein you say God has revealed the duty of masters: —

> "Masters, give unto your servants that which is just and equal, knowing that ye also have a Master in heaven." — Col. 4: 1.

"Neither be ye called masters; for one is your master, even Christ; and all ye are brethren." — Matt. 23: 8, 10.

"Whatsoever ye would that men should do unto you, do ye even so unto them." — Matt. 7: 12.

"Is not this the fast that I have chosen, to loose the bands of wickedness, to undo the heavy burdens, and to let the oppressed go free, and that ye break every yoke?" — Isa. 58: 6.

"They have given a boy for a harlot, and sold a girl for wine, that they might drink." — Joel 3: 3.

"He that oppresseth the poor, reproacheth his Maker." — Prov. 14: 31.

"Rob not the poor, because he is poor; neither oppress the afflicted. For the Lord will plead their cause, and spoil the soul of those who spoiled them." — Prov. 22: 22, 23.

"Woe unto him that useth his neighbor's service without wages, and giveth him not for his work." — Jer. 22: 13.

"Let him that stole, steal no more, but rather let him labor, working with his hands." — Eph. 4: 28.

"Woe unto them that decree unrighteous decrees, and that write grievousness which they have prescribed; to turn aside the needy from judgment, and to take away the right from the poor, that widows may be their prey, and that they may rob the fatherless." — Isa. 10: 1, 2.

"If I did despise the cause of my man-servant or of my maid-servant, when they contend with me, what then shall I do when God riseth up? and when he visiteth, what shall I answer Him?" — Job 31: 13, 14.

"Thou hast sent widows away empty, and the arms of the fatherless have been broken. Therefore snares are round about thee, and sudden fear troubleth thee; and darkness, that thou canst not see." — Job 22: 9, 10, 11.

"Behold, the hire of your laborers, who have reaped down your fields, which is of you kept back by fraud, crieth; and the cries of them which have reaped are entered into the ears of the Lord of sabaoth. Ye have lived in pleasure on the earth, and been wanton; ye have nourished your hearts as in a day of slaughter; ye have condemned and killed the just." — James 5: 4.

If the appropriateness of these texts is not apparent, I will try to make it so, by evidence drawn entirely from *Southern* sources. The Abolitionists are not such an ignorant set of fanatics as you suppose. They *know* whereof they affirm. They are familiar with the laws of the Slave States, which are alone sufficient to inspire abhorrence in any humane heart or reflecting mind not perverted by the prejudices of education and custom. I might fill many letters with significant extracts from your statute-books; but I have space only to glance at a few, which indicate the *leading* features of the system you cherish so tenaciously.

The universal rule of the slave State is, that "the child follows the condition of its *mother.*" This is an index to many things. Marriages between white and colored people are forbidden by law; yet a very large number of the slaves are brown or yellow. When Lafayette visited this country in his old age, he said he was very much struck by the great change in the colored population of Virginia; that at the time of the Revolution, nearly all the household slaves were black, but when he returned to America, he found very few of them black. The advertisements in

Southern newspapers often describe runaway slaves that "pass themselves for white men." Sometimes they are described as having "straight, light hair, blue eyes, and clear complexion." This could not be, unless their fathers, grandfathers, and great-grandfathers had been white men. But as their *mothers* were slaves, the law pronounces *them* slaves, subject to be sold on the auction-block whenever the necessities or convenience of their masters or mistresses require it. The sale of one's own children, brothers, or sisters, has an ugly aspect to those who are unaccustomed to it; and, obviously, it cannot have a good moral influence, that law and custom should render licentiousness a *profitable* vice.

Throughout the Slave States, the testimony of no colored person, bond or free, can be received against a white man. You have some laws, which, on the face of them, would seem to restrain inhuman men from murdering or mutilating slaves; but they are rendered nearly null by the law I have cited. Any drunken master, overseer, or patrol, may go into the negro cabins, and commit what outrages he pleases, with perfect impunity, if no white person is present who chooses to witness against him. North Carolina and Georgia leave a large loophole for escape, even if white persons are present, when murder is committed. A law to punish persons for "maliciously killing a slave" has this remarkable qualification: "Always provided that this act shall not extend to any slave dying of moderate correction." We at the North find it difficult to understand how *moderate* punishment can cause *death*. I have read several of your law-books attentively, and I find no cases of punishment for the murder of a slave, except by fines paid to the *owner*, to indemnify him for the loss of his *property*: the same as if his horse or cow had been killed. In the South Carolina Reports is a case where the State had indicted Guy Raines for the murder of a slave named Isaac. It was proved that William Gray, the owner of Isaac, had given him *a thousand lashes*. The poor creature made his escape, but was caught, and delivered to the custody of Raines, to be carried to the county jail. Because he refused to go, Raines gave him five hundred lashes, and he died soon after. The counsel for Raines proposed that he should be allowed to acquit himself by his *own oath*. The Court decided against it, because *white witnesses* had testified; but the Court of Appeals afterward decided he *ought* to have been exculpated by his own oath, and he was *acquitted*. Small indeed is the chance for justice to a slave, when his own color are not allowed to testify, if they see him maimed or his children murdered; when he has slaveholders for Judges and Jurors; when the murderer can exculpate himself by his own oath, and when the law provides that it is no murder to kill a slave by "moderate correction"!

Your laws uniformly declare that "a slave shall be deemed a chattel personal in the hands of his owner, to all intents, constructions, and purposes whatsoever." This, of course, involves the right to sell his children, as if they were pigs; also, to take his wife from him "for any intent or purpose whatsoever." Your laws also make it death for him to resist a white man, however brutally he may be treated, or however much his family may be outraged before his eyes. If he attempts to run away, your laws allow any man to shoot him.

By your laws, all a slave's earnings belong to his master. He can neither receive donations nor transmit property. If his master allows him some hours to work for himself, and by great energy and perseverance he earns enough to buy his own bones and sinews, his master may make him pay two or three times over, and he has no redress. Three such cases have come within my own knowledge. Even a written promise from his master has no legal value, because a slave can make no contracts.

Your laws also systematically aim at keeping the minds of the colored people in the most abject state of ignorance. If white people attempt to teach them to read or write, they are punished by imprisonment or fines; if they attempt to teach others, they are punished with from twenty to thirty-nine lashes each. It cannot be said that the anti-slavery agitation produced such laws, for they date much further back; many of them when we were Provinces. They are the *necessities* of the system, which, being itself an outrage upon human nature, can be sustained only by perpetual outrages.

The next reliable source of information is the advertisements in the Southern papers. In the North Carolina (Raleigh) *Standard*, Mr. Micajah Ricks advertises, "Runaway, a negro woman and her two children. A few days before she went off, I burned her with a hot iron on the left side of her face. I tried to make the letter M." In the Natchez *Courier*, Mr. J. P. Ashford advertises a runaway negro girl, with "a good many teeth missing, and the letter A branded on her cheek and forehead." In the Lexington (Ky.) *Observer*, Mr. William Overstreet advertises a runaway negro with "his left eye out, scars from a dirk on his left arm, and much scarred with the whip." I might quote from hundreds of such advertisements, offering rewards for runaways, "dead or alive," and describing them with "ears cut off," "jaws broken," "scarred by rifle-balls," &c.

Another source of information is afforded by your "Fugitives from Injustice," with many of whom I have conversed freely. I have seen scars of the whip and marks of the branding-iron, and I have listened to their heart-breaking sobs, while they told of "piccaninnies" torn from their arms and sold.

Another source of information is furnished by emancipated slaveholders. Sarah M. Grimké, daughter of the late Judge Grimké, of the Supreme Court of South Carolina, testifies as follows: "As I left my native State on account of Slavery, and deserted the home of my fathers to escape the sound of the lash and the shrieks of tortured victims, I would gladly bury in oblivion the recollection of those scenes with which I have been familiar. But this cannot be. They come over my memory like gory spectres, and implore me, with resistless power, in the name of a God of mercy, in the name of a crucified Saviour, in the name of humanity, for the sake of the slaveholder, as well as the slave, to bear witness to the horrors of the Southern prison-house." She proceeds to describe dreadful tragedies, the actors in which she says were "men and women of the first families in South Carolina"; and that their cruelties did not, in the slightest degree, affect their standing in society. Her sister, Angelina Grimké, declared: "While I live, and Slavery lives, I *must* testify against it. Not merely for the sake of my poor brothers and sisters in bonds; for even were Slavery no curse to its victims, the exercise of arbitrary power works such fearful ruin upon the hearts of slaveholders, that I should feel impelled to labor and pray for its overthrow with my latest breath." Among the horrible barbarities she enumerates is the case of a girl thirteen years old, who was flogged to death by her master. She says: "I asked a prominent lawyer, who belonged to one of the first families in the State, whether the murderer of this helpless child could not be indicted, and he coolly replied that the slave was Mr. ——'s property, and if he chose to suffer the *loss*, no one else had anything to do with it." She proceeds to say: "I felt there could be for me no rest in the midst of such outrages and pollutions. Yet I saw nothing of Slavery in its most vulgar and repulsive forms. I saw it in the city, among the fashionable and the honorable, where it was garnished by refinement and decked out for show. It is my deep, solemn, deliberate conviction that this is a cause worth dying for. I say so from what I have seen, and heard, and known, in a land of Slavery, whereon rest the darkness of Egypt and the sin of Sodom." I once asked Miss Angelina if she thought Abolitionists exaggerated the horrors of Slavery. She replied, with earnest emphasis: "They *cannot* be exaggerated. It is impossible for imagination to go beyond the facts." To a lady who observed that the time had not yet come for agitating the subject, she answered: "I apprehend if thou wert a *slave*, toiling in the fields of Carolina, thou wouldst think the time had *fully* come."

Mr. Thome, of Kentucky, in the course of his eloquent lectures on this subject, said: "I breathed my first breath in an atmosphere of Slavery. But though I am heir to a slave inheritance, I am bold to denounce the whole system as an outrage, a complication of crimes, and wrongs, and cruelties, that make angels weep."

Mr. Allen, of Alabama, in a discussion with the students at Lane Seminary, in 1834, told of a slave who was tied up and beaten all day, with a paddle full of holes: "At night, his flesh was literally pounded to a jelly. The punishment was inflicted within hearing of the Academy and the Public Green. But no one took any notice of it. No one thought any wrong was done. At our house, it is so common to hear screams from a neighboring plantation, that we think nothing of it. Lest any one should think that the slaves are *generally* well treated, and that the cases I have mentioned are exceptions, let me be distinctly understood that cruelty is the *rule*, and kindness is the exception."

In the same discussion, a student from Virginia, after relating cases of great cruelty, said: "Such things are common all over Virginia; at least, so far as I am acquainted. But the planters generally avoid punishing their slaves before *strangers*."

Miss Mattie Griffith, of Kentucky, whose entire property consisted in slaves, emancipated them all. The noble-hearted girl wrote to me: "I shall go forth into the world penniless; but I shall work with a light heart, and, best of all, I shall live with an easy conscience." Previous to this generous resolution, she had never read any Abolition document, and entertained the common Southern prejudice against them. But her own observation so deeply impressed her with the enormities of Slavery, that she was impelled to publish a book, called "The Autobiography of a Female Slave." I read it with thrilling interest; but some of the scenes made my nerves quiver so painfully, that I told her I hoped they were too highly colored. She shook her head sadly, and replied: "I am sorry to say that every incident in the book has come within my own knowledge."

St. George Tucker, Judge and Professor of Law in Virginia, speaking of the legalized murder of runaways, said: "Such are the cruelties to which a state of Slavery gives birth — such the horrors to which the human mind is capable of being reconciled by its adoption." Alluding to our struggle in '76, he said: "While we proclaim our resolution to live free or die, we imposed on our fellow-men, of different complexion, a Slavery ten thousand times worse than the utmost extremity of the oppressions of which we complained."

Governor Giles, in a Message to the Legislature of Virginia, referring to the custom of selling free colored people into Slavery, as a punishment for offences not capital, said: "Slavery must be admitted to be a *punishment of the highest order*; and, according to the just rule for the apportionment of punishment to crimes, it ought to be applied only to *crimes of the highest order*. The most distressing reflection in the application of this punishment to female offenders is, that it extends to their offspring; and the innocent are thus punished with the guilty." Yet one hundred and twenty thousand innocent babes in this country are annually subjected to a punishment which your Governor declared "ought to be applied only to crimes of the highest order."

Jefferson said: "One *day* of American Slavery is worse than a *thousand years* of that which we rose in arms to oppose." Alluding to insurrections, he said: "The Almighty has no attribute that can take side with us in such a contest."

John Randolph declared: "Every planter is a sentinel at his own door. Every Southern mother, when she hears an alarm of fire in the night, instinctively presses her infant closer to her bosom."

Looking at the system of slavery in the light of all this evidence, do you candidly think we deserve "two-fold damnation" for detesting it? Can you not believe that we may hate the system, and yet be truly your friends? I make allowance for the excited state of your mind, and for the prejudices induced by education. I do not care to change your opinion of me; but I do wish you could be persuaded to examine this subject dispassionately, for the sake of the prosperity of Virginia, and the welfare of unborn generations, both white and colored. For thirty years, Abolitionists have been trying to reason with slaveholders, through the press, and in the halls of Congress. Their efforts, though directed to the *masters only*, have been met with violence and abuse almost equal to that poured on the head of John Brown. Yet surely we, as a portion of the Union, involved in the expense, the degeneracy, the danger, and the disgrace, of this iniquitous and fatal system, have a *right* to speak about it, and a right to be *heard* also. At the North, we willingly publish pro-slavery arguments, and ask only a fair field and no favor for the other side. But you will not even allow your own citizens a chance to examine this important subject. Your letter to me is published in Northern papers, as well as Southern; but my reply will not be allowed to appear in any Southern paper. The despotic measures you take to silence investigation, and shut out the light from your own white population, prove how little reliance you have on the strength of your cause. In this enlightened age, all despotisms *ought* to come to an end by the agency of moral and rational means. But if they resist such agencies, it is in the order of Providence that they *must* come to an end by violence. History is full of such lessons.

Would that the veil of prejudice could be removed from your eyes. If you would candidly examine the statements of Governor Hincks of the British West

Indies, and of the Rev. Mr. Bleby, long time a Missionary in those Islands, both before and after emancipation, you could not fail to be convinced that Cash is a more powerful incentive to labor than the Lash, and far safer also. One fact in relation to those Islands is very significant. While the working people were slaves, it was always necessary to order out the military during the Christmas holidays; but, since emancipation, not a soldier is to be seen. A hundred John Browns might land there, without exciting the slightest alarm.

To the personal questions you ask me, I will reply in the name of all the women of New England. It would be extremely difficult to find any woman in our villages who does *not* sew for the poor, and watch with the sick, whenever occasion requires. We pay our domestics generous wages, with which they can purchase as many Christmas gowns as they please; a process far better for their characters, as well as our own, than to receive their clothing as a charity, after being deprived of just payment for their labor. I have never known an instance where the "pangs of maternity" did not meet with requisite assistance; and here at the North, after we have helped the mothers, *we do not sell the babies.*

I readily believe what you state concerning the kindness of many Virginia matrons. It is creditable to their hearts: but after all, the best that can be done in that way is a poor equivalent for the perpetual wrong done to the slaves, and the terrible liabilities to which they are always subject. Kind masters and mistresses among you are merely lucky accidents. If any one *chooses* to be a brutal despot, your laws and customs give him complete power to do so. And the lot of those slaves who have the kindest masters is exceedingly precarious. In case of death, or pecuniary difficulties, or marriages in the family, they may at any time be suddenly transferred from protection and indulgence to personal degradation, or extreme severity; and if they should try to escape from such sufferings, anybody is authorized to shoot them down like dogs.

With regard to your declaration that "no Southerner ought henceforth to read a line of my composition," I reply that I have great satisfaction in the consciousness of having nothing to lose in that quarter. Twenty-seven years ago, I published a book called "An Appeal in behalf of that class of Americans called Africans." It influenced the minds of several young men, afterward conspicuous in public life, through whose agency the cause was better served than it could have been by me. From that time to this, I have labored too earnestly for the slave to be agreeable to slaveholders. Literary popularity was never a paramount object with me, even in my youth; and, now that I am old, I am utterly indifferent to it. But, if I cared for the exclusion you threaten, I should at least have the consolation of being exiled with honorable company. Dr. Channing's writings, mild and candid as they are, breathe what you would call arrant treason. William C. Bryant, in his capacity of editor, is openly on our side. The inspired muse of Whittier has incessantly sounded the trumpet for moral warfare with your iniquitous institution; and his stirring tones have been answered, more or less loudly, by Pierpont, Lowell, and Longfellow. Emerson, the Plato of America, leaves the scholastic seclusion he loves so well, and, disliking noise with all his poetic soul, bravely takes his stand among the trumpeters. George W. Curtis, the brilliant writer, the eloquent lecturer, the elegant man of the world, lays the wealth of his talent on the altar of Freedom, and makes common cause with rough-shod reformers.

The genius of Mrs. Stowe carried the outworks of your institution at one dash, and left the citadel open to besiegers, who are pouring in amain. In the church, on the ultra-liberal side, it is assailed by the powerful battering-ram of Theodore Parker's eloquence. On the extreme orthodox side is set a huge fire, kindled by the burning words of Dr. Cheever. Between them is Henry Ward Beecher, sending a shower of keen arrows into your entrenchments; and with him ride a troop of sharp-shooters from all sects. If you turn to the literature of England or France, you will find your institution treated with as little favor. The fact is, the whole civilized world proclaims Slavery an outlaw, and the best intellect of the age is active in hunting it down.

L. Maria Child

Suggestions for Further Reading

Clinton, Catherine. *The Plantation Mistress: Woman's World in the Old South.* New York: Pantheon Books, 1982.

Fox-Genovese, Elizabeth. *Within the Plantation Household: Black and White Women of the Old South.* Chapel Hill: University of North Carolina Press, 1988.

Holt, Michael F. *The Political Crisis of the 1850s.* New York: John Wiley & Sons, 1978.

Oates, Stephen B. *To Purge This Land with Blood: A Biography of John Brown.* 2d ed. Amherst: University of Massachusetts Press, 1984.

Potter, David M. *The Impending Crisis, 1848–1861.* New York: Harper and Row, 1977.

Walters, Ronald G. *The Antislavery Appeal: American Abolitionism after 1830.* Baltimore: Johns Hopkins University Press, 1976.

Welter, Barbara. "The Cult of True Womanhood, 1820–1869." *American Quarterly* 18 (summer 1966): 151–74.

Wyatt-Brown, Bertram. *Southern Honor: Ethics and Behavior in the Old South.* New York: Oxford University Press, 1976.

Yellin, Jean Fagan. *Women & Sisters: The Antislavery Feminists in American Culture.* New Haven, Conn.: Yale University Press, 1989.

CHAPTER FOURTEEN

THE CIVIL WAR

The Minds and Hearts
of the Southern People

WhEN decades of sectional conflict and animosity finally exploded into
violence and Americans fought Americans in a bloody civil war, the
overwhelming majority of white Southerners supported the Confederacy. Even many who had opposed secession rallied to the support of their state
and region when the fighting began. There were, however, many pockets of
Unionists within the South, especially in Texas and in the border states. And of
course, millions of African Americans in the South supported the Union; thousands of black Southerners — both free men and former slaves — fought in the
Union army.

The war brought great suffering to both North and South: the bloodiest war
the world had ever seen, it remained unparalleled in the number of people killed
until World War I. Because most of the war was fought on their soil, however,
Southerners faced particular difficulties. Many of their cities were occupied and
several burned; destruction of plantations, farms, and fields, compounded by federal blockades of the harbors, led to extreme shortages of food and supplies. Southerners of every class, color, and creed were affected. Women faced major challenges as they coped with these scarcities, took on unfamiliar duties, nursed the
wounded, confronted enemy soldiers, or fled with their children; few escaped the
trauma of losing loved ones.

In addition, the South faced an enemy vastly superior in industrial strength,
material resources, and numbers of fighting men. Aside from major battles between the regular armies, the border states experienced violence between civilians
supporting the Confederacy and those supporting the Union. And the gradual dis-
integration of slavery with progressing Union penetration of the South brought
freedom — but also much uncertainty and suffering — for black Southerners, as

Union policies fluctuated and African Americans encountered prejudice and violence from all sides.

The might of the Union and the miseries of the home front did not deter the Confederates from waging a four-year battle against considerable odds. According to historian James M. McPherson, much of this tenacity derived from ideology: throughout the war, soldiers (on both sides) remained strongly convinced of the ideas for which they fought. Indeed, Confederate soldiers were more vocal in their patriotism than many on their home front and resented the defeatist attitude of many civilians. They looked back to ideals of the Revolution, convinced that they were the true defenders of the Constitution and the rights of states. They blamed the North for causing the war, believing that the federal government was in the hands of despots who, in attacking slavery, were abusing the rights of southern individuals as well as states. Racial prejudice was another source of their determined resistance: most southern whites of all classes not only recognized that their economy was dependent on slavery, they could not abide the idea of living amid a free black population. Confederates also went to battle out of a sense of duty to the South, deriving emotional fervor from the sense that their land was being invaded, their homes, families, and property threatened. References to Yankees in their letters and diaries reveal the impact of decades of proslavery rhetoric depicting Northerners as ruffianly, uncouth, and cowardly. Southern soldiers saw themselves as fighting for their honor and manhood, to retain the respect of families, friends, and comrades. Finally, religion was a major factor: like the Northerners, Southerners were firmly convinced that God was on their side.

White women of the Confederacy shared many of these feelings. They were praised extravagantly by Confederate men for their patriotism and willingness to sacrifice for the cause. They had a reputation for hating Yankees with a passion and for making their feelings clear, a fact that General Benjamin Butler, in charge of occupied New Orleans, found intolerable. He became notorious throughout the South, the nation, and even abroad for his decree that women who insulted Union soldiers be treated as prostitutes. Drew Gilpin Faust, George Rable, and other historians have effectively challenged the idea that southern white women were indefatigable supporters of the war; letters to the Confederate government attest otherwise, as does their participation in bread riots in the streets of southern cities. Nonetheless, letters and diaries do clearly indicate that at the outset of the war and for much of its duration — before it became abundantly clear that the bloodbath was for naught — southern white women were passionate partisans indeed.

There were passionate partisans among southern Unionists, as well. Some, like those in West Virginia, East Tennessee, Northwest Arkansas, and parts of Texas, were from regions with few slaves and resented the power of the slaveholding elite. Others, like W. G. "Parson" Brownlow of Tennessee, were former

Whigs who thought national greatness depended on a strong central government and blamed the war on southern extremists.

Inspired by the prospect of freedom, enslaved African Americans eagerly seized opportunities to attain it. Many masters tried to prevent escape by sending their slaves far from Yankee positions. But a steady stream of African Americans sought freedom behind Union lines, despite the shabby treatment "contrabands" received. More than one hundred thousand freedmen joined the Union army once it finally decided to accept them, serving alongside free blacks from the South and elsewhere. Black soldiers from all parts of the nation were determined to demonstrate their courage and manhood and claim all their rights and privileges as American citizens.

The readings in this chapter, but a small sample of the Civil War documents available, tell us much about the varied experiences of Southerners during the war and why they supported the Confederacy or the Union. The examples from the Confederate perspective consist of letters from an upper-class white man from Mississippi fighting as an officer in the Confederate army; excerpts from a journal written by an infantryman from Virginia who participated in Pickett's famous charge at Gettysburg; and diary entries written by an upper-class Jewish girl living in New Orleans during the Union occupation. Illustrating the pro-Union view are sections of a book written to explain the position of Union supporters from the border states, and letters and a petition written by African Americans from New Orleans.

As you read, think about the ideas that motivated these writers. What led southern men to fight for the Confederacy and to continue fighting despite so many defeats? What did they think would happen if they lost? What was the response of Confederate women who found themselves in occupied territory? What led African American men to fight for the Union? What rights did they hope to gain from such demonstrations of loyalty and service to the Union?

50. A Confederate Officer

WILLIAM L. NUGENT
Letters to Eleanor Smith Nugent
1861–1865

An intelligent, articulate, and educated lawyer, Colonel William Nugent was not himself a slaveholder, but his wife's family (with whom the young couple lived) was a politically prominent and wealthy one that owned both a plantation and slaves. Nugent clearly considered his fortunes bound up in the continued existence of slavery. He enlisted in March 1862 and returned home in May 1865. During that time federal troops occupied the area in northwestern Mississippi where he lived, burned the town (Greenville) and his family's plantation, and killed his father-in-law, an elderly civilian. His young wife, Nellie, weakened by bearing two children and the privations of the war, died in early 1866. Nugent's letters to her, written at the beginning, middle, and near the end of the Civil War, reveal ideas widely shared among Confederates about the war's causes, the enemy's intentions, and the righteousness of the Confederate cause as well as expectation of political upheaval in the North or foreign intervention that kept Confederate hopes alive despite many defeats.

The letters also make it clear that he regarded life in a South without slavery as unthinkable, expecting whites to be disfranchised and impoverished. After the war, he played an active role in returning state politics to white control, for which he was revered by white Mississippians until his death in 1897.

Washington Hotel,
August 19th, 1861

My dear wife,

After rather a pleasant trip on the packet I reached this place, and have been engaged all the evening looking at the parades & evolutions of several companies that are going off for the wars. The emotions and thoughts that swelled my heart, as I looked at the stalwart frames of those who had embarked their all in the service of their Country, were conflicting and nearly overwhelming. And along with these feelings there is a kind of vindictive spirit that impels me to want to engage in the service of my Country right away. I feel that I would like to shoot a Yankee, and yet I know that this would not be in harmony with the Spirit of Christianity, that teaches to love our enemies & do good to them that despitefully use us and

My Dear Nellie: The Civil War Letters of William L. Nugent to Eleanor Smith Nugent, ed. William M. Cash and Lucy Somerville Howorth (Jackson: University Press of Mississippi, 1977), 45–47, 76–81, 86–89, 112–14, 128–33, 179–81, 196–99, 232–34.

entreat us. The North will yet suffer for this fratricidal war she has forced upon us — Her fields will be desolated, her cities laid waste and the treasures of her citizens dissipated in the vain attempt to subjugate a free people. Our armies will yet teach the Quakers of the Keystone State that they are not inaccessible. The two boats *Prince* & *Charm* go up tomorrow with the Warren Artillery & Swamp Rangers. They go up the Arkansas or St. Francis River on the way to Missouri, and from their appearance will acquit themselves with credit.

There is no war news here of any movement. Beauregard[1] is gradually advancing upon Washington City, preparing everything for the grand attack, and will level the Capitol to the ground. The necessity for destroying the city is imperative. In Europe it will give us a great advantage, will destroy the resources of the Federal government and conquer a peace. It is useless, I think, to base any calculations upon the reaction at the North; the peace party wants *reconstruction* and not the recognition of the Southern Confederacy. We must whip the North and in my opinion we can do it. There is no use in disguising the truth. The contest is narrowed down to [a] single issue; with us it is life or death. A great many sanguine persons think otherwise; I cannot.

You must not think, my dear wife, that I forget you while my head is so much engaged in cogitations about the war. The persuasion that it will be the cause of a temporary separation from you is very afflicting to me indeed. I cannot think of leaving for the war without sad emotions. I could much more readily die if I had the satisfaction of leaving an heir behind me to take my name and represent me hereafter in the affairs of men. What boots this tho'? One cannot die too soon in the discharge of his duty, and then the chances are rather favorable to escape. The God who protects me in the peaceful walks of every day life, can avert from my person the balls & bullets of the enemy.

I leave for Yazoo City tomorrow at noon and will return as soon as possible so as to get the *Quitman* on Friday night & be at home on Saturday. Love & Kisses to all.

May God in his infinite mercy, bless, comfort & protect you is the daily prayer of

Your devoted husband
W. L. Nugent

Jackson, Miss.
May 26, 1862

My darling Nellie,

Judge Yerger has arrived, and although I have forwarded you a letter & a baby dress by Dr. Beden this evening, I have concluded to send along a few lines

---

[1] **Beauregard:** General Pierre Gustave Toutant Beauregard, a New Orleans–born former superintendent of West Point who resigned to join the Confederate army; led troops at engagements at Fort Sumter, Bull Run, and Shiloh, among others, and also participated in the defense of Richmond.

more. I am in hearing of the voices of fifteen Yankee Prisoners, who are singing "Nellie Gray" and the thoughts suggested by the music are not of the best. These poor deluded victims of a false and aggrandizing policy, far away from home, in the hands of enemies and hedged in by bayonets, are singing to relieve the dull tedium of the day. And while I am listening to them comes obtrusively the thought will I ever be in a like predicament. . . .

The enemy do not appear to fancy a fight at all. Twice have we offered battle and twice has it been declined. They are concentrating their forces from every available point & preparing for a desperate struggle for Empire. With Beauregard for our Leader, and a good God for Protector, our armies will prevail over theirs, and terrible will be the retribution for all their devastation. . . . While we have had reverses, we have had successes. Sleeping upon a fancied security at New Orleans we were suddenly aroused from our fancied security and are being taught the hourly lesson that liberty is the price of ceaseless watchfulness. In fact we needed some lessons that only defeats could teach us. . . . In the army there is none of the despondency manifested by the non-combatants at home. The homespun volunteer feels a patriotic ardor which reverses cannot dampen; and the people at home must not complain, if they are called upon to suffer inconveniences. Privations are ennobling to any people if willingly endured for the sake of a public good. Eternal shame should mantle the cheek of the skulking coward, who hopes nothing and does nothing; and while his nerveless arm is not raised in defence of his Country, his croaking voice should be palsied instead of breathing its dolorous accents into the ears of the timid. God bless the women of the South, God bless them! With delicate frames not made to face the pitiless storm of battle, they yet uncomplainingly bear the brunt of privation at home, and hover, like ministering angels around the couches of those whom war has crushed beneath the iron orbs of his intolerable car. Rallying from the effects of each reverse they gather courage in misfortune, and inspire us with the ardor of their patriotism and the enthusiasm of their souls. If our men of stout frames had but the staunch hearts of our women, Nell, we would indeed be a nation of heroes worthy of the name. We have too long "laid supinely upon our backs and hugged the delusive phantom of hope to our bosoms." We have well nigh suffered ourselves to be defeated. The wonder is that God has blessed us so wonderfully — even beyond our deserts. . . .

Everything indicates . . . a speedy termination to the present war. The battle at Corinth will decide the duration of the present contest and if entirely successful there our enemies will be disposed to cease their attempt at our subjugation. They will be satisfied with war and will like to try the cultivation of peaceful pursuits for a time; to which end let us all unitedly lend our prayers and ceaseless efforts. . . .

May God Almighty have you, my dear Nell, in his watchful care and keeping & keep you secure unto the perfect day is the prayer of

Yr. devoted husband
Will

Jackson, Miss.
May 29th, 1862

My own dear wife,

The quasi poetic sentiment that strikes me at times, broke out on yesterday and I send enclosed the result. Keep it until baby can read, and write, & let her learn it by heart. . . .The news, this morning, is that they have left Vicksburg declining to take it, until after the fall of Fort Pillow, which is looked forward to as a very easy matter. A Federal army is marching down on the other side of the River without opposition at present, but if Price & Van Dorn[2] get after them they will move backwards. Unquestionably the grand object of attack will be the Mississippi defences. The Yankees fondly imagine that we will be whipped as they get control of the Father of Waters. Cotton is what the Lincoln Dynasty wants. The distress & suffering in England and Ireland consequent upon the failure of the cotton supply is opening the eyes of England & France; and unless soon pacified, there will be some demonstration from across the water that will astound us all. The war must be ended soon. The commercial interests of the old world inwrought in our social fabric require it; the dictates of humanity require it; the happiness and material prosperity of the whole world almost absolutely demand it. Lincoln will sooner or later be satisfied of this & rest in his career of anticipated conquest. If the news that one of the New England States has refused to send any more troops to the army without abolitionism engrafted into the war policy of the Federal Government as its peculiar characteristic be true, the signs are hopeful. That this will be the result I have no doubt; & then we will see of what material the great Northwest & the border states are made. Things are rapidly culminating & there will be a general explosion in the Northern Camp soon. Not all the adhesive and cohesive power of the great national debt will save it: and when that time does come, as come, I pray, it may soon, you may hear of Southern & Western soldiers together marching to the proud emporium of Northern trade — New York. If in the Providence of God, abolitionism be put down, the design will be accomplished in some way or other. "God moves in a mysterious way, His wonders to perform" — and we may expect a deliverance from all our present woes in a way we little dream of.

The weather still continues to be warm, and the prospect for a dreadfully hot summer is brightening. Yellow fever will invade the city of New Orleans, and will entail a vast deal of suffering on the vandals.

There are a great many sick in our army at Corinth and a Northern trip is the most efficacious remedy for it. From Genl. Beauregard's recent orders I incline to the opinion that he is meditating some bold movement into Kentucky; where he will gather an army of determined men who will march wherever he orders.

---

[2] **Price & Van Dorn:** Major General Sterling Price, a Virginian and the former governor of Missouri; Commander Earl Van Dorn, a Mississippian.

My health still continues good. Have a pleasant time with the army officers all of whom I find to be gentlemen.—Wouldn't be surprised if we are kept here all summer. Love & Kisses.

Your affec. husband
Will

Hd. Qrs. Camp Mayson
Near V.Burg June 13th, 1862

My own dear wife,

I wrote you the other day by Mr. Wolfe of our Company, and learning that there will be another [opportunity] tomorrow of communicating with you, avail myself of it. And I do this with the greater pleasure since the news from all of our armies is of an encouraging character. Maj. Gen. Stonewall Jackson has defeated three columns of the enemy's armies, Gen. Johnston has driven back McClellan, Gen. Beauregard has completely checkmated Halleck by his retrograde movements from Corinth, and Gen. Kirby Smith is prepared for them at Chattanooga. Our Gen. Smith is confident of his ability to drive the Federals back from this city, and we are looking out every day to hear that the Yellow Fever has broken out in New Orleans. Butler's infamous proclamation is thought by the *New York Herald* to be a forgery, and the English papers are denouncing it as unparalleled by anything that ever emanated from Nero himself. These flagrant, unwarranted & demoniac violations of the usage of a civilized warfare are having, as they should have, a recalcitrating effect; and if the rebound doesn't accomplish some good in our favor, I don't know what will. Every calculation, has however, up to this time, been more or less defeated; seemingly and really, as I believe, to teach us to rely more upon Divine aid than human foresight. Our armies are getting into the best possible fighting trim — discarding all superfluous baggage, accustoming themselves to physical endurance by rapid marches and learning the art of fighting with their legs — an art much practiced by Napoleon, tho' sorely neglected in these latter days. Gen. Price has adopted the idea that breastworks in the open field are useless, and the idea is a good one. If an army is kept busy it will not have the time, nor will the enemy have an opportunity of making regular approaches by parallels & all the other trenches & ditches known to engineering art. Give me an open field, rapid marches, heavy blows, constant skirmishes, incessant annoyings, and I will be better pleased than now. I have no possible fear of the result, however, my mind is fully impressed with the belief that all things are rapidly culminating towards a speedy & successful end to this war: and when the crushing blow falls upon the unprotected shoulders of the North, the effects will be terrible. The Yankee Despotism will be utterly annihilated and a new Empire will spring up in the West.

We have received intelligence that France, Spain, & England have determined to intervene in our war, and have submitted to both Governments a proposition to arrange the whole matter. The propositions are,

1st. Reconstruction of the Union upon primitive principles — 2nd Cessation of hostilities — 3rd General Amnesty — 4th Evacuation of all Southern ports & 5th The Decision of the question of *Secession* by an election in all of the Southern States. These propositions have all been accepted by our Government, but the last has been refused by the United States Government, thus leaving the matter to be settled by the foreign Governments; and the result will be the annihilation of Northern commerce & her navy; and the speedy establishment of Southern independence. England & France are bound to play their hands openly very soon, and no one can doubt that they will indirectly favor a severance of the Old Government. United the old union could have defeated the world in arms, and had really grown too powerful for the good of the human family. Strength brings in its train lust of power and disregard of the rights of the weak; and the preservation of the balance of power is necessary to the security of nations. Here let my lucubrations terminate. . . .

I think of you Nellie *all the time* and long to see you, and pet you & kiss you till you would make me quit: and I hope to see you soon. Kiss our dear little baby often for me & show her my picture when she is old enough to notice it. Tell her I love her now, and will love with all the fullness of a Father's heart when I see her. . . . May God Almighty bless, comfort & protect & preserve you & our baby is the prayer of

Yr. devoted husband
Will

Camp near Mechanicsburg
June 24, '63

My own darling wife,
Again I have been exposed to the missiles of the enemy, and again, by the blessing of God, have escaped. A *spent* grape shot struck my right arm but didn't hurt me at all. May our all wise & all merciful Providence continue this protection to me ward and preserve me to rejoin you before long amidst all the blessings of peace. . . .

When Genl. Johnston will move it is impossible to tell. He is preparing to raise the siege of the Hill City as soon as possible and I have every reason to think he will accomplish his purpose. He is confident of discomfiting Genl. Grant. Genl. Lee is reported to be at or near the Capital of Pennsylvania with 90,000 men. Business is suspended in Philadelphia and the whole state is in an uproar. Genl. Bragg is near Nashville and Rosecrans retreating; and now if we can only defeat Grant the Yankees will, I hope, let us alone for awhile. At least I earnestly hope so. — Matters are becoming very complicated up in the Northwestern States, and there will be a civil war soon between the Democrats & Abolitionists. I confidently look forward to a cessation of hostilities as soon as the next Congress meets; and if the war fever has a short time to cool off the Yanks can never revive it. — They are keeping up the drooping spirits of their soldiers by exciting their fears of our vengeance and encouraging hopes of the speedy capture of our stronghold. This, I trust, they will never accomplish. —

My health is pretty good, tho' I have for several days past been afflicted with the camp diarrhoea that gives me a little trouble. My greatest discomfort arises from the want of the means of Grace. I hear no sermons, hear none of the Songs of Zion, and am verily a stranger in a strange land. I find it almost impossible to *enjoy* religion surrounded by everything that is evil, and cheered by very little that is good.

Clarence & Jack are both well & hearty and send their love to all. I learn you have all moved back to the plantation; and on this subject am very much of Judge Yerger's opinion. I scarcely think Alf can succeed in taking the negroes to Texas. If not he had better move them to the interior of the State and behind our army. I think it would be better to take them all to Texas & dispose of them there if practicable. I understand they command very *high prices*. . . .

Our camp fare is limited in the number and kind of food. Cornbread, bacon & beef generally rules the roost. Occasionally we have chickens; now & then butter & eggs — Biscuits are a rarity; but the incoming wheat crop will remedy this defect. Love & Kisses and may God bless, comfort, direct & preserve you is the ardent prayer of

Yr. devoted husband
Will

Have Maria, Agnes & Uncle Frank deserted you?
Let me know the names of all who have gone.

Hd. Qrs. Ferguson's Cavalry
Okolona, Miss. August 27th, 1863

My own darling wife,
Bride I was on the point of writing for with the thought of you in my mind insensibly recurs to the days *lang syne* when first I "wooed & wed"; and were it not that the flashing flame of my affection some years agone had steadied to the burning glow of a continually increasing love, and the youthful bride become the gentle, trustful & confiding wife I would so have written it: as it is, my darling Nellie, let me always call you wife; and let that endearing appellation continue the watchword of my life and the conservator of my purity of purpose & constancy of love. May the remembrance that I have so gentle and noble a creature for my life companion ever buoy me up amid the many trials through which I am called to pass and nerve my arm in the dread hour of a battle. Dear is my country to me, yet dearer far in that I have a treasure in a little woman who bears her trials bravely far away surrounded by the invading foeman. Let the legions of our relentless enemy come on. . . . They count time & men & money as nothing, esteeming the length of the war as of no moment. Well, if it is necessary, so be it. If they are determined to fight it to the bitter end, let them go ahead. It is difficult to conquer and possess so widely extended a country as that which we hold. They may & doubtless will impoverish the people as they go along; but this only leaves a thousand foes behind them who will rise upon their stragglers and put an end to their

useless lives. Every hollow will resound to the alarm of the Guerilla's gun, and every bush by the roadside will conceal a relentless pursuer. They might avoid this by a different policy, but their maxim is rule or ruin and they haven't judgment enough to pursue a different course. If they would respect private rights & private property, abolish their unholy alliance with our negroes, put them back upon the plantations and make them work as heretofore, they would do more to end this war than by five years hard fighting. Of this, however, they could not be persuaded "though one were to rise from the dead" — What good will it do us if we submit? Our land will be a howling waste, wherever it has been invaded & we will be forced to abandon it to the *freed negroes* & the wild beasts. The humble tiller of the bleak hillsides in the interior may manage to eke out a miserable existence, but the growers of cotton & sugar, the staple products of the country, will be forgotten as a class — The commerce of the South will be nothing and certainly no one, unless his pretensions be very humble, will be content to live in a land where the inter-mixture of races will breed a long train of evils which were fairly illustrated in the history of Jamaica. What the end will be of course no one knows. Of one thing, I feel assured, if we pursue the proper policy all will yet be well. . . .

You cannot imagine how comforting your letters are, and how great a satisfaction it is to me to know that you are a patriot still, when your husband fails to gird his sword upon him gladly to meet the invader, you may then feel disheartened. . . .

Hd. Qrs. Cavalry Brigade
Tupelo, Miss. Sept. 7th, 1863

My darling wife,

The hour of your trial is approaching and I feel very very uneasy on your account. I hope and trust in the Giver of all good, though the thought that you are so far away, so near the enemy's lines and surrounded by so many dangers makes me feel quite blue at times: and were it not for the elasticity of mind & heart which characterizes me, I should have long since grown utterly despondent.

War is fast becoming the thing natural, tho' abhorrent to my feelings. I go at it just as I used to go at law-suits. Still I am not by any manner of means fond of the profession. The idea of being continually employed in the destruction of human life is revolting in the extreme. Necessity imperious and exacting, forces us along and we hurry through the dreadful task apparently unconscious of its demoralizing influences and destructive effects both upon the nation & individuals. I wish *Uncl. Saml.* would recognize his nephew and give us peace. I do not desire a reconstruction & a hollow truce, a servile place in the family of nations and to eat the bread of dependence while I am denied all the privileges of a freeman. The Yankees say, that when we are conquered they cannot afford to let us have the right of trial by jury, because they say a "secesh" jury would clear us all, neither can we have our own judges or exercise the elective franchise. This is the doctrine held by their main supporters and is the one which will be practiced by them if they are successful. And yet our weak-minded friends are willing to lick the hand that would smite them and pay court to the hardhearted minions of abolitionism. I own no slaves and can freely express my notions, without being taxed with any motive of self interest. I know that this country without slave labor would be wholly worthless, a barren waste and desolate plain — We can only live & exist by this species of labor: and hence I am willing to continue the fight to the last. If we have to succumb we must do it bravely fighting for our rights; and the remnant must migrate. If the worst comes, we must go over to England or France, and become Colonies again. Never will I be content to submit to Yankee rule. The Russian yoke would be preferable. The close fisted Yankees would filch our pockets at every turn — France I would prefer. Her policy is more enlightened than that of England and she would give us the rights and privileges of freemen. It would be her policy and doubtless when her affairs are straightened in Mexico, she will recognize the importance of a more decided policy in American affairs. . . .

Give my love & kisses to all. Do the best you can, and ever remember that you are supreme in my affections. May God Almighty bless, comfort, protect & preserve you is the prayer of

Your devoted husband
Will

Hd. Qrs. Ferguson's Brigade
N. Lost Mountain, Ga. June 9th, 1864

My precious Nellie,

Another day of rest from the fatiguing duties on *Outpost* has nearly elapsed and I hasten to consume the little remnant left by writing to you. I had off my coat and was sitting out in the sun fixing up my papers and reports when your last letter reached me, in company with one from Ma. Instantly my spirits went up like a shot and I felt as if the war was really over. The whole atmosphere seemed changed, and I was far away in dreamland busying about the garden at our once loved home and listening again to the plashing of the Mississippi's waves. I could not help indulging the refreshing train of thought and dropping my head, gave free scope to my imaginings. Ah! little do those, who live in peace provided with everything that heart could desire, know what a torrent of feeling the bowed head of a Southern Soldier indicates. Sustained alone by a patriotism that has been purified by fire, in camp he often dreams of loved ones at home and wakes to the dread reality that encompasses him with a firm trust in the God of battles and a fixed purpose to abide his holy will. On the lonely picket post, in the damp & noisome trenches, sweeping over the open plain in a charge, or covertly seeking a tree to pick off & destroy the Yankee sharp shooters who continually annoy him in a fight, he is actuated by one moving impulse continually and that is to do and dare everything for the independence of his country. A soldier's life is very tame except when on a *raid* or in a skirmish and then the danger of being killed by any stray bullet that comes along is not very encouraging. It is absolutely shocking to witness the horrors of war; to see the number of the dead and dying scattered all around; to inhale the sickening stench of bodies in every state of decomposition;

and listen to the obscenity & blasphemies that are being continually uttered all around. I have, however, been greatly pleased since I came to the Army of Tenn. There is a better moral tone exhibited here than I have ever seen among soldiers. Thousands have been converted and are happy Christians. Nearly all our first Generals have joined the Church and the army is fast becoming literally a God-fearing soldiery. This I regard as a very favorable omen and as strongly indicative of our success. . . .

You don't know how I long to see you & our darling *Nellie*. How I fervently wish to pet her, dandle her on my knee, and witness her playful humors. I hope she resembles her Mother more than me, tho' I am perfectly willing for her to wear my smile if it pleases you. Teach her to know my picture and call my name as soon as she begins to talk. I hope our baby is beautiful, but I do want her, above all things else, to be good and intelligent. Purity of heart and an active acquisitive mind are preferable to mere beauty of person. I am afraid if I was at home I should help you spoil her. While I am on the subject I think you had better wean Nellie, if the Dr. thinks she can get along without nursing. If your system becomes enfeebled your milk may be an injury to her. . . .

I am recommended for promotion to a Majority and hope to have a star on my collar when next you see me: and maybe ere long I will have two or even three. . . . Love & kisses to Ma, Evie, Abe, Kate & the baby and may God abundantly bless comfort, protect and preserve you is the prayer of

Your devoted husband
W. L. Nugent

Hd. Qrs. Brigade
Near Atlanta, Ga. Aug. 8/64

My darling Nellie:

I received two letters from you last night and a pair of saddle bags filled with clothing. The clothes were very acceptable, supplying, as they did, a want which it was utterly impossible to gratify in Georgia. . . . I regret very much to hear of your bad health. I would be satisfied with my present disagreeable mode of life if you could only be spared the great affliction of ill-health, because I feel that God will spare me to see you and enjoy your society for many long years after the war is over. Still it grieves me to hear that you suffer. I am too far off and too strongly bound by regulations to fly to your relief and minister to your comfort; and it is this thought which adds to the poignancy of feeling. I sometimes am inclined to kick at the laws which effect a compulsory separation between man and wife and to esteem it all wrong. Still, my own precious Nellie, what can I do? A cruel, relentless war is waged for our annihilation, and unless we present a bold front to the enemy, contesting every inch of ground, we may expect nothing but vassalage and slavery all our lives. Our rights and privileges will be totally destroyed and military governors and Yankee judges will govern us, while our lands will be parcelled out among a horde of foreign adventurers and mercenary soldiers. This is a fate to which we can never submit. The alternative of taking the oath, kissing the hand that has so severely smitten us, and bowing to the triumphant chariot of Abe Lincoln is more than freemen can endure until they have exhausted every resource which the God of Nature has placed in their power. To me it would be an ignominious fate were I compelled to rear a family forever ignored in the land of their birth, and I must still battle for freedom a little longer. My candid opinion is, that we are fast approaching the goal and that the present campaigns in Virginia and Georgia will terminate the war. We may have a desultory warfare along the border for some months thereafter; but the hard fighting will be over by the last of November. . . . May God bless, comfort, protect and preserve you is the

Prayer of your devoted husband
W. L. Nugent

I do not think it would be a good idea to bring the negroes back before something definite occurs. The Yankees are very busy recruiting darkies. Can't Ma get Jack's negroes back and turn off ours that have gone off? She had better wait awhile and trust to the Providence of God. Respects to all inquiring friends.

Hd. Qrs. Ferguson's Brigade
On the March January 16, 1865

My dear wife,
Your last letter reached me in camp near Robertsville, South Carolina, and relieved my mind considerably — I will endeavor to practice your philosophy and not "swim the rivers until we come to them." . . . I visited Charleston and from the top of *St. Michael's steeple* had a grand view of the "broad" Atlantic, the forts guarding the harbor approaches, and the blockading fleet in the offing. The sight was inspiriting enough to one who has never enjoyed the sight. As far out as the eye could reach there was nothing but a limitless expanse of water relieved at intervals by the bare masts of a ship at anchor. The ingenuity of the Yankee alone could have invented and built a *Monitor*. Through a powerful telescope I could discover nothing but the smoke stack, the turret, and a long dark line just above the water. The hulk, machinery, berths & magazine are all below the water level. The Yankees were not shelling at the time, or I might have [seen] the turrets revolving & sending their terrible shells on the mission of destruction. The old city is pretty well battered. I couldn't help moralizing from my *exalted* position, and as I descended the dark and spiral stairway wondered when the carnival of blood and the desolation of our homes would cease. We have been dreadfully scourged as a people and from present appearances are doomed to still greater woes. We believed in the beginning that God would intervene in our behalf and yet left undone those things essential to secure that intervention.

We hear very discouraging accounts of Hood, who with his army, is at Tupelo on the Mobile & Ohio Railroad in No. East Miss. The result of this movement will be to inaugurate a new campaign thro' Miss. & Alabama and destroy the only country left from which our supplies of corn & meal are drawn. What the effect of this will be, no one can determine. The people in South Eastern Georgia are already beginning to hold conventions with a view to go back into the Union and from all I hear, the disposition to stop the war at all hazards is fast taking hold of the minds of the people. If they take the bit, we are gone up. Our hopes are alone with our armies in the field. That in Virginia is in excellent spirits & condition; Hood's Army needs a new commander in the person of Beauregard or Johnston.[3] We fear that the President will not make the appointment because of some unhappy prejudices he is said to entertain against these able officers. I hope for the best.

My health is very good at present, save a little cold which keeps me from sleeping comfortably on the ground. . . . I hardly think Sissie will make her debut in society until the war is over. I believe she is now about sixteen and *mateable* beaux are *scarce*. I will make the effort to get home as soon as there is the remotest probability. My horses are now all "gone up" from hard service & I will have to get another before starting. Love & kisses to all. Tell Sis to be careful of her heart & not suffer her affections to become fixed on an unworthy object. Kiss baby often for me and tell her Pa wants to see a good child when he comes home. May God bless, comfort & preserve you is the prayer of

Your devoted husband
Will

[3]**Johnston:** Confederate General Joseph E. Johnston.

51. A Confederate Soldier

JOHN DOOLEY
Journal Entries
1862 and 1863

A soldier in the Old First Virginia Infantry Regiment (which was part of General Robert E. Lee's Army of Northern Virginia), John Dooley was the son of Irish immigrant parents who prospered in Richmond. He left Georgetown College to enlist in the Confederate army in August 1862 — just before the beginning of Lee's invasion of Maryland, which ended in the bloody battle at Antietam. Dooley was again with Lee's army when it pushed up into the North in 1863. As an infantryman in General George Pickett's regiment, he participated in its famous frontal charge into

John Dooley: Confederate Soldier: His War Journal, ed. Joseph T. Durkin (Washington, D.C.: Georgetown University Press, 1945), 26–29, 104–7.

enemy fire: in thirty minutes, ten thousand of the fifteen thousand Confederate sol-
diers were killed. Dooley was wounded in both thighs and spent the night on an open
field fearing he would bleed to death; he was taken prisoner in the morning. While
imprisoned, he rewrote and expanded the journal he had kept at the front. These pas-
sages from it reveal a Confederate soldier's ideas about what the South stood for and
describe what it was like to participate in the war's devastating battles.

Invading Maryland, September 1862

About noon today, Sunday 7th, we move towards Frederick, near which we arrive about 4 P.M. We bivouacked just at Monocacy Station on the bank of the river and close by the bridge which our men immediately began to prepare for destruction.—Here we remained two days.

Ned Haines, our black servant boy who had made the campaigns of the 1st Manassas and the Peninsular with my Father and Brother, arrived bringing me letters, money, and other necessary articles, the most grateful of which was an excellent pair of shoes. These I needed more than anything else, and Ned declared himself forthwith ready to take care of me as he had done of my father before me.

While staying here I paid a visit to Frederick to look for some of my kind old Professors and Friends of Georgetown memory. As I approached the Novitiate I met Fr. Paresce a few paces from the door, and although he had never spoken to me but once before, he immediately recognized me, called me by name and invited me to come in. Here I was feasted and clothed anew. They insisted on supplying me with clean clothing, and indeed I needed underclothing as much as a poor dirty Confederate ever did. I bathed from head to foot and returned refreshed to camp, feeling clean all over. Perhaps I felt as if I too should be immured in those quiet halls; certainly it was my place, and if I was spared to reach it again after long weary wanderings, I might well exclaim, "They have said Thy mercy, O Lord, is above all Thy works."

There was a good deal of noise and cheering among our particular friends [as the Confederate troops passed thru Frederick] on this occasion; but it was not difficult to discern that this enthusiasm was roused only for the display, and that the large majority of the people were silent in regard to giving demonstrations of opinion; many because they were really hostile to us, and some because they knew that every one was narrowly watched by Spies, by the remnant of Yankee forces on parole in the town, and most of all by their own neighbors.

This was one of the vilest evils produced and encouraged by our Civil War, that it often made the oldest and nearest neighbors the bitterest enemies and mutual spies. This most disgraceful evil, though not universal, might be found existing partially in every portion of our poor afflicted and invaded territory. It was not enough that grim visaged war swept with fire and sword through a defenceless country, that rich and abundant crops were wantonly ravaged and down trodden by a savage soldiery; that blooming fields and fragrant gardens, luscious orchards and verdant lawns withered and died like accursed things beneath the singeing flame of the lawless invaders; that hamlets and whole towns were plundered, their peoples outraged and the houses left masses of charred and smoking ruins; that through every portion of this devastated land the homesteads of the poor and the mansions of the rich were pillaged, fired and on their smoking ruins the most abominable and fiendish outrages perpetrated upon the poor defenceless women and children. . . .

So many evils were not sufficient for the enemies of the Southern States, and for those foes of the human race, but there arose even amid such misery men and women who to curry favor with the invader pointed out their neighbors for still more dreadful punishments as being guilty of some special acts of disloyalty to that most enlightened and glorious government that the sun ever rejoiced to shine upon!

But there were many in Frederick bold enough to cheer as we passed, feeling that we were the last representatives of free government, and that when we fell the right of self government or the rights of States and peoples to govern themselves would fall with us; and despotism more galling than any tyranny of Europe would be forced upon the land by a party of brutal men, uneducated, unrefined, unprincipled, inhuman, criminal, and perjured.

I stopped today, *en passant*,[1] at the Novitiate to bid the kind Fathers good-bye. Father Maguire is here and Jack Davis, an old class-mate. They are trying to get passports to carry him through to Baltimore. . . . Jack's entire sentiments are Northern and he candidly told me so. I felt a little hurt, but endeavoured to shew myself as cordial towards him as he seemed to feel towards me, for I knew that his kind heart could never really beat in unison with those who had been so cruelly harassing our land. He wanted to do many things for me, and even tried to induce me to accept some of his clothing. Good-hearted Jack! I shall always remember your kindness and only wish that the infamous Yankee had no such brave heart among his degraded troops. . . .

Gettysburg, July 3, 1863

The sun poured down his fiercest beams and added to our discomfort. Genl. Dearing was out in front with his flag waving defiance at the Yankees and now and then rushing forward to take the place of some unfortunate gunner stricken down at his post. The ammunition wagons fly back and forth bringing up fresh supplies of ammunition, and still the air is shaking from earth to sky with every missile of death fired from the cannon's mouth. Around, above, beneath, and on all sides they schreech, sing, scream, whistle, roar, whirr, buzz, bang and whizz, and we are obliged to lie quietly tho' frightened out of our wits and unable to do any thing in our own defence or any injury to our enemies. . . .

Our artillery has now ceased to roar and the enemy have checked their fury, too. The time appointed for our charge is come.

---

[1] *en passant*: in passing.

I tell you, there is no romance in making one of these charges. You might think so from reading "Charlie O'Malley," that prodigy of valour, or in reading of any other gallant knight who would as little think of riding over *gunners and sich like* as they would of eating a dozen oysters. But when you rise to your feet as we did today, I tell you the enthusiasm of ardent breasts in many cases *ain't there*, and instead of burning to avenge the insults of our country, families and altars and firesides, the thought is most frequently, *Oh,* if I could just come out of this charge safely how thankful *would I be!*

We rise to our feet, but not all. There is a line of men still on the ground with their faces turned, men affected in 4 different ways. There are the gallant dead who will never charge again; the helpless wounded, many of whom desire to share the fortunes of this charge; the men who have charged on many a battlefield but who are now helpless from the heat of the sun; and the men in whom there is not sufficient courage to enable them to rise, — but of these last there are but few.

Up, brave men! Some are actually *fainting* from the heat and dread. They have fallen to the ground overpowered by the suffocating heat and the terrors of that hour. Onward — steady — dress to the right — give way to the left — steady, not too fast — don't press upon the center — how gentle the slope! steady — keep well in line — there is the line of guns we must take — right in front — but how far they appear! Nearly one third of a mile, off on Cemetery Ridge, and the line stretches round in almost a semicircle. Upon the center of this we must march. Behind the guns are strong lines of infantry. You may see them plainly and now they see us perhaps more plainly.

To the right of us and above the guns we are to capture, black heavy monsters from their lofty mountain sites belch forth their flame and smoke and storms of shot and shell upon our advancing line; while directly in front, breathing flame in our very faces, the long range of guns which must be taken thunder on our quivering melting ranks. Now truly does the work of death begin. The line becomes unsteady because at every step a gap must be closed and thus from left to right much ground is often lost.

Close up! Close up the ranks when a friend falls, while his life blood bespatters your cheek or throws a film over your eyes! Dress to left or right, while the bravest of the brave are sinking to rise no more! Still onward! Capt. Hallinan has fallen and I take his place. So many men have fallen now that I find myself within a few feet of my old Captain (Norton). His men are pressing mine out of place. I ask him to give way a little to the left, and scarcely has he done so then he leaps into the air, falling prostrate. Still we press on — oh, how long it seems before we reach those blazing guns. Our men are falling faster now, for the deadly musket is at work. Volley after volley of crashing musket balls sweeps through the line and mow us down like wheat before the scythe.

On! men, on! Thirty more yards and the guns are ours; but who can stand such a storm of hissing lead and iron? What a relief if earth, which almost seems to hurl these implements of death in our faces, would open now and afford a secure retreat from threatening death. Every officer is in front, Pickett with his long curls streaming in the fiery breath from the cannons' mouth. Garnett on the right,

Kemper in the center and Armistead on the left; Cols., Lieut. Cols., Majors, Captains, all press on and cheer the shattered lines.

Just here — from right to left the remnants of our braves pour in their long reserved fire; until now no shot had been fired, no shout of triumph had been raised; but as the cloud of smoke rises over the heads of the advancing divisions the well known southern battle cry which marks the victory gained or nearly gained bursts wildly over the blood stained field and *all that line of guns is ours.*

Shot through both thighs, I fall about 30 yards from the guns. By my side lies Lt. Kehoe, shot through the knee. Here we lie, he in excessive pain, I fearing to bleed to death, the dead and dying all around, while the division sweeps over the Yankee guns. Oh, how I long to know the result, the end of this fearful charge! We seem to have victory in our hands; but what can our poor remnant of a shattered division do if they meet beyond the guns an obstinate resistance?

There — listen — we hear a new shout, and cheer after cheer rends the air. Are those fresh troops advancing to our support? No! no! That huzza never broke from southern lips. Oh God! Virginia's bravest, noblest sons have perished here today and perished all in vain!

Oh, if there is anything capable of crushing and wringing the soldier's heart it was this day's tragic act and all in vain! But a little well timed support and Gettysburg was ours. The Yankee army had been routed and Pickett's division earned a name and fame not inferior to that of the Old Guard of Bonaparte. I will not attempt to describe. . . .

52. A Young Woman in Occupied New Orleans

CLARA SOLOMON
From Her Diary
1862

Seventeen-year-old Clara Solomon was a member of a wealthy and socially prominent New Orleans Jewish family. They were staunch supporters of the Confederacy, which suffered a major blow early in the war when a flotilla of warships and gunboats under Captain David G. Farragut broke through Confederate defenses at the

The Civil War Diary of Clara Solomon: Growing Up in New Orleans, 1861–1862, ed. Elliott Ashkenazi (Baton Rouge: Louisiana State University Press, 1995), 343–51, 354–56, 367–70.

mouth of the Mississippi, forcing New Orleans to surrender. The occupying troops were commanded by General Benjamin Butler, who was despised by the residents of the city for his series of "General Orders," especially No. 28 better known as his "Woman Order," which decreed that any woman who by word or gesture insulted any Union soldier would be "held liable to be treated as a woman of the town [i.e., a prostitute], plying her vocation." A friend of the Solomon family, Eugenia Levy Phillips, was later arrested under this act and imprisoned at Fort Massachusetts on Ship Island.

These entries from her diary reveal Solomon's fear and indignation after the capture of her beloved New Orleans, her confidence that the Confederacy would yet prevail, and her passionate resentment of the occupying forces.

Sunday, May 4th, 1862

6½ A.M.   Who can penetrate into that unknown future? Who can remove the veil in which a kind Providence has enfolded it? . . . Oh! from the depths of my heart my gratitude ascends to God for so veiling the "coming time." Oh! Philomen,[1] a gloom has settled o'er my spirit, a gloom envelopes our dearly-beloved city. My breaking heart but aches the more, when I am prepared to record events, which can never fade from my memory, & did I not consider it a duty, I should spare myself the unpleasant task. . . . Last Thursday, Ma, F. & I were seated up stairs in the pursuance of our vocations, when Mrs. N. came in. Ma & F. went out, & my curiosity being excited by hearing F. remark, "They will think you foolish," I went out & learned that it was her determination to send for Josh, as rumor had said that the *Yankees had passed our forts, & were on their way to the city.* We scorned the idea, but simultaneously in came Sallie, quaking with terror, & informed us that the whole School was alarmed & about to be dismissed. Oh! my God! our fears were then awakened. We went by the door & the excitement & commotion was an indication that something was the matter. Uniformed men were hurrying to & fro, & we gained from them that the whole military was ordered out. Oh! my God! Imagine my feelings as the Idea of a battle arose before me, but I immediately abandoned such ideas for what resistance could we offer to them on the water. Mrs. N. was frantic with terror, for the safety of her husband. Oh! never have I experienced such emotions as in those moments, never did my heart sink so deep within me. . . . Beyond doubt, the Yankees had passed our forts & were on their way to our city, it having been decided to be the most daring naval exploit ever attempted, as they passed under our fires, our brave men, fighting to the last. Mr. "D" left with a promise to see us again at an early period. We went home. But little sleep that night visited our eyes. At every sound we would startle & jump up & were patiently waiting for the dawn of the morning. It came, & our

[1] **Philomen:** Clara's name for her diary.

first impulse was to get the paper, which contained no news. Friday, we decided upon going out. . . . It was cloudy, but we hastily made our toilettes, & were on our way down town, the omnibuses having ceased to run, the stores closed, & everything betoking the calamity which was to befall us. Ma having sent a telegraph to Pa, we went to the Office, but no answer had been received, & they expected momentarily to close. But certainly Pa knew of it. It had been telegraphed. . . . To add to our gloom, the rain began to fall, & in the midst of it were we. We stopped at Mrs. D., borrowed umbrellas, & in the mean time there was a general stampede & hundreds of persons running & exclaiming "They are coming!!!" We joined in the crowd, but soon extricating ourselves, made our way through the pouring rain. The tents were all removed from the Square & we were informed that the Confederates had gone some place up the road. Mrs. N. was distracted. Standing at a corner we saw one of our finest boats, of our own accord committed to the flames. Oh! *never* shall I forget the 25th of Apr. 1862. Such expressions of woe as were on the faces of every one, & such sadness as reigned in every heart. Oh! that that day should ever come! We reached home, very wet, changed our clothes, & then began *to pack*. I was of little assistance being so excited, & I sat by the window, watching the rain which was pouring in torrents, for the heavens indeed were in tears. We sent for A. & she came, & remained home. After dinner went to Mrs. N.'s who did not know what to do. The rain ceased & Mr. D. came up. No train left & it was not known when we would & we were again undetermined about going. He remained some time & promised to come up again, he, not knowing what he was going to do, & telling us that Pa would come over. . . . Did not sleep well. In the paper there was the correspondence between the Mayor & Com. Farragut. The Mayor's document was ably written. All our chief men had left, Gov., Lieut. Gov., etc. & everything devolved upon the Mayor, & *his* conduct will ever be remembered. He surrendered the city to a more powerful force without resistance, but would not consent to our lowering the flag which waved so proudly from the dome of our City Hall. They wished to humiliate us, but could not. We had fallen, but not disgraced. . . . Mrs. N. brought no news with the exception of our determination not to take down our flag, to die first. Oh! how glorious. They are content with our submission. There is not a man in our midst whose hand would not be palsied in the act. Dinner very light, as it is impossible to purchase anything, stores all closed. What are we to do for provisions. . . . With heavy & aching hearts we retired to bed. Oh! how terrible to think of. I awake in the morning & imagine it to be all a dream, but too soon the illusion was dispelled. Mrs. N. had been assured that Mr. N. was safe & would be back, but she could not be consoled. We were hopeful on Monday, when Ma came in with the tidings that "D" had just communicated to her. Com. F. had allowed the women & children 48 hours to leave the city, as it was to be shelled, we refusing to haul down our flag. . . . Now, in what a predicament were we. No male around to assist & protect. . . . I had great hopes that the worst would not come to pass, but still we had to prepare for the emergency. We intended to take but a few clothes with us & were willing to make any sacrifice to behold our prided city reduced to ruins rather than it should fall into the hands of the barbarous invaders. . . . In the afternoon Mr. E. came up & told us not to be alarmed, as they would not dare to shell in consequence of the many foreign subjects. . . . In the morning no wiser were we, until about 11 o'clock when we heard that Forts Jackson & St. Philip had surrendered & the enemy had consented *themselves* to lower our flag. . . . Now it was at an end. We had maintained our dignity to the last, & though humiliated were not disgraced. In the night I was eating supper when E. came for me, saying that Mr. da P. wished to see me. I went & he informed me that he was going to leave the city probably on the morrow. He was so despondent, so sad. He gave us an account of the events of the day & the tears in the eyes of men, as our flag was lowered. He held the consultation with the Fed. officers. I pitied him for I knew his feelings. Mr. D. was with him, his intention being to leave. The next morning *Mr. N. came.* What does it not express! He had been since Saturday on his way home, & had come by the way of Baton Rouge, leaving L. there. The Reg. [Home Guard] had disbanded. Oh! how happy was Mrs. N. He gave us an account of his adventures, his fears & uneasiness for his family & he was as delighted to see us as we were to see him. . . . Father! When, oh! when, shall we meet again. The rolling stock of the R.R. has been removed, but if he wishes, he can effect a passage someway. . . . The following day Fed. transports arrived, & have been continually. Gen. Picayune Butler being in command, a gentleman with whom "D" was at one time on terms of the closest intimacy. "D" did not wish to remain after a Yankee foot had polluted our soil. In the morning he & M.A.B. stepped out of a carriage & ascended our steps & entered. Mr. Duncan was to remain, to be in the office. The publication of the paper will continue, but it will be but a chronicler of city items, cut off as we are from all the world. Affairs in Tennessee, & Vir. we will never know. . . . I sewed in the afternoon, with a heavy heart. Oh! to think we are in a captured city. But how disappointed are they! Not a bale of cotton fell into their hands for $2,000,000 worth was consigned to the flames. Nothing Friday. Finished our dresses. In the humor for anything but dressing. Never intend to again. . . . They [the Yankees] informed the proprietor of the St. Charles that if he did not open it, Gen. B. & staff would occupy it any hour. It is now their headquarters. They are quartering at Odd Fellows Hall, & have seized a private house on Poydras St. which they have converted into a hospital. In the heart of the city! They seized the Telegraph Offices, but happily all the implements had been removed. The supply of this large population with the necessaries of life is a question of the greatest moment to our people. The land forces of U.S. have occupied Opelousas R.R. & forbid communication by that, our principal means of transportation of fresh supplies. We have since learned that they have made arrangements for us to receive provisions, so ideas of starvation are now abandoned. They are camping in Lafayette Square! What a contrast to its late occupants! . . . Saturday, we attended Synagogue.

Mr. G. prayed earnestly for the S. Confederacy! I suppose they will interfere with the Churches. I wonder with the School? I pray, for the Normal. Oh! I hate to go. When I am in the street I do not seem to breathe a free atmosphere. It is not free. Laden with the breath of those invaders. I am sick at heart. What a victory. The taking of N.O. The Fed. flag over our Custom House. They have the valley of the Mississippi at their command. I am alarmed to walk the street & would not be out after dark. In fact, all citizens are requested to be in doors by 9. We are conquered but not subdued; & our independence *will yet* be recognized by the leading powers of the world. Poor Beauregard.[2] What a blow it was to him. On my return from Syn. I dressed S. & went to Mrs. N. where I dined. She got in some provisions for herself & Ma. Beef is 40 cts. a pound. Everything in proportion. No bread at all. There is no flour. Gen. B.'s Proclamation [Butler at first allowed the mayor to exercise civil power] appeared in the evening paper. It was not very arbitrary, but we must remember that it is his first. . . . It was anticipated that when their flag was hoisted there would be cheers for "Lincoln," but instead, when they had accomplished the act, there arose upon the air, one deafening, rousing cheer for Jeff. Davis, & the Southern Confederacy, which was represented to be by a witness a "truly sublime spectacle." And now, how inadequate a conception have I given you of our trials & adventures of the past, never to be forgotten week. But remember that the fullest heart is that which does not admit of expression & this, with your knowledge of my want of command of language, will, I know, acquit me in your eyes. How ignorant are we as to what will be the contents of each succeeding page, for never did the idea once present itself to me that I should ever relate the particulars of New Orleans, the Queen City of the South.

Thursday, May 8th, 1862

6½ A.M. Two weeks have elapsed since the intelligence was first received that the Federal gun-boats had passed our forts. The time has seemed like months, but I am confident that when years shall elapse my recollection of that memorable time will be as vivid. . . . Eat dinner & then departed on my loathsome way. With what different feeling had I last trod that path. Then I breathed the air of a free city, now I breathed the air tainted by the breath of 3,000 Federals & trod a soil polluted by their touch. My thoughts & feelings I can assure you were none of the pleasantest, & assumed no better a nature when I entered the Institution. The 10 min. before the commencement I spent with A. Mrs. P. expressed her pleasure at seeing so large an attendance, the best for many days. Some so excited my displeasure by wearing upon their shoulders black crepe bows. How silly! All know that our hearts are in mourning, but why make any outward demonstration. Do we go in black for a very sick person? Our *cause* is not *dead*, it is only *sick*. The Yankees are here on a *visit*. I also disapprove of Confederate flags about the persons for they are well aware of the feelings & sentiments of Southern women. . . . Mrs. N. told us that she heard from a reliable source that Butler had opened the prison & allowed all the negroes to be released. It is this fear which alarms me. I fear more from the negroes than Yankees & an insurrection is my continual horror. But oh! so many rumors are afloat. We should make up our minds to believe *nothing*. Yesterday was a fine day & being desirous of seeing something & of getting out, she concluded to go down town, & I & S. was to accompany her. . . . Canal St. did not present the same spectacle as in former times. There was a dearth of

[2] **Beauregard:** General Pierre Gustave Toutant Beauregard.

ladies, & everything reminded me of a ruin. For the benefit of R.'s — we took a ride in the cars, & frequently would spy a Yankee. One tore my dress. A live Yankee stepped on it. They are subjected to every silent insult by the ladies. A car on Camp St. containing a number of the last named articles was hailed by some Fed. officers & as they walked in the ladies walked out. As some officers came into their pews in Church they vacated them, & it is said that they seemed to feel the insult. . . . Had the good fortune to come up on the 'bus with Emile Jarreau! He is so handsome, & the circumstance of his having fought in the battle of Manassas tends to render him doubly attractive. . . . Gen. Butler has allowed the Mayor & c. to resume their authorities, promising not to interfere with civil powers, but no confidence is placed in his word, & it is anticipated that he may at any moment violate it. . . .

Saturday, May 17th, 1862

6¾ A.M.   I have been up for some time, & in obedience to A.'s orders, the Paper was brought to her, & the general orders No. 29 & 30 were so unexpected & startling that they completely unnerved me, & I was unable to continue my toilette. I was not quite right in saying that they were unexpected for do we place any reliance on the word of that unprincipled Butler? Order No. 29, "On the 27th day of May, all circulation of or trade in Con. notes & bills will cease within this department, & all sales or transfers made on that day will be void, & the property confiscated to the U.S.!!" Now, how terrible a blow is this. The greater part of the money now in circulation is the Con. notes, & the loss to many will be enormous. None, I presume, will now be received in payment & what substitute are we to have. The "Wretch" said in his proclamation that he would allow them as a legal tender, & see how he has violated his word. I have no doubt but it will produce a great commotion in the city & why shouldn't it, when it will involve the ruin of thousands. General order No. 30. The N.O. *Delta* having published in today's issue, an article discussing the cotton question in a manner which violates the terms of the Proclamation, from these headquarters, *the office of that paper will be taken possession of & its business conducted under direction of the U.S. authorities.* They knew that it would eventually come to this & they should have suspended it. . . . Now the old driver [Butler] is beginning to draw his reins. For a while he was quite willing that the papers should continue, but now his object is accomplished & paper after paper will depart. The taking of this city & the burning of our cotton will be the making of our Confederacy, for it will show the foreign nations that we are in *earnest* & willing to make any sacrifices, that we are a brave determined people imbued with the same spirit as were those 13 little colonies who triumphed over the greatest nation on earth. There were gloomier days than this during the Revolution, for says a London paper, "the capture of Charleston or N.O. itself would, if the Southerners intend to hold out, be but the commencement of the war. Let it be remembered that we took all these cities & Boston & N.Y. besides during the war of Independence. We had nothing to conquer but the Atlantic coast & we found after a fair trial that it was impossible. It was not so much the volunteers as the *country* which beat us. We had a much more desperate battle & a much more glorious success at Bunker Hill, than the Fed. had at Fort Donelson but it had little value towards the conquest of Massachusetts." This seems as though they were decidedly in our favor. That cotton is But.'s tender point, & may it often be assailed. Oh! my head is so filled with them that every other topic sinks into insignificance. . . . When I arrived in School, I noticed an unusual stir & commotion & when I inquired the cause, there was some astonishment expressed that I had not heard the news, the General order, No. 28. I was informed of it & when Miss B. came she read it. "Be silent that you may hear. As the soldiers of the U.S. have been subject to insults offered to them by the women (calling themselves ladies) of N.O., I hereby order that should any female treat with contempt, or insult in word, gesture or movement any officer & private under my command, she shall be liable to be treated as a woman of the town, plying her vocation." Oh! Philomen, I cannot express to you the indignation this thing awakened, my feelings are akin to a lady, who speaking of the subject, said "I cannot tell you how I feel or what I think." I hear that the men were perfectly exasperated for you know the insult offered to us is also to them. The cowardly wretches! to notice the insults of ladies! But the news will get abroad & then we shall be praised for our actions. They will see the spirit of our women, aged, even children, but they *dare* not notice their insults. And how did they expect to be treated. Can a woman, a Southern woman, come in contact with one of them & allow her countenance to retain its wonted composure. Will not the scornful feelings in our hearts there find utterance. They may control our actions, but looks, they never can. . . . A long argument & discussion was kept up, upon patriotism, the different ways of showing it, etc., etc. Truly, I would have made any sacrifice rather than those —— should have had possession of our city. Shall it? yes [burn it] to the ground. . . . No one came at night & after the usual programme retired. Endeavored to kill as few mosquitoes as possible. For two reasons, the first being that we should be polluted by being touched by "Yankee blood," & secondly each one increases the number & aids in biting & tormenting them. I wonder how they like them! . . .

53. A Unionist from Tennessee

W. G. Brownlow
Explaining Union Support from the Border States
1862

W. G. "Parson" Brownlow was the editor of the Knoxville Whig, *a Methodist minister, and a staunch Union supporter from East Tennessee. After Tennessee seceded, East Tennesseans — who had rejected secession by more than three to one — were furious when the state government began requiring a loyalty oath and announced that it would confiscate the property of "alien enemies." Many fled to Kentucky to escape the mass arrests that followed, but the ever-defiant Brownlow remained. He was imprisoned in the Knoxville jail, then released to "exile" in the North, where he wrote* Sketches of the Rise, Progress, and Decline of Secession *(excerpted here) to explain the views of the loyal people of the border states. When Unionists continued to be harassed by Confederate soldiers and by their neighbors, they responded with guerrilla warfare. Federal troops gained control of the area in 1863, prompting many Confederates to flee and allowing prominent Unionists, including Brownlow, to return. He later became governor.*

PREFACE

I have prepared this work from the single stand-point of uncompromising devotion to the American Union as established by our fathers, and unmitigated hostility to the armed rebels who are seeking its destruction. My ancestors fought in its defence; and while their blood flows in my veins I shall instinctively recoil from bartering away the glory of its past and the prophecy of its future for the stained record of that vile thing, begotten by fraud, crime, and bad ambition, christened a Southern Confederacy. I cannot exchange historic renown for disgrace, national honor for infamy, how splendid soever may be the bribe or how violent soever may be the compulsion. This is my faith as an American citizen; and this book will show how sorely it has been put to the test. I claim, however, no merit, further than that arising from the discharge of a simple duty both of religion and patriotism. Thousands of my fellow-citizens have been equally faithful among the faithless. Their sufferings may be conceived from this narrative of my own.

Indeed, it is not from the slightest desire of self-glorification that I have spoken so freely of myself. It would have been sheer affectation of modesty to attempt by circumlocution of speech to do otherwise. For I have, in this matter, rather re-

W. G. Brownlow, *Sketches of the Rise, Progress, and Decline of Secession; with a Narrative of Personal Experiences among the Rebels* (Philadelphia: George W. Childs of Applegate & Co., 1862), 5–10, 114–20.

garded myself as a type of the large body of loyal people in the border States, and have, accordingly, been the more unreserved, inasmuch as I felt that I might assume to some extent to speak in their behalf. It is important that our countrymen of the North should clearly understand the embarrassing position of this class, and the peculiar privations they have been compelled to undergo. It is chiefly due to them that the battle-field of the Rebellion has not been transferred to Northern homes. Their geographical location and political elements are such that, upon the soil which they inhabit, loyalty and treason have overlapped, and, being thus confronted face to face, they have been plunged into all the horrors of discord and anarchy, of divided communities and sundered households. In many respects, however, we of that region do not wholly sympathize with the North any more than with the extreme South. We deprecate alike the fanatical agitators of one section and the Disunion demagogues of the other. I believe I represent the views of multitudes of ever-true and now suffering patriots when I declare that, Southern man and slave-holder as I am, if the South in her madness and folly will force the issue upon the country, of Slavery and no Union, or a Union and no Slavery, I am for the Union, though every other institution in the country perish. I am for sustaining this Union if it shall require "coercion" or "subjugation," or, what is worse, the annihilation of the rebel population of the land. These peculiarities in my position, as an East-Tennessean, it will be seen, have contributed to mould the views which I have expressed.

I am, therefore, prepared to expect that many readers will not concur in all that I have said. But I do verily believe that, as a National man, — having had an opportunity, as from an intermediate eminence, to view this question on both sides, — and having observed the bearings of the whole subject for thirty years past, I am enabled to suggest something worthy the consideration of my countrymen. Hence I have not consulted the opinions of others, nor reflected whether what I say would be acceptable or unacceptable, would render the writer popular or unpopular. I seek only to utter the profound convictions of my own mind, in order that, God willing, I may be of some benefit in my day and generation, and, without fear or favor, come weal or woe, may have the sad privilege of warning my fellow-citizens, even if I may not enjoy the cheerful satisfaction of convincing them.

I have suffered deeply in person and estate, have avoided no responsibility, have endured evil treatment and imprisonment, and been compelled day by day to contemplate the near prospect of a brutal death upon the gallows, — all in behalf of the sacred cause I have espoused. I avouch these things as evidence of sincerity. Not only so, but they have left me in no mood for the use of softened forms of speech in narrating such acts or depicting the actors. Hence I have spoken plainly. Extreme fastidiousness of taste may, perhaps, shrink with over-sensitiveness from some of the language I have employed. But it was no time for dalliance with polished sentences or enticing words; for an imminent necessity — like the "burden" of the old Hebrew prophets — was upon us, and the cause of our LORD and LAND could be best served by the sturdy rhetoric of defiance and the unanswerable logic of facts. The traitors merited a sword-thrust style, and deserved the strongest epithet I have applied. My persecution by them was such that I had a fair right to handle them roughly: they were not worth any other mode of treatment; and I have written what I have written.

I cannot close this preface without expressing my thanks for the generous reception I have met with at the North. In Cincinnati, Columbus, Chicago, Philadelphia, New York, — indeed, wherever I have gone, — I have been welcomed by individuals and by public bodies with demonstrations of honor and kindness which seem like a providential recompense for all I have endured. I shall preserve a life-long recollection of such universal and spontaneous sympathy, and leave its precious memory and memorials as an heir-loom to the latest generation of my descendants. I bear this testimony all the more willingly, because these courtesies vindicate me from aspersions, and are occasioned by no modification or concealment of my opinions. I have, everywhere, condemned the disorganizing propagandists of the North, and have publicly proclaimed that I was a Southerner by birth, education, and habits; yet, when I also announced that I was a National man and uncompromisingly for the Union, I found that other things were forgotten, and that I had touched a chord which made us all of kin.

God grant that we may, as Sections, Churches, and Individuals, realize how great a share each of us has had in bringing about our present calamities, and, consequently, how much of the responsibility falls upon *self* as well as upon others! When this shall be felt, and when a proper spirit shall accompany the conviction, the horrors of this wicked war will be appreciated, the hand of vengeance will be stayed, and

"Returning Justice lift aloft her scale."

Doctors Will Differ

The following correspondence will explain itself. We take the writer of the letter to us to be a clever man carried astray upon the Secession wave that has swept over the land, blinding the eyes of honest men to all sense of duty, and burying beneath it the last remnant of the privileges of the Constitution: —

"Cedar Grove, Fla., June 15, 1861

"Dr. Brownlow: —

"As a freeman, you have a right to your opinions, in common with other men, but, sir, you have no right to defame those who are laboring to throw off the yoke of Northern oppression. I have ever been an admirer of yours, and of your principles; but permit me to tell you this morning that you are doing more injury to the Cotton States than any of the Greeleys or Webbs of Yankeedom. I do not believe you to be an Abolitionist, as some do in this quarter. These being my honest opinions, I do not wish to read your paper longer. If there be any thing due me on my subscription, I wish it applied to the family of Jackson the martyr.

Very truly, &c.,
"R. M. Scarborough"

Knoxville, June 25, 1861

Mr. Scarborough: —

I received your letter of the 15th only on yesterday, and I hasten to reply very briefly. Upon examination, I find thirty cents due you on my book, and I enclose you the amount in United States stamps, which you can transmit to "the family of Jackson the martyr," who can use them in their locality.

You are correct in supposing me free from the taint of Abolitionism. I have fought the agitators of the Slavery question at the North for the last two-and-twenty years, during which time I have edited a Whig paper in Tennessee. With my *Government*, and its *Constitution* and *laws*, I intend to stand or fall, having no regard to who may be President for the time being. This rebellion is utterly without cause. Nothing but force will put it down; and hence there never was a more necessary, just, and lawful war than this, to preserve a necessary, just, and noble Government against inexcusable, unnatural, and villainous rebellion. This rebellion, on the part of the South, originated in falsehood, fraud, and perjury, and the men who inaugurated it, and are now at its head, are as bad men as ever agitated the Slavery question in New England, or any who suffer the vengeance of eternal fire for having flagrantly violated God's law through a long and eventful life of wickedness! Knowing this, or rather believing it, as I honestly do, I can have no sympathy with the men in the South who have brought about this war and are urging it on. No mad-dog cry of the invasion of the sacred soil of the South by the Vandals of the North can blind my eyes to the *facts* in the case, or shift the responsibilities of its origin upon those who are fighting to preserve the Government. Men need not talk to me about the unnatural, fratricidal, and horrible war Lincoln is waging! Why is it unnatural? I think it the most natural thing in the world for a nation to fight for its Government against a vile rebellion which has never yet been able to allege an excuse. That any portion of the people should stand aloof from such a cause, is indeed unnatural, but that does not make the war unnatural.

That any people should rebel against so benign a Government, and make war upon it, is most unnatural. It is the greatest crime that could be committed against humanity, for it and its consequences include all other crimes. It was not the falsely-alleged Slavery question that excited the Cotton States to the *fatal* point, and brought about their acts of secession. It was because they lost the race for the Presidency, and with it the spoils and power of a Government they had been plundering and living off of for years. Hence, it was only when the Government changed hands, and, in the legitimate exercise of its lawful powers, resorted to the only means that would preserve it and a vestige of liberty to the American people, that the war became unnatural, fratricidal, and horrible to the advocates of a Southern Confederacy. Southern-Rights politicians and hypocritical clergymen may ejaculate that their heads may be made water, and their eyes fountains of tears, that they may weep day and night over the unnatural war of the best Government that has ever existed, against the most villainous rebellion that history gives any account of, and they can never excite my sympathies but in favor of the Government.

The Secessionists, for the purpose of hiding their traitorous course, create a false issue before the people. They assert that the effort to preserve the Government is an attempt on the part of the North to crush the South, and that a sectional fight is the real issue before the people. This attempt to create a false issue is an acknowledgment on their part that they dare not meet the true one. The effort to enforce the law is not a fight against the South, but it is a fight against the traitors to the General Government; and, whether they appear North or South, it is the duty of the Government to crush the treason. When Southern traitors resist the laws of the land, they call all attempts on the part of the Administration to enforce those laws, outrageous acts of oppression, — attempts to invade and subjugate the free and independent people of fifteen sovereign States. Rebellion with this class of men is liberty, whilst they denounce all attempts to execute the laws of the land as the essence of despotism. To such subterfuges are Secessionists driven to sustain the rebellious course they have entered upon under a Southern Confederacy.

For daring to oppose Secession, the chivalry of my own section have denounced me in unmeasured terms, and declared me less sane than the inmates of Bedlam. And because I have refused to lavish volumes of whimsical abuse upon the North for their defence of the National Government, I have been pelted with a most horrible bombardment of uncleanly epithets by the veracious chroniclers who control the pensioned press of the South. The complaint against me is, that my paper has not teemed with bragging and fantastical lies about the origin of this war, and the ability of one Southern soldier to whip five Yankees. I have been even required by my Southern subscribers to declare, upon the receipt of the news of every engagement by scouting-parties, that the Yankees took to their heels, and that soon the Southern troops would have the Yankees harnessed tandem-fashion, and with their own hands conveying them back to their Southern plantations in a Broadway omnibus! I have been expected to state in every issue of my paper, that the mantle of Washington sits well on Jeff Davis! This would be a funny publication. The bow of Ulysses in the hands of a pigmy! The robes of the giant adorning Tom Thumb! The curls of a Hyperion on the brow of a Satyr! The Aurora Borealis of a cotton farm melting down the icy North! This would be to metamorphose a *minnow* into a WHALE!

I never look through telescopes made of cotton-stalks, and hence I never make these ridiculous discoveries. And I tell the misguided men of the South, who have been laboring to make a demi-god of Davis, to undeceive themselves, and look at men "as trees walking." Look at battles as they occur, and at chances as they are. The deception they are imposing upon the honest masses is only temporary. It will become more and more apparent, as their humbugged victims draw near to the sober realities of a war which must terminate fatally for the interests of the South.

I assure you, my dear sir, that I am honest in my convictions of right, and that in advocating my Government I am not looking to a reward in dollars and cents. Indeed, I am a loser by my course, as I knew I would be; but I feel tranquil under losses incurred in the manly defence of PRINCIPLES. I shall look on the progress of affairs with as much interest as any one man in the country. If the Federal Government prevails, it will prove that the Union was a nationality; if the Cotton

States make good their independence, it will prove that the Union was a partnership during pleasure. In other words, if we have a Government, I want to know it; and this war will determine the issue.

I am, sir, very truly,
W. G. Brownlow

Knoxville Whig, June 29, 1861

54. Black Loyalists in Louisiana

Letters and Petition
1862 and 1864

The famous Louisiana Native Guards were originally composed of men from the free black community in New Orleans — a prosperous, well-educated, and proud group that included professionals, artisans, merchants, and some slaveholders; eighty percent of them were of mixed African and European ancestry. Their ranks were soon swelled by escaped slaves who responded to a call for volunteers early in the war. The Native Guards' extraordinary bravery under fire at Port Hudson in May 1863 won national attention and paved the way for participation by northern blacks and freedmen. After Port Hudson, the Guards' black line officers were persuaded or forced to resign, but they immediately petitioned for reinstatement and the right to recruit and lead black troops, as in the three letters included here.

More than one thousand free black civilians in New Orleans also fought to ensure equality in the government at war's end. Delivered in person to President Abraham Lincoln in 1864, their petition to be registered as voters that they might "participate in the reorganization of civil government" concludes the chapter.

CAPTAIN JAMES H. INGRAHAM TO THE *NEW ORLEANS DELTA*

[November 29, 1862]

Desiring to appease the fears of the friends and relations of the First Regiment Louisiana Volunteer Native Guards, Col. Spencer H. Stafford, commanding, I ad-

New Orleans Daily Delta, 7 November 1862. Reprinted in the *National Anti-Slavery Standard,* 23, no. 29 (29 November 1862): 1.

dress you this letter, hoping that you may publish it in your columns, which are read daily by at least five or six hundred of their friends. When we left the city on the 30th ult.,[1] we were from 850 to 875 strong. We arrived at this place on the 1st inst.,[2] 800 to 845 strong — only about thirty men having fallen out, and these from sickness. We have not, as yet, had the pleasure of exchanging shots with the enemy. But we are still anxious, as we have ever been, to show the world that the latent courage of the African is aroused, and that, while fighting under the American flag, we can and will be a wall of fire and death to the enemies of this country, our birth-place. When we enlisted we were hooted at in the streets of New Orleans as rabble of armed plebians and cowards. I am proud to say that if any cowardice has been exhibited since we left Camp Strong, at the Louisiana Race Course, it has been exhibited by the rebels. They have retreated from Boutee Station beyond Ter-rebonne Station, on the line we have marched, burning bridges and destroying culverts, which, no sooner than coming to the knowledge of Col. Thomas, of the Eighth Vermont Regiment, have been repaired as quickly as they were destroyed.

I am not of a disposition to claim for our regiment more than its share of praise, but I venture the assertion that there is not a regiment in the service more willing to share the hardships of marching and bivouacking, and more desirous of meeting the enemy than this regiment, led by Col. E. H. Stafford and Maj. C. F. Bassett.

Hoping these few lines may appease the anxiety of our friends and relations.

I am yours, with highest respect,
J. H. I.

[1] **ult.:** ultimo, that is, the previous month.
[2] **inst.:** instant, that is, the current month.

SIXTEEN OFFICERS TO THE COMMANDER
OF THE DEPARTMENT OF THE GULF

New-Orleans. Feb. 19th 1863

General,   The following circumstances renders It an Imparitive duty to ourselves, to herewith tender our Ressignations, unconditional and Immediate.

At the time we entered the army It was the expectation of ourselves, and men, that we would be treated as soldiers. [W]e did not expect, or demand to be putt on a Perfect equality In a social point of view, with the whites, But we did most certainly expect the Priviledges, and respect due to a soldier who had offered his services and his life to his government, ever ready and willing to share the com-

Freedom: A Documentary History of Emancipation, 1861–1867, ed. Ira Berlin, selected from the Holdings of the National Archives of the United States, Series II, The Black Military Experience (Cambridge: Cambridge University Press, 1982), 316–17, 329–30.

mon dangers of the Battle field. This we have not received, on the contrary, we have met with scorn and contempt, from both military and civillians. If we are forced to ask for Information, from the generality of white Officers, we Invariably, receive abrupt, and ungentlemanly answers, when in maney Instances It is their legitimate business to give the Information required. To be Spoken to, by a colord Officer, to most of them, seams an Insult. Even our own Regimental commander has abused us, under cover of his authority. Presuming upon our limited Knoledge of military Discipline, all combine to make our Position Insupportable.

General, This treatment has sunk deep Into our hearts. [W]e did not expect It and therefore It is intolerable. [W]e cannot serve a country In which we have no more rights and Priviledges given us.

Therefore, we most Respectfully beg of you, to accept This Tender. We have the honor, Sir, to be most Respectfully your obedient servants,

[*16 signatures*]

HLS

Ten Former Officers to the Commander of the Department of the Gulf

New Orleans April 7th 1863

Sir   we the undersigned in part resigned officers of the Third (3rd) regt La vol native guards and others desiring to assist in putting down this wicked rebelion. And in restoring peace to our once peaceful country. And wishing to share with you the dangers of the battle field and serve our country under you as our forefathers did under Jackson in eighteen hundred and fourteen and fifteen — On part of the ex officers we hereby volunteer our services to recruit A regiment of infantry for the United Satates army — The commanding Gen[era]l may think that we will have the same difficulties to surmount that we had before resigning. But sir give us A commander who will appreciate us as men and soldiers, And we will be willing to surmount all outer difficulties. We hope allso if we are permitted to go into the service again we will be allowed to share the dangers of the battle field and not be Kept for men who will not fight[.] If the world doubts our fighting give us A chance and we will show then what we can do — We transmit this for your perusal and await your just conclusion. And hope that you will grant our request[.] We remain respectfully your obedient servants

Adolph. J. Gla	James. E. Moore
Samuel. Lauence	William. Hardin
Joseph G Parker	William. Moore
Joseph. W. Howard	Charles A. Allen
Charles. W. Gibbons	Danl W. Smith Jr

ALS

R. H. Isabelle to the Commander
of a Louisiana Brigade

New Orleans   June 12th 1863

Sir   Permit me to inform you that there [are] more than one thousand free colored citizens in this city who are anxious to Enlist in the united states army to share their blood & lives in the common cause of their country. among them are some who are very wealthey, having graduated in Eroupe as well as having considerable experience of the Military tactics, being capable of passing before a board of examination to prove their qualifications as to they being lines officers.

This is all they ask, is the privilege of selecting their own lines officers or for you to select from our own race such persons as you might find qualified[. T]his privilege our fathers enjoyed in 1812 & 15 and as the late battles of East Pascagoola Miss & Port Hudson has proved that the colored officers are capable of commanding as officers[.]

I hope that you will pardon me for my familarness but as I feel that it is the duty of every man to come forward and aid in putting down this unholy rebellion and save our country from her awful threatened doom. I have no doubt but that we can raise a regiment in less than one week of able bodid well educated men

Hoping that this application will meet with your due consideration[.] Respectfully Your humble Servant

R. H. Isabelle

ALS

Petition to Abraham Lincoln

January 5, 1864

To His Excellency Abraham Lincoln, President of the United States, and to the Honorable the Senate and House of Representatives of the United States of America in Congress assembled:
The undersigned respectfully submit the following:
That they are natives of Louisiana, and citizens of the United States; that they are loyal citizens, sincerely attached to the Country and the Constitution, and ardently desire the maintenance of the national unity, for which they are ready to sacrifice their fortunes and their lives.

That a large portion of them are owners of real estate, and all of them are owners of personal property; that many of them are engaged in the pursuits of commerce and industry, while others are employed as artisans in various trades; that

The Liberator, 1 April 1864. Reprinted in *A Documentary History of the Negro People in the United States*, ed. Herbert Aptheker, preface by W. E. B. Du Bois (New York: The Citadel Press, 1951), 494–95.

they are all fitted to enjoy the privileges and immunities belonging to the condition of citizens of the United States, and among them may be found many of the descendants of those men whom the illustrious Jackson styled "his fellow citizens" when he called upon them to take up arms to repel the enemies of the country.[1]

Your petitioners further respectfully represent that over and above the right, which, in the language of the Declaration of Independence, they possess to liberty and the pursuit of happiness, they are supported by the opinion of just and loyal men, especially by that of Hon. Edward Bates, Attorney-General, in the claim to the right of enjoying the privileges and immunities pertaining to the condition of citizens of the United States; and, to support the legitimacy of this claim, they believe it simply necessary to submit to your Excellency, and to the Honorable Congress, the following considerations, which they beg of you to weigh in the balance of law and justice. Notwithstanding their forefathers served in the army of the United States, in 1814–15, and aided in repelling from the soil of Louisiana the haughty enemy, over-confident of success, yet they and their descendants have ever since, and until the era of the present rebellion, been estranged, and even repulsed-excluded from all franchises, even the smallest. . . . During this period of forty-nine years, they have never ceased to be peaceable citizens, paying their taxes on an assessment of more than fifteen millions of dollars.

At the call of General Banks, they hastened to rally under the banner of Union and Liberty; they have spilled their blood, and are still pouring it out for the maintenance of the Constitution of the United States; in a word, they are soldiers of the Union, and they will defend it so long as their hands have strength to hold a musket.

While General Banks was at the seige of Port Hudson, and the city threatened by the enemy, his Excellency, Governor Shepley, called for troops for the defence of the city, and they were foremost in responding to the call, having raised the 1st regiment in the short space of forty-eight hours.

In consideration of this fact, as true and as clear as the sun which lights this great continent — in consideration of the services already performed, and still to be rendered by them to their common country, they humbly beseech your Excellency and Congress to cast your eyes upon a loyal population; awaiting, with confidence and dignity, the proclamation of those inalienable rights which belong to the condition of citizens of the great American Republic.

Theirs is but a feeble voice claiming attention in the midst of the grave questions raised by this terrible conflict; yet confident of the justice which guides the action of the Government, they have no hesitation in speaking what is prompted by their hearts — "We are men; treat us as such."

Mr. President and Honorable members of Congress: The petitioners refer to your wisdom the task of deciding whether they, loyal and devoted men, who are ready to make every sacrifice for the support of the best Government which man has been permitted to create, are to be deprived of the right to assist in establish-

---

[1] The ancestors of the free black soldiers in the Louisiana Home Guards fought in the Battle of New Orleans in 1815 and under the French and Spanish previously.

ing a civil government in our beloved State of Louisiana, and also in choosing their Representatives, both for the Legislature of the State and for the Congress of the nation.

Your petitioners aver that they have applied in respectful terms to Brig. Gen. George F. Shepley, Military Governor of Louisiana, and to Major Gen. N. P. Banks, commanding the Department of the Gulf, praying to be placed upon the registers as voters, to the end that they might participate in the reorganization of civil government in Louisiana, and that their petition has met with no response from those officers, and it is feared that none will be given; and they therefore appeal to the justice of the Representatives of the nation, and ask that all the citizens of Louisiana of African descent, born free before the rebellion, may be, by proper orders, directed to be inscribed on the registers, and admitted to the rights and privileges of electors.

And your petitioners will ever pray.

Suggestions for Further Reading

Boles, John B. *The South through Time: A History of an American Region.* Englewood Cliffs, N.J.: Prentice Hall, 1995. See especially chapter 3, "The Southern Nation," pp. 281–336.

Campbell, Edward D. C., Jr., and Kym S. Rice. *A Woman's War: Southern Women, Civil War, and the Confederate Legacy.* Charlottesville: University Press of Virginia, 1996.

Faust, Drew Gilpin. *Mothers of Invention: Women of the Slaveholding South in the American Civil War.* Chapel Hill: University of North Carolina Press, 1996.

Hollandsworth, James G., Jr. *The Louisiana Native Guards: The Black Military Experience during the Civil War.* Baton Rouge: Louisiana State University Press, 1995.

McPherson, James M. *For Cause and Comrades: Why Men Fought in the Civil War.* New York: Oxford University Press, 1997.

Rable, George C. *Civil Wars: Women and the Crisis of Southern Nationalism.* Urbana: University of Illinois Press, 1989.

CHAPTER FIFTEEN

RECONSTRUCTION

Black Freedom and
the Ku Klux Klan

The end of the Civil War raised basic questions about African American civil and political rights. What would be the position of newly freed slaves in national life? What rights would they possess? Who would define these rights? What would the role of the national government be in assuring civil and political rights for freed people? Should African Americans participate fully in the political dialogue about the South's future? If so, what should their role be? Beyond the mandates of the Fourteenth and Fifteenth Amendments — which declared that freed slaves were citizens and enfranchised all male citizens over the age of twenty-one — there was considerable room for disagreement among whites and blacks, Northerners and Southerners, Democrats and Republicans. After 1865, these clashing expectations manifested themselves violently in the Ku Klux Klan.

Historians, too, have disagreed about the role African Americans played in Reconstruction. Many of those writing near the turn of the twentieth century were sharply critical of a "tragic era" during which, they believed, southern blacks plunged headlong and disastrously into politics; implicit in this interpretation was a racist assumption that African Americans were ill-prepared and unsuited for political participation and leadership. Describing Reconstruction's successes, later historians contested this view. Even more recent scholars, emphasizing the centrality of the freed slaves' quest for freedom, have been less charitable about the results of Reconstruction — much of which they have portrayed as a failure.

Although historians have disagreed in these interpretations, they have agreed that African Americans were at the core of the issues of the day. A central thread of Reconstruction lies in the attempt of black people to secure their freedom from slavery — and the ways in which southern and northern whites responded to these attempts. The war had been a liberating experience; thousands of black soldiers served in it and participated in the invasion of the South. Thousands more remained under slavery, to be sure, but they too witnessed the erosion of slavery as a system. Emancipation was a joyous experience, but black leaders were determined to secure their freedom by seeking out a full measure of civil and political equality. African Americans became politically mobilized almost immediately: soon after the war, many black leaders, convinced that the destruction of slavery was not fully possible without political empowerment, fought to obtain the vote for African Americans. They believed that their new status as freed people depended on it.

Many southern whites, in contrast, greeted the new, postemancipation turmoil in race relations with disbelief. Northern whites expressed responses ranging from indifference, fear of black emigration out of the South, or sympathy for African Americans. But southern whites had lived under a system of slavery in which the assumed inferiority of African Americans, free and slave, was embedded in law, custom, politics, and economic life. Most resented black political participation and opposed efforts by blacks to obtain other dimensions of freedom in working conditions, schools, and churches. Despite emancipation, the status of black people remained unclear, and many southern white leaders sought to reestablish — without reestablishing slavery — the old system of white supremacy. These clashing expectations set the stage for violent conflict. In many states of the South, anti-Reconstruction "conservative" parties came into existence during the late 1860s. And a secret terrorist organization, the Ku Klux Klan, formed to intimidate African Americans and white Republicans as part of a concerted effort to end Reconstruction.

The Klan first appeared in eastern Tennessee during the spring or summer of 1866, and white paramilitary organizations began to spring up elsewhere in the South within a year. By 1868, the Klan was fully organized in most of the South and operated campaigns of terror across the region. With the peak of Klan violence in the late 1860s and early 1870s, scores of African Americans became victims of organized terror. The intent of the violence was to upend Reconstruction and unseat Republicans spearheading it. As part of this objective, the Klan sought to limit black civil and political freedom. In a number of states, white opponents of Reconstruction used the KKK and terrorism — beatings, whippings, lynchings — as tools to overturn Republican rule, capitalizing on white fears and unease about civil and political equality for African Americans, in the process exposing divisions among black and white Republicans. Although its actions had specific political ends, the Klan struck at the basic definition of freedom.

For the most part, Klan violence elicited ineffective — or even counterproductive — responses from southern Republican regimes. The federal government did little to intervene before the early 1870s; what was necessary was armed protection in areas of Klan activity. But by then the damage to African American groups and Republican Party infrastructure had already been done. By April 1871, Klan outrages were so common that Congress organized a special Joint Select Committee to investigate the situation. Meanwhile, new federal anti-Klan legislation empowered prosecutions during 1871–72, and that put a temporary end to the reign of terror, although not to the Klan. In February 1872, the Joint Select Committee concluded its investigation and issued reports. The minority report — written by the Democrats on the committee — denied the existence of an organized uprising and maintained that the Klan represented the reaction of liberty-loving people to their repression.

But the majority report, written by the committee's Republicans, described a widespread Klan conspiracy that connected terror with a broader political effort to upend Reconstruction and Republican influence. Based on vast documentation, it ultimately convinced the northern public and provided a basis for an expanded federal prosecution effort. With strong backing from Congress and President Ulysses S. Grant, federal officials began a concerted effort to uproot the Klan. But the federal intervention was largely too little and too late, for a pattern of political oppression and intimidation of black voters and their white Republican allies had been well established.

The documents in this chapter examine the impact of the Klan on African American aspirations to freedom during Reconstruction. Testimony from two Mississippi blacks illustrates the ways in which their efforts to define the boundaries of freedom met determined and violent resistance from local whites. The extent to which the Klan spread throughout the South is indisputable; its effects on northern public opinion are shown in an excerpt from *Harper's Weekly*. Efforts to educate freed people, largely spearheaded by northern women such as Maria Waterbury, also became targets for terrorist violence. And as Albion W. Tourgée suggests in an excerpt from *The Invisible Empire*, the rise of the Klan was broad-ranging and extensive in scope, rooted in fundamentally different expectations between whites and blacks about the meaning of freedom.

As you read, keep in mind the differing backgrounds and perspectives of the authors of these documents. According to the sources, what did black people want from freedom? How did white people (northern and southern) differ in their expectations? In what ways do the sources agree or disagree about the causes and consequences of Klan activity?

55. The Rise of the Klan

ALEXANDER K. DAVIS AND LYDIA ANDERSON
Testimony for the Joint Select Committee in Macon, Mississippi
1871

In Mississippi, tensions between whites and blacks were particularly acute because that state possessed an African American majority, many of whom actively participated in politics. Violence and terror against blacks were rampant across the state in the spring of 1871. Because these outrages seemed to take place with impunity in Mississippi and elsewhere, Congress acted and in April 1871 organized a Joint Select Committee composed of seven senators and fourteen representatives to conduct an investigation of the Klan. It dispatched subcommittees to southern states "lately in insurrection" to interview scores of black and white witnesses to Klan violence. The following two excerpts from this testimony are from Noxubee County, a center of Mississippi's white terror. As these African American witnesses suggest, white intimidation tactics targeted the diverse ways in which blacks sought out freedom.

Macon, Mississippi, *November* 6, 1871

ALEXANDER K. DAVIS (colored) sworn and examined.
By the Chairman:
Question: State your place of residence.
Answer: Macon, Noxubee County, Mississippi.
Question: State your occupation.
Answer: I am, you might say, a law-student. I have been admitted to the bar; I claim that for my occupation.
Question: Are you a candidate for the legislature at this time?
Answer: Yes, sir.
Question: Have you ever been a member of the legislature?
Answer: Yes, sir; I represented this county in the last legislature.
Question: How long have you lived in Noxubee County?
Answer: I have lived here since June, 1869.
Question: Where did you live previous to that time?
Answer: I lived in Shelby County, Tennessee, sir.
Question: What opportunities have you enjoyed of knowing the condition of affairs in this county as to peace and good order, and the observance of the laws?

Alexander K. Davis and Lydia Anderson, "Report of the Joint Select Committee to Inquire into the Condition of Affairs in the Late Insurrectionary States," 42d Cong., 2d sess., 1871, H. Rept. 22, 13 vols., 11:469–79, 510–12.

Answer: Well, sir, I can only say that the only opportunities I have had to know them was as a grand juror of the United States court, of the district court for the northern district of Mississippi.

Question: Are you pretty generally acquainted with the colored people of this county?

Answer: In all the counties in the eastern tier of counties I am pretty well acquainted — Kemper, Lowndes, Monroe, and Chickasaw; and I am pretty well known, and know a great many prominent colored men through these counties.

Question: Are you pretty well acquainted through the different townships of this county?

Answer: I am pretty thoroughly acquainted in the county, but I do not know that I know a great deal of the township and section lines.

Question: I mean the different neighborhoods in the county?

Answer: O, yes; I am as thoroughly acquainted, probably, as any man in the county.

Question: You may state whether you know, or have been informed, of any outrages committed upon colored people of this county by combinations of disguised men.

Answer: I could not state that I know of any of my own knowledge. I have seen parties who have been whipped, with scars on their backs, and they stated that it had been done by disguised parties.

Question: You may give to the committee such cases as have been reported to you, with the particulars so far as you are informed.

Answer: I will have to refresh my memory a little, in order to state dates and names, there are so many of them. Probably I could better furnish you a list of the different parties themselves, and you could examine them.

Question: Have you any such list prepared?

Answer: I can prepare one, sir, through the course of the day, and furnish it to the committee.

Question: For the present you may give such cases as occur to you, and when you have opportunity you may prepare the list you speak of.

Answer: The first case that came to my knowledge was a woman by the name of Betsey Lucas, who lives here in Macon now. She then lived at a Mr. Robert Jackson's, in the northern portion of this county, near the Lowndes County line, about eight miles north of this place.

Question: What were the particulars of her case?

Answer: She was living with Mr. Jackson, and a party of men came there. It was in the month of March, 1870, I think, or maybe a little later. It may have been as late as — it was between the months of March and May; I don't remember just when it was, but I think I can find that out at home, as I took a note of it at the time. They took her out and put a rope around her neck, a bridle-rein, and whipped her, and gave her a certain number of days to get away. That I learned from her; that was her sworn testimony, too.

Question: Did you learn from her whether the men were disguised?

Answer: All disguised. She said she recognized some of the parties by — some of them had only their faces disguised, but their clothing, their pants and coats, she recognized, and their voices. She recognized some of them. . . .

Question: What did Betsey tell you she was whipped for, or what did she say the men who inflicted the whipping said was the cause?

Answer: She said she could not account for the whipping at all. One white man, who was along with the party when she was whipped, and was a member of the klan, stated that she was whipped for messing with this man, Jackson, she lived with, or was hired to. That was his story about it. . . .

Question: If you have finished all you have to say about the case of Betsey Lucas, you may pass on to the next case which occurs to you.

Answer: The next case occurred about the same time, I think on the same night. It was the ordering off of some colored families that had been settled upon what was called the bottom place, here in this county, of Mr. William May. Mr. May settled a lot of colored people on a place of his there, and gave them lands for a term of years, to clear them up, and, I believe, gave them some assistance in building and improving, and they were all run off on that night — at least ordered off and notified that if they were there at a certain stated night or day, what would be the consequence, and they moved off.

Question: Was that done by the same party that whipped Betsey Lucas?

Answer: The same party. All the men were there, I believe, with one exception; that one exception was the captain; he was not present that night — the captain of the squad.

Question: What was his name?

Answer: He was said to be the captain, and was a man by the name of C. M. Doss.

Question: How many families were driven off from that bottom place?

Answer: I think there were five — I can't be positive as to the number.

Question: Is Mr. Doss living still in the county?

Answer: Yes, sir.

Question: Did these families leave pursuant to this warning?

Answer: Yes, sir.

Question: Go on.

Answer: The same night — or the next raid they made. I merely give this as evidence I have had, and from reports of the parties who were along and know.

Question: Do you regard the information you have of these transactions as reliable?

Answer: I do; there isn't any of it of my own knowledge. I never saw one of these parties.

Question: That is proper evidence. You may proceed.

Answer: They went to — I have forgotten whose plantation it was, now — but they were there to look up some parties, and there was a colored man killed by the name of Coger. It seems that this man, Sam, they had nothing against him, or didn't want him, but he talked to them a little plain, and they just fired into him and killed him. It was all the same raid. . . .

Question: Do you recollect any other cases of whipping or murder or other outrages in this county?

Answer: Yes, sir; about the latter part of March or 1st of April, 1871, there was a half a dozen cases of whipping down here about Mushulaville, in this county. The most noted of them was the whipping of Aleck Hughes. Aleck had rented a place down near Mushulaville. He was a very industrious young fellow, and made a crop there last year. This year he bought some stock and they whipped him and run him off. They whipped him nearly to death, or so he was not able to go. They left him for dead. They hung him up, and I saw his back two months afterwards, and it was a perfect scab then. He said that after they hung him up he begged them not to kill him, and they gave him his choice to take five hundred lashes or be shot or hung. He consented to take five hundred lashes, and he said he guessed they gave them to him. They whipped him, and he didn't know when they quit — didn't know anything about it. That is his own story. He is in the county now. He was a witness, and was a very prominent witness, and thought it was not safe for him to come back, and he is over at Holly Springs now; but his team and everything is out here. He had a crop in; eighteen or twenty acres in cotton, about thirty acres in corn; I believe he has instituted a suit in the United States court for damages against the parties. He recognized two or three of the parties. One of the parties that he recognized on account of a little horse that he rode, that he (Aleck) had owned himself, and had sold him. He claims that he hadn't paid him for it, and he thought that may be was one of the reasons for his whipping, because he had asked him for the money. He had owned a little horse, and sold it to a man in the neighborhood; and he got after him for the money, and he abused him and struck him, and a few nights afterward told him he had got a little too saucy and impudent, and they had come down to correct him.

Question: Who told him?

Answer: He named the party that told him this. I think it was the same man that rode his horse. I don't remember which one now; there was so many. There were only five though that whipped him. They went to his house and took his gun and pistol after they had whipped him. They didn't catch him at his house at all. He was looking for them — expecting them. He had heard they were coming for him, and he went off that night. He was staying over at another colored man's house in the neighborhood.

Question: And they took his gun that night?

Answer: Yes, sir; after they whipped him; and they went to his house and got his gun and pistol. He told them where it was, and they went and got it. I am just giving the outlines. I do not know the particulars. . . .

Question: What is the sentiment of the whites in this county as to the colored schools?

Answer: Well, sir, in a portion of the county the majority of the whites, I think, are favorable; in all the northeast portion of the county, and Macon beat here, and probably Shuqualak and that district down there, the majority of the whites, I think, are favorable to the free schools; but in the southeast corner, and southwest corner, and the northwest corner of the county, and all the west part of the county, the most of the whites are opposed to free schools for anybody, white or black. I have met a great many persons and talked with them. I met a leading man in the northwest corner of the county who keeps a store up there, a wealthy man, and he told me he thought it an outrage. He thought the principle was wrong that he should be taxed to educate other people's children; he said he had to educate his own, and he did not think it was right. It is generally said that what he says is the sentiment of his whole community. He is a very quiet man, though, and I have never heard of his participating in the disturbances. That is pretty generally the feeling.

Question: Is that the sole objection made to the free schools, the expense it entails in the shape of taxes?

Answer: That is the only public objection they make. What their private views are I do not pretend to say at all. The only objection I have heard of their making to any of the friends of the system is that they did not think they ought to be taxed to support them.

Question: Do you hear any opposition to colored suffrage?

Answer: Well, no, sir; there is no open opposition in this county, scarcely; our paper here opposes it; it has at its head a motto, "All the time in opposition to negro suffrage"; that is, it raised it after the election of 1869, and pulled it down a few weeks ago. I presume they will raise it again after this election is over; everybody that is a candidate now for every party claims to be a friend to universal suffrage. We have three or four tickets in the field, all claiming to be friends to negro suffrage.

Question: That was the motto of the democratic paper published here from 1869 until within a few weeks past, I understand you?

Answer: Yes, sir; they raised it right after the election in 1869; I think the motto was, "Uncompromising opposition to negro suffrage"; that is the substance, but not the exact language.

Question: Have you heard any considerable number of democrats denounce that motto as not representing the sentiments of the democratic party in this county?

Answer: No, sir; I have heard some few. I have heard it myself, that motto, and I have heard one or two say that it did not represent the sentiments of their party. The most prominent democrats here now claim that there is no opposition to universal suffrage or free schools, and that they are not opposed to radicalism.

Question: Do you believe them to be sincere in the sentiments they express?

Answer: No, sir; I don't believe them.

Question: Have there been any cases in which any white men, implicated in the various outrages you have detailed, have ever been brought to justice and punished?

Answer: None; I never have heard of one yet being punished. I have heard of several attempts to investigate, but they have never succeeded. I have had witnesses tell me that they have gone before grand juries here — I know witnesses that told me they were going before grand juries to report certain parties that they recognized that had committed outrages, and they went before the grand juries and have seen parties on that grand jury that they knew were connected with the Klan, or were members of the bands that had committed these outrages; and they then and there stated that they didn't know anything about it — just heard of it. They said they didn't think it was safe to do so, and I know it was so. There are white men in this town; I know a man that has lived here always, and probably has at stake as much as anybody in this county; he told me this morning that he wouldn't testify what he knew before this committee, because, he said, it would be published; he said he didn't intend to be slaughtered. There are plenty of men here, sir, that will not do it. They don't believe that there will be any effort made — that their testimony before this committee will simply amount to informing the outside world as to these outrages, and that is about all; and that they will not lend any aid at all to bring these parties to justice, and it will only place them in the position of being more obnoxious to these men and more liable to be killed.

Macon, Mississippi, *November* 6, 1871

LYDIA ANDERSON (colored) sworn and examined.
By the Chairman:
Question: Where do you live?
Answer: I live here now. I have been living between Winston and Noxubee, in the edge of Noxubee, about three miles above Mushulaville.
Question: What induced you to come here?
Answer: Well, I don't know whether they threatened my life or not, but I was told I had better go to Macon, and I did so.
Question: Had you been threatened?
Answer: No, sir; only in this way.
Question: Had you ever been whipped?
Answer: Yes, sir.
Question: When were you whipped?
Answer: It has been about five months, as well as I can recollect.
Question: Where were you living when you were whipped?
Answer: At Massa Anderson's; Killes (Achilles) Anderson.
Question: Who whipped you?
Answer: It is what they call the Ku-Klux.
Question: At night?
Answer: Yes, sir.
Question: Was it in your own house?
Answer: They took me out of my bed — out of my house.
Question: How many men were concerned in it?
Answer: There was four.
Question: Had they disguises on?
Answer: Yes, sir; they all wore dresses.
Question: Had gowns on?
Answer: Yes, sir; all had gowns on, and one of them had a sheet over him.
Question: Was there anything over their faces?

Answer: Yes, sir; they had horns here and here, at the corners of the head, [illustrating].

Question: So you could not see the faces at all?

Answer: No, sir; I couldn't see the faces.

Question: Did they come to your house on foot or on horseback?

Answer: On horses.

Question: Did they have any pistols or guns?

Answer: Yes, sir; they had pistols.

Question: Was anybody in the house with you at the time?

Answer: No, sir; not then. My daughter was staying at the house, and she was at the washing-place washing, and she spied them, but she didn't tell me. She thought she would go and wake up sister. She brought her the news and went back to her — and went back after her soap. She saw them coming and went into her sister's house. She says, "I believe them nasty things is about here. Where's mother?" She said, "Mother is asleep," so she goes into her sister's house. She wasn't there no time before they came tearing through the yard as hard as they could stave, right up to my son-in-law's house door.

Question: Were you living with your son-in-law?

Answer: Yes, sir. He jumped up in his sleep and says, "What's the matter?" She says, "There's the Ku-Klux." As she said that he opened the door, and Fuller — that's my son-in-law's name — said he, "Yes, sir." He said, "Is Aunt Liddy here?" Fuller says, "Yes, sir." He said, "Where is she?" Fuller said, "In her own house." Said he, "Is she asleep?" "Yes, I expect she has gone to bed." "Tell her to come out; we want to see her; we just want to ask her some questions; we are not going to hurt a hair of her head." As quick as I stepped out, as soon as I put my foot on the step, he says, "March to them woods there, or I'll blow your God damned brains out." That scared my son-in-law, and he run to the house and waked up my young master, and he asked him what was the matter, and he told him the Ku-Klux was there. He said, "Fuller, did you know them?" He says, "No, I didn't." "Well," says he, "I can't do nothing."

Question: That was what your young master said?

Answer: Yes, sir. He couldn't do nothing; if the boy could he would. I raised him; I nursed him and fed him, and he thought as much of me almost as he did of his mother; but they took me out there and whipped me.

Question: How long did they whip you?

Answer: They didn't whip me very long. It has been about five months since they whipped me. I stayed there two weeks, and it has been four months and two weeks since I have been here; that makes five months. I was living at the factory last Christmas. My son-in-law said, "Mother, you have worked and hired long enough without pay, and I am able to take you in my own house and take care of you." After I went there — old Mr. Richards is about a mile below — and I went to work with Mrs. Richards; I hired to her. Mrs. Richards says, "Why not stay with me?" I said I would just as quick as any other. She says, "I just want such an old woman as you to help me about cooking and milking"; and I said I would stay with the old lady. She said it would not be hard, and I was there a week. She wanted to go up to Choctaw to see her children, and she said, "Now, if I go away, will you take care of my things good?" I said, "Yes, I would." My old master had recommended me for a good hand; he had raised me from a little thing. She said, "I want to go to see my children, I have been gone so long, and if you will stay here and take care of my things I will give you a good present when I get back." The old creature started Monday morning, and then Monday night and Tuesday morning her husband commenced some of his talk. I didn't understand him. He says, "The witches rode me last night." I says, "I have heard of witches riding folks, but they never have rode me." I didn't know what he meant. He says, "You ought to come in and keep me company." Says I, "I am not afraid of staying around there." He says, "The old lady told you to take good care of me." I says, "I am going to cook your victuals and make your bed and take care of you." He kept talking that way, and finally I found out what he was talking about, and I said, "No, sir; my old master raised me like his own child; that's one thing that they never accused me of, and never shall, and that's not my disposition." In that week my daughter came there; she wanted to live there; the foolish child wants always to stay with me. I says, "Child, you may stay if they hire you," and says I, "Mrs. Richards, my daughter is come, and if you would like a house-girl she will stay with you." She says, "If she will stay on the same terms as you do I will take her." I had a baby girl about so high, [illustrating], and when she came he dropped off with me and flies to this young girl, young woman grown. She is the one I was telling you of was there, and this little girl told me what her sister said this old man said to her. I never let on; I said if he became too free she will tell me after a while. I made no fuss. On Friday morning he was coming down here, last court, and they thought I was gone out milking, but I stopped behind the chimney, and I heard him say, "What do you want me to fetch you from Macon?" She said, "Nothing; I don't want nothing you have got." She says, "If I did such a thing as that that you want, she would beat me nearly to death." Says he, "O, your mother won't know it." She says, "Yes, she will; my mother don't allow no such bother, nor any of the other girls to do it, and I am right to mind my mother." He went off and he told me then he wanted me to make the children do it, and I made them do it, and Friday evening my young master came up. My old master was to have a dinner with the neighbors, and he sent his son to ask, "Where is old Mr. Richards?" and I says, "He went to Macon to-day." He says, "Tell him to come up to dinner, and ma wants you to come, for you have always been ma's cook." I said I would come, and when night come I told him about it; when he came home. He never said nothing, and so my daughter, Saturday morning, says, "Ma, are you going to the dinner?" I says, "I don't know; I promised the old lady I would stay and take care of her things until she comes back. If you want to go I will stay here." She says, "I want to go." I says, "Now don't you think because you are free you can go off. You go and ask the old man, no odds if you are free; you ask him if you can go." She went and done it. He said, "No; you were gone to dinner last Saturday, and I hired you to work." She says, "Mr. Richards, I have done all you told me." He says, "You go to work." Well, there was not a thing to do. Says I, "Martha, you sweep these weeds around here." She says after a while to him, "I know the reason you want to keep me from going; I won't let you keep me." He says, "You hush." I was in the kitchen and heard it. I says, "You tell me right here what that was, or I'll knock you down," and she told me and I went and set down on the doorstep, and he jumped up and went off and came back with a great hickory stick, as big as your thumb. She was at the gate sweeping, and he came in and drawed down on Martha three times. She run back, and I stepped up and asked, "What's the matter?" She said, "Mr. Richards is whipping me." I says, "Mr. Richards, what's the matter? Didn't I tell you when them children come here, if they didn't mind you, all you had to do was to tell me and I would make them mind you? What are you whipping her for?" He says, "I'll whip her again." Says I to her, "Martha, get your things and go." He says, "She had better go." Says I, "She is a woman, and I'm going too. I told you that if my children didn't mind you, you should come to me and tell me, and I would make them mind, and now what are you whipping that girl for? You think I don't know, but I do know. She shan't stay and I shan't stay." There was a black man living on the plantation; he moved down on that same place. I went back up to the owner of the factory; his wife had never wanted me to leave; I cooked until I tired myself down; I said I would rest myself awhile; she asked me to come there again awhile; the woman sent her husband after me and I went up next day. This black man told my son-in-law, and told me, that they had been trying to catch me ever since I had been going back and forward; that's what made me know who they were, and I could tell them by the voices, because it was nobody else but them.

Question: You say there were four who were concerned in whipping you?

Answer: Yes, sir; but only one whipped, but he whipped me enough for all.

Question: How many licks did they strike you?

Answer: Nine licks and cut my skin, and the marks is on my back.

Question: What did they say it was for?

Answer: They said I talked of the Ku-Klux.

Question: Did you know that man?

Answer: No, sir; he said I did; he jabbed a pistol at me and said, "God damn you, do you know me?"

Question: Who do you think these men were?

Answer: Old master's sons.

Question: The sons of old man Richards?

Answer: Yes, sir; I will say it until I die; they were his sons; they were the ones the black man told my son-in-law were trying to catch me ever since I was gone to the factory.

Question: Has anybody ever been taken up for this whipping?

Answer: No, sir; not that I know of.

Question: Did you ever make any complaint to a justice of the peace?

Answer: No, sir; I was afraid to speak a word.

Question: Did they warn you not to tell of it?

Answer: No, sir; they told me, "Go on now, and I'll see you again in a few days, and I'll give you five hundred lashes the next time I see you."

Question: Did they tell you to leave the county?

Answer: No, sir; the water was up then and I couldn't cross, and that kept me as long as I did stay there; then I came away. . . .

56. A Northern View

HARPER'S WEEKLY
"The Ku-Klux Conspiracy"
1872

The majority report of the Joint Select Committee appointed by Congress in 1871 determined that the Klan engaged in a widespread effort to turn back Reconstruction in the South. This view, which came to dominate northern perceptions, has in fact been borne out by recent historians, who conclude that the chief implication of Klan violence was the erosion of political support for the Republicans. The following excerpt from a Harper's Weekly article on the Klan reflects that view. Yet, in some respects, the emphasis here — how political factors weighed heavily in the Klan — stands in contrast to the concerns of many of the Joint Select Committee's witnesses, who stressed the social impact of white terror.

. . . The Congressional reports on the Ku-Klux conspiracy show the real causes of the decline in the value of every kind of property in the Southern States, and the dangers that threaten the future of their industry and trade. The Democratic party has fallen under the control of a murderous faction: its more intelligent and prudent members have not sufficient courage to free themselves from the tyranny of robbers and assassins; the colored population and the white Republicans, the industrious and the honest, in many parts of the South are disfranchised by intimidation and open violence; the governments of several States are plain usurpations; a minority of lawless men rule over the powerless majority, and once more threaten rebellion, defy the national government, and bring ruin upon their fellow-citizens. The Ku-Klux conspiracy has extended its mysterious links through

Harper's Weekly, 19 October 1872. Reprinted in *African American History in the Press, 1851–1899: From the Coming of the Civil War to the Rise of Jim Crow as Reported and Illustrated in Selected Newspapers of the Time*, vol. 2, *1870–1899*, ed. Robert L. Harris Jr., David Dennard, Cynthia Neverdon-Morton, and Jacqueline Rose, The Schneider Collection (Detroit: Gale, 1996), 705–8.

every Southern State: it has usually flourished before and after every election with a sudden vigor, and has then sunk into obscurity until the hour for new efforts arrived; its measures are always the same, whether in Texas or Missouri; its members ride around at night in strange disguises; their victims are white and colored Republicans, their wives and children, honest working-men, teachers, and active Baptist or Methodist ministers; sometimes United States officials or State judges and Senators have fallen before their rifles; sometimes the clergyman has been shot in his pulpit or the lawyer in his court-house; but oftener they are content to rob and burn the negro cabin, to seam the backs of its unlucky tenants with pitiless lashes, or leave the husband and the father bleeding and dying in the midst of his horror-stricken family. The pitiless cruelty of these Southern Democrats — for the chief object of the Ku-Klux assassins is always to insure the election of the Democratic officials — surpasses the barbarity of the savage. . . .

In several of the counties of South Carolina the Ku-Klux ruled for a long period unchecked; hundreds of persons suffered from their unparalelled malignity; the sick, the aged, and the feeble were torn from their beds at night, whipped, tortured, or shot; women were often the express objects of their cruelty. Scarcely a year ago, disguised with masks, horns upon their heads, long dresses, and fantastic ornaments, these representatives of the fallen chivalry dashed along the roads of South Carolina in the depth of night, committed their atrocities upon the harmless and the innocent, and tormented the helpless and the weak. They openly declared to their bleeding victims that they must promise to vote for the Democratic party, or they would return and kill them. Many, after severe whippings, yielded to their dreadful argument. The newspapers were filled with the recantations of white and black Republicans, who had been converted to Democratic principles by stripes and wounds. One aged victim, beaten and bruised, crawled to the court-house steps, and there pronounced in faltering words his abjuration of Republican heresy. And if for a moment the murderous association seems suppressed in South Carolina, there can be no doubt that it would at once renew its outrages should the national government fall into the hands of its friends.

In Alabama the rage of the Democratic politicians seems chiefly turned against school-teachers, Methodist and Baptist preachers, and white Republicans who strive to elevate the colored race. The Ku-Klux labors have proved successful: a Democratic Governor has been elected (Lindsay), who denies the existence of any Ku-Klux conspiracy, and will see nothing of the brutal system of intimidation by which he has won an office; the State is ominously quiet. Governor Lindsay boasts of his power over the colored voters; the Democratic politicians assert that they are fast winning the negroes to their side — by what means who can fail to see? and that it can not be by any known train of argument is shown from the open assertion of leading Democrats that, had they the power, they would take from the colored population the right to vote at all.

The measures employed by the Democrats to recruit their party from the Republican side is best shown in the testimony of the Rev. Mr. Lakin, and his narrative of the fearful deeds of the Ku-Klux in Alabama is sustained and made probable by the long series of their similar crimes in every Southern State. Mr. Lakin was sent to Alabama by Bishop Clark, of Ohio, to renew the Methodist Episcopal Church in that State. He seems to have been unusually successful. He traveled over nearly all the counties of the State. He numbered seventy ministers or teachers among his assistants; he was presiding elder of his district, and was gladly welcomed in many humble cottages on the mountains, and in every negro cabin. He was chosen president of the State university. But in 1868 the Ku-Klux were awakened by the approaching election, and by the cheering words of their friends in the North, of Seymour, Buckalew, Kernan, and Wood;[1] they drove the Rev. Mr. Lakin from the university; they threatened death to every Republican student. In the *Independent Monitor*, of Tuscaloosa, Alabama, appeared a leading article warning the new president to leave the State at once, and a cut was given, in which the Rev. Mr. Lakin was represented as hanging from the limb of a tree. It was also suggested that the end of "negroism" was near, and that there was room on the same limb for every "Grant negro." The Ku-Klux now renewed their terrible career, nor have we space even to allude to the details of their frightful deeds. Judge Thurlow was shot at Hunstville, where the disguised assassins had ridden in openly and in "line of battle"; Judge Charlton, another active Republican, was pursued and shot; a band of Ku-Klux rode into the town of Eutaw, in irresistible strength, seized a Mr. Boyd in his room at the hotel, and murdered him. The Rev. Mr. Lakin was threatened, shot at, and finally driven to take refuge in the mountains. The fate of many of his assistant preachers revives the image of the persecutions of Decius or Diocletian.[2] A Mr. Sullivan was barbarously whipped; the Rev. J. A. M'Cutchen, a presiding elder, was driven from Demopolis; the Rev. James Buchanan, and the Rev. John W. Tailly, another presiding elder, were expelled by force; the Rev. Jesse Kingston was shot in his pulpit; the Rev. James Dorman whipped; Dean Reynolds whipped and left nearly dead, with both arms broken; a colored preacher and his son were murdered on the public road; the Rev. Mr. Taylor severely beaten; six churches were burned in one district; schoolhouses were every where destroyed, and the teachers, male or female, driven away or infamously ill treated; while in many a negro cabin disguised assassins murdered the unoffending inmates, and spread terror beyond conception in all the colored population of Alabama. Such were the means by which Alabama was converted to Democracy, and by which Mr. Greeley[3] and his associates must hope to gain the Southern vote.

The Ku-Klux sprang up almost at the same moment through all the Southern States. It terrified and subdued Louisiana; it swept over Texas; mounted and disguised ruffians rode through Mississippi in 1871, breaking up the colored schools, and driving away preachers and teachers; they covered Western Tennessee; they murdered, whipped, and tormented in North Carolina. In Georgia,

---

[1] **Seymour . . . Wood:** northern Democratic leaders Horatio Seymour, Charles R. Buckalew, Francis Kernan, and Fernando Wood.
[2] **Decius . . . Diocletian:** Roman emperors who persecuted Christians.
[3] **Mr. Greeley:** Horace Greeley, New York newspaper editor and, in 1872, Democratic presidential nominee.

we are told by Mr. Stearnes,[4] whole counties of colored voters are disfranchised by the terrors of their fearful orgies. Not even the Congressional Committee has been able to pierce the depths of this widespread conspiracy. The Democratic leaders of the South, who profit by its secret influence, endeavor to hide in doubt and obscurity the means by which they forced Republican States to vote for Seymour and Blair,[5] and by which they hope again to drive them to vote for Greeley and the Democracy. They pretend that the period of license is past; that a year of the rigid intervention of the national government has suffered to dissolve forever the wide spread conspiracy which in 1871 was active in its enormities in every Southern State; that every colored citizen may vote safely in Alabama, and every white Republican till his plantation in Georgia in peace. He may; but it is on the condition that he will support the Democratic candidates and the Democratic policy. Whatever be the opinion of Northern or Southern politicians, the colored and the white Republicans of the South know that the Ku-Klux conspiracy is not dissolved; that the men who rode last year in masks and grotesque disguises over Georgia and Mississippi are more ready now than they were then to murder an aged Fowler almost in the arms of his wife ("He was so old a gentleman," she said, "that she did not think they could do it"); to shoot Methodist ministers in their pulpits; to whip Republican voters until they profess Democracy, and drive them to proclaim their shame, in faltering accents, on the steps of a court-house, or in the public papers; to disfranchise counties and States. And he can scarcely deserve the confidence of honest men who professes to believe that because the Ku-Klux has hidden from justice, it is not yet firmly united, pledged to rebellion, resolute to effect its aim; that it has not its allies at the North as cruel and as barbarous as in its own section; that an organized conspiracy does not still exist in every Southern State, laboring to provoke civil war and to destroy the Union. We might learn in every negro family, and in the home of every true Republican at the South, the universal terror of the midnight assassins by which the Democracy has risen to power. . . .

It is certain that a large majority of the Southern people would rejoice to see these "pests of society" swept away forever by the rigorous hand of the government. The merchant and the mechanic, the farmer and the laborer, had they dared, would long ago have suppressed the infamous association. But they are terrified into silence. It is not improbable that most of the honest Democrats have no sympathy with their murderous allies. And the whole colored population awaits, in prayerful silence, the result of the approaching election. . . .[6] What freeman is there but will give his vote against that faction whose only hope of success lies in ruling the Southern States by violence and fraud? What honest man but will

---

[4] **Mr. Stearnes:** Eben Sperry Stearns, Massachusetts educator who later headed the State Normal School in Nashville, Tennessee.

[5] **Seymour and Blair:** Horace Seymour and Francis Preston Blair Jr., the Democratic nominees for president and vice president in 1868.

[6] **the approaching election:** the presidential election of 1872, in which incumbent Ulysses S. Grant would be reelected by an overwhelming majority.

labor with ceaseless energy to set free the South from these enemies of industry, knowledge, liberty, and Union? . . .

57. Missionary Women and Black Education

Maria Waterbury
From *Seven Years among the Freedmen*
1890

An important part of African Americans' search for freedom focused on education. During and after the Civil War, schools were founded to teach slaves who had been liberated by the Union army. Some of these schools were operated by the Freedmen's Bureau, a federal agency established in 1865 to supervise the transition from slavery to freedom; northern church groups — as well as interdenominational organizations such as the American Missionary Association — ran many other schools. Scores of missionary teachers, many of them northern white women, arrived in the South. They received an enthusiastic greeting from African Americans, but their reception from southern whites was more qualified. In a number of states, the efforts of northern teachers were seen as meddling; they became the subject of political attacks and, sometimes, even violence.

In this memoir, Maria Waterbury, a missionary teacher from Illinois who arrived in the South sometime in the 1870s, describes her experiences in rural Mississippi, where missionary schools became the targets of Klan terror.

Journal — 1877
Ku-Klux Outrages

A well-educated man from South Carolina, who had taught all the white school in the place for fourteen years; his wife not able to read a word; five children, three of whom are women in size. The mother, though not book learned,

Maria Waterbury, *Seven Years among the Freedmen* (1890), 2d ed., rev. and enl., The Black Heritage Library Collection (Freeport, N.Y.: Books for Libraries Press, 1971), 129–31, 133–34, 136–38.

teaches her daughters to do all kinds of work. In a small cook-house, in the rear of the dwelling, each of the daughters take turns in cooking. Here we saw rice used as a vegetable, eaten with meat, as in Carolina, where it grows so abundantly. The bread and coffee were excellent, and the kindness of this family drew every one to them.

Here, for want of a county poor-house, were boarded the poor, who were a county charge, and here the northern teachers found a boarding place.

The family is large, and Mr. Sandsby, the father, having returned from the town, twenty-five miles away, is standing with his back to the great fire-place, telling the home circle of the doings in the county.

"The Ku-Klux have whipped the colonel, madam," addressing the teacher, "and have sent me word they will call on you. Of course I will defend you and my family, with my gun and dogs, as well as I can," said the tall South Carolina gentleman; "but they'll burn the house immediately, and what now is our wisest course, that's the question! There are many colored people here, and very much attached to the school they are; but it isn't safe to trust them in an emergency. They are not well armed, and they haven't dogs at their command; and the Ku-Klux have both arms and dogs, and they know if they are half of them killed, there is no jury in this state that will give them justice.

"It's never thought much of a sin to kill a colored man in a southern state, and one of the proverbs of the secret society known as the Ku-Klux, is, that '*Dead men tell no tales.*' The other proverb, that mostly governs them, is, '*This is a white man's government*'; and so, with some whisky on board, they manage to intimidate the blacks, and make them vote mostly their own way.

"There's an election close at hand, and this raid is to scare them to vote the ticket they give them. So much for freedom in old Mississippi, madam; and you'll find, too, they are bent on so scaring the blacks, that the children will be afraid to attend the school.

"They've killed the colored man who ferried them over the Tombigbee, and now, what's best to be done? We must act promptly; they'll be here by to-morrow night."

All night the blacks had a prayer-meeting, and at sunrise, sent Uncle Billy to see the teacher, and try to persuade her to stay.

Morning exercises in the school-room; Scripture lesson: "Let not your heart be troubled; ye believe in God, believe also in me. In my Father's house are many mansions: I go to prepare a place for you." "In the world ye shall have tribulation: but be of good cheer; I have overcome the world." "The angel of the Lord encampeth round about them that fear him, and delivereth them."

Singing, prayer, and calling the roll. The teacher tells the scholars she is going to take a vacation, and will send them word when the school is to begin again; gives each pupil a beautiful Scotch Bible, donated by the Y. M. C. A. of Scotland, which she has been saving to give at the end of the term. . . .

We had slept but little all night, as the blacks had an all-night prayer-meeting, and we could hear their shouts, songs, and prayers, sounding on the still night air; but we made the journey without much inconvenience, save that we crossed over a dozen streams, some of them so swollen we had to jump up on the saddle, and let the horse nearly swim through. A colored boy rode a mule, and went with the teacher, to show the way.

Arriving at the town, which was the county seat of a large county, we found the colonel, superintendent of schools, also government officer, had been badly whipped by a hundred masked men. They detailed ten of their number to do the whipping, which was done with a leather strap. The colonel had gone a dozen miles from town, taking with him two northern teachers; had located them in their school, and stopped at a house three miles on his homeward journey, to stay all night. The house was surrounded by a hundred masked men on horseback. A few of these *brave ones* entered the house, took the colonel, tied him to a tree, and mercilessly whipped him, he telling them if they killed him, it would bring more war to their homes, as he was a government officer, and the government was bound to punish the offense. The colonel, more dead than alive, was left at the house, while the riders returned to their homes. A driver was found to drive for the school officer, and ere morning he reached home, and soon his neighbors filled the house with their calls, proffering their sympathy, and loud in denouncing such work in their state. Here were members of the same church the colonel had joined, on going South to live; here was the grocery man who supplied the colonel's family with eatables; here were many living close around the dwelling of this man, who, though a government officer, was devoting his hours, when not on duty for the government, to benefiting both white and colored, in the capacity of head officer of the free-school system they were trying to establish in this state; all these, and some others, who had come to proffer their condolence, *were found to be the very Ku-Klux who whipped their neighbor.*

The case was brought before the civil courts, but the lawyers adjourned it from time to time for *three years,* then a southern jury *acquitted the Ku-Klux,* and when they returned from the trial, a company of ladies met them at the depot, with a flag, and band of music. . . .

Another Raid

Miss Ada was a devoted Christian girl, the daughter of a first-class lawyer in Illinois. The missionary spirit had fired her soul, and filled with desires to benefit the ex-slaves, she left a home of luxury to come South and be a despised teacher of the colored race. She lived in one room of an old house. Aunt Melinda, a colored woman occupied a part of the house, cooked the food of the teacher, and carried it to her room. The school taught by the lady was a short distance away, in an uncomfortable shed-like building. The scholars were learning fast, and greatly attached to the teacher. A night school for adults was taught, and good progress was being made by all the pupils.

The school had gone on not yet two months, when at two o'clock in the morning, the sound of many horsemen was heard, and soon a rap at the door announced the presence of the Ku-Klux. They ordered the door opened immediately, speaking in a guttural tone, behind a mask, saying they were in haste, as they had a long ways to go.

"Yes, yes," said Miss Ada, who had sprung from her bed at the first rap, and thrown on a wrapper, "as soon as I light a lamp," taking the precaution to secrete her gold watch and chain, which lay on the table.

"Open the door or we'll break it open," came from the hasty night riders, and with a prayer for help, the teacher opened the door, to be greeted by a dozen masked and armed men. Masks of white, trimmed with black, and their pistols at half cock, they entered the room. The lady invited them to sit down, and said she felt such a sense of the presence of God with her, that a thought of fear never entered her mind. With pistol in hand the captain of the band gave his orders for her to leave in three days saying, "This is a white man's government," also inquiring if she had a home, and why she should leave it to engage in so mean a calling.

"We will not have white people mixed up with niggers," said the Captain, and after inquiring the time of her, thinking to get sight of her watch, said they must go. As they went out, one said to another, "She wa'n't scared a bit."

Miss Ada in relating it, said, "I shed tears when they were gone, to think I was worthy to feel the mighty presence of God so much." "The angel of the Lord encampeth round about them that fear him, and delivereth them."

58. The Legacy of the Klan

ALBION W. TOURGÉE
"The Causes, Character, and Consequences of the Ku-Klux Organization"
1880

Thousands of Northerners migrated to the South during Reconstruction. They were tarred with the derogatory title of carpetbagger *because they supposedly arrived with all their possessions in a carpetbag, with the intention of enriching themselves at the expense of the local citizenry. In fact, many moved South for humanitarian reasons or because their war experience exposed them to the region, although others came because of economic opportunity. Albion W. Tourgée, a carpetbagger from Ohio, served in the Union army and moved to North Carolina in 1865. He almost immediately became deeply involved in Republican politics, and between 1869 and*

Albion Winegar Tourgée, *The Invisible Empire*, introduction and notes by Otto H. Olsen (Baton Rouge: Louisiana State University Press, 1989), 131–33, 136–40, 144–45.

1871, as a state judge, mounted a heroic effort to prosecute Klan activity. Although the Klan disappeared in North Carolina after 1871, Tourgée eventually became so frustrated that he left in disgust in 1879.

Soon after his departure, Tourgée wrote the best-selling novel A Fool's Errand, *which described fictionally his experiences in North Carolina. The* Invisible Empire, *a supplement to the novel, spells out the Klan's impact with startling clarity. In this excerpt, Tourgée summarizes his explanation for its rise and success.*

The Causes

The reader who has followed us thus far has obtained some faint idea of the most wonderful combination of armed men for unlawful purposes which the civilized world has ever known. There have been conspiracies and revolutions more desperate and daring, but none so widespread, secret, universal among so great a people, and above all so successful. It may be well to review briefly in conclusion the causes, character, purpose, and effect of this remarkable organization.

The cause — or to speak more accurately, the occasion — of its rise and sudden growth is, no doubt, somewhat complex. Its objective point was the overthrow of what is known as the reconstructionary legislation, including the abrogation or nullification of the thirteenth, fourteenth, and fifteenth amendments to the Federal Constitution; and the cause of its sudden spread was the almost universal hostility, on the part of the whites of the South, to this legislation and its *anticipated* results. For it should be kept constantly in mind that this organization was instituted and *in active operation in at least four States before a single one of the reconstructed State governments had been organized.*

Effects of the War

The reason of this hostility is not difficult to assign, though its elements are almost as various as the classes of mind and temperament which were affected by it. With some it was probably exasperation and chagrin at the results of the war. No doubt this was the chief incentive acting upon the minds of those who originally instituted in Tennessee this famous scheme of secret resistance to the policy of the government. Not only the sting of defeat but the shame of punishment without its terror combined to induce those who had cast all their hopes of honor and success upon the Confederate cause to lend themselves to any thing that would tend to humiliate the power which, in addition to the fact of conquest, had endeavored to impose upon them the stigma of treason. There is no doubt that the disfranchisement of those who had engaged in rebellion — or a "war for secession," as they prefer that it should be termed — was almost universally deemed an insult and an outrage only second in infamy to the enfranchisement of the colored man, which was contemporaneous with it. It is a matter of the utmost difficulty for a Northern man to realize the strength and character of this sentiment at the South. . . .

The "Carpet-Bagger" and "Caste"

This feeling was of course intensified by that pride of caste and prejudice of race, as well as the accustomed intolerance of diverse opinions which have already been considered as characteristic of the South. The antipathy to Northern men became laughable in its absurdity. The cry of "Carpet-bag" governments has been bandied about until it has become a synonym for oppression and infamy. That the reconstructionary governments were failures goes without denial; that incompetency and extravagance characterized them is a most natural result of their organization; but that any one of them was controlled by men of Northern birth is an idea of the sheerest folly and absurdity. In hardly one of them were there a score of officers, great and small, who were of Northern birth. . . .

The Fear of Servile Insurrection

There was another cause for the sudden spread of the Klan throughout the South which it is hard for the Northern mind to appreciate. Despite the marvelous peacefulness and long-suffering of the colored race, the people of the South had come to entertain an instinctive horror of servile or negro insurrections. Under the old slave *régime* this feeling was no doubt, in a measure, the product of that conscience which "doth make cowards of us all"; for it is unlikely that one could practice that "sum of all villainies," as Wesley[1] vigorously phrased the description of Slavery, without doing violence to that moral mentor. It was, however, much more the result of that demagogic clamor which had for fifty years or more dwelt with inexhaustible clamor upon the inherent and ineradicable savageness of the gentle and docile race that was held in such carefully guarded subjection. This feeling was manifested and deepened in those days by the terrible enactments in which the "Black Codes" of the South abounded, all designed to check disobedience of any kind, and especially that which might lead to organized resistance. The constant repetition of this bugbear of a servile insurrection as a defensive argument for the institution of Slavery had impressed every man, woman, and child at the South with a vague and unutterable horror of the ever-anticipated day when the docile African should be transformed into a demon too black for hell's own purlieus.[2] Year after year, for more than one generation, the Southern heart had been fired by the depiction of these horrors. In every political campaign the opposing orators upon the stump had striven to outdo each other in portraying the terrors of San Domingo and the Nat Turner insurrection, until they became words used to frighten children into good behavior. It came to be the chronic nightmare of the Southern mind. Every wayside bush hid an insurrection.

[1] **Wesley:** John Wesley, English Methodist and antislavery reformer.
[2] **purlieus:** environs.

Men were seized with a frenzy of unutterable rage at the thought, and women became delirious with apprehension at its mere mention. It was the root of much of that wild-eyed lunacy which bursts forth among the Southern people at the utterance of the magic slogan of to-day, "a war of races." There is no doubt but very many otherwise intelligent men and women are confirmed lunatics upon this subject. It has become a sort of holy horror with them. No greater offence can be given in a Southern household than to laugh at its absurdity. The race prejudice has been fostered and encouraged for political effect, until it has become a part of the mental and moral fiber of the people. There is no doubt but this feeling, taken in connection with the enfranchisement of the blacks, induced thousands of good citizens to ally themselves with the Klan upon the idea that they were acting in self-defence in so doing, and especially that they were securing the safety of their wives and children thereby.

Need of a Patrol

The old "patrol" system of the ante-bellum days and a devout belief in its necessity was also one of the active causes of the rapid spread of the Klan. This system was established by legislative enactment in all the Southern States. It varied somewhat in its details and in the powers conferred upon the patrolmen, or "patrollers" as they were popularly called. The purpose of the system, however, was declared to be "the preservation of order, and proper subordination among the colored population." The patrol generally consisted of a certain number of men, appointed for each captain's district or other local subdivision of the county, whose duty it was to patrol the public highway at night; to arrest and whip all negroes found beyond the limits of their masters' plantations after dark without a pass from the owner or overseer; to visit the "nigger quarters" on the plantations and see that no meetings or assemblies were held without the presence of a white man; and, in general, to exercise the severest scrutiny of the private life and demeanor of the subject-race. This system of espionage and the enforcement of the code designed for the control of the blacks without form of trial, had a great influence upon the mental status of both races. It deprived the person, house, and property of the freedmen of all that sanctity which the law throws around the person, home, and possessions of the white man, in the minds of both the Caucasian and the African. The former came to believe that he had the right to trespass, and the latter that he must submit to this claim. As the spirit of the new era did not admit of such statutory espionage and summary correction of the black as had been admitted by all to be necessary in the days of Slavery, and as it was undeniable that emancipation had not changed the nature of the inferior race nor removed all grounds for disaffection on his part, it was but natural that there should be a general sentiment that some volunteer substitute was necessary. As the power to whip and chastise for any infraction of the code of slave-etiquette was conferred upon the patrol, it was equally natural that they should regard the exercise of such authority by the Klan as not only necessary but quite a fit and proper thing to be done by them.

The Brutality of Slavery

The chief ground of doubt at the North in regard to the atrocities of the Klan, the Bull-dozers, and the Rifle Clubs,[3] is that it seems altogether incredible that the being so long and loudly self-vaunted as the very incarnation of all that is noble, generous, brave, and Christianlike — the ideal "Southern gentleman"— should assent to or engage in such atrocities. The trouble about this reasoning is that the "Southern gentleman," according to the Northern conception of him, is an almost mythical personage. The North has mistaken the terms used in self-description by the Southern aristocrat, who was at no time economical of adjectives. The perfect gentleman of the South is very apt, along with many splendid qualities and noble impulses, to possess others which at the North would be accounted very reprehensible. He is simply like other men, good according to the style and measure of his era and surroundings. In the old days a man might be a perfect gentleman and yet a cruel master, a keen speculator in human flesh, the sire of his own slaves, — and literally a dealer in his own flesh and blood. The Northern mind was horrified at such a combination. Yet it should not have been. The greatest evil of slavery was that it brutified the feelings of the master-race and lowered and degraded their estimate of humanity. . . .

It should be remembered that the institution of Slavery so warped and marred the common-law that grave and reverend — yea, conscientious, learned, and Christian men announced from the bench, with all the solemn sanction of the judicial ermine, doctrines with regard to the master's power over the person of the slave which are now considered barbarous and unlawful when applied to his brute possessions. In some States it was held that slavery vested the master with absolute power over the life of the slave; and, in all, that he might kill him to enforce obedience or to punish insolence. It is true that the slave was protected to a certain extent from the violence and passion of those not entitled to exercise mastery over him, but that was merely or chiefly for the sake of the master whose property he was. . . .

The Controlling Powers

The idea which has prevailed that the Ku-Klux were simply rough, lawless, irresponsible young rowdies is a singularly absurd reflection on the "best" classes — their power and inherited authority over their poorer neighbors. The minority which forced an overwhelming majority into what the victims themselves termed "the rich man's war and the poor man's fight," is still omnipotent in the domain of Southern public opinion. If they had disapproved of the doings of these men, the Klan would have shrivelled before the first breath of denunciation. But that breath never came with any earnestness or sincerity of tone until the object of the organization, the *destruction of the negro's political power*, had been fully ac-

---

[3] **Bull-dozers . . . Rifle Clubs:** along with the Klan, these were white paramilitary groups seeking to intimidate African Americans and Republicans.

complished. It is a reflection on the power of the best citizens to indulge the idea that the rabble could do any thing in opposition to their wishes. Professedly, they feebly "deplored" what was done, but in fact they either directly encouraged or were discreetly silent. That thousands of them loaned their horses for poor men to ride upon raids is just as certain as that they should put substitutes into the army under "the twenty-nigger law."[4]

Another thing which shows that the claim made in extenuation — that it was merely the work of rough spirits of the lower classes — is a libel on the common people of the South, is the fact that the best classes never prosecuted nor denounced these acts, but were always their apologists and defenders. Besides that, they kept the secrets of the Klan better than the Masons have ever kept the mysteries of their craft. It was an open secret in families and neighborhoods. Ladies met together in sewing-circles to make the disguises. Churches were used as places of assembly. Children were intrusted with secrets which will make them shudder in old age. Yet the freemasonry of a common impulse kept them as true as steel. As a rule, the only ones who flinched were a few of the more unfortunate or more cowardly of its members. Not a woman or a child lisped a syllable that might betray the fatal secret. It was a holy trust which the Southern cause had cast upon them, and they would have died rather than betray it. . . .

There is no sort of doubt that it originated with the best classes of the South, was managed and controlled by them, and was at all times under their direction. It was their creature and their agent to work out their purposes and ends. . . .

[4]"the twenty-nigger law": refers to the exemption from the draft that the Confederate government granted to owners of twenty or more slaves.

Suggestions for Further Reading

Du Bois, W. E. B. *Black Reconstruction.* New York: Harcourt and Brace, 1935.

Edwards, Laura F. *Gendered Strife and Confusion: The Political Culture of Reconstruction.* Urbana: University of Illinois Press, 1997.

Foner, Eric. *Reconstruction: America's Unfinished Revolution, 1863–1877.* New York: Harper & Row, 1988.

Litwack, Leon F. *Been in the Storm So Long: The Aftermath of Slavery.* New York: Alfred A. Knopf, 1979.

Trelease, Allen W. *White Terror: The Ku Klux Klan Conspiracy and Southern Reconstruction.* New York: Harper & Row, 1971. Reprint, Westport, Conn.: Greenwood Press, 1979.

DATE DUE

MR 18 '06			

DEMCO 38-296